THE WORLD OF MYTH

THE WORLD OF MYTH

David Adams Leeming

OXFORD UNIVERSITY PRESS
New York   Oxford

Oxford University Press

Oxford New York Toronto
Delhi Bombay Calcutta Madras Karachi
Petaling Jaya Singapore Hong Kong Tokyo
Nairobi Dar es Salaam Cape Town
Melbourne Auckland

and associated companies in
Berlin Ibadan

First published in 1990 by Oxford University Press, Inc.,
200 Madison Avenue, New York, New York 10016

First issued as an Oxford University Press paperback, 1992

Oxford is a registered trademark of Oxford University Press

Library of Congress Cataloging-in-Publication Data
Leeming, David Adams, 1937–
The world of myth / David Adams Leeming.
p. cm. Includes bibliographical references.
ISBN 0-19-505601-9
1. Myth 2. Mythology. I. Title.
BL311.L328 1990 291.1'3—dc20 89-48070

The following pages are regarded as an extension
of the copyright page

ISBN 0-19-507475-0 (pbk.)

4 5 6 7 8 9 10

Printed in the United States of America

Text Credits:

New American Library for excerpts from Thomas Bulfinch, *Mythology: The Age of Chivalry* and *Mythology: The Age of Fable*.

Grafton Books for excerpts from Rex Warner, *The Stories of the Greeks*.

Search Press, Ltd., for excerpts from *Butler's Lives of the Saints*.

Charles Boer, translator, for excerpts from *The Homeric Hymns*, published by Swallow Press and in revised edition by Spring Books.

Excerpts from Cornelia Dimmitt and J. A. B. Van Buitenen, eds., *Classical Hindu Mythology*. © 1978 by Temple University. Reprinted by permission of Temple University Press.

The University of California Press and Bowes and Bowes, Ltd., for excerpts from *The Prose Edda* of Snorri Sturluson, ed. by Jean Young. © 1954 Bodley Head, Ltd., and © 1964 The Regents of the University of California.

Sidgwick and Jackson, Ltd., for excerpts from *The Wonder that was India*, translated by A. L. Basham.

Parabola and Paul Jordan-Smith for excerpts from the *Popol Vuh*.

Oxford University Press, Ltd., for excerpts from Julius Eggeling, *Sacred Books of the East*, and James Lovelock, *Gaia: A New Look at Life on Earth*.

Oxford University Press, Ltd., and Everyman's Library for excerpts from the *Bhagavad-Gita*, translated by R. C. Zaehner.

Houghton Mifflin Company for excerpts from Longfellow's "Song of Hiawatha."

The University of Chicago Press for excerpts from Sophocles, *Oedipus the King*, translated by David Grene, © 1942, by The University of Chicago; Sophocles, *Antigone*, translated by Elizabeth Wycoff, © 1954 by The University of Chicago. Both in *Sophocles 1: The Complete Greek Tragedies*, ed. David Grene and Richard Lattimore, © 1954, by The University of Chicago.

Dennis Hirota, translator, and Ryukoku University Translation Center for excerpts from Shinran, *Tannisho: A Primer*.

American Philosophical Society for excerpts from S. N. Kramer, *Sumerian Mythology*.

By permission from G. M. Mullett, *Spider Woman Stories*, The University of Arizona Press, Copyright 1979.

J. M. Dent and Sons, Ltd., for excerpts from *The Koran*.

Dover Publications, Inc., for excerpts from A. K. Coomaraswamy and Sister Nivedita, *Myths of the Hindus and Buddhists*.

Harrap, Ltd., for excerpts from Ramsay Smith, *Myths and Legends of the Australian Aborigines*, and Ananda Coomaraswamy, *Buddha and the Gospel of Buddhism*.

University of Nebraska Press for excerpts from George Bird Grinnell, *Blackfoot Lodge Tales*.

Excerpts from Jerome Rothenberg, "The Flight of Quetzalcoatl" in *Shaking the Pumpkin*. Copyright © 1972 by Jerome Rothenberg. Reprinted by permission of Sterling Lord Literistic, Inc.

Cooper Square Publishers for excerpts from Louis Grey, ed., *The Mythology of All Races*.

W. B. Yeats, "Leda and the Swan." Reprinted with permission of Macmillan Publishing Company from *The Poems of W. B. Yeats: A New Edition*, edited by Richard J. Finneran. Copyright 1928 by Macmillan Publishing Company; renewed 1956 by Georgie Yeats.

Excerpts from Hesiod's *Theogony*. Reprinted with permission of Macmillan Publishing Company from *Hesiod's Theogony*, translated and edited by Norman O. Brown. Copyright 1953 by Macmillan Publishing Company. Copyright renewed 1981 by Norman O. Brown.

Excerpts from R. T. Rundle Clark, *Myth and Symbol in Ancient Egypt*. © 1959 Thames and Hudson Ltd., London.

Excerpts from Edith Hamilton, *Mythology*. Copyright 1942 by Edith Hamilton, © renewed 1969 by Dorian Fielding Reid and Doris Fielding Reid. By permission of Little, Brown and Company.

Methuen and Co. for excerpts from H. J. Rose, *A Handbook of Greek Mythology*.

Excerpts from *Mythologies of the Ancient World* by Samuel N. Kramer, copyright © 1961 by Doubleday, a division of Bantam, Doubleday, Dell Publishing Group, Inc. Used by permission of the publisher.

American Anthropological Association for excerpts from T. P. Coffin, ed., *Indian Tales of North America*.

Alfred A. Knopf, Inc., for excerpts from Otto Rank, *The Myth of the Birth of the Hero and Other Writings*, edited by Philip Freund. Copyright 1932, 1936, © 1959 by Alfred A. Knopf, Inc. Copyright renewed, 1960, 1964, by Alfred A. Knopf, Inc.

Bear and Company, Inc., Santa Fe, New Mexico, for excerpts from Brian Swimme, *The Universe Is a Green Dragon: A Cosmic Creation Story*. Copyright © 1984 by Bear and Company, Inc.

Excerpts from *Lost Goddesses of Early Greece* by Charlene Spretnak. Copyright © 1978 by Charlene Spretnak. Reprinted by permission of Beacon Press and the author.

For
Pam
Margaret
Juliet
and Paul

PREFACE

This collection of world myths, although comprehensive, is not intended to be exhaustive and might well be supplemented by a good general encyclopedia or dictionary of mythology, as well as by modern editions of the major Greek and Roman epics and the Greek tragedies. The myths selected are representative of the cultures in question, with some emphasis on myths that have influenced the creative arts in Western culture. These myths are used to illustrate a process by which an approach to myth is gradually revealed. This approach, essentially archetypal in nature, will be of particular use to students of literature and the other arts. It should also be of interest to a general, nonacademic, audience, as it stresses the connections between myth and our own everyday lives.

    I wish to thank my daughter, Margaret Leeming, for researching the facts in this volume. Thanks also to Christine Jopeck for her editorial assistance as proofreader and indexer.

Stonington, Conn.
December 1989

D.A.L.

CONTENTS

Introduction: The Dimensions of Myth, 3

* Select Bibliography, 8

PART I   COSMIC MYTHS   11

The Creation, 15

* The Creation Stories, 17

EGYPTIAN: THE BEGINNINGS, 17
MESOPOTAMIAN: *ENUMA ELISH*, 18
HEBREW: GENESIS, 24
INDIAN: THE *RIG VEDA* AND THE *BRIIADARANYAKA UPANISHAD*, 29
GREEK: HESIOD'S *THEOGONY*, 32
CHRISTIAN: JOHN'S GOSPEL, 35
HOPI: SPIDER WOMAN, 36
BOSHONGO (BANTU): BUMBA'S CREATION, 39
MODERN: THE BIG BANG, 41

* Bibliography, 42

The Flood, 43

* The Flood Stories, 44

MESOPOTAMIAN: UTNAPISHTIM, 44
HEBREW: NOAH, 47
CHINESE: YÜ, 53
INDIAN: MANU, 55
GRECO-ROMAN: DEUCALION AND PYRRHA, 56
MAYAN: THE *POPOL-VUH*, 60

* Bibliography, 62

The Afterlife, 64

● The Afterlife Stories, 65

   EGYPTIAN: OSIRIS, 65
   GRECO-ROMAN: LANDS OF THE DEAD, 67
   JUDEO-CHRISTIAN: HELL, PURGATORY, HEAVEN, 68
   MUSLIM: HELL AND HEAVEN IN THE KORAN, 68
   BUDDHIST: THE PURE LAND, 69
   HOPI: THE KACHINAS, 72

● Bibliography, 75

The Apocalypse, 76

● The Apocalypse Stories, 77

   HEBREW: THE DAY OF YAHWEH, 77
   CHRISTIAN: ST. JOHN'S BOOK OF REVELATION, 79
   INDIAN: THE END OF THE KALI AGE, 81
   HOPI: EMERGENCE TO THE FIFTH WORLD, 84
   NORSE: RAGNARÖK, 85
   MODERN: ENTROPY AND HEAT DEATH, 88

● Bibliography, 89

PART II   MYTHS OF THE GODS   91

The Pantheons, 95

● The Pantheonic Stories, 95

   EGYPTIAN, 95
   The Gods of Heliopolis, 96
   The Separation of Geb and Nut, 97
   GREEK, 98
   The Olympians, 98
   The Originators, 99
   The Children of Kronos and Rhea, 100
   The Children of Zeus, 103
   ROMAN: THE RENAMED OLYMPIANS, 117
   NORSE (ICELANDIC): THE AESIR, 118

● Bibliography, 121
● The God as Archetype, 123
● Stories of Archetypal Gods, 124
● The Supreme Being, 124

   INDIAN: KRISHNA-VISHNU-BRAHMAN, 125

HEBREW: YAHWEH, 130
MODERN: IMMANENT MIND, 133

* The Great Mother, 134
MESOPOTAMIAN: INANNA-ISHTAR, 136
MODERN: GAIA AS EARTH, 145

* The Dying God, 146
EGYPTIAN: OSIRIS AND ISIS, 147
BABYLONIAN–GRECO-ROMAN: ADONIS AND APHRODITE, 153
PHRYGIAN: ATTIS, 155
GREEK: DIONYSOS, 156
AZTEC/TOLTEC: QUETZALCOATL, 157
CHRISTIAN: JESUS, 157
NORSE (ICELANDIC): ODIN, 162

* The Trickster, 163
GREEK: HERMES, 163
INDIAN: KRISHNA, 165
SHOSHONI: OLD MAN COYOTE, 169
FON (DAHOMEY): LEGBA, 171

* Bibliography, 172

Gods, Goddesses, and Lesser Spirits, 175

* Stories of Gods, Goddesses, and Lesser Spirits, 175
GRECO-ROMAN, 175
Prometheus, 175
Pandora, 177
Tiresias, Echo, and Narcissus, 178
Hyacinthus, 183
Eros and Psyche, 185
Daphne and Apollo, 185
Pan, 188
The Muses, 192
The Eumenides, 192
Zeus and Io, 192
Zeus and Europa, 196
NON-GREEK, 197
PERSIAN: MITHRAS, 197
JAPANESE: AMATERASU AND SUSANOWO, 199
POLYNESIAN: PELE AND HIIAKA', 202
INDIAN: INDRA AND THE PARADE OF ANTS, 207

* Bibliography, 213

PART III   HERO MYTHS   215

* The Hero Stories, 221
* The Conception, Birth, and Childhood of the Hero, 221
  NATIVE AMERICAN (TEWA): WATER JAR BOY, 221
  GREEK: THESEUS, 224
  INDIAN: KRISHNA, 225
  INDIAN: KARNA, 226
  GREEK: HERAKLES, 228
  INDIAN: THE BUDDHA, 229
  IRISH: CUCHULAINN, 233
  BANTU: LITUOLONE, 234

* The Journey Quest of the Hero, 235
  FRENCH: JOAN OF ARC, 235
  GREEK: OEDIPUS, 237
  GREEK: ANTIGONE, 239
  CELTIC: KING ARTHUR, 243
  GREEK: THESEUS, 244
  HEBREW: MOSES, 248
  CELTIC: PARCIVAL, 252
  HEBREW: JONAH, 255
  GREEK: JASON, 257
  ROMAN: AENEAS, 258
  HEBREW: SAMSON AND DELILAH, 260
  INDIAN: THE BUDDHA, 262
  NATIVE AMERICAN: WUNZH, OR HIAWATHA, 267
  GREEK: HERAKLES, 274
  AFRICAN: WANJIRU, 281
  AUSTRALIAN ABORIGINAL: THE PLEIADES, 283
  HEBREW: ABRAHAM AND ISAAC, 287
  MESOPOTAMIAN: GILGAMESH, 288
  GREEK: ORPHEUS AND EURYDICE, 292
  GREEK: ODYSSEUS, 295

* The Rebirth, Return, and Apotheosis of the Hero, 298
  BLACKFOOT: KUTOYIS, 298
  CHRISTIAN: JESUS, 304
  GREEK: HERAKLES, 307
  AZTEC/TOLTEC: QUETZALCOATL, 307
  CHRISTIAN: MARY, 308
  GREEK: ALCESTIS, 309

* Bibliography, 311

PART IV PLACE AND OBJECT MYTHS 313

* Stories of Places and Objects, 316
* The Mountain, 316
  HEBREW: MOUNT SINAI, 316

* The City, 319
  GREEK: TROY, 319
  HEBREW: JERUSALEM, 330
  GREEK: DELPHI, 332

* The Temple, 333
  JUDEO-CHRISTIAN: THE TEMPLE AT JERUSALEM, 333
  EUROPEAN: THE CHAPEL PERILOUS, 335

* The Genitals, 336
  GREEK: TIRESIAS, 336
  APACHE: THE VAGINA GIRLS, 337
  GREEK: THE FIG PHALLUS OF DIONYSOS, 338

* The Stone, 338
  PHRYGIAN: THE AGDOS ROCK, 338
  AUSTRALIAN ABORIGINAL: ERATHIPA, 339
  HEBREW: THE BETHEL, 340

* The Tree, 341
  INDIA: THE COSMIC TREE, 342
  NORSE: YGGDRASIL, 343
  HEBREW: THE TREE OF KNOWLEDGE, 344

* The Garden, the Grove, and the Cave, 344
  MUSLIM: MUHAMMAD'S CAVE, 345

* The Labyrinth, 347
  GREEK: DAEDALUS AND ICARUS, 347

* Bibliography, 348

Index, 349

THE WORLD OF MYTH

INTRODUCTION:
THE DIMENSIONS OF MYTH

In common parlance, a myth is an "old wives' tale," a generally accepted belief unsubstantiated by fact. Thus, it is a myth that professors are absent-minded or that women are intuitive rather than rational. We also classify as myths the stories of gods and heroes of cults in which we do not believe, tales that once had religious significance. The stories of the exploits of Zeus and Hera, Theseus, Perseus, and Odysseus are in this sense myths. Collections of the myths of particular cultures are called mythologies: the exploits of the characters just mentioned form parts of Greek mythology; the stories of Osiris and Isis are part of Egyptian mythology. We also use the word "mythology" to refer to the academic field concerned with the study of myths and mythologies. We can also speak of myth as an abstract reality, like religion or science.

In the Western world, myths have traditionally been tales of pagan (i.e., non–Judeo-Christian) religions. We speak of Egyptian and Greek myths and sometimes of Hindu and Buddhist myths, but until recently even atheists have rarely spoken of Jewish or Christian myths. Yet if "myth" has always implied falsehood, if we have not believed in Zeus or the Golden Fleece, we have accepted the mythical tales of cultures we value—especially Greco-Roman culture—as somehow important and worth teaching our children. One of the assumptions of this book is that Greco-Roman myths (and those of other cultures) are not only worth teaching but are essential to our education.

The English word "myth" is derived from the Greek *mythos*, meaning word or story. Human beings have traditionally used stories to describe or explain things they could not explain otherwise. Ancient myths were stories by means of which our forebears were able to assimilate the mysteries that occurred around and within them. In this sense, myth is related to metaphor, in which an object or event is compared to an apparently dissimilar object or event in such a way as to make its otherwise inexplicable essence clear: Thus, when Yeats speaks of "Two girls in silk kimonos, both / Beautiful, one a gazelle," the girl in the poem is, in fact, not a gazelle; but something true about her grace and her presence is conveyed when the image of a gazelle is substituted in our minds. In the same way, something of the sense of loss and death we may feel in winter is conveyed by the story of the abduction of Persephone. In short, both as story and as extended metaphor, myth is the direct ancestor of what we think of today as literature. The meaning of myths, like the meaning of any literature, is, as Northrop Frye has said, "inside them, in the implications of their incidents" (*Fables of Identity*, p. 32).

But, as has already been implied, in its explanatory or etiological aspect myth is also a form of history, philosophy, theology, or science. Myths helped early societies understand such phenomena as the movement of the sun across the sky and the changing of the seasons, as well as such events as the ancient struggle for the control of the Dardanelles and such mysteries as the Creation and the nature of the gods. Myths also served as the basis for rituals by which the ways of humanity and those of nature could be psychologically reconciled. Many of these myths and rituals are still operative in the world's religions. The anthropologist or sociologist will properly study a myth as the expression of a social ethos. For example, the Sumerian myth of Inanna perhaps indicates a matriarchal tradition, whereas the myths of Narcissus and Hyacinth might suggest a practice of ritual human sacrifice.

In recent times we have gradually broadened our understanding of myth. Psychologists, linguists, and anthropologists have taken us beyond an appreciation of myths as primitive literature, science, or history to a realization of their importance in our own lives today. When we study mythology now, we tend to concern ourselves with basic assumptions that define a person, a family, or a culture—with the informing reality that resides at the center of being. We find ourselves talking not only about pagan tales but also about national, religious, and aesthetic essences. We find architects like Bruno Zevi discussing the mythic implications of architecture, or scientists discussing Newtonian mythic structure as opposed to that of "the new physics." We can refer to the common millennial myth that pervades the Judeo-Christian and Marxist traditions or to the myth of the American Dream. In each case we are considering something intangible, perhaps not literally real, that is nevertheless "true" in some higher sense. In other words, we have come to think of myths as conveyors of information rather than odd examples of pagan superstition, and we have learned that the mythic tales of particular cultures are masks for a larger, less tangible mythic substructure that we all share.

Throughout recorded history, the stories and patterns that we call myths have dominated human experience. If the purpose of our existence in the larger organism we call earth is to make that organism conscious of itself, we have tended to do so by means of myths—contained in stories,

songs, rituals, and paintings—that accomplish such real tasks as the justi-
fication of power, authority, ideologies, and political acts. God, personified
as the patriarchal figure with the long white beard is not merely a superstition but the embodiment of a myth, possessing real power, who has
dominated our spiritual and temporal world for millennia. He inhabits not
only our churches and temples but our male-dominated governments, families, and schools, from London to Djakarta. Similarly, the story of the
quest has been used to justify not only denial of physical needs for the sake
of spiritual growth but even murder and genocide.

Joseph Campbell has written that "the chronicle of our species, from
its earliest page, has been not simply an account of man the tool-maker,
but—more tragically—a history of the pouring of blazing visions into the
minds of seers and the efforts of earthly communities to incarnate
unearthly covenants" (*The Masks of God*, I,3). Thus, myths are not to be
regarded lightly. The stories in this book are cultural versions of universal
tendencies. They are sometimes funny, occasionally bizarre, but they must
always be taken seriously. One culture's cleansing ritual, based on myth,
can become another culture's holocaust. Never was this dangerous aspect
of myth so obvious as in Germany during the Third Reich, when Hitler
used Germanic myths, particularly as popularized by Wagner in his operas,
to justify the concept of an Aryan master race in a German fatherland.

A more positive impetus for the reemergence of myth as a phenomenon to be taken seriously was provided by a host of great anthropologists
and psychologists around the turn of the century, who saw in myth a rich
source of material for their study of human nature. Such names as Sir
James Frazer, E. B. Tylor, Franz Boas, Bronislaw Malinowski, Adolf Bastian, and Ernst Cassirer come to mind, as do those of the two great founders of modern psychology, Sigmund Freud and Carl Jung. The emergence
of psychology as a science has probably done more than any other recent
development to remind us of the significance of myth in our own lives.
Both Freud and Jung recognized motifs and patterns that were common
to the mythic and subconscious worlds. Such phrases as "Oedipus complex" and the "Elektra complex," which arise from Freudian psychology,
are now a part of our general vocabulary. Jung, in particular, made use of
myths in his approach to questions of self-realization, stressing the existence of archetypes, or inherent psychic tendencies, in our "collective unconscious"—tendencies that take form as motifs or themes common to individual dreams and tribal myths. Among such archetypal themes are the
femme fatale, the journey quest, the figure of the wise old guide, and many
others.

The connection between dreams and myths is crucial for a proper
understanding of the significance of the latter. An assumption of modern
psychology popular at the turn of the century was that dreams are a symbolic language by which information about the dreamer is conveyed. More
specifically, with the help of an analyst—a sort of modern-day shaman—
the individual can find reflected in dreams messages drawn from the inner

self, the self buried beneath the debris of childhood training, adult repression, and mental prejudice. When the dreams of an individual are studied as a whole, a pattern—a personal mythology—emerges. When the dreams of many individuals are compared, a universal dream language, a language of dream symbols, takes form.

Like the dreams of an individual, the myths of a given group are created unconsciously, as it were. As Claude Lévi-Strauss has written, "Myths are anonymous . . . they exist only as elements embodied in a tradition," they develop on their own, they come from "nowhere" (*The Raw and the Cooked*, p. 18). Yet few anthropologists would deny that to read a culture's myths is to gleam information about that culture—about its inner identity, hidden beneath the mask of its everyday concerns. To go one step further, when we study the world's mythologies and discover the archetypal patterns (also common to our individual dreams) that essentially unite those mythologies, we study what we might reasonably call the dreams of humankind, in which we find information about the nature of humanity itself. In a real sense, the world reveals its inner self through its common mythology.

When we study a dream or a myth, or a series of dreams or myths, we are simultaneously studying difference and commonality. On the surface of a dream we find material reflecting the dreamer's immediate circumstances and environment. The setting and the characters of the dream will contain mysteries, to be sure, but they will also reflect people and places known to the dreamer. By the same token, the external surface of a myth is likely to reflect the experience of the culture in question. American Indian myths are populated by ravens, buffalo, and other North American animals, while in East Indian myths we find elephants and cobras. But at a deeper level, the dreams of an African, the myths of a Native American, and those of an East Indian are unified by a common symbolic and archetypal "language" or "deep structure."

This psychological analogy can be taken one step further. Just as dreams help us to determine our identity as individuals and tribal myths help to establish a tribe's identity, so world mythology, considered as a whole, is the eternal story of humanity's quest for self-fulfillment in the face of entropy, the universal tendency toward disorder. Whether the hero of a myth is Indian, Norse, African, or Polynesian, whether he or she is on a quest for nirvana, self, the Kingdom of God, or the Golden Fleece, this figure is on a universal human quest for identity and individuation, as Joseph Campbell and Mircea Eliade, two of our greatest modern mythologists, have so eloquently taught us. This is a quest that we all understand, for only humans are endowed with the ability to be conscious, at any given time, of the universal scheme of things, of *mythos*, of the beginning, middle, and end of a given process. In that sense we are all ultimately questers, voyagers on the mythical "road of life," the "path," the "Tao."

A question that inevitably arises in connection with mythology is that of authorship. Who wrote the myths or, more accurately, who first told them? Almost invariably the answer must be the people themselves. The myth, like its close relative the fairy tale, has its origins in the collective "folk" mind. Perhaps it was individual priests or shamans who gave some specific form to the "primitive" speculations concerning the reason for spring, the origin of earth, and the nature of death; but the essential similarities within those various forms, irrespective of chronology and geography, indicate a collective authorship, the human mind wrestling en masse with the mysteries, attempting to make earth conscious of itself. Of course, much later there arose great literary mythmakers, early poets who, like the shamans, medicine men, and priests, were somehow individually inspired—even possessed—to the point that they could achieve self-identity only by breathing a new conscious literary life into the old tales. These poets were, like the folk mind itself, true mythmakers to the extent that they found new ways to convey the universal human story in terms suited to their own cultures. It was at about the time of Homer—himself a figure of mythic proportions—that human beings began to associate particular names with their mythmakers. We do not know the name of the poet of the Gilgamesh epic, through which much of Sumerian mythology is known to us. There are many literary versions—which were eventually written down—of Indian, Chinese, Egyptian, and Hebrew myths as well, but we do not know their authors. If there was a historical Homer, he can be called the first identifiable mythmaker, unless it was the Indian counterpart of Homer, the legendary Vyasa, who was said to have composed the *Mahabharata*. The Greek poet Hesiod is among the first truly historical mythmakers, renowned for his descriptions of the mythological past in such works as the *Theogony*.

After Homer the mythmakers become more consciously literary, better known, and further removed from their folk sources. The Romans, primarily Virgil (the *Aeneid*) and Ovid (the *Metamorphoses*), are perhaps more accurately described as professional poets than mythmakers; the creators of the oral epic tradition, such as Homer and Vyasa were still straddling the folk world and the self-conscious literary world. In the *Odyssey*, Homer gives us a brief portrait (perhaps a self-portrait) of one of these inspired voices of the folk mind, a mythmaking minstrel at the court of the Phaiakians, who in his songs gave new form and life to the ancient tales of prehistory:

> *The crier soon came, leading that man of song*
> *whom the Muse cherished; by her gift he knew*
> *the good of life, and evil—*
> *for she who lent him sweetness made him blind.*
>   . . .
> *In time, when hunger and thirst were turned away,*
> *the Muse brought to the minstrel's mind a song*
> *of heroes whose great fame rang under heaven.*

(*Odyssey*, VIII, p. 139 [trans. Robert Fitzgerald])

Like the Homer of legend, Demodocus, the minstrel described, is blind. He may lack sight but he possesses insight, being closer to the gods, as it were, and to the folk imagination than to what we usually think of as "literature." In the *Odyssey* itself, Odysseus is certainly a literary hero, but he is also a mytho-religious figure whose journey is firmly rooted in a ritual pattern involving loss, descent, and rebirth. In this sense he resembles Job in the Old Testament or the Pandava brothers in the *Mahabharata*. In a way, the early poetic mythmakers told stories that the collective mind already knew. In those stories humanity could see itself in proper perspective; creation could step back and look at itself. It should be pointed out here that the modern artist is a direct descendant of the ancient mythmaker. The true artist explores the inner myth of life in the context of a particular local experience. If the story of Odysseus is humanity's story of loss and rebirth leading to transformation, so is *War and Peace* in a nineteenth-century Russian context and so, perhaps, is Picasso's *Guernica* in a twentieth-century European one.

In this book the great mythic tales of the world are introduced and arranged in such a way as to make the universal tale they tell as clear as possible. Four types of myths serve as the organizing principle: cosmic myths, theistic myths, hero myths, and place and object myths. Cosmic myths are concerned with the great facts of existence (e.g., the Creation, the Flood, the apocalypse). The theistic myths involve cultural hierarchies (e.g., the Twelve Olympians, the Egyptian gods). Hero myths, perhaps the best known, are stories dealing with individuals (e.g., Achilles, Odysseus, Theseus, Jesus, Moses). Place and object myths concern either mythical places (e.g., Atlantis, the Labyrinth) or objects (e.g., King Arthur's sword, the Golden Fleece).

As we explore the world of myth, we should remember that we are journeying not through a maze of falsehood but through a marvelous world of metaphor that breathes life into the essential human story: the story of the relationship between the known and the unknown, both around and within us, the story of the search for identity in the context of the universal struggle between order and chaos. The metaphors themselves may be Indian, Greek, Native American, or Egyptian. The story they convey belongs to us all. It is what Joseph Campbell called "the wonderful song of the soul's high adventure" (*The Hero with a Thousand Faces*, p. 19).

Select Bibliography

The following works are intended as background reading not only for this introduction but also for the subject of mythology as a whole. The selection of individual titles reflects the approach adopted by the author. Additional bibliographical listings may be found at the end of each section of the book.

Aarne, A. A. *Types of the Folktale: A Classification and Bibliography*. Trans. Stith Thompson. Helsinki, 1961.

Beltz, Walter. *God and the Gods: Myths of the Bible*. New York, 1983.

Bodkin, Maude. *Archetypal Patterns in Poetry*. Oxford, 1934.

Campbell, Joseph. *The Hero with a Thousand Faces*. 1959. Princeton, N.J., 1968.

———. *The Masks of God*. 4 vols. New York, 1970.

———. *The Mythic Image*. Princeton, N.J., 1974.

———. *The Way of the Animal Powers*. San Francisco, 1983.

———. *Transformations of Myth Through Time*. New York, 1990.

Cassirer, Ernst. *Language and Myth*. New York, 1946.

Chase, Richard. *Quest for Myth*. Baton Rouge, La., 1949.

De Santillana, Giorgio, and Hertha von Dechend. *Hamlet's Mill: An Essay on Myth and the Frame of Time*. 1969. Boston, 1977.

Doane, T. W. *Bible Myths and Their Parallels in Other Religions*. New York, 1971.

Eisenberg, Diane, et al. *Transformations of Myth Through Time: An Anthology of Readings*. New York, 1990.

Eliade, Mircea. *Birth and Rebirth*. New York, 1958.

———. *Mephistopheles and the Androgyne*. New York, 1965.

———. *Myth and Reality*. New York, 1963.

———. *The Myth of the Eternal Return*. New York, 1954.

———. *Patterns in Comparative Religion*. New York, 1958.

———. *The Sacred and the Profane*. New York, 1959.

———, ed. *The Encyclopedia of Religion*. 16 vols. New York, 1987.

Frazer, Sir James. *The Golden Bough*. 12 vols. London, 1905–17.

Freud, Sigmund, *Totem and Taboo*. New York, 1918.

Frye, Northrop. *Anatomy of Criticism*. New York, 1970.

———. *Fables of Identity: Studies in Poetic Mythology*. New York, 1963.

———. *The Great Code: The Bible and Literature*. New York, 1983.

Gaster, Theodor. *Myth, Legend and Custom in the Old Testament*. New York, 1969.

Grimal, Pierre, ed. *Larousse World Mythology*. New York, 1973.

Hamilton, Edith. *Mythology*. 1942. New York, 1953.

Harrison, Jane. *Mythology*. New York, 1963.

Hillman, James. *The Myth of Analysis: Essays on Psychological Creativity*. New York, 1978.

Jung, Carl Gustav. *The Archetypes and the Collective Unconscious*. Princeton, N.J., 1959.

———. *Symbols of Transformation*. Princeton, 1956.

———, ed. *Man and His Symbols*. New York, 1968.

Leeming, David A. *Mythology*. New York, 1976.

———. *Mythology: The Voyage of the Hero*. New York, 1981.

Lévi-Strauss, Claude. *Myth and Meaning*. New York, 1979.

———. *The Naked Man: Introduction to a Science of Mythology*. New York, 1981.

———. *The Raw and the Cooked*. Trans. John and Doreen Weightman. New York, 1969.

Luke, Helen M. *Woman Earth and Spirit: The Feminine in Symbol and Myth*. New York, 1987.

Thompson, Stith. *The Folktale*. New York, 1946.

———. *Motif-Index of Folk Literature*. Bloomington, Ind., 1958.

Thompson, William Irwin. *The Time Falling Bodies Take to Light: Mythology, Sexuality and the Origins of Culture*. New York, 1981.

Walker, Barbara. *The Woman's Encyclopedia of Myths and Secrets*. New York, 1983.

Watts, Alan. *Myth and Ritual in Christianity*. Boston, 1968.

PART I

COSMIC
MYTHS

Cosmic myths are myths of the cosmos (Greek *kosmos*, meaning "order"). They belong to a science called cosmology, the study of the order of the universe as a whole. Under this category can be included such myths as those of Creation and the Fall, the Flood, the other life or afterlife, and the end of the world. Each culture has its own mythic cosmology. Each cosmology reflects the experience of the culture that produced it. At the same time, all cosmologies reflect a universal human concern with the outer boundaries of existence. In our cosmologies, we humans have established ourselves at the very center of time-space. The cosmic myths give us purpose and significance in the larger perspective of the universe itself. In creation stories we are given a context; in flood myths we express a cosmic basis for the pervasive idea of the cleansing sacrifice; in afterlife and apocalypse myths we celebrate the immortality of human consciousness against the background of personal and universal physical decay.

THE CREATION

A myth of creation, a cosmogony *(Greek* kosmos, *meaning "order," and* gen-esis, *meaning "birth"), is a story of how the cosmos began and developed. Typ-ically, though not always, cosmogonies include the creation of the world, the creation of humankind, and the fall of humankind from a state of perfection, or the struggle in heaven between various groups of immortals.*

Each person's birth is the subject of a story that is somehow revealing about that person. The events surrounding one's birth are a celebration of the miracle of individuality. The same applies to cultural myths of origin. Origin stories are sacramental—outward and visible signs of an inner truth about the individual or culture in question. Mircea Eliade has called the creation myth the "narration of a sacred history," the story of the "breakthrough of the sacred" into time (Myth and Reality, *p. 6).*

That the creation story is a metaphor for birth is indicated further by the frequent presence in cosmogonies from around the world of the motifs of the primal egg or the primal waters. These essential female symbols remind us that it is the Great Mother, perhaps breathed on by an intangible ultimate source, who gives form to life. It is she who is the prima materia *without which life cannot be born:*

> *The mother of us all*
> *the oldest of all,*
> *hard,*
> > *splendid as rock*
>
> *"The Hymn to the Earth,"*
> (Homeric Hymns, *trans. Charles Boer, p. 5*)

In the analogous mythic motif of the hero's birth, even God, if he chooses to participate in the human experience, must be born of a Maya or a Mary or an Isis, the living embodiment of Creation itself.

For us, the creation myth, like the myth of the hero's birth, inevitably has a psychological meaning. In the fact that cosmos is born out of chaos or no-thing-ness, or the fact that a hero is born of a virgin, we find a metaphor for the awakening of consciousness from the unconscious. In the Creation myths themselves, the creation of the human being is a necessary step. In the Judeo-Christian Genesis myth we find explicitly stated what is nearly always implied in creation myths, the idea that human beings are created to be namers, to apply their godlike powers of consciousness to recording creation and thereby providing it with significance.

The creation myth, then, establishes our reason for being, the source of our significance. As such, it is often used to help individuals or groups to regain health or order. When we are broken, we return to our origins to become whole again, whether on the psychiatrist's couch or in the shaman's hut. So it is that the ancient Sumero-Babylonian creation myth, the Enuma elish, *was read aloud at the Babylonian New Year festival. And so it is that many curing ceremonies, such as the Navajo and Buddhist sand-painting ceremonies, begin with the recitation of the creation myth. The sand painting is itself a mandala, a sacred circle representing creation in its original wholeness. When the patient sits in the sand painting and has the creation myth recited over him by the sha-man (medicine man), he is returning to the womb of nature in the hope of being reborn into nature's wholeness, of reenacting the creation myth in his own life. An equivalent of the curative sand painting for the Christian, for example, would be the church building. It is in "Mother Church," where the sacred meal is administered or "celebrated" by a priest—the spiritual descendant of a hero born of the Virgin Mother—that the Christian is reborn into spiritual health. There is obvious significance in the fact that in certain branches of the church, the Christian version of the creation story from the first book of John's Gospel ("In the beginning was the Word . . .") is recited before the dismissal of the congregation at the end of the Eucharist, the sacred soul-curing liturgy.*

But if humans are born to make Earth conscious of itself, why must they (or warring immortals) fall from grace so soon after creation? The answer would seem to lie in the nature of the created world. Life, by definition, implies death. To be alive is to be imperfect, to be on an evolving path toward death, toward the entropic equilibrium of chaos. To be in the world is to be a part of the life-defining struggle to create order out of chaos. The bodies we live in, the chairs we sit in—all in process of decaying—are models of that struggle and, as such, models of creation. Works of art are even more obviously so. A poem lives insofar as its form holds chaos at bay, and its very being is a celebration of the skill that enables it to do so. The fall from grace at the end of the creation story perhaps suggests this necessary freedom of the created sphere of time and space from the formless perfection of the supreme source.

THE CREATION STORIES

Egyptian: The Beginnings

The Egyptian cosmogony developed in various directions over the centuries between the beginning of the Old Kingdom in c. 3000 B.C.E. and the end of the ancient civilization in the third century C.E. Our sources for Egyptian mythology are the ancient Pyramid Texts inscribed in hieroglyphs on inner chamber walls of Old Kingdom (3000–2200 B.C.E.) pyramids, the somewhat later Coffin Texts of the Middle Kingdom (2134–1660 B.C.E.), and the *Book of Going Forth by Day* (often called the *Book of the Dead*), an early New Kingdom work (c. 1550 B.C.E.) that is derived from the earlier texts.

The central priestly source for the Egyptian creation myth is the cult of Atun or Re, the sun god of Heliopolis (near Cairo). In the various versions of the myth we find an original spirit or Word; the High God as an emerging deity called Khoprer or Khepri (meaning "form"); a cosmic egg; a creating eye (the sun); creation by way of the High God's androgynous act of masturbation; and creation through the god Shu's separation of Sky (Nut) and Earth (Geb). We also find a primeval mound of earth, sometimes in fusion with the sun—a combination perhaps symbolized by the great pyramids themselves. We are not surprised to learn that rituals and myths of the Creation were repeated by the ancient Egyptians at funerals as well as at coronations and other important rites of passage.

What follows is a series of fragments that convey some idea of the Egyptian sense of the Creation. Many of these motifs of the Egyptian cosmogony are found in the creation myths of later cultures.

*

I am the Eternal Spirit,
I am the sun that rose from the Primeval Waters.
My soul is God, I am the creator of the Word.
Evil is my abomination, I see it not.
I am the Creator of the Order wherein I live,
I am the Word, which will never be annihilated
in this my name of "Soul."

. . .

The Word came into being.
All things were mine when I was alone.
I was Rê in [all] his first manifestations:
I was the great one who came into being of himself,

R. T. Rundle Clark, *Myth and Symbol in Ancient Egypt* (London, 1959; 1978), pp. 77, 79, 92, 93

who created all his names as the Companies of the [lesser] gods,
he who is irresistible among the gods.
The battleship of the gods was made according to what I said.
Now I know the name of the great god who was therein.
   [An early gloss adds, "Perfume of Rê is his name."]
I was that great Phoenix who is in Heliopolis,
who looks after the decision of all that is.
   [An early gloss adds, "That is Osiris, while as to all that is,
   that is eternity and everlastingness."]

                                    . . .

I fulfilled all my desires when I was alone,
before there had appeared a second to be with me in this place;
I assumed form as that great soul wherein I started being creative
while still in the Primeval Waters in a state of inertness,
before I had found anywhere to stand.
I considered in my heart, I planned in my head how I should
   make every shape
—this was while I was still alone—I planned in my heart how I
   should create
other beings—the myriad forms of Khopri—and that there
   should come into being their children and theirs.
So it was I who spat forth Shu and expectorated Tefnut
so that where there had been one god there were now three as
   well as myself
and there were now a male and a female in the world.
Shu and Tefnut rejoiced thereat in the Primeval Waters in which
   they were.
After an age my Eye brought them to me and they approached
   me and joined my body, that they might issue from me.
When I rubbed with my fist my heart came into my mouth in
   that I spat forth Shu and expectorated Tefnut.
But, as my father was relaxed . . . ages . . . serpents . . .
I wept tears . . . the form of my Eye; and that is how mankind
   came into existence.
I replaced it with a shining one [the sun] and it became enraged
   with me when it came back and found another growing in its
   place.

Mesopotamian: *Enuma elish*

One of the world's oldest written creation myths is the Babylonian *Enuma elish* ("When on high"), composed no later than the reign of Nebuchad-rezzar in the twelfth century B.C.E. and perhaps much earlier. It is in part a creation myth and in part a celebration of the high god Marduk. As a creation myth, it contains several familiar motifs: the emergence of order from chaos, the primal waters as a source of creation, a war in heaven, the emergence of a king god, and the creation of earthly matter from the body of the first mother.

Much has been made of the connection between this myth and that of the Old Testament story of Genesis. Several scholars have pointed out the inevitable diffusion of ideas in the early days of the great Middle Eastern cultures.

*

When on high the heaven had not been named,
Firm ground below had not been called by name,
Naught but primordial Apsu,[1] their begetter,
(And) Mummu[2]-Tiamat,[3] she who bore them all,
Their waters[4] commingling as a single body;
No reed hut had been matted, no marsh land had appeared,
When no gods whatever had been brought into being,
Uncalled by name, their destinies undetermined—
Then it was that the gods were formed within them.[5]
Lahmu and Lahamu[6] were brought forth, by name they were called.
For aeons they grew in age and stature.
Anshar and Kishar[7] were formed, surpassing the others.
They prolonged the days, added on the years.
Anu[8] was their son, of his fathers the rival;
Yea, Anshar's first-born, Anu, was his equal.
Anu begot in his image Nudimmud.[9]
This Nudimmud was of his fathers the master;
Of broad wisdom, understanding, mighty in strength,
Mightier by far than his grandfather, Anshar.
He had no rival among the gods, his brothers.
The divine brothers banded together,
They disturbed Tiamat as they surged back and forth,
Yea, they troubled the mood of Tiamat
By their hilarity in the Abode of Heaven.
Apsu could not lessen their clamour
And Tiamat was speechless at their ways.
Their doings were loathsome unto [. . .].
Unsavoury were their ways; they were overbearing.
Then Apsu, the begetter of the great gods,

Mircea Eliade, *Gods, Goddesses, and Myths of Creation* (New York, 1974), pp. 98–109.

Cried out, addressing Mummu, his vizier:
"O Mummu, my vizier, who rejoicest my spirit,
Come hither and let us go to Tiamat!"
They went and sat down before Tiamat,
Exchanging counsel about the gods, their first-born.
Apsu, opening his mouth,
Said unto resplendent Tiamat:
"Their ways are verily loathsome unto me.
By day I find no relief, nor repose by night.
I will destroy, I will wreck their ways,
That quiet may be restored. Let us have rest!"
As soon as Tiamat heard this,
She was wroth and called out to her husband.
She cried out aggrieved, as she raged all alone,
Injecting woe into her mood:
What? Should we destroy that which we have built?
Their ways are indeed troublesome, but let us attend kindly!"
Then answered Mummu, giving counsel to Apsu;
Ill-wishing and ungracious was Mummu's advice:
"Do destroy, my father, the mutinous ways.
Then shalt thou have relief by day and rest by night!"
When Apsu heard this, his face grew radiant
Because of the evil he planned against the gods, his sons.
As for Mummu, by the neck he embraced him
As (that one) sat down on his knees to kiss him.
(Now) whatever they had plotted between them
Was repeated unto the gods, their first born.
When the gods heard (this), they were astir,
(Then) lapsed into silence and remained speechless.
Surpassing in wisdom, accomplished, resourceful,
Ea,[10] the all-wise, saw through their[11] scheme.
A master design against it he devised and set up,
Made artful his spell against it, surpassing and holy.
He recited it and made it subsist in the deep,[12]
As he poured sleep upon him. Sound asleep he lay.
When Apsu he had made prone, drenched with sleep,
Mummu, the adviser, was impotent to move.
He loosened his band, tore off his tiara,
Removed his halo (and) put it on himself.
Having fettered Apsu, he slew him.
Mummu he bound and left behind lock.
Having thus upon Apsu established his dwelling,
He laid hold on Mummu, holding him by the nose-rope.

After he had vanquished and trodden down his foes,
Ea, his triumph over his enemies secured,
In his sacred chamber in profound peace he rested.
He named it "Apsu,"[13] for shrines he assigned (it).
In that same place his cult hut he founded.
Ea and Damkina, his wife, dwelled (there) in splendour.
In the chamber of fates, the abode of destinies,
A god was engendered, most potent and wisest of gods.
In the heart of Apsu[14] was Marduk created,
In the heart of holy Apsu was Marduk created.
He who begot him was Ea, his father;
She who conceived him was Damkina, his mother.
The breast of goddesses did she suck.
The nurse that nursed him filled him with awesomeness.
Alluring was his figure, sparkling the lift in his eyes.
Lordly was his gait, commanding from of old.
When Ea saw him, the father who begot him,
He exulted and glowed, his heart filled with gladness.
He rendered him perfect and endowed him with a double godhead.
Greatly exalted was he above them, exceeding throughout.
Perfect were his members beyond comprehension,
Unsuited for understanding, difficult to perceive.
Four were his eyes, four were his ears;[15]
When he moved his lips, fire blazed forth.
Large were all hearing organs,
And the eyes, in like number, scanned all things.
He was the loftiest of the gods, surpassing was his stature;
His members were enormous, he was exceeding tall.
"My little son, my little son!
My son, the Sun! Sun of the heavens!"
Clothed with the halo of ten gods, he was strong to the utmost,
As their awesome flashes were heaped upon him.

.   .   .

Disturbed was Tiamat, astir night and day.
The gods, in malice, contributed to the storm.
Their insides having plotted evil,
To Tiamat these brothers said:
"When they slew Apsu, thy consort,
Thou didst not aid him but remaindest still.
Although he fashioned the awesome Saw,[16]
Thy insides are diluted and so we can have no rest.
Let Apsu, thy consort, be in thy mind
And Mummu, who has been vanquished! Thou art left alone."

. . .

Then joined issue Tiamat and Marduk, wisest of gods,
They swayed in single combat, locked in battle.
The lord spread out his net to enfold her,
The Evil Wind, which followed behind, he let loose in her face.
When Tiamat opened her mouth to consume him,
He drove in the Evil Wind that she close not her lips.
As the fierce winds charged her belly,
Her body was distended and her mouth was wide open.
He released the arrow, it tore her belly,
It cut through her insides, splitting the heart.
Having thus subdued her, he extinguished her life.
He cast down her carcass to stand upon it. . . .
The lord trod on the legs of Tiamat,
With his unsparing mace he crushed her skull.
When the arteries of her blood he had severed,
The North Wind bore (it) to places undisclosed.
On seeing this, his fathers were joyful and jubilant,
They brought gifts of homage, they to him.
Then the lord paused to view her dead body,
That he might divide the monster and do artful works.
He split her like a shellfish into two parts:
Half of her he set up and ceiled as sky,
Pulled down the bar and posted guards.
He bade them to allow not her waters to escape.
He crossed the heavens and surveyed (its) regions.
He squared Apsu's quarter, the abode of Nudimmud,
As the lord measured the dimensions of Apsu.
The Great Abode, its likeness, he fixed as Esharra,
The Great Abode, Esharra, which he made as the firmament.
Anu, Enlil,[17] and Ea he made occupy their places.

. . .

When Marduk hears the words of the gods,
His heart prompts (him) to fashion artful works.
Opening his mouth, he addresses Ea
To impart the plan he addresses Ea
To impart the plan he had conceived in his heart:
"Blood I will mass and cause bones to be.
I will establish a savage, 'man' shall be his name.
Verily, savage-man I will create.
He shall be charged with the service of the gods
     That they might be at ease!
The ways of the gods I will artfully alter.
Though alike revered, into two (groups) they shall be divided."

Ea answered him, speaking a word to him.
To relate to him a scheme for the relief of the gods:
"Let but one of their brothers be handed over;
He alone shall perish that mankind may be fashioned.[18]
Let the great gods be here in Assembly,
Let the guilty be handed over that they may endure."
Marduk summoned the great gods to Assembly;
Presiding graciously, he issued instructions.
To his utterance the gods pay heed.
The king addresses a word to the Anunnaki:
"If your former statement was true,
Do (now) the truth on oath by me declare!
Who was it that contrived the uprising,
And made Tiamat rebel, and joined battle?
Let him be handed over who contrived the uprising.
His guilt I will make him bear that you may dwell in peace!"
The Igigi, the great gods, replied to him,
To Lugaldimmerankia,[19] counsellor of the gods, their lord:
"It was Kingu who contrived the uprising,
And made Tiamat rebel, and joined battle."
They bound him, holding him before Ea.
They imposed on him his guilt and severed his blood (vessels).
Out of his blood they fashioned mankind.
He[20] imposed the service and let free the gods.

Notes

1. God of subterranean waters; the primeval sweet-water ocean.
2. An epithet of Tiamat; perhaps meaning "mother."
3. A water-deity; the primeval salt-water ocean.
4. I.e., the fresh waters of Apsu and the marine waters of Tiamat.
5. The waters of Apsu and Tiamat.
6. The first generation of gods.
7. Gods.
8. The sky-god.
9. One of the names of Ea, the earth- and water-god.
10. Ea, the earth- and water-god.
11. That of Apsu and his vizier Mummu.
12. I.e., caused it to be in the waters of Apsu.
13. "The Deep."
14. See note 13.
15. Cf. Ezekiel 1:6.
16. The weapon of the sun-god.

17. The god of the wind, i.e., of the earth.
18. Out of his blood.
19. Meaning "The king of the gods of heaven and earth."
20. Ea.

Hebrew: Genesis

The watery chaos or "deep" (*tehom*) of the Hebrew creation story, part of which was probably composed during and soon after the Babylonian captivity (that is, during the sixth and fifth centuries B.C.E.), owes something to the concept of Tiamat in the Babylonian *Enuma elish*. If the Tiamat–*tehom* connection is not clear in the official Hebrew creation story, it is evident enough elsewhere in Hebrew scripture. When we read these words from Psalm 89 (9–10), we are reminded of the Babylonian wars in heaven and of the creative splitting of the primal mother:

> Thou rulest the raging of the sea: when
> the waves thereof arise, thou stillest them.
> Thou hast broken Rahab in pieces, as one
> that is slain; thou hast scattered thine
> enemies with thy strong arm.

But if the Babylonian creation myth was meant to establish the rule of Marduk, the Hebrew Genesis seems to be more concerned with the establishment of humanity's role in the universe. Genesis is in fact made up of two somewhat distinct myths. Genesis I contains the version composed probably as late as the fifth century B.C.E.; Genesis II is a much earlier text, perhaps as early as 950 B.C.E.. The differences to be particularly noted are those that concern the creation of the first humans. The story of the first humans in both of the Genesis versions continues to affect the relationship between men and women today.

*

Chapter 1

In the beginning God created the heaven and the earth.

2 And the earth was without form, and void; and darkness *was* upon the face of the deep. And the spirit of God moved upon the face of the waters.

3 And God said, Let there be light: and there was light.

Genesis 1–3.

4 And God saw the light, that it was good: and God divided the light from the darkness.

5 And God called the light Day, and the darkness he called Night. And the evening and the morning were the first day.

6 ¶ And God said, Let there be a firmament in the midst of the waters, and let it divide the waters from the waters.

7 And God made the firmament, and divided the waters which were under the firmament from the waters which were above the firmament: and it was so.

8 And God called the firmament Heaven. And the evening and the morning were the second day.

9 ¶ And God said, Let the waters under the heaven be gathered together unto one place, and let the dry land appear: and it was so.

10 And God called the dry land Earth; and the gathering together of the waters called he Seas: and God saw that it *was* good.

11 And God said, Let the earth bring forth grass, the herb yielding seed, and the fruit tree yielding fruit after his kind, whose seed *is* in itself, upon the earth: and it was so.

12 And the earth brought forth grass, and herb yielding seed after his kind, and the tree yielding fruit, whose seed was in itself, after his kind: and God saw that it was good.

13 And the evening and the morning were the third day.

14 ¶ And God said, Let there be lights in the firmament of the heaven to divide the day from the night; and let them be for signs, and for seasons, and for days, and years:

15 And let them be for lights in the firmament of the heaven to give light upon the earth: and it was so.

16 And God made two great lights; the greater light to rule the day, and the lesser light to rule the night: he made the stars also.

17 And God set them in the firmament of the heaven to give light upon the earth,

18 And to rule over the day and over the night, and to divide the light from the darkness: and God saw that it was good.

19 And the evening and the morning were the fourth day.

20 And God said, Let the waters bring forth abundantly the moving creature that hath life, and fowl that may fly above the earth in the open firmament of heaven.

21 And God created great whales, and every living creature that moveth, which the waters brought forth abundantly, after their kind, and every winged fowl after his kind: and God saw that it was good.

22 And God blessed them, saying, Be fruitful, and multiply, and fill the waters in the seas, and let fowl multiply in the earth.

23 And the evening and the morning were the fifth day.

24 ¶ And God said, Let the earth bring forth the living creature after his kind, cattle, and creeping thing, and beast of the earth after his kind: and it was so.

25 And God made the beast of the earth after his kind, and cattle after their kind, and every thing that creepeth upon the earth after his kind: and God saw that it was good.

26 ¶ And God said, Let us make man in our image, after our likeness: and let them have dominion over the fish of the sea, and over the fowl of the air, and over the cattle, and over all the earth, and over every creeping thing that creepeth upon the earth.

27 So God created man in his own image, in the image of God created he him; male and female created he them.

28 And God blessed them, and God said unto them, Be fruitful, and multiply, and replenish the earth, and subdue it: and have dominion over the fish of the sea, and over the fowl of the air, and over every living thing that moveth upon the earth.

29 ¶ And God said, Behold, I have given you every herb bearing seed, which is upon the face of all the earth, and every tree, in the which is the fruit of a tree yielding seed; to you it shall be for meat.

30 And to every beast of the earth, and to every fowl of the air, and to every thing that creepeth upon the earth, wherein there is life, I have given every green herb for meat: and it was so.

31 And God saw every thing that he had made, and, behold, it was very good. And the evening and the morning were the sixth day.

Chapter 2

Thus the heavens and the earth were finished, and all the host of them.

2 And on the seventh day God ended his work which he had made; and he rested on the seventh day from all his work which he had made.

3 And God blessed the seventh day, and sanctified it: because that in it he had rested from all his work which God created and made.

4 ¶ These are the generations of the heaves and of the earth when they were created, in the day that the Lord God made the earth and the heavens.

5 And every plant of the field before it was in the earth, and every herb of the field before it grew: for the Lord God had not caused it to rain upon the earth, and there was not a man to till the ground.

6 But there went up a mist from the earth, and watered the whole face of the ground.

7 And the Lord God formed man of the dust of the ground, and breathed into his nostrils the breath of life; and man became a living soul.

8 ¶ And the Lord God planted a garden eastward in Eden; and there he put the man whom he had formed.

9 And out of the ground made the Lord God to grow every tree that is pleasant to the sight, and good for food; the tree of life also in the midst of the garden, and the tree of knowledge of good and evil.

10 And a river went out from Eden to water the garden; and from thence it was parted, and became into four heads.

11 The name of the first *is* Pī'-sŏn: that is it which compasseth the whole land of Hăv'-i-läh, where there is gold;

12 And the gold of that land is good: there is bdellium and the onyx stone.

13 And the name of the second river is Gī'-hŏn: the same is it that compasseth the whole land of Ethiopia.

14 And the name of the third river is Hĭd'-dĕ-kĕl: that is it which goeth toward the east of Assyria. And the fourth river is Eû-phrā'-tēṡ.

15 And the Lord God took the man, and put him into the garden of Eden to dress it and to keep it.

16 And the Lord God commanded the man, saying, Of every tree of the garden thou mayest freely eat:

17 But of the tree of the knowledge of good and evil, thou shalt not eat of it: for in the day that thou eatest thereof thou shalt surely die.

18 ¶ And the Lord God said, It is not good that the man should be alone; I will make him an help meet for him.

19 And out of the ground the Lord God formed every beast of the field, and every fowl of the air; and brought them unto Adam to see what he would call them: and whatsoever Adam called every living creature, that was the name thereof.

20 And Adam gave names to all cattle, and to the fowl of the air, and to every beast of the field; but for Adam there was not found an help meet for him.

21 And the Lord God caused a deep sleep to fall upon Adam, and he slept: and he took one of his ribs, and closed up the flesh instead thereof;

22 And the rib, which the Lord God had taken from man, made he a woman, and brought her unto the man.

23 And Adam said, This is now bone of my bones, and flesh of my flesh: she shall be called Woman, because she was taken out of Man.

24 Therefore shall a man leave his father and his mother, and shall cleave unto his wife: and they shall be one flesh.

25 And they were both naked, the man and his wife, and were not ashamed.

Chapter 3

Now the serpent was more subtil than any beast of the field which the Lord God had made. And he said unto the woman, Yea, hath God said, Ye shall not eat of every tree of the garden?

2 And the woman said unto the serpent, We may eat of the fruit of the trees of the garden:

3 But of the fruit of the tree which is in the midst of the garden, God hath said, Ye shall not eat of it, neither shall ye touch it, lest ye die.

4 And the serpent said unto the woman, Ye shall not surely die:

5 For God doth know that in the day ye eat thereof, then your eyes shall be opened, and ye shall be as gods, knowing good and evil.

6 And when the woman saw that the tree was good for food, and that it was pleasant to the eyes, and a tree to be desired to make one wise, she took of the fruit thereof, and did eat, and gave also unto her husband with her; and he did eat.

7 And the eyes of them both were opened, and they knew that they were naked; and they sewed fig leaves together, and made themselves aprons.

8 And they heard the voice of the Lord God walking in the garden in the cool of the day: and Adam and his wife hid themselves from the presence of the Lord God amongst the trees of the garden.

9 And the Lord God called unto Adam, and said unto him, Where art thou?

10 And he said, I heard thy voice in the garden, and I was afraid, because I was naked; and I hid myself.

11 And he said, Who told thee that thou wast naked? Hast thou eaten of the tree, whereof I commanded thee that thou shouldest not eat?

12 And the man said, The woman whom thou gavest to be with me, she gave me of the tree, and I did eat.

13 And the Lord God said unto the woman, What is this that thou hast done? And the woman said, The serpent beguiled me, and I did eat.

14 And the Lord God said unto the serpent, Because thou hast done this, thou art cursed above all cattle, and above every beast of the field; upon thy belly shalt thou go, and dust shalt thou eat all the days of thy life:

15 And I will put enmity between thee and the woman, and between thy seed and her seed; it shall bruise thy head, and thou shall bruise his heel.

16 Unto the woman he said, I will greatly multiply thy sorrow and thy conception; in sorrow thou shalt bring forth children; and thy desire shall be to thy husband, and he shall rule over thee.

17 And unto Adam he said, Because thou hast hearkened unto the

voice of thy wife, and hast eaten of the tree, of which I commanded thee, saying, Thou shalt not eat of it: cursed is the ground for thy sake; in sorrow shalt thou eat of it all the days of thy life;

18 Thorns also and thistles shall it bring forth to thee; and thou shalt eat the herb of the field;

19 In the sweat of thy face shalt thou eat bread, till thou return unto the ground; for out of it wast thou taken: for dust thou art, and unto dust shalt thou return.

20 And Adam called his wife's name Eve; because she was the mother of all living.

21 Unto Adam also and to his wife did the Lord God make coats of skins, and clothed them.

22 ¶ And the Lord God said, Behold, the man is become as one of us, to know good and evil: and now, lest he put forth his hand, and take also of the tree of life, and eat, and live for ever:

23 Therefore the Lord God sent him forth from the garden of Eden, to till the ground from whence he was taken.

24 So he drove out the man; and he placed at the east of the garden of Eden Chĕr'-ū-bims, and a flaming sword which turned every way, to keep the way of the tree of life.

Indian: The *Rig Veda* and the *Brhadaranyaka Upanishad*

Like Egypt, India has many ancient creation myths. These are to be found in the Vedas, Brahamanas, Upanishads, and epics of the Hindus. They contain many familiar motifs: the creator god (Brahma or Prajapati), creation by the "spilling" of the creator god's seed, the sacrifice of a single being into two, the cosmic egg, the cosmic eye, the primal waters, and many others. Their dominant theme seems to be that of the emergence of reality as Mind (*manas*) or Soul (*atman*) from nothingness. The stories here are from the *Rig Veda* (c. 2000–1700 B.C.E.) and the *Brhadaranyka Upanishad* (c. sixth century B.C.E.).

*

1. Then[1] even nothingness was not, nor existence.[2]
     There was no air then, nor the heavens beyond it.
   What covered it? Where was it? In whose keeping?
     Was there then cosmic water, in depths unfathomed?
2. Then there were neither death nor immortality,
     nor was there then the torch of night and day.

Mircea Eliade, *Gods, Goddesses, and Myths of Creation* (New York, 1974), p. 110.

The One[3] breathed windlessly and self-sustaining.[4]
There was that One then, and there was no other.

3. At first there was only darkness wrapped in
darkness.
All this was only unillumined water.[5]
That One which came to be, enclosed in nothing,
arose at last, born of the power of heat.[6]

4. In the beginning desire descended on it—
that was the primal seed, born of the mind.
The sages who have searched their hearts with
wisdom
know that which is, is kin[7] to that which is not.

5. And they have stretched their cord across the void,
and know what was above, and what below.
Seminal powers made fertile mighty forces.
Below was strength, and over it was impulse.[8]

6. But, after all, who knows, and who can say
whence it all came, and how creation happened?
The gods themselves are later than creation,
so who knows truly whence it has arisen?

7. Whence all creation had its origin,
he, whether he fashioned it or whether he did not,
he, who surveys it all from highest heaven,
he knows—or maybe even he does not know.

Notes

1. In the beginning.
2. *Asat* nor *sat*.
3. *Tad ekam*, "That One," who "breathes without air."
4. *Svadhā*, energy, intrinsic power which makes self-generation possible.
5. Fluid (*salila*) and indistinguishable (*apraketa*).
6. *Tapas*, an archaic word which also defines those human austerities or techniques which, like this cosmic heat, generate power.
7. From "bond" (*bandhu*).
8. This stanza is obscure. A. A. Macdonell suggests that the "cord" (*rashmi*) implies the bond of the preceding stanza; thought measures out of the distance between the non-existent and the existent and separates the male and female cosmogonic principles: impulse (*prayati*) above and energy (*svadhā*) below. (*A Vedic Reader for Students*, London: Oxford University, 1917, p. 210.)

In the beginning, this universe was Soul [*ātman*] in the form of the Man [Purusa]. He looked around and saw nothing other than himself. Then, at first, he said, "I am," and thus the word "I" was born. Therefore even now when one is addressed he first says, "It is I," and then he speaks whatever other name he has. Since he, preceding [*pūrva*] all this universe, burnt up [*uṣ*] all evils, he is the Man [Puruṣa]. He who knows this burns up anyone who would precede him.

He was afraid; therefore one who is all alone is afraid. He reflected, "Since there is nothing other than me, of what am I afraid?" Then his fear vanished, for of what could he have been afraid? One becomes afraid of a second. He did not rejoice; therefore one who is all alone does not rejoice. He desired a second. He was of the same size and kind as a man and a woman closely embracing. He caused himself to fall [*pat*] into two pieces, and from him a husband and a wife [*pati* and *patnī*] were born. Therefore Yājñavalkya has said, "Oneself is like a half-fragment." Therefore this space was filled by a woman. He united with her, and from this mankind was born.

She reflected, "How can he unite with me after engendering me from himself? For shame! I will conceal myself." She became a cow; he became a bull and united with her, and from this all the cattle were born. She became a mare; he became a stallion. She became a female ass; he became a male ass and united with her, and from this all whole-hooved animals were born. She became a she-goat; he became a billy-goat; she became a ewe; he became a ram and united with her, and from this goats and sheep were born. Thus he created all the pairs, even down to the ants.

He knew that he was creation, for he created all of this. Thus creation arose. Whoever knows this is born in that creation of his. Then he churned. From his mouth as the fire-hole [*yoni*] and from his two hands he created fire. Therefore both mouth and hands are without hair on the inside, for the fire-hole is without hair on the inside. When people speak of him, saying, "Sacrifice to this god!" "Sacrifice to this god!," speaking of one single god and then of another single god, it is his own creation, and he himself is all the gods. Now, whatever is moist he created from semen, and that is Soma. All this universe is food and the eater of food. For Soma is food, and Agni is the eater of food. This was the surpassing creation of Brahmā, for he created the gods, who were better than him, when he, being mortal, created immortals. Therefore it was a surpassing creation. Whoever knows this is born in that surpassing creation of his.

Wendy Doniger O'Flaherty, *Hindu Myths*, trans. W. D. O'Flaherty (New York, 1975), pp. 34–35.

Greek: Hesiod's *Theogony*

Hesiod probably lived in the eighth century B.C.E. His *Theogony* contains the preclassical Greek view of the founding of the universe. Essentially, Hesiod gave voice to an early Greek understanding of the myths of Homer and the mythic lore of the ancient Near East in general. Not surprisingly, then, we find in Hesiod's cosmogony a number of familiar themes: creation out of chaos, a war in heaven, and the establishment of an organized monarchy in heaven. What Hesiod adds, as Norman O. Brown points out ("Introduction," *Theogony* p. 43), is a reconciliation between that monarchy—that patriarchal order— and the female creative principle represented by Earth (Gaia). In this reconciliation we may have the birth of classical humanism.

•

[II, 116–53]

First of all, the Void came into being, next broad-bosomed Earth, the solid and eternal home of all, and Eros [Desire], the most beautiful of the immortal gods, who in every man and every god softens the sinews and overpowers the prudent purpose of the mind. Out of Void came Darkness and black Night, and out of Night came Light and Day, her children conceived after union in love with Darkness. Earth first produced starry Sky, equal in size with herself, to cover her on all sides. Next she produced the tall mountains, the pleasant haunts of the gods, and also gave birth to the barren waters, sea with its raging surges—all this without the passion of love. Thereafter she lay with Sky and gave birth to Ocean with its deep current, Coeus and Crius and Hyperion and Iapetus; Thea and Rhea and Themis [Law] and Mnemosyne [Memory]; also golden-crowned Phoebe and lovely Tethys. After these came cunning Cronus, the youngest and boldest of her children; and he grew to hate the father who had begotten him.

Earth also gave birth to the violent Cyclopes—Thunderer, Lightner, and bold Flash—who made and gave to Zeus the thunder and the lightning-bolt. They were like the gods in all respects except that a single eye stood in the middle of their foreheads, and their strength and power and skill were in their hands.

There were also born to Earth and Sky three more children, big, strong, and horrible, Cottus and Briareus and Gyes. This unruly brood had a hundred monstrous hands sprouting from their shoulders, and fifty heads on top of their shoulders growing from their sturdy bodies. They had monstrous strength to match their huge size.

Hesiod, *Theogony*, trans. Norman O. Brown (Indianapolis, Ind., 1953), pp. 56–59, 62–68, 70–73.

[III, 154–210]

Of all the children born of Earth and Sky these were the boldest, and their father hated them from the beginning. As each of them was about to be born, Sky would not let them reach the light of day; instead he hid them all away in the bowels of Mother Earth. Sky took pleasure in doing this evil thing. In spite of her enormous size, Earth felt the strain within her and groaned. Finally she thought of an evil and cunning stratagem. She instantly produced a new metal, gray steel, and made a huge sickle. Then she laid the matter before her children; the anguish in her heart made her speak boldly: "My children, you have a savage father; if you will listen to me, we may be able to take vengeance for his evil outrage: he was the one who started using violence."

This was what she said; but all the children were gripped by fear, and not one of them spoke a word. Then great Cronus, the cunning trickster, took courage and answered his good mother with these words: "Mother, I am willing to undertake and carry through your plan. I have no respect for our infamous father, since he was the one who started using violence."

This was what he said, and enormous Earth was very pleased. She hid him in ambush and put in his hands the sickle with jagged teeth, and instructed him fully in her plot. Huge Sky came drawing night behind him and desiring to make love; he lay on top of Earth stretched all over her. Then from his ambush his son reached out with his left hand and with his right took the huge sickle with its long jagged teeth and quickly sheared the organs from his own father and threw them away, backward over his shoulder. But that was not the end of them. The drops of blood that spurted from them were all taken in by Mother Earth, and in the course of the revolving years she gave birth to the powerful Erinyes [Spirits of Vengeance] and the huge Giants with shining armor and long spears. As for the organs themselves, for a long time they drifted round the sea just as they were when Cronus cut them off with the steel edge and threw them from the land into the waves of the ocean; then white foam issued from the divine flesh, and in the foam a girl began to grow. First she came near to holy Cythera, then reached Cyprus, the land surrounded by sea. There she stepped out, a goddess, tender and beautiful, and round her slender feet the green grass shot up. She is called Aphrodite by gods and men, because she grew in the *froth*, and also Cytherea, because she came near to Cythera, and the Cyprian, because she was born in watery Cyprus. Eros [Desire] and beautiful Passion were her attendants both at her birth and at her first going to join the family of the gods. The rights and privileges assigned to her from the beginning and recognized by men and gods are these: to preside over the whispers and smiles and tricks which girls employ, and the sweet delight and tenderness of love.

Great Father Sky called his children the Titans, because of his feud with them: he said that they blindly had *tightened* the noose and had done a savage thing for which they would have to pay in time to come.

. . .

[VIII, 453–506]

Rhea submitted to the embraces of Cronus and bore him children with a glorious destiny: Hestia, Demeter, and Hera, who walks on golden sandals; Hades, the powerful god whose home is underground and whose heart is pitiless; Poseidon, the god whose great blows make the earth quake; and Zeus the lord of wisdom, the father of gods and men, whose thunder makes the broad earth tremble. As each of these children came out of their mother's holy womb onto her knees, great Cronus swallowed them. His purpose was to prevent the kingship of the gods from passing to another one of the august descendants of Sky; he had been told by Earth and starry Sky that he was destined to be overcome by his own son. For that reason he kept a sleepless watch and waited for his own children to be born and then swallowed them. Rhea had no rest from grief; so, when she was about to give birth to Zeus, the father of gods and men, she begged her own dear parents, Earth and starry Sky, to help her contrive a plan whereby she might bear her child without Cronus' knowing it, and make amends to the vengeful spirits of her father Sky. Earth and Sky listened to their daughter and granted her request; they told her what was destined to happen to King Cronus and to his bold son. When she was about to give birth to great Zeus, her youngest child, they sent her to the rich Cretan town of Lyctus. Huge Mother Earth undertook to nurse and raise the infant in the broad land of Crete. Dark night was rushing on as Earth arrived there carrying him, and Lyctus was the first place where she stopped. She took him and hid him in an inaccessible cave, deep in the bowels of holy Earth, in the dense woods of Mount Aegeum. Then she wrapped a huge stone in baby blankets and handed it to the royal son of Sky, who then was king of the gods. He took the stone and swallowed it into his belly—the fool! He did not know that a stone had replaced his son, who survived, unconquered and untroubled, and who was going to overcome him by force and drive him from his office and reign over the gods in his place.

The young prince grew quickly in strength and stature. After years had passed Cronus the great trickster fell victim to the cunning suggestions of Mother Earth and threw up his own children again. The first thing he vomited was the stone, the last thing he had swallowed; Zeus set it up on the highways of the earth in holy Pytho under the slopes of Parnassus, to be a sign and a wonder to mankind thereafter.

Zeus also set free his father's brothers from the cruel chains in which their father Sky had in foolish frenzy bound them. They gratefully remembered his kindness and gave him the thunder and the lightning-bolt and flash, which huge Earth had kept hidden till then. In these weapons Zeus trusts; they make him master over gods and men.

Christian: John's Gospel

Traditionally, the Fourth Gospel (from the Greek *evangelion,* meaning "good news")—the last of the approved early biographies of Jesus included in the New Testament—was written by the disciple John in Ephesus. Papyrus fragments of John's Gospel found in Egypt indicate that the work was written about 100 C.E.

The prologue to John's Gospel begins with the words "In the beginning was the Word" (Greek *Logos,* the creative and controlling principle of the universe)—that which turned the void (*chaos*) into order (*cosmos*). The significance for Christians of John's prologue is his suggestion that Jesus and Logos are somehow one, that what took human form as Jesus had always been ultimate reality. This creation myth incorporates the new sense of Jesus' divinity.

The somewhat mystical tone of the Gospel suggests possible Gnostic influence and reminds us of the Egyptian High God's words in the most popular chapter (17) of the *Book of the Dead:* "The Word came into being. / All things were mine when I was alone."

*

Chapter 1

In the beginning was the Word, and the Word was with God, and the Word was God.

2 The same was in the beginning with God.

3 All things were made by him; and without him was not any thing made that was made.

4 In him was life; and the life was the light of men.

5 And the light shineth in darkness; and the darkness comprehended it not.

6 ¶ There was a man sent from God, whose name was John.

7 The same came for a witness, to bear witness of the Light, that all men through him might believe.

8 He was not that Light, but was sent to bear witness of that Light.

John 1:1–14.

9 That was the true Light, which lighteth every man that cometh into the world.

10 He was in the world, and the world was made by him, and the world knew him not.

11 He came unto his own, and his own received him not.

12 But as many as received him, to them gave he power to become the sons of God, even to them that believe on his name:

13 Which were born, not of blood, nor of the will of the flesh, nor of the will of man, but of God.

14 And the Word was made flesh, and dwelt among us, (and we beheld his glory, the glory as of the only begotten of the Father,) full of grace and truth.

Hopi: Spider Woman

The dominance of Spider Woman, the female creative principle, befits a culture that remains to this day matrilineal. The Hopi creation myth uses many familiar motifs: the creative female principle itself, associated with the Earth; the more mysterious divine spirit, the sun god Tawa; the division of the divine parents into new creative forms; and creation by thought, a motif common to many Native American mythologies. An interesting development is the notion of creation by song, an innovation that seems to owe something to Anasazi-Hopi ritual song-dances.

Most important, the Spider Woman story is an example of an emergence myth, a type of creation myth popular among Native American tribes. The emergence story stresses the idea of the Earth as a womb from which the people emerge gradually, as in childbirth. At each stage they grow in knowledge and ability, and only when fully born are they bathed by the light of the sun god's power, the power of *Logos*, the principle that allows for proper social ordering.

•

First Tale

In the beginning there were only two: Tawa, the Sun God, and Spider Woman, the Earth Goddess. All the mysteries and power in the Above belonged to Tawa, while Spider Woman controlled the magic of the Below. In the Underworld, abode of the gods, they dwelt and they were All. There was neither man nor woman, bird nor beast, no living thing until these Two willed it to be.

G. M. Mullett, *Spider Woman Stories: Legends of the Hopis* (Tucson, Ariz., 1979), pp. 1–6.

In time it came to them that there should be other gods to share their labors. So Tawa divided himself and there came Muiyinwuh, God of All Life Germs; Spider Woman also divided herself so that there was Huzrui-wuhti, Woman of the Hard Substances, the goddess of all hard ornaments of wealth such as coral, turquoise, silver and shell. Huzruiwuhti became the always-bride of Tawa. They were the First Lovers and of their union there came into being those marvelous ones the Magic Twins—Puukon-hoya, the Youth, and Palunhoya, the Echo. As time unrolled there followed Hicanavaiya, Ancient of Six (the Four World Quarters, the Above and Below), Man-Eagle, the Great Plumed Serpent and many others. But Masauwuh, the Death God, did not come of these Two but was bad magic who appeared only after the making of creatures.

And then it came about that these Two had one Thought and it was a mighty Thought—that they would make the Earth to be between the Above and the Below where now lay shimmering only the Endless Waters. So they sat them side by side, swaying their beautiful bronze bodies to the pulsing music of their own great voices, making the First Magic Song, a song of rushing winds and flowing waters, a song of light and sound and life.

"I am Tawa," sang the Sun God, "I am Light. I am Life. I am Father of all that shall ever come."

"I am Kokyanwuhti," the Spider Woman crooned in softer note. "I receive Light and nourish Life. I am Mother of all that shall ever come."

"Many strange thoughts are forming in my mind—beautiful forms of birds to float in the Above, of beasts to move upon the Earth and fish to swim in the Waters," intoned Tawa.

"Now let these things that move in the Thought of my lord appear," chanted Spider Woman, the while with her slender fingers she caught up clay from beside her and made the Thoughts of Tawa take form. One by one she shaped them and laid them aside—but they breathed not nor moved.

"We must do something about this," said Tawa. "It is not good that they lie thus still and quiet. Each thing that has a form must also have a spirit. So now, my beloved, we must make a mighty Magic."

They laid a white blanket over the many figures, a cunningly woven woolen blanket, fleecy as a cloud, and made a mighty incantation over it, and soon the figures stirred and breathed.

"Now, let us make ones like unto you and me, so that they may rule over and enjoy these lesser creatures," sang Tawa, and Spider Woman shaped the Thoughts of her lord into man figures and woman figures like unto their own. But after the blanket magic had been made the figures still stayed inert. So Spider Woman gathered them all in her arms and cradled them in her warm young bosom, while Tawa bent his glowing eyes upon them. The two now sang the magic Song of Life over them, and at last each man figure and woman figure breathed and lived.

"Now that was a good thing and a mighty thing," quoth Tawa. "So now all this is finished, and there shall be no new things made by us. Those things we have made shall multiply, each one after his own kind. I will make a journey across the Above each day to shed my light upon them and return each night to Huzruiwuhti. And now I shall go to turn my blazing shield upon the Endless Waters, so that the Dry Land may appear. And this day will be the first day upon the Earth."

"Now I shall lead all these created things to the land that you shall cause to appear above the waters," said Spider Woman.

Then Tawa took down his burnished shield from the turquoise wall of the kiva and swiftly mounted his glorious way to the Above. After Spider Woman had bent her wise, all-seeing eyes upon the thronging creatures about her, she wound her way among them, separating them into groups.

"Thus and thus shall you be and thus shall you remain, each one in his own tribe forever. You are Zunis, you are Kohoninos, you are Pah-Utes—." The Hopis, all, all people were named by Kokyanwuhti then.

Placing her Magic Twins beside her, Spider Woman called all the people to follow where she led. Through all the Four Great Caverns of the Underworld she led them, until they finally came to an opening, a sipapu, which led above. This came out at the lowest depth of the Pisisbaiya (the Colorado River) and was the place where the people were to come to gather salt. So lately had the Endless Waters gone down that the Turkey, Koyona, pushing eagerly ahead, dragged his tail feathers in the black mud where the dark bands were to remain forever.

Mourning Dove flew overhead, calling to some to follow, and those who followed where his sharp eyes had spied out springs and built beside them were called "Huwinyamu" after him. So Spider Woman chose a creature to lead each clan to a place to build their house. The Puma, the Snake, the Antelope, the Deer, and other Horn creatures, each led a clan to a place to build their house. Each clan henceforth bore the name of the creature who had led them.

Then Spider Woman spoke to them thus: "The woman of the clan shall build the house, and the family name shall descend through her. She shall be house builder and homemaker. She shall mold the jars for the storing of food and water. She shall grind the grain for food and tenderly rear the young. The man of the clan shall build kivas of stone under the ground where he shall pay homage to his gods. In these kivas the man shall make sand pictures which will be his altars. Of colored sand shall he make them and they shall be called 'ponya'. After council I shall whisper to him; he shall make prayer sticks or paho to place upon the ponya to bear his prayers. There shall be the Wupo Paho, the Great Paho, which is mine.

There shall be four paho of blue, the Cawka Paho—one for the great Tawa, one for Muiyinwuh, one for Woman of the Hard Substances and one for the Ancient of Six. Each of these paho must be cunningly and secretly wrought with prayer and song. The man, too, shall weave the clan blankets with their proper symbols. The Snake clan shall have its symbol and the Antelope clan its symbol; thus it shall be for each clan. Many shall fashion himself weapons and furnish his family with game."

Stooping down, she gathered some sand in her hand, letting it run out in a thin, continuous stream. "See the movement of the sand. That is the life that will cause all things therein to grow. The Great Plumed Serpent, Lightning, will rear and strike the earth to fertilize it, Rain Cloud will pour down waters and Tawa will smile upon it so that green things will spring up to feed my children."

Her eyes now sought the Above where Tawa was descending toward his western kiva in all the glory of red and gold. "I go now, but have no fear, for we Two will be watching over you. Look upon me now, my children, ere I leave. Obey the words I have given you and all will be well, and if you are in need of help call upon me and I will send my sons to your aid."

The people gazed wide-eyed upon her shining beauty. Her woven upper garment of soft white wool hung tunic-wise over a blue skirt. On its left side was woven a band bearing the woman's symbols, the Butterfly and the Squash Blossom, in designs of red and yellow and green with bands of black appearing between. Her beautiful neck was hung with heavy necklaces of turquoise, shell and coral, and pendants of the same hung from her ears. Her face was fair, with warm eyes and tender red lips, and her form most graceful. Upon her small feet were skin boots of gleaming white, and they now turned toward where the sand spun about in whirlpool fashion. She held up her right hand and smiled upon them, then stepped upon the whirling sand. Wonder of wonders, before their eyes the sands seemed to suck her swiftly down until she disappeared entirely from their sight.

Boshongo (Bantu): Bumba's Creation

The dominant theme in this myth is that of creation out of the male principle. Bumba's vomiting reminds us of the Egyptian High God's creation by spitting and seed spilling. The absence of the female principle here suggests a patrilineal culture. The fact that Bumba is white suggests that this is a late myth, affected, like so much African mythology, by the presence of the white race in colonial Africa.

•

In the beginning, in the dark, there was nothing but water. And Bumba was alone.

One day Bumba was in terrible pain. He retched and strained and vomited up the sun. After that light spread over everything. The heat of the sun dried up the water until the black edges of the world began to show. Black sandbanks and reefs could be seen. But there were no living things.

Bumba vomited up the moon and then the stars, and after that the night had its light also.

Still Bumba was in pain. He strained again and nine living creatures came forth; the leopard named Koy Bumba, and Pongo Bumba the crested eagle, the crocodile, Ganda Bumba, and one little fish named Yo; next, old Kono Bumba, the tortoise, and Tsetse, the lightning, swift, deadly, beautiful like the leopard, then the white heron, Nyanyi Bumba, also one beetle, and the goat named Budi.

Last of all came forth men. There were many men, but only one was white like Bumba. His name was Loko Yima.

The creatures themselves then created all the creatures. The heron created all the birds of the air except the kite. He did not make the kite. The crocodile made serpents and the iguana. The goat produced every beast with horns. Yo, the small fish, brought forth all the fish of all the seas and waters. The beetle created insects.

Then the serpents in their turn made grasshoppers, and the iguana made the creatures without horns.

Then the three sons of Bumba said they would finish the world. The first, Nyonye Ngana, made the white ants; but he was not equal to the task, and died of it. The ants, however, thankful for life and being, went searching for black earth in the depths of the world and covered the barren sands to bury and honour their creator.

Chonganda, the second son, brought forth a marvellous living plant from which all the trees and grasses and flowers and plants in the world have sprung. The third son, Chedi Bumba, wanted something different, but for all his trying made only the bird called the kite.

Of all the creatures, Tsetse, lightning, was the only trouble-maker. She stirred up so much trouble that Bumba chased her into the sky. Then mankind was without fire until Bumba showed the people how to draw fire out of trees. "There is fire in every tree," he told them, and showed them how to make the firedrill and liberate it. Sometimes today Tsetse still leaps down and strikes the earth and causes damage.

When at last the work of creation was finished, Bumba walked through the peaceful villages and said to the people, "Behold these wonders. They belong to you." Thus from Bumba, the creator, the First Ancestor, came forth all the wonders that we see and hold and use, and all the brotherhood of beasts and man.

Mircea Eliade, *Gods, Goddesses, and Myths of Creation* (New York, 1974), pp. 91–92.

Modern: The Big Bang

Creation stories are treated as truth by the culture from which they emerge—at least until they are "exposed" as mere myths. One creation story of modern culture is the "Big Bang" theory. Like all other creation myths, this one reveals the priorities of a culture; it is a record of our culture's understanding of its own place in the universe and its sense of what the universe is. It is told here by Brian Swimme in the form of an interview between a man called Thomas, whose ideas reflect those of the philosopher Thomas Berry, and a youth who is simultaneously the author and the collective voice of our curiosity.

YOUTH: Where should we start?

THOMAS: At the beginning. We need to start with the story of the universe as a whole. Our emergent cosmos is the fundamental context for all discussions of value, meaning, purpose, or ultimacy of any sort. To speak of the universe's origin is to bring to mind the great silent fire at the beginning of time.

Imagine that furnace out of which everything came forth. This was a fire that filled the universe—that *was* the universe. There was no place in the universe free from it. Every point of the cosmos was a point of this explosion of light. And all the particles of the universe churned in extremes of heat and pressure, all that we see about us, all that now exists was there at the beginning, in that great burning explosion of light.

YOUTH: How do we know about it?

THOMAS: We can see it! We can see the light from the primeval fireball. Or at least the light from its edge, for it burned for nearly a million years. We can see the dawn of the universe because the light from its edge reaches us only now, after traveling twenty billion years to get here.

YOUTH: We can see the actual light from the fireball?

THOMAS: When you see a candle's flame, you see the light from the candle. In that sense, we see the fireball. We are able to interact physically with photons from the beginning of time.

YOUTH: So we're in direct contact with the origin of the universe?

THOMAS: That's right.

YOUTH: I can't believe I didn't know this.

THOMAS: Scientists have only just learned to see the fireball. The light has always been there, but the ability to respond to it required a tremendous development of the human senses. Just as an artist

Brian Swimme, *The Universe Is a Green Dragon: A Cosmic Creation Story* (Santa Fe, N.M., 1984), pp, 27–29.

learns to see a lakeshore's subtle shades and contours, the human race learns to develop its sensitivities to what is present. It took millions of years to develop, but humans can now interact with the cosmic radiation from the origin of the universe. We can now see the beginnings of time—a stupendous achievement.

YOUTH: It's amazing.

THOMAS: Most amazing is this realization that every thing that exists in the universe came from a common origin. The material of your body and the material of my body are intrinsically related because they emerged from and are caught up in a single energetic event. Our ancestry stretches back through the life forms and into the stars, back to the beginnings of the primeval fireball. This universe is a single multiform energetic unfolding of matter, mind, intelligence, and life. And all of this is new. None of the great figures of human history were aware of this. Not Plato, or Aristotle, or the Hebrew Prophets, or Confucius, or Thomas Aquinas, or Leibniz, or Newton, or any other world-maker. We are the first generation to live with an empirical view of the origin of the universe. We are the first humans to look into the night sky and see the birth of stars, the birth of galaxies, the birth of the cosmos as a whole. Our future as a species will be forged within this new story of the world. . . .

Bibliography

The most important contribution to the study of cosmogonic myths has been made by Mircea Eliade, who sees the creation story as the basis for all myth. See especially *Cosmos and History: The Myth of the Eternal Return* (New York, 1954); *Gods, Goddesses, and Myths of Creation* (New York, 1974; *Myth and Reality* (New York, 1963); and *Patterns in Comparative Religion* (New York, 1958). See also Charles H. Long's *Alpha: The Myths of Creation* (New York, 1963) for a comprehensive collection of creation myths. Also useful is Long's overview entitled "Cosmogony" in *The Encyclopedia of Religion*, ed. Mircea Eliade (New York, 1987), vol. 4, pp. 94–100).

THE FLOOD

The flood myth is common to many cultures, partly because floods, like great earthquakes and other natural disasters, are distinctly memorable. Floods do occur, and when they do, the destruction and loss are frequently so total as to suggest a cosmic conspiracy of some sort and, necessarily, the hope of a new beginning. The flood myths that emerge from the human psyche, therefore, tend to be dual in nature. The pattern behind the many forms that the flood myth takes is the archetype of the productive sacrifice. Thus, Jung could write of the "Noah's Ark that crosses the waters of death and leads to a rebirth of all life" (The Archetypes and the Collective Unconscious, p. 353). *The Deluge cleanses and gives birth to new forms even as it destroys the old. It is the breaking of the eternal waters of the Great Mother—the destructive mother who, whether her name is Kali or Demeter, sweeps away the old life but preserves the germ of a new beginning. The Noah or the Utnapishtim or the Manu who is spared is the hero of new life who is born of the cosmic waters of the womb of the Great Mother. The flood myth, like the myths of the Destroyer-Mother herself, reminds us that life depends on death, that without death there can be no cycle, no birth.*

That the new creation is preceded by a flood is appropriate, since the first life itself emerged from the waters. The flood myth, like the original creation myth, is what Mircea Eliade calls a "festival" of productive chaos, a "restoration of primordial chaos, and the repetition of the cosmogonic act" (The Myth of the Eternal Return, pp. 57–59).

The flood myth has personal as well as universal ramifications. Rituals of purification by water are microcosmic versions of the Deluge. The baptized "sinner" immersed in the waters of the font-womb dies to the old life and on emerging is born into the new. Just as the hero descends into the underworld to confront death itself, the baptized individual symbolically overcomes the destructive powers of chaos. J. Danielou writes,

The flood . . . was an image which baptism comes to fulfill. . . . Just as Noah had confronted the Sea of Death in which sinful humanity had been destroyed, and had emerged from it, so the newly baptized man descends into the baptismal piscina to confront the water Dragon in a supreme combat from which he emerges victorious" (Sacramentum futuri, p. 65).

Finally, in psychological terms, the flood myth, like the story of the hero's descent into the underworld, can be seen as a metaphor for the individual's necessary time in the dark world of the unconscious before the rebirth that is the achievement of individuation.

THE FLOOD STORIES

Mesopotamian: Utnapishtim

In the eleventh tablet of the Semitic Babylonian epic of the legendary king Gilgamesh, we find a flood story which is clearly the source for the Old Testament Noah story. The Gilgamesh story itself is based on an earlier, third-millennium B.C.E. myth of the Sumerians. In the Sumerian myth, the gods decide to destroy humankind with a flood. The god Enki, disagreeing with this decision, instructs a worthy man named Ziusudra, who narrates the tale, to build a great boat in which to save himself, his family, and a few other people, as well as animals. In the later second-millennium B.C.E. Babylonian version, Ziusudra has become Utnapishtim, Enki has become Ea.

•

"You know the city Shurrupak, it stands on the banks of Euphrates? That city grew old and the gods that were in it were old. There was Anu, lord of the firmament, their father, and warrior Enlil their counsellor, Ninurta the helper, and Ennugi watcher over canals; and with them also was Ea. In those days the world teemed, the people multiplied, the world bellowed like a wild bull, and the great god was aroused by the clamour. Enlil heard the clamour and he said to the gods in council, 'The uproar of mankind is intolerable and sleep is no longer possible by reason of the babel.' So the gods agreed to exterminate mankind. Enlil did this, but Ea because of his oath warned me in a dream. He whispered their words to my house of reeds, 'Reed-house, reed-house! Wall, O wall, hearken reed-house, wall reflect; O man of Shurrupak, son of Ubara-Tutu; tear down your house and build a boat, abandon possessions and look for life, despise worldly

N. K. Sandars, trans. *The Epic of Gilgamesh*, rev. ed. (Harmondsworth, Eng., 1972), pp. 108–13.

goods and save your soul alive. Tear down your house, I say, and build a boat. These are the measurements of the barque as you shall build her: let her beam equal her length, let her deck be roofed like the vault that covers the abyss; then take up into the boat the seed of all living creatures.'

"When I had understood I said to my lord, 'Behold, what you have commanded I will honour and perform, but how shall I answer the people, the city, the elders?' Then Ea opened his mouth and said to me, his servant, 'Tell them this: I have learnt that Enlil is wrathful against me, I dare no longer walk in his land nor live in his city; I will go down to the Gulf to dwell with Ea my lord. But on you he will rain down abundance, rare fish and shy wild-fowl, a rich harvest-tide. In the evening the rider of the storm will bring you wheat in torrents.'

"In the first light of dawn all my household gathered round me, the children brought pitch and the men whatever was necessary. On the fifth day I laid the keel and the ribs, then I made fast the planking. The ground-space was one acre, each side of the deck measured one hundred and twenty cubits, making a square. I built six decks below, seven in all, I divided them into nine sections with bulkheads between. I drove in wedges where needed, I saw to the punt-poles, and laid in supplies. The carriers brought oil in baskets, I poured pitch into the furnace and asphalt and oil; more oil was consumed in caulking, and more again the master of the boat took into his stores. I slaughtered bullocks for the people and every day I killed sheep. I gave the shipwrights wine to drink as though it were river water, raw wine and red wine and oil and white wine. There was feasting then as there is at the time of the New Year's festival; I myself anointed my head. On the seventh day the boat was complete.

"Then was the launching full of difficulty; there was shifting of ballast above and below till two thirds was submerged. I loaded into her all that I had of gold and of living things, my family, my kin, the beast of the field both wild and tame, and all the craftsmen. I sent them on board, for the time that Shamash had ordained was already fulfilled when he said, 'In the evening, when the rider of the storm sends down the destroying rain, enter the boat and batten her down.' The time was fulfilled, the evening came, the rider of the storm sent down the rain. I looked out at the weather and it was terrible, so I too boarded the boat and battened her down. All was now complete, the battening and the caulking; so I handed the tiller to Puzur-Amurri the steersman, with the navigation and the care of the whole boat.

"With the first light of dawn a black cloud came from the horizon; it thundered within where Adad, lord of the storm was riding. In front over hill and plain Shullat and Hanish, heralds of the storm, led on. Then the gods of the abyss rose up; Nergal pulled out the dams of the nether waters, Ninurta the war-lord threw down the dykes, and the seven judges of hell, the Annunaki, raised their torches, lighting the land with their livid flame. A stupor of despair went up to heaven when the god of the storm turned daylight to darkness, when he smashed the land like a cup. One whole day the tempest raged, gathering fury as it went, it poured over the people like the tides of battle; a man could not see his brother nor the people be seen from heaven. Even the gods were terrified at the flood, they fled to the highest heaven, the firmament of Anu; they crouched against the walls, cowering like curs. Then Ishtar the sweet-voiced Queen of Heaven cried out like a woman in travail: 'Alas the days of old are turned to dust because I commanded evil; why did I command this evil in the council of all the gods? I commanded wars to destroy the people, but are they not my people, for I brought them forth? Now like the spawn of fish they float in the ocean.' The great gods of heaven and of hell wept, they covered their mouths.

"For six days and six nights the winds blew, torrent and tempest and flood overwhelmed the world, tempest and flood raged together like warring hosts. When the seventh day dawned the storm from the south subsided, the sea grew calm, the flood was stilled; I looked at the face of the world and there was silence, all mankind was turned to clay. The surface of the sea stretched as flat as a roof-top; I opened a hatch and the light fell on my face. Then I bowed low, I sat down and I wept, the tears streamed down my face, for on every side was the waste of water. I looked for land in vain, but fourteen leagues distant there appeared a mountain, and there the boat grounded; on the mountain of Nisir the boat held fast, she held fast and did not budge. One day she held, and a second day on the mountain of Nisir she held fast and did not budge. A third day, and a fourth day she held fast on the mountain and did not budge; a fifth day and a sixth day she held fast on the mountain. When the seventh day dawned I loosed a dove and let her go. She flew away, but finding no resting-place she returned. Then I loosed a swallow, and she flew away but finding no resting-place she returned. I loosed a raven, she saw that the waters had retreated, she ate, she flew around, she cawed, and she did not come back. Then I threw everything open to the four winds, I made a sacrifice and poured out a libation on the mountain top. Seven and again seven cauldrons I set up on their stands, I heaped up wood and cane and cedar and myrtle. When the gods smelled the sweet savour, they gathered like flies over the sacrifice. Then, at last, Ishtar also came, she lifted her necklace with the jewels of heaven that once Anu had made to please her. 'O you gods here present, by the lapis lazuli round my neck I shall remember these days as I remember the jewels of my throat; these last days I shall not forget. Let all the gods gather round the sacrifice, except Enlil. He shall not approach this offering, for without reflection he brought the flood; he consigned my people to destruction.'

"When Enlil had come, when he saw the boat, he was wrath and swelled with anger at the gods, the host of heaven, 'Has any of these mortals escaped? Not one was to have survived the destruction.' Then the god of the wells and canals Ninurta opened his mouth and said to the warrior Enlil, 'Who is there of the gods that can devise without Ea? It is Ea alone who knows all things.' Then Ea opened his mouth and spoke to warrior Enlil, 'Wisest of gods, hero Enlil, how could you so senselessly bring down the flood?

> Lay upon the sinner his sin,
> Lay upon the transgressor his transgression,
> Punish him a little when he breaks loose,
> Do not drive him too hard or he perishes;
> Would that a lion had ravaged mankind
> Rather than the flood,
> Would that a wolf had ravaged mankind
> Rather than the flood,
> Would that famine had wasted the world
> Rather than the flood,
> Would that pestilence had wasted mankind
> Rather than the flood.

It was not I that revealed the secret of the gods; the wise man learned it in a dream. Now take your counsel what shall be done with him.'

"Then Enlil went up into the boat, he took me by the hand and my wife and made us enter the boat and kneel down on either side, he standing between us. He touched our foreheads to bless us saying, 'In time past Utnapishtim was a mortal man; henceforth he and his wife shall live in the distance at the mouth of the rivers.' Thus it was that the gods took me and placed me here to live in the distance, at the mouth of the rivers."

Hebrew: Noah

The Hebrew story, although clearly based on the older Babylonian one, emphasizes the idea of humanity's sinfulness. The Flood is a punishment, and Noah is saved so that humankind can be reborn in a cleansed state. Whereas the Babylonian flood is the result of a whim of the gods, the Hebrew flood is harsh but constructive.

•

Chapter 6

And it came to pass, when men began to multiply on the face of the earth, and daughters were born unto them,

2 That the sons of God saw the daughters of men that they were fair; and they took them wives of all which they chose.

3 And the Lord said, My spirit shall not always strive with man, for that he also is flesh: yet his days shall be an hundred and twenty years.

4 There were giants in the earth in those days; and also after that, when the sons of God came in unto the daughters of men, and they bare children to them, the same became mighty men which were of old, men of renown.

5 And God saw that the wickedness of man was great in the earth, and that every imagination of the thoughts of his heart was only evil continually.

6 And it repented the Lord that he had made man on the earth, and it grieved him at his heart.

7 And the Lord said, I will destroy man whom I have created from the face of the earth; both man, and beast, and the creeping thing, and the fowls of the air; for it repenteth me that I have made them.

8 But Noah found grace in the eyes of the Lord.

9 ¶ These are the generations of Noah: Noah was a just man and perfect in his generations, and Noah walked with God.

10 And Noah begat three sons, Shem, Ham, and Jā'-phĕth.

11 The earth also was corrupt before God, and the earth was filled with violence.

12 And God looked upon the earth, and, behold, it was corrupt; for all flesh had corrupted his way upon the earth.

13 And God said unto Noah, The end of all flesh is come before me; for the earth is filled with violence through them; and, behold, I will destroy them with the earth.

14 Make thee an ark of gopher wood; rooms shalt thou make in the ark, and shalt pitch it within and without with pitch.

15 And this is the fashion which thou shalt make it of: The length of the ark shall be three hundred cubits, the breadth of it fifty cubits, and the height of it thirty cubits.

16 A window shalt thou make to the ark, and in a cubit shalt thou finish it above; and the door of the ark shalt thou set in the side thereof; with lower, second, and third stories shalt thou make it.

17 And, behold, I, even I, do bring a flood of waters upon the earth, to destroy all flesh, wherein is the breath of life, from under heaven; and every thing that is in the earth shall die.

Genesis 6–9.

18 But with thee will I establish my covenant; and thou shalt come into the ark, thou, and thy sons, and thy wife, and thy sons' wives with thee.

19 And of every living thing of all flesh, two of every sort shalt thou bring into the ark, to keep them alive with thee; they shall be male and female.

20 Of fowls after their kind, and of cattle after their kind, of every creeping thing of the earth after his kind, two of every sort shall come unto thee, to keep them alive.

21 And take thou unto thee of all food that is eaten, and thou shalt gather it to thee; and it shall be for food for thee, and for them.

22 Thus did Noah; according to all that God commanded him, so did he.

Chapter 7

And the Lord said unto Noah, Come thou and all thy house into the ark; for thee have I seen righteous before me in this generation.

2 Of every clean beast thou shalt take to thee by sevens, the male and his female: and of beasts that are not clean by two, the male and his female.

3 Of fowls also of the air by sevens, the male and the female; to keep seed alive upon the face of all the earth.

4 For yet seven days, and I will cause it to rain upon the earth forty days and forty nights; and every living substance that I have made will I destroy from off the face of the earth.

5 And Noah did according unto all that the Lord commanded him.

6 And Noah was six hundred years old when the flood of waters was upon the earth.

7 And Noah went in, and his sons, and his wife, and his sons' wives with him, into the ark, because of the waters of the flood.

8 Of clean beasts, and of beasts that are not clean, and of fowls, and of every thing that creepeth upon the earth.

9 There went in two and two unto Noah into the ark, the male and the female, as God had commanded Noah.

10 And it came to pass after seven days, that the waters of the flood were upon the earth.

11 In the six hundredth year of Noah's life, in the second month, the seventeenth day of the month, the same day were all the fountains of the great deep broken up, and the windows of heaven were opened.

12 And the rain was upon the earth forty days and forty nights.

13 In the selfsame day entered Noah, and Shem, and Ham, and Jā'-

phĕth, the sons of Noah, and Noah's wife, and the three wives of his sons with them, into the ark;

14 They, and every beast after his kind, and all the cattle after their kind, and every creeping thing that creepeth upon the earth after his kind, and every fowl after his kind, every bird of every sort.

15 And they went in unto Noah into the ark, two and two of all flesh, wherein *is* the breath of life.

16 And they that went in, went in male and female of all flesh, as God had commanded him: and the Lord shut him in.

17 And the flood was forty days upon the earth; and the waters increased, and bare up the ark, and it was lift up above the earth.

18 And the waters prevailed, and were increased greatly upon the earth; and the ark went upon the face of the waters.

19 And the waters prevailed exceedingly upon the earth; and all the high hills, that *were* under the whole heaven, were covered.

20 Fifteen cubits upward did the waters prevail; and the mountains were covered.

21 And all flesh died that moved upon the earth, both of fowl, and of cattle, and of beast, and of every creeping thing that creepeth upon the earth, and every man:

22 All in whose nostrils was the breath of life, of all that was in the dry land, died.

23 And every living substance was destroyed which was upon the face of the ground, both man, and cattle, and the creeping things, and the fowl of the heaven; and they were destroyed from the earth: and Noah only remained alive, and they that were with him in the ark.

24 And the waters prevailed upon the earth an hundred and fifty days.

Chapter 8

And God remembered Noah, and every living thing, and all the cattle that was with him in the ark: and God made a wind to pass over the earth, and the waters assuaged;

2 The fountains also of the deep and the windows of heaven were stopped, and the rain from heaven was restrained;

3 And the waters returned from off the earth continually: and after the end of the hundred and fifty days the waters were abated.

4 And the ark rested in the seventh month, on the seventeenth day of the month, upon the mountains of Ararat.

5 And the waters decreased continually until the tenth month: in the

tenth month, on the first day of the month, were the tops of the mountains seen.

6 And it came to pass at the end of forty days, that Noah opened the window of the ark which he had made:

7 And he sent forth a raven, which went forth to and fro, until the waters were dried up from off the earth.

8 Also he sent forth a dove from him, to see if the waters were abated from off the face of the ground;

9 But the dove found no rest for the sole of her foot, and she returned unto him into the ark, for the waters were on the face of the whole earth: then he put forth his hand, and took her, and pulled her in unto him into the ark.

10 And he stayed yet other seven days; and again he sent forth the dove out of the ark;

11 And the dove came in to him in the evening; and, lo, in her mouth was an olive leaf plucked off: so Noah knew that the waters were abated from off the earth.

12 And he stayed yet other seven days; and sent forth the dove; which returned not again unto him any more.

13 And it came to pass in the six hundredth and first year, in the first month, the first day of the month, the waters were dried up from off the earth: and Noah removed the covering of the ark, and looked, and, behold, the face of the ground was dry.

14 And in the second month, on the seven and twentieth day of the month, was the earth dried.

15 And God spake unto Noah, saying,

16 Go forth of the ark, thou, and thy wife, and thy sons, and thy sons' wives with thee.

17 Bring forth with thee every living thing that is with thee, of all flesh, both of fowl, and of cattle, and of every creeping thing that creepeth upon the earth; that they may breed abundantly in the earth, and be fruitful, and multiply upon the earth.

18 And Noah went forth, and his sons, and his wife, and his sons' wives with him:

19 Every beast, every creeping thing, and every fowl, and whatsoever creepeth upon the earth, after their kinds, went forth out of the ark.

20 And Noah builded an altar unto the Lord; and took of every clean beast, and of every clean fowl, and offered burnt offerings on the altar.

21 And the Lord smelled a sweet savour; and the Lord said in his heart, I will not again curse the ground any more for man's sake; for the imagination of man's heart is evil from his youth; neither will I again smite any more every thing living, as I have done.

22 While the earth remaineth, seedtime and harvest, and cold and heat, and summer and winter, and day and night shall not cease.

Chapter 9

And God blessed Noah and his sons, and said unto them, Be fruitful, and multiply, and replenish the earth.

2 And the fear of you and the dread of you shall be upon every beast of the earth, and upon every fowl of the air, upon all that moveth upon the earth, and upon all the fishes of the sea; into your hand are they delivered.

3 Every moving thing that liveth shall be meat for you; even as the green herb have I given you all things.

4 But flesh with the life thereof, which is the blood thereof, shall ye not eat.

5 And surely your blood of your lives will I require; at the hand of every beast will I require it, and at the hand of man; at the hand of every man's brother will I require the life of man.

6 Whoso sheddeth man's blood, by man shall his blood be shed: for in the image of God made he man.

7 And you, be ye fruitful, and multiply; bring forth abundantly in the earth, and multiply therein.

8 And God spake unto Noah, and to his sons with him, saying,

9 And I, behold, I establish my covenant with you, and with your seed after you;

10 And with every living creature that is with you, of the fowl, of the cattle, and of every beast of the earth with you; from all that go out of the ark, to every beast of the earth.

11 And I will establish my covenant with you; neither shall all flesh be cut off any more by the waters of a flood; neither shall there any more be a flood to destroy the earth.

12 And God said, This is the token of the covenant which I make between me and you and every living creature that is with you, for perpetual generations:

13 I do set my bow in the cloud, and it shall be for a token of a covenant between me and the earth.

14 And it shall come to pass, when I bring a cloud over the earth, that the bow shall be seen in the cloud:

15 And I will remember my covenant, which is between me and you and every living creature of all flesh; and the waters shall no more become a flood to destroy all flesh.

16 And the bow shall be in the cloud; and I will look upon it, that I

may remember the everlasting covenant between God and every living creature of all flesh that is upon the earth.

17 And God said unto Noah, This is the token of the covenant, which I have established between me and all flesh that *is* upon the earth.

18 And the sons of Noah, that went forth of the ark, were Shem, and Ham, and Jā'-phĕth: and Ham is the father of Cā'-nă-ăn.

19 These are the three sons of Noah: and of them was the whole earth overspread.

20 And Noah began to be an husbandman, and he planted a vineyard:

21 And he drank of the wine, and was drunken; and he was uncovered within his tent.

22 And Ham, the father of Cā'-nă-ăn, saw the nakedness of his father, and told his two brethren without.

23 And Shem and Jā'-phĕth took a garment, and laid it upon both their shoulders, and went backward, and covered the nakedness of their father; and their faces were backward, and they saw not their father's nakedness.

24 And Noah awoke from his wine, and knew what his younger son had done unto him.

25 And he said, Cursed be Cā'-nă-ăn; a servant of servants shall he be unto his brethren.

26 And he said, Blessed be the Lord God of Shem; and Cā'-nă-ăn shall be his servant.

27 God shall enlarge Jā'-phĕth, and he shall dwell in the tents of Shem; and Cā'-nă-ăn shall be his servant.

28 And Noah lived after the flood three hundred and fifty years.

29 And all the days of Noah were nine hundred and fifty years: and he died.

Chinese: Yü

The flood theme is one of the very oldest in Chinese mythology. A flood myth from the *Shu ching* in the Chou Dynasty—perhaps from as early as 1000 B.C.E.—reveals a distinctly nonmystical sense of the gods and is clearly earth-oriented. The emphasis is on a very practical matter, the channeling of unruly water in such a way as to make cultivation of the land possible. There is less of a sense here than in most other flood myths of the waters as an ultimately just or beneficial force. The myth is summarized here by Derk Bodde.

•

"Everywhere the tremendous flood waters were wreaking destruction. Spreading afar, they embraced the mountains and rose above the hills. In a vast flow they swelled up to Heaven. The people below were groaning."

In response to their appeals, a being who in the *Shu ching* is referred to simply as Ti, "Lord," rather reluctantly (because he had reservations about his ability) commanded Kun to deal with the flood. (By the commentators this "Lord" is equated with the sage ruler Yao; in all probability, however, he was none other than the supreme divinity, Shang Ti, the "Lord on High.")

For nine years Kun labored without success to dam up the waters. At the end of that time either Yao or his successor Shun (the texts differ) had Kun executed at the Feather Mountain (Yü-shan), and ordered Kun's son, Yü, to continue the task. The latter, instead of trying to dam up the waters in the manner of his father, adopted the new technique of channeling passages for them to drain off to the sea. In this way he eventually conquered the flood and made the land fit for habitation. As a reward, he was given the throne by Shun and became founder of the Hsia dynasty.

In contrast to this "historical" account, we can, by piecing together the fragments found both in Chou and Han literature, produce another version which is much more "mythological":

On being ordered to deal with the flood, Kun stole from the Lord the "swelling mold" (*hsi jang*)—a magical kind of soil which had the property of ever swelling in size. With this he tried to build dams which, through their swelling, would hold back the waters. When his efforts failed, the Lord, angered by his theft, had him executed at Feather Mountain, a sunless place in the extreme north. There his body remained for three years without decomposing, until somebody (unspecified) cut it open with a sword, whereupon Yü emerged from his father's belly. (One tradition says that Yü was born from a stone, which would apparently signify that Kun's body had turned to stone.) Following Yü's birth, Kun became transformed into an animal—variously said to be a yellow bear, black fish, three-legged turtle, or yellow dragon—and plunged into the Feather Gulf (Yü-yüan). A cryptic line in the *T'ien wen* poem, however, suggests that he subsequently managed to get to the west, where he was restored to life by a shamanness.

Yü, we are told, "came down from on high" to continue his father's work. He was helped by a winged dragon which, going ahead of him, trailed its tail over the ground and thus marked the places where channels should be dug. For some eight or ten years Yü labored so intensely that, though several times passing the door of his home, he had no time to visit his family within. He wore the nails off his hands, the hair off his shanks, and developed a lameness giving him a peculiar gait which in later times came to be known as the "walk of Yü." Nonetheless, he eventually succeeded in draining the great rivers to the sea, expelling snakes and dragons

Derk Bodde, "Myths of Ancient China," in *Mythologies of the Ancient World*, ed. Samuel Noah Kramer (New York, 1961), pp. 399–400.

from the marshlands, and making the terrain fit for cultivation. So great, indeed, were his achievements that the *Tso chuan* history, under the year 541 B.C., reports a noble as exclaiming: "Were it not for Yü, we would indeed be fish!"

Indian: Manu

The story of Manu, who alone is saved from the great flood, must remind us of the Utnapishtim and Noah stories. Like the other flood heroes, Manu receives supernatural help and is saved by remaining in a ship until he is able to tie up on an Indian version of Mount Ararat. The story is told in the *Shatapatha-Brahmana*.

•

1. In the morning they brought to Manu water for washing, just as now also they (are wont to) bring (water) for washing the hands. When he was washing himself, a fish came into his hands.

2. It spake to him the word, "Rear me, I will save thee!" "Where-from wilt thou save me?" "A flood will carry away all these creatures: from that I will save thee!" "How am I to rear thee?"

3. It said, "As long as we are small, there is great destruction for us: fish devours fish. Thou wilt first keep me in a jar. When I outgrow that, thou wilt dig a pit and keep me in it. When I outgrow that, thou wilt take me down to the sea, for then I shall be beyond destruction."

4. It soon became a *ghasha* (a great fish); for that grows largest (of all fish). Thereupon it said, "In such and such a year that flood will come. Thou shalt then attend to me (i.e. to my advice) by preparing a ship; and when the flood has risen thou shalt enter into the ship, and I will save thee from it."

5. After he had reared it in this way, he took it down to the sea. And in the same year which the fish had indicated to him, he attended to (the advice of the fish) by preparing a ship; and when the flood had risen, he entered into the ship. The fish then swam up to him, and to its horn he tied the rope of the ship, and by that means he passed swiftly up to yonder northern mountain.

6. It then said, "I have saved thee. Fasten the ship to a tree; but let not the water cut thee off whilst thou art on the mountain. As the water subsides, thou mayest gradually descend!" Accordingly he gradually descended and hence that (slope) of the northern mountain is called "Manu's descent." The flood then swept away all these creatures, and Manu alone remained here.

Mircea Eliade, *Gods, Goddesses, and Myths of Creation* (New York, 1974), p. 151.

Greco-Roman: Deucalion and Pyrrha

Ovid tells the story of Jupiter's decision to punish humanity for its sins by means of a great cleansing flood. Only one righteous couple, Deucalion and Pyrrha, are saved. Their boat eventually lands on Mount Parnassus, a mountain sacred to the ancient Greeks. It seems likely that this story was directly influenced by those of the Hebrews and Babylonians.

•

"One house has fallen, but far more than one have deserved to perish. To the ends of the earth, the dread Fury holds sway. You would think men had sworn allegiance to crime! They shall all be punished, forthwith, as they deserve. Such is my resolve."

Some of the gods shouted their approval of Jove's words, and sought to increase his indignation: others played the part of silent supporters. Yet all were grieved at the thought of the destruction of the human race, and wondered what the earth would be like, in future, when it had been cleared of mortal inhabitants. They inquired who would bring offerings of incense to their altars, whether Jove meant to abandon the world to the plundering of wild beasts. In answer to their questions, the king of the gods assured them that they need not be anxious, for he himself would attend to everything. He promised them a new stock of men, unlike the former ones, a race of miraculous origin.

Now he was on the point of launching his thunderbolts against every part of the earth, when he felt a sudden dread lest he should set light to the pure upper air by so many fiery bolts, and send the whole vault of heaven up in flames. He remembered, too, one of fate's decrees, that a time would come when sea and earth and the dome of the sky would blaze up, and the massive structure of the universe collapse in ruins. So he laid aside the weapons forged by the hands of the Cyclopes, and resolved on a different punishment, namely to send rain pouring down from every quarter of the sky, and so destroy mankind beneath the waters.

He wasted no time, but imprisoned the North wind in Aeolus' caves, together with all the gusts which dispel the gathering clouds; and he let loose the South wind. On dripping wings the South wind flew, his terrible features shrouded in pitchy darkness. His beard was heavy with rain, water streamed from his hoary locks, mists wreathed his brow, his robes and feathers dripped with moisture. When he crushed the hanging clouds in his broad hand, there was a crash; thereafter sheets of rain poured down from heaven. Juno's messenger Iris, clad in rainbow hues, drew up water and supplied nourishment to the clouds. The corn was laid low, and the

Ovid, *Metamorphoses*, trans. Mary M. Innes (London, 1955), pp. 35–40.

crops the farmer had prayed for now lay flattened and sadly mourned, the long year's toil was wasted and gone for nothing.

Nor was Jupiter's anger satisfied with the resources of his own realm of heaven: his brother Neptune, the god of the sea, lent him the assistance of his waves. He sent forth a summons to the rivers, and when they entered their king's home: "No time now for long exhortations!" he cried. "Exert your strength to the utmost: that is what we need. Fling wide your homes, withdraw all barriers, and give free course to your waters." These were his orders. The rivers returned to their homes and, opening up the mouths of their springs, went rushing to the sea in frenzied torrents.

Neptune himself struck the earth with his trident; it trembled and by its movement threw open channels for the waters. Across the wide plains the rivers raced, overflowing their banks, sweeping away in one torrential flood crops and orchards, cattle and men, houses and temples, sacred images and all. Any building which did manage to survive this terrible disaster unshaken and remain standing, was in the end submerged when some wave yet higher than the rest covered its roof, and its gables lay drowned beneath the waters. Now sea and earth could no longer be distinguished: all was sea, and a sea that had no shores.

Some tried to escape by climbing to the hilltops, others, sitting in their curved boats, plied the oars where lately they had been ploughing; some sailed over cornlands, over the submerged roofs of their homes, while some found fish in the topmost branches of the elms. At times it happened that they dropped anchor in green meadows, sometimes the curved keels grazed vineyards that lay beneath them. Where lately sinewy goats cropped the grass, now ugly seals disported themselves. The Nereids wondered to see groves and towns and houses under the water; dolphins took possession of the woods, and dashed against high branches, shaking the oak trees as they knocked against them. Wolves swam among the flocks, and the waves supported tawny lions, and tigers too. The lightning stroke of his strong tusk was of no use, then, to the wild boar, nor his swift legs to the stag— both alike were swept away. Wandering birds searched long for some land where they might rest, till their wings grew weary and they fell into the sea. The ocean, all restraints removed, overwhelmed the hills, and waves were washing the mountain peaks, a sight never seen before. The greater part of the human race was swallowed up by the waters: those whom the sea spared died from lack of food, overcome by long-continued famine.

There is a land, Phocis, which separates the fields of Boeotia from those of Oeta. It was a fertile spot while it was land, but now it had become part of the sea, a broad stretch of waters, suddenly formed. In that region a high mountain, called Parnassus, raises twin summits to the stars, and its ridges pierce the clouds. When the waters had covered all the rest of the earth, the little boat which carried Deucalion and his wife ran aground here. Of all the men who ever lived, Deucalion was the best and the most upright, no woman ever showed more reverence for the gods than Pyrrha, his wife. Their first action was to offer prayers to the Corycian nymphs, to the deities of the mountain, and to Themis, the goddess who foretold the future from its oracular shrine.

Now Jupiter saw the earth all covered with standing waters. He perceived that one alone survived of so many thousand men, one only of so many thousand women, and he knew that both were guiltless, both true worshippers of god. So, with the help of the North wind he drove away the storm clouds and, scattering the veils of mist, displayed heaven to earth and earth to heaven. The sea was no longer angry, for the ruler of ocean soothed the waves, laying aside his trident. Then he called to the sea-god Triton, who rose from the deep, his shoulders covered with clustering shellfish. Neptune bade him blow on his echoing conch shell, and recall waves and rivers by his signal. He lifted his hollow trumpet, a coiling instrument which broadens out in circling spirals from its base. When he blows upon it in mid-ocean, its notes fill the furthest shores of east and west. So now, too, the god put it to his lips, which were all damp from his dripping beard, and blew it, sending forth the signal for retreat as he had been bidden. The sound was heard by all the waters that covered earth and sea, and all the waves which heard it were checked in their course. The sea had shores once more, the swollen rivers were contained within their own channels, the floods sank down, and hills were seen to emerge. Earth rose up, its lands advancing as the waves retreated, and after a long interval the woods displayed their treetops uncovered, the mud left behind still clinging to their leaves.

The world was restored: but when Deucalion saw its emptiness, the desolate lands all deeply silent, tears started to his eyes, and he said to Pyrrha: "My cousin, my wife, the only woman left alive, related to me first by birth and blood, then joined to me in marriage—now, Pyrrha, our very dangers unite us. We two are the sole inhabitants of all the lands which east and west behold. The sea has taken the rest. Indeed, even yet, I feel no certainty that we shall survive; even now the clouds strike terror to my heart. What would your feelings be now, my poor wife, had fate snatched you to safety, without saving me? How could you have endured your fears, had you been left all alone? Who would have comforted you in your grief? For believe me, if the sea had taken you with the rest, I should follow you, my dear one, and the sea would have me too. If only I could create the nations anew, by my father's skill! If only I could mould the earth and give it breath: now the human race depends upon us two. It is god's will: we have been left as samples of mankind." So he spoke, and they wept together.

Then they decided to pray to the god in heaven, and to seek help from the holy oracle. Without delay, they went side by side to the waters of

Cephisus which, though not yet clear, were already flowing in their accustomed channel. When they had sprinkled their heads and garments with water drawn from the river they turned their steps to the shrine of the holy goddess. The gables of the temple were discoloured with foul moss, and its altars stood unlit. At the temple steps they both fell forward, prone upon the ground, and timidly kissed the chill rock, saying: "If the gods may be touched and softened by the prayers of the righteous, if divine anger may be thus turned aside, tell us, O Themis, how we may repair the destruction that has overtaken our race. Most gentle goddess, assist us in our distress."

The goddess pitied them, and uttered this oracle. "Depart from my temple, veil your heads, loosen the girdles of your garments and throw behind you the bones of your great mother." For long they stood in speechless wonder at this reply. Pyrrha was the first to break the silence, by declaring that she would not obey the commands of the goddess. With trembling lips she prayed to be excused: for she was afraid to injure her mother's ghost by disturbing her bones. But meanwhile they considered again the words of the oracle, so puzzling and obscure, and pondered them deeply: till after a time the son of Prometheus soothed the fears of Epimetheus' daughter with these comforting words: "Oracles are righteous, and never advise guilty action; so, unless my intuition deceives me, our great mother is the earth, and by her bones I think the oracle means the stones in the body of the earth. It is those we are instructed to throw behind our backs." The Titan's daughter was impressed by her husband's surmise; but she did not trust her hopes, for neither of them had any confidence in heaven's counsels. Still, there could be no harm in putting the matter to the test.

They went down the hillside, veiled their heads, loosened their tunics, and threw the stones behind them, as they had been bidden. Who would believe what followed, did not ancient tradition bear witness to it? The stones began to lose their hardness and rigidity, and after a little, grew soft. Then, once softened, they acquired a definite shape. When they had grown in size, and developed a tenderer nature, a certain likeness to a human form could be seen, though it was still not clear: they were like marble images, begun but not yet properly chiselled out, or like unfinished statues. The damp earthy parts, containing some moisture, were adapted to make the body: that which was solid and inflexible became bone. What was lately a vein in the rock kept the same name, and in a brief space of time, thanks to the divine will of the gods, the stones thrown from male hands took on the appearance of men, while from those the woman threw, women were recreated. So it comes about that we are a hardy race, well accustomed to toil, giving evidence of the origin from which we sprang.

Other animals of different kinds were produced by the earth, of its own accord, when the long-lingering moisture was warmed through by the rays of the sun. Then the mud and soggy marshes swelled under the heat, and fertile seeds, nourished in the life-giving earth as in a mother's womb, grew and in the fullness of time acquired a definite shape. This is what happens when the Nile, the river with seven mouths, recedes from the flooded fields and returns its streams to their original bed. The new mud becomes burning hot under the sun's rays, and the farmers, as they turn over the sods of earth, come upon many animals. Among these creatures they see some just begun, but already on the point of coming alive, others unfinished, lacking their full complement of limbs; and often in one and the same body one part is alive, while another is still only raw earth. Indeed, when heat and moisture have reached the proper balance, they bring forth life, and all things are born from these two elements. Although fire and water are always opposites, none the less moist heat is the source of everything, and this discordant harmony is suited to creation. . . .

Mayan: The *Popol-Vuh*

The *Popol-Vuh*, the sacred book of the Mayas, contains this strange creation story, which includes the destruction of an early, experimental form of humanity. The Flood here is used to erase a mistake rather than to punish sins.

•

In the very beginning, there was only the still sky and the still sea. Nothing moved, and there was no sound because there were no living creatures. There was no earth and no sun or moon to give light. Only God was surrounded with His own light, and He was in the heart of the still, dark sky and in the heart of the still, dark sea. In the sky He was called Hurricane, the Heart of Heaven; and in the depths of the water, where He seemed to shimmer as if covered by green and blue feathers, He was called The Feathered Serpent.

And God planned about making life and light. He knew that man and the dawn must appear together. He planned to make man so that the light could dawn.

First He said: "Let the emptiness be filled! Let the earth appear!"

And the earth appeared, with mountains, valleys, rivers, lakes, grass and trees and vines. But there was still no sound in the darkness.

Then God said: "Shall there be only silence under the trees?"

Then the animals appeared, the deer and the birds and the snakes and the jaguars and all the others, and God gave them all their places to live and told them to speak each in his own way. So they began to call and sing

Paul Jordan Smith, "In the Very Beginning," *Parabola*, 2, no. 2 (Spring 1977), 41–43.

and hiss and snarl and scream, each in his own way; but they couldn't speak to each other, or understand each other. God saw that they couldn't talk together and they couldn't say any of His names, and He saw that that wasn't enough.

So God said: "I will try again. You animals are not able to speak to each other nor to Me; so it will be that you will kill each other. But I need a creature who can speak to Me, who can know me and obey Me and love Me. It is nearly time for the dawn to come. I will make man out of mud."

He made some men out of mud. But they were very soft and limp and couldn't see. They could speak, but what they said didn't make sense. When they got wet they couldn't even stand up. God saw that they were no use, so He broke them up and said: "I will try again."

Then He made men out of wood. The wooden men were better; they could walk and talk. They built houses and had children, and there were very many of them. But they were dry and yellow, and their faces had no expression, because they had no minds nor souls nor hearts. They beat their dogs and they burned the bottoms of their cooking pots. They had forgotten how they were made, and could not remember any of the names of God. So He said: "These men will not do either. I must destroy them also."

And He sent a great flood, and the houses of the wooden men fell down. The wooden men wanted to escape, but the animals they had starved and beaten, and cooking pots they had burned, and the trees whose branches they had chopped off, all turned against them and wouldn't help them. Only a few of them escaped from the flood, and it is said that their descendants are the monkeys.

And still it hadn't dawned; and God wanted to make real men when the dawn came and the sun rose.

He thought about it, and He saw that the earth and the sky were not yet ready and that there were things that had to be done before the sun could move and make light and man could be made. He saw that He had to send two parts of Himself to put things in order. These two needed two sons of their own to help them, but at last all was ready, and the two sons entered the sun and moon to make them move.

Then God said: "It is time. I need men on the earth who will know My names, who will obey Me and love Me; and that will nourish and sustain Me."

He pondered deeply and discovered the way to make man.

He found a beautiful valley full of many plants and fruits, and He took ears of yellow corn and of white corn and ground them into meal. With the corn meal He made nine kinds of liquor, and these became man's strength and energies. With the dough of the meal He shaped the body. And He made four men, very strong and handsome.

While the men slept, he made four women very carefully, and when the men woke, each found at his side a beautiful wife. And they were very happy when they saw their wives.

The Creator said to the four men:

"You are alive. What do you think about it? You can see, and hear, and move, and speak. Do you like it? Look at the world! Try to see!"

The men looked and they were able to see the whole world and everything that was in it. They could see the whole sky. They could see everything. They began to give thanks to the Creator.

"Thank you for our life!" they said. "We can see, we can hear, we can move and think and speak, we feel and know everything, we can see everything in the earth and in the sky. Thank you for having made us, O our Father!"

Then the Creator was troubled, for He realized that these men could see too much and too far, so that they would not really be men, but gods. He saw that He had to change them so that they could be what He needed. So He leaned down and blew mist in their eyes and clouded their vision, like breathing on a mirror, and from then on nothing was clear to their sight except what was close to them.

The four men and their wives went up on a mountain and waited for the dawn. First they saw the shining face of the great star, the Morning Star which comes ahead of the sun, and they burned incense and unwrapped three gifts to offer the sun.

And then the sun came up.

Then the puma and the jaguar roared, and all the birds stretched their wings and sang, and the men and their wives danced with joy because the sun had risen.

Bibliography

For an overview of the flood myth, see Jean Rudhardt's article on the flood in *The Encyclopedia of Religion*, ed. Mircea Eliade (New York, 1987, vol. 5, pp. 353–57). An important work on the relationship between the Babylonian and Hebrew floods is Alexander Heidel's *The Gilgamesh Epic and Old Testament Parallels* (Chicago, 1949, 1967). For an account of the development of the Gilgamesh flood story itself, see Jeffrey H. Tigay, *The Evolution of the Gilgamesh Epic* (Philadelphia, 1982). Samuel Noah Kramer's *Mythologies of the Ancient World* (New York, 1961) and his *Sumerian Mythology* (New York, 1961) are also useful on the Babylonian flood. For the significance of the Flood and its connection with baptism, see Alan Watts, *Myth and Ritual in Christianity* (Boston, 1968). Carl Jung provides a psychological perspective in *Symbols of Transformation* (Princeton, N.J., 1956, 1976) and in *The Archetypes and the Collective Unconscious* (Princeton, N.J., 1959, 1976). Mircea Eliade has perceptive comments on aquatic symbolism and the paradigmatic history of baptism in *The Sacred and the Profane* (New York, 1959) and on the Flood and cosmic rhythm in *The Myth of the Eternal Return* (Princeton, N.J., 1954, 1974). Eliade's *Patterns in Comparative Religion* (New York, 1958, 1974) contains a thorough discussion of water symbolism, and of deluge symbolism in particular.

THE AFTERLIFE

The belief in some sort of afterlife is ubiquitous. The human being finds the concept of total dissipation of self after death more difficult to accept than the notion of conscious existence after death. The Land of the Dead need not be pleasant; one of the earliest literary examples of an afterlife is the one recorded in Homer's Odyssey. *The Land of the Dead that Odysseus visits is a place of darkness, sadness, and despair. Yet it is not primarily a place of punishment. The religious cultures that stress the struggle between good and evil in this world are the ones that divide the afterworld into areas of suffering and bliss. The Christian and Muslim concept of heaven and hell is only one example of this tendency. In the more mystical religions that stress the illusory nature of life, the afterlife may be a distinctly nonphysical realm, even a place where self loses its individual identity in a larger Self. In fact, such concepts as nirvana do not include a sense of place and are not properly thought of as myths of the afterlife, any more than is the Christian idea of the Kingdom of God. In one way or another, all afterlife myths, and even the lack of such myths, reflect cultural perceptions of this world.*

Part of the need for belief in an afterlife can probably be traced to humanity's experience of the cycles of nature. As a functioning part of the organism called Earth, we do not like to be left out. The paths of the sun and the moon, the rhythms of the tides, the menstrual process, and the seasons, all suggest a natural return of whatever is lost and lead naturally to the concept of life after death and ultimately some kind of restoration of life.

Perhaps an even more important factor is consciousness itself. Of all species, only humans are capable of conceiving of life as a complete process, including birth and death. It might be said that consciousness of the total life process—of life's beginning, middle, and end as a single plot—is our defining characteristic. Without that consciousness, existence itself—certainly our existence—is threatened. That being the case, it is perhaps ultimately impossible to conceive of the permanent loss of consciousness. Even if we do not go so far as to believe in the physical restoration of our individual lives, we tend to have difficulty conceiving of life without the consciousness by which we perceive it. The afterlife is an almost inevitable result. And it should be noted that more often than not, the souls in the various underworlds—the heavens and hells of world mythology—are nearly always, in death, freed from the restrictions on knowledge of the future that are necessarily associated with the physical life— with mortality itself. In the afterlife individual consciousness comes into its own as part of a larger consciousness that informs all things and all actions.

THE AFTERLIFE STORIES

Egyptian: Osiris

Given its general emphasis on death and rebirth, it is not surprising that ancient Egyptian civilization has the afterlife as a predominant theme. Osiris, the resurrection god, is the central figure in the afterlife myth and in Egyptian mythology as a whole. To die and be properly prepared for the other life is to become one with Osiris in the underworld over which he rules. Thus, at a funeral, the name Osiris was attached to the name of the mummified dead person. In this new identity the individual could be reborn as a soul. Our sources for the Egyptian afterlife myth are the Pyramid and Coffin texts and the *Book of the Dead*. R. T. Rundle Clark creates a single narrative from these sources.

●

The ancients thought of death as the essential prelude to life. The two form a polarity; one is meaningless without the other, and they alternate in all spheres of nature—among men, animals, vegetation and stars. Death is a passing from one kind of time to another—from life yesterday to life tomorrow. What is in the Underworld belongs to death, but it is in a state of becoming, where the "form" or shape of things is given in which they will later "appear." Life can be seen, becoming is hidden. The chief instance of this great process is the sun, which must somehow be refitted or remoulded beneath the earth or beyond the visible sky. The place where these things happened was called by the Egyptians the *Dat*, which for convenience is called the Underworld. The Egyptians, however, do not seem to have given a fixed location to the Dat; it is usually under the earth but sometimes beyond the visible sky vault ("the belly of Nut") or in the waters which they imagined to extend everywhere beneath the land. The Dat is without light and beyond the reach of man. It is the place of the formation

R. T. Rundle Clark. *Myth and Symbol in Ancient Egypt* (London, 1959, 1978), pp. 165–67

of the living out of the dead and the past, the true meeting-place of time before and after. Being mysterious, the anxieties of the living were easily transposed. If it was the source of new life it was also the lair of demons who symbolized the forces of annihilation which threatened re-creation in the early and crucial stages. The demons must be kept at bay, so the gates of the Underworld are protected by still more grisly creatures, the tamed forces of chaos, represented by the authors of the Underworld literature as poisonous fire-spitting serpents, lions, lakes of fire and dragons of mixed form.

Osiris is the spirit of becoming, but in the Dat he has largely lost his accidental characteristics. He is no longer the Dead King, Fertility Daimon or Inundation Spirit but the personification of the coming into being of all things. He is generalized as the secret of what lies beneath the surface and is represented as a mummy figure without any distinguishing marks, the symbol which the Egyptians called "irw"—"form." He is the embodiment of the positive aspect of the Dat. A journey to the Underworld is a descent either to the recumbent Osiris or to view the various stages through which he has to go to be reconstituted.

During the Middle Kingdom the Underworld became a much more frightening place than had been imagined by the authors of the Pyramid Texts. It was divided into sections, each of which was guarded by fearful monsters. The earliest of the special works which deal with these horrors must date from before the Twelfth Dynasty. One of them, the so-called Book of the Two Ways, is a guide through the subterranean paths to the places where the sun and moon are reconstituted, apparently in the far north beneath the world axis. The second is Spell 336 of the Coffin Texts, which divides up the Underworld journey into a series of obstacles or gates which must be passed through by means of magical formulae. In these early Underworld texts the journey is made by the soul, but in the developed works which appear on the tombs of the New Kingdom, the theme is the night journey of the sun. As the latter goes through the subterranean ways it lights up the denizens of the dark. It has been the custom of recent commentators to dismiss these sombre productions as trivial expressions of fear and deficient imagination. This is to misunderstand their intention and overlooks the fact that they remained popular until almost the end of the civilization. When the sun passes along it illumines all the forms which must be in the Underworld and belong to the past or future. As an imaginative exercise it is also a journey into the inner reaches of the mind and an attempt to penetrate to the reality which underlies phenomena. The temptation to people the darkness with the unredeemed dead has appealed to nearly every culture—witness the Underworlds of Homer and Virgil. The Egyptians, too, thought it a place destitute of light and hope, the domain of unregulated power, phantoms and terror. Nevertheless, the Underworld is one of the abiding symbols of mankind. Life must come from elsewhere and revival of the heavenly bodies must take place beyond human knowledge. The Underworld may be a limbo or a hell, but it is also the source of new life.

Greco-Roman: Lands of the Dead

In Homer's *Odyssey* (Book XI) Odysseus visits the Land of the Dead, providing us with the most complete vision of the Greek concept of the afterlife. The great hero Achilles has become lord over this land, but he reminds the visiting Odysseus that "I would rather follow the plow as thrall to another / man, one with no land alloted him and not much to live on, / than be a king over all the perished dead. . . ." The Land of the Dead is a place marked by emptiness and despair, a land in which the shades of heroes wander aimlessly, longing for a life lost to them forever.

But another view of the afterlife, which Homer also knew, emerged in the Greek world. In Book IV of the *Odyssey* we hear of the Elysian Field, where Menelaos, as the husband of a daughter of Zeus (Helen), will be privileged to spend his afterlife:

> . . . the gods intend you for Elysion
> with golden Rhadamanthos at the world's end,
> where all existence is a dream of ease.
> Snowfall is never known there, neither long
> frost of winter, nor torrential rain,
> but only mild and lulling airs from Ocean
> bearing refreshment for the souls of men—
> the West Wind always blowing

(*Odyssey*, IV, p. 81 [trans. Robert Fitzgerald])

Gradually this underworld, in which Rhadamanthos, a former king of Crete and son of Zeus and Europa, was to become a judge, would emerge as a place where the dead would be punished or rewarded for their lives on earth. This is the familiar classical Hades, reached when the river Acheron, the River of Woe, is crossed by means of Charon's ferry. Other rivers, such as Lethe, the River of Forgetfulness, and the mysterious Styx, must also be crossed. Hades is presided over by the brother of Zeus, who is himself called Hades. The gates of Hades are guarded by the monster Cerberus. The reader will find a comic version of Hades in Aristophanes' *The Frogs*, where Herakles describes the underworld to the god Dionysos.

The Roman Virgil's epic, the *Aeneid*, (Book VI) contains a vision of the afterlife that places emphasis on reward and punishment. It is an extension of the two visions of the Underworld provided by Homer, the *Aeneid* itself being in a sense a Roman version of the *Iliad* and the *Odyssey*.

The Roman afterlife reflects the Roman view of an orderly, law-abiding culture dominated by a sense of justice.

In Virgil's story Aeneas travels under the guidance of the Virgin Sybil (as he and the Virgin Beatrice will guide Dante in the *Divine Comedy*), allowing us to share his experience of an underworld in which sins are appropriately punished and virtues rewarded. The next stage in Western civilization's view of the afterlife is found in the Bible.

Judeo-Christian: Hell, Purgatory, Heaven

Judaism does not emphasize the idea of an afterlife, but the concept of Sheol—the abyss or underworld where "the shades writhe in fear" (Job 26:5)—was an ancient one that persisted in Jewish thought. Sheol is not unlike the Homeric Greek underworld in that the shades who abide there are without hope, regardless of their behavior while alive. Sheol is a metaphor for the nothingness that follows life. The proud kings who deny the Hebrew God and who will become mere dust in Sheol must remind even the righteous of the importance of life in this world rather than in the other: "Whatever task lies to your hand, do it with all your might; because in Sheol, for which you are bound, there is neither doing nor thinking, neither understanding nor wisdom" (Eccles. 9:10).

The early Christians were, of course, influenced by the concept of Sheol as well as the Greco-Roman dualistic underworld. But the central message of Christianity—influenced in part by the Osiris cult and other Middle Eastern fertility cults—has to do with the overcoming of death through an acceptance of and ritual participation in the resurrection of Jesus and through a following of his commandments and teachings. By the Middle Ages, the Catholic version of the afterworld as expressed, for instance, in Dante's *Divine Comedy*, had become three places—Hell, Purgatory, and Heaven—to any one of which the deceased might be sent, depending on his or her former conduct in life.

Muslim: Hell and Heaven in the Koran

The vision of heaven and hell in the Koran, the sacred book containing the teachings of the prophet Muhammad, is much like that of the Christians. Heaven is for the true believer; hell is for the infidel or the sinner.

•

With this cleansing did we cleanse them—the remembrance of the abode of Paradise.

And verily, they were, in our sight, of the elect and of the good.

Koran, Saura 37ff.

And remember Ishmael and Elisha and Dhoulkefl, for all these were of the just.

This is a monition: and verily, the pious shall have a goodly retreat:

Gardens of Eden, whose portals shall stand open to them:

Therein reclining, they shall there call for many a fruit and drink:

And with them shall be virgins of their own age, with modest retiring glances:

"This is what ye were promised at the day of reckoning."

"Yes! this is our provision: it shall never fail."

Even so. But for the evil doers is a wretched home—

Hell—wherein they shall be burned: how wretched a bed!

Even so. Let them then taste it—boiling water and gore,

And other things of kindred sort!

To their leaders it shall be said, "This company shall be thrown in headlong with you. No greetings shall await them, for they shall be burned in the fire."

They shall say: "But ye, too! there shall be no welcome for you. It was ye who prepared this for us, and wretched is the abode!"

They will say: "O our Lord! increase twofold in the fire, the punishment of him who hath brought this upon us."

And they will say: "Why see we not the men whom we numbered among the wicked—

Whom we used to treat with scorn? Have they escaped our eyes?"

Verily this is truth—the wrangling together of the people of the fire.

SAY: I am but a warner; and there is no God but God the One, the Almighty!

Lord of the Heavens and of the Earth, and of all that is between them, the Potent, the Forgiving!

SAY: this is a weighty message,

From which ye turn aside!

Buddhist: The Pure Land

The popularization of Buddhism in twelfth-century Japan led to the rapid growth of a sect associated with Amida, the Buddha of Boundless Light, who promised to the devout a "Pure Land" or "Western Paradise" to which they could go for eternal rest after the trials of life. In the Buddhist view, derived from Hinduism, an individual builds up good or bad Karma (self-identity and destiny) through actions and thoughts. The concept of "Pure Land," like the Christian redemption through Christ, is a means by which even apparent destiny can be overcome. "Just say the name and be saved by Amida," the would-be devotee is told. Even those whose "Karmic evil" is great can be saved by physically and spiritually calling on the name

of Amida (performing the *nembutsu*). The spiritual nature of the Pure Land
is suggested by the thirteenth-century Japanese sage Shinran in the *Tannishō*.

*

1

"Saved by the inconceivable working of Amida's Vow, I shall realize birth
into the Pure Land": the moment you entrust yourself thus, so that the
mind set upon saying the Name arises within you, you are brought to share
in the benefit of being grasped by Amida, never to be abandoned.

Know that the Primal Vow of Amida makes no distinction between
people young and old, good and evil; only the entrusting of yourself to it
is essential. For it was made to save the person in whom karmic evil is
deep-rooted and whose blind passions abound.

Thus, entrusting yourself to the Primal Vow requires no performance
of good, for no act can hold greater virtue than saying the Name. Nor is
there need to despair of the evil you commit, for no act is so evil that it
obstructs the working of Amida's Primal Vow.

Thus were his words.

2

Each of you has crossed the borders of more than ten provinces to come
to see me, undeterred by concern for your bodily safety, solely to inquire
about the way to birth in the land of bliss. But if you imagine in me some
special knowledge of a way to birth other than the nembutsu or a familiar-
ity with writings that teach it, you are greatly mistaken. If that is the case,
you would do better to visit the many eminent scholars in Nara or on
Mount Hiei and inquire fully of them about the essentials for birth. I simply accept and entrust myself to what a good teacher told me, "Just say
the Name and be saved by Amida"; nothing else is involved.

I have no idea whether the nembutsu is truly the seed for my being
born in the Pure Land or whether it is the karmic act for which I must fall
into hell. Should I have been deceived by Hōnen Shōnin and, saying the
Name, plunge utterly into hell, even then I would have no regrets. The
person who could have attained Buddhahood by endeavoring in other practices might regret that he had been deceived if he said the nembutsu and
so fell into hell. But I am one for whom any practice is difficult to accomplish, so hell is to be my home whatever I do.

Shinran, *Tannishō: A Primer*, trans. Dennis Hirota (Kyoto, 1982), pp. 22–24.

If Amida's Primal Vow is true and real, Śākyamuni's teaching cannot be lies. If the Buddha's teaching is true and real, Shan-tao's commentaries cannot be lies. If Shan-tao's commentaries are true and real, can what Hōnen said be a lie? If what Hōnen said is true and real, then surely my words cannot be empty.

Such, in essence, is the shinjin of the foolish person that I am. Beyond this, whether you entrust yourself, taking up the nembutsu, or whether you abandon it, is your own, individual decision.

Thus were his words.

3

Even a good person can attain birth in the Pure Land, so it goes without saying that an evil person will.

Though such is the truth, people commonly say, "Even an evil person attains birth, so naturally a good person will." This statement may seem well-founded at first, but it runs counter to the meaning of the Other Power established through the Primal Vow. For a person who relies on the good that he does through his self-power fails to entrust himself wholeheartedly to Other Power and therefore is not in accord with Amida's Primal Vow. But when he abandons his attachment to self-power and entrusts himself totally to Other Power, he will realize birth in the Pure Land.

It is impossible for us, filled as we are with blind passions, to free ourselves from birth-and-death through any practice whatever. Sorrowing at this, Amida made the Vow, the essential intent of which is the attainment of Buddhahood by the person who is evil. Hence the evil person who entrusts himself to Other Power is precisely the one who possesses the true cause for birth.

Accordingly he said, "Even the virtuous man is born in the Pure Land, so without question is the man who is evil."

4

In the matter of compassion, the Path of Sages and the Pure Land path differ. Compassion in the Path of Sages is to pity, sympathize with, and care for beings. But the desire to save others from suffering is vastly difficult to fulfill.

Compassion in the Pure Land path lies is saying the Name, quickly attaining Buddhahood, and freely benefiting sentient beings with a heart of great love and great compassion. In our present lives, it is hard to carry out the desire to aid others however much love and tenderness we may feel; hence such compassion always falls short of fulfillment. Only the saying of the Name manifests the heart of great compassion that is replete and thoroughgoing.

Thus were his words.

Hopi: The Kachinas

Nearly every Native American tribe has its highly complex version of the afterlife. One such version is this Hopi Indian myth as told to Alice Marriott and Carol Rachlin by two Hopi "informants" who, given the Hopi tendency to be secretive with outsiders about religious matters, were willing to reveal only a part of the story. The context of this myth includes the land of the good spirits (*Kachinas*), whom the single-hearted (i.e., good) Hopis will join in death, and the Hopi hell, known as the "Country of the Two Hearts" (two hearts signifying falseness—a deviation from single-heartedness) where evil people go.

•

The San Francisco Peaks stand north of Flagstaff, Arizona, and for many centuries they have been the most sacred places known to the Hopis, except parts of the Grand Canyon.

Within the San Francisco Peaks, the kachinas* live. They have a very beautiful world. The corn grows thickly every year; the squashes and melons grow at every joint of the vines; nobody knows how many different kinds of beans the kachinas have. There are lakes of water—there are springs, too, like those on the mesas—but there are really lakes of water, where the cattails grow tall and sweet.

The hills are covered with all the plants the Hopis use: wild spinach and wild potatoes for food, rabbit brush and yucca for baskets, and all the plants the Hopis need to make dyes for their basketry.

Highest up of all grow the sacred trees, blue spruce and juniper and mountain mahogany and piñon. The kachinas can go out whenever they like and gather everything they need for their ceremonies.

During the growing months, from February to July, the kachinas live in the villages with the Hopis. Nobody can see them, except when they come out of the kivas to dance in the plaza, but the Hopis know the kachinas are there, and they feel that they and their crops are safe.

---

*A kachina may be one of the forces of nature: life, death, fire, flood, or famine. A kachina may be the spirit of a much-loved ancestor who, as the Hopis say, has "passed beyond." A kachina may be man dancing to impersonate one of these spirits. Or a kachina, as is most frequently said, may be what the Hopis call a "kachin tihu"—a doll carved and painted to represent a spirit. These dolls are given to children as a combination toy–cathechism book, with which they play but from which they also learn the essentials of their religion.

Alice Marriott and Carol K. Rachlin, *American Indian Mythology* (New York, 1968), pp. 233–37.

Late in July, the kachinas go home to the San Francisco Peaks. They dance for the people one last time, and give presents to all the children. Then the kachinas go over the edge of the mesa, and you can see the tall rain columns marching across the desert to the San Francisco Peaks.

Naturally, every Hopi wishes to join the spirits of his loved ones who have passed beyond. To that end he keeps his heart pure and is kind and generous to other people.

When a bad person—one who is known as ka-Hopi, or not Hopi—dies, his fate is very different. The Two Hearts, or witches, take him by the hand as soon as the breath is out of his body, and they lead him away to their own country. The country of the Two Hearts is as bad as they are themselves. You may live in a village all your life with a Two Heart, and the only way that you can tell he is a witch is that the people in his family keep dying off. Every time a Two Heart works his wickedness and hurts somebody else, he must give up one of his own kinfolk.

The country of the Two Hearts is a desert. It is dry, dry, and it has no water holes. The ka-Hopi must crawl through it on his hands and knees; when he is too weak, he crawls on his belly. Sometimes the ka-Hopi has a vision of someone he loved and he begs and pleads for water, for shade, for rest. But no matter how much his loved one wants to help the ka-Hopi, he cannot do so.

That is what happens to Hopis who do wrong, and who are selfish and cruel. No Hopi wants to suffer that way.

There was a young couple who married, many years ago. Naturally, the husband went to live in his wife's mother's house. At first everything went very well, but then the husband began to feel nervous. He felt as if someone were looking at him all the time. He glanced here and there, over his shoulder, up at the sky, down at the earth, but he could see nobody.

They lived on the very top of the mesa, and down at its foot was the old cemetery. When people were wrapped in their blankets, their faces covered over with cloud cotton, and they were buried, their relatives smashed pottery bowls on their graves, and gave away everything the dead ones had owned. Nobody ever went near the cemetery at any other time, unless he took the burro trails from the spring that led past its outer edge. Only Two Hearts went there, to gather more power to hurt people.

Presently the young husband noticed that his wife's relatives were dying off. They were young people, hard workers, and lived good lives, but they would sicken and die, leaving their children to be taken care of by the women of the children's clans.

The young wife did not mourn aloud—that is not the Hopi way. But often in the night her husband woke to find his wife's body shaking with sobs, at his side. When the husband asked her what was wrong, the wife told him that she was crying because they had no children. That was true,

although they loved each other very much, and wanted children, and tried
to have them.

This went on for a long time—about four years. The husband grew
more and more disturbed. Once he went back to his mother's house, in
another village, but his wife followed him, crying and begging him to come
home, so at last he gave up and went with her.

One night it was getting dark, and the wife said to her husband, "I
wonder where my mother is? I don't think she should be out so late."

"I don't know where she's gone," the husband answered. "I've been
in the fields all day. How would I know what you women are doing?"

"Well, I wish you'd go and look for her," his wife said.

"Not till I eat my dinner," the husband answered.

She gave him beans boiled with mutton, and some baked corn, and a
cup of coffee. When he had finished he got up and said, "That was a good
meal. I'll go and look for your mother now."

"All right," said his wife. "Will you take the water canteen with you
and fill it at the spring? I'm almost out of water."

The husband grumbled a little, but he finally took the flat-sided canteen and slung it with a strap across his forehead, the way a woman would
carry it. It was dark, and none of the other men would see him carrying
water the way a woman would.

The young man climbed down the track toward the spring, feeling his
way very carefully, because the pebbles were rough under his moccasins.
He reached the spring safely, and held the canteen under its trickle until
the jar was full. Then he slung it across his forehead and down his back,
and started back toward the village to look for his wife's mother. He
thought she might be visiting some relatives.

Just as he reached the edge of the old cemetery, something struck him
in the back, and he felt legs locked around his hips.

"I'm going to take you," a voice hissed in his ear. The man couldn't
tell if it was a man's or a woman's "I'm going to take you right now, away
from here. All of us Two Hearts are holding a meeting, and it's my turn,
to bring in a new member. I'm going to take you to the Two Heart kiva
and make you one of us. If I don't, they'll kill me."

"You can't do that," the man answered. "I'm a kachina priest, and
the kachinas will protect me."

"I'm going to ride you like a mule," the Two Heart hissed. It began
beating him with a clump of yucca. "Do what I tell you and go where I
tell you to go. I've captured you, and now you'll be one of us."

"The kachinas will protect me," the man insisted.

Again the Two Heart beat him with the yucca. "Do what I say," it
insisted.

The man struggled again, and tried to throw the Two Heart off, but
in vain. It only beat him more, and at last he gave up and followed its

directions to the Two Heart kiva. In his heart he was praying to the kachinas, telling them he had tried to be a good man and take care of his family, that he was studying to be their priest, and that he believed that their power was stronger than that of the Two Hearts.

At last the wall of the mesa loomed in front of them. The Two Heart slipped from the man's back, and knocked four times against the rock. It opened in front of them. Inside, the man saw many people he knew sitting in council. Outside, in the dim light from the fire in the kiva, when he turned his head, he saw his wife's mother. Between the man and his mother-in-law stood the Sun God kachina, the strongest of all the good kachinas.

"Go home to your wife," said the Sun God. "You will always be safe."

The husband, with his water canteen still on his back, went home. "I couldn't find your mother anywhere," was all that he said as he put it down.

They went to bed, then, and late at night they heard the door open and the old lady come in. She slipped into her own bed very quietly, but they knew she was there. The husband prayed to the kachinas all night; he dared not sleep with a Two Heart in the house.

From that day on, the old woman withered and shriveled. The younger members of the family grew round and strong and healthy again, but she wasted away. The only time she spoke she cried for water, but when they gave it to her she could not swallow it, not even when they tried to drop it into her mouth with a yucca blade. Within the year she died.

Bibliography

Richard Cavendish's *Visions of Heaven and Hell* (London, 1977) contains useful commentary and an excellent bibliography. *Psyche and Death* (New York, 1958) by Edgar Herzog utilizes a psychological approach to the question. S. G. F. Brandon's *The Judgement of the Dead* (London, 1967) and James Mew's *Traditional Aspects of Hell* (Mich., 1903, 1971) are also valuable works on the subject of the afterlife.

THE APOCALYPSE

An apocalypse, strictly speaking, is a revelation (from the Greek apocalypsis, *a revealing), a prophetic vision. In common usage it has come to mean a vision of the catastrophic end of the world. Apocalypse myths, then, are eschatological (Greek* eschatos, *last, and* eschata, *the last things), and the study of the end of things is called eschatology.*

The idea of a catastrophic end to the world is common in human culture. In most cases the apocalypse marks the end of an old world and the emergence of a new. But the emphasis is on the end of the current order of things: "The sun will be turned to darkness, and the moon to blood, before the great and terrible day of the Lord comes" (Joel 2:31).

Through their myths of the apocalypse human societies express a sense that the higher powers of the universe must intervene definitively to put an end to the failure of humanity. In some cases the righteous will be allowed to survive, but usually in a nonworldly state.

Apocalyptic writers tend to make heavy use of symbol and fantasy. Their writings are, above all, visionary and prophetic. Apocalypses contain strange beasts and a resurrection of the dead.

The apocalypse motif must be seen as closely related to the deluge archetype. The apocalypse is a ritual cleansing of cosmic proportions, a large-scale expression of the human fascination with the death and resurrection process. Psychologically, it speaks to a need to confront reality, to make ultimate decisions. In our culture the literary archetype for this aspect of the apocalyptic process is Armageddon (Hebrew Haer Megiddon, the famous battlefield of ancient Israel in Judges and Kings). In the Book of Revelation (16:16) Armaggedon becomes the symbolic battlefield where good and evil must finally fight it out at the time of the Last Judgment. We speak metaphorically of Armaggedon in reference to great moments of decision or confrontation. Much of the Christian view of the apocalypse is related to the Persian Zoroastrian Day of Judgment, on which the forces of light confront those of darkness and the dead arise to be judged. A still more important influence is that of the apocalyptic visions of the Old Testament prophets.

If the apocalypse of the Western world stresses the end of things and a final establishment of the Kingdom of God, if the Western view is essentially millennial, the Eastern view is more cyclical, placing less emphasis on human failings justly punished and more on the rhythm of the universe itself. Existence for the Hindu, for instance, is a cosmic breathing, with creation and apocalypse endlessly repeating themselves.

Apocalyptic imagery is very much a part of the way we see reality today. The recent experience of genocidal holocaust and the ever-present threat of a nuclear one bring the myth all too close to home, and science itself teaches an eventual descent into "heat death," before Earth returns, as all systems eventually must, to a natural state of entropic equilibrium or no-thing-ness.

THE APOCALYPTIC STORIES

Hebrew: The Day of Yahweh

The apocalyptic mode is common in the Old Testament. Daniel (7–12), Isaiah (24–27), Ezekiel (37), and Joel (3) all contain apocalyptic moments, as does the Zechariah selection (14) included here. The Hebrew prophets, when berating the Hebrews for their failure to follow their God, speak in dire terms of the Day of Yahweh, when the dead will return to be judged and the enemies of God will be destroyed before the true Kingdom is established. The Old Testament prophets establish the motifs of which John will make full use in the New Testament Book of Revelation.

•

Behold, the day of the Lord cometh, and thy spoil shall be divided in the midst of thee.

2 For I will gather all nations against Jerusalem to battle; and the city shall be taken, and the houses rifled, and the women ravished; and half of the city shall go forth into captivity, and the residue of the people shall not be cut off from the city.

3 Then shall the Lord go forth, and fight against those nations, as when he fought in the day of battle.

4 And his feet shall stand in that day upon the mount of Olives, which is before Jerusalem on the east, and the mount of Olives shall cleave in the

Zechariah 14.

midst thereof toward the east and toward the west, and there shall be a very great valley; and half of the mountain shall remove toward the north, and half of it toward the south.

5 And ye shall flee to the valley of the mountains; for the valley of the mountains shall reach unto Azal: yea, ye shall flee, like as ye fled from before the earthquake in the days of Ŭz-zī'-ăh king of Judah: and the Lord my God shall come, and all the saints with thee.

6 And it shall come to pass in that day, that the light shall not be clear, nor dark.

7 But it shall be one day which shall be known to the Lord, not day, nor night: but it shall come to pass, that at evening time it shall be light.

8 And it shall be in that day, that living waters shall go out from Jerusalem; half of them toward the former sea, and half of them toward the hinder sea: in summer and in winter shall it be.

9 And the Lord shall be king over all the earth: in that day shall there be one Lord, and his name one.

10 All the land shall be turned as a plain from Geba to Rimmon south of Jerusalem: and it shall be lifted up, and inhabited in her place, from Benjamin's gate unto the place of the first gate, unto the corner gate, and from the tower of Hăn'-ă-neel unto the king's winepresses.

11 And men shall dwell in it, and there shall be no more utter destruction; but Jerusalem shall be safely inhabited.

12 And this shall be the plague wherewith the Lord will smite all the people that have fought against Jerusalem; Their flesh shall consume away while they stand upon their feet, and their eyes shall consume away in their holes, and their tongue shall consume away in their mouth.

13 And it shall come to pass in that day, that a great tumult from the Lord shall be among them; and they shall lay hold every one on the hand of his neighbour, and his hand shall rise up against the hand of his neighbour.

14 And Judah also shall fight at Jerusalem; and the wealth of all the heathen round about shall be gathered together, gold, and silver, and apparel, in great abundance.

15 And so shall be the plague of the horse, of the mule, of the camel, and of the ass, and of all the beasts that shall be in these tents, as this plague.

16 And it shall come to pass, that every one that is left of all the nations which came against Jerusalem shall even go up from year to year to worship the King, the Lord of hosts, and to keep the feast of tabernacles.

17 And it shall be, that whoso will not come up of all the families of the earth unto Jerusalem to worship the King, the Lord of hosts, even upon them shall be no rain.

18 And if the family of Egypt go not up, and come not, that have no rain; there shall be the plague, wherewith the Lord will smite the heathen that come not up to keep the feast of tabernacles.

19 This shall be the punishment of Egypt, and the punishment of all nations that come not up to keep the feast of tabernacles.

20 In that day shall there be upon the bells of the horses, HOLINESS UNTO THE LORD; and the pots in the Lord's house shall be like the bowls before the altar.

21 Yea, every pot in Jerusalem and in Judah shall be holiness unto the Lord of hosts: and all they that sacrifice shall come and take of them, and seethe therein: and in that day there shall be no more the Cā'nă-ăn-īte in the house of the Lord of hosts.

Christian: St. John's Book of Revelation

The last book of the New Testament, the Book of Revelation of the Apocalypse of St. John the Divine, was probably composed at Ephesus in about 95 C.E. It is contemporaneous with such late Hebrew apocalypses as those in Esdras (2) and Baruch (2), and it owes much to Old Testament symbology and tone in general. Like most apocalypses, it predicts the coming of the Kingdom, the raising of the dead, and a final judgment. It is from John's mysterious work that our literature takes such terms as the "Antichrist" and "the hour of fulfillment is near." John establishes for the early Christians what the four Gospels had only suggested, that the Kingdom of God is at hand, that the Second Coming of Christ is imminent. John's vision was to color Western culture from the first century on. Through John, the millennial outlook of the Hebrews took precedence over the less historically oriented and less visionary Greek attitude in the Christian world view. The effects remain with us today, even in the atheistic but millennial and visionary philosophy of Marxism.

*

Chapter 15

And I saw another sign in heaven, great and marvellous, seven angels having the seven last plagues; for in them is filled up the wrath of God.

2 And I saw as it were a sea of glass mingled with fire: and them that had gotten the victory over the beast, and over his image, and over his mark, and over the number of his name, stand on the sea of glass, having the harps of God.

Revelation 15–16.

3 And they sing the song of Moses the servant of God, and the song of the Lamb, saying, Great and marvellous are thy works, Lord God Almighty; just and true are thy ways, thou King of saints.

4 Who shall not fear thee, O Lord, and glorify thy name? for thou only art holy: for all nations shall come and worship before thee; for thy judgments are made manifest.

5 And after that I looked, and, behold, the temple of the tabernacle of the testimony in heaven was opened:

6 And the seven angels came out of the temple, having the seven plagues, clothed in pure and white linen, and having their breasts girded with golden girdles.

7 And one of the four beasts gave unto the seven angels seven golden vials full of the wrath of God, who liveth for ever and ever.

8 And the temple was filled with smoke from the glory of God, and from his power; and no man was able to enter into the temple, till the seven plagues of the seven angels were fulfilled.

Chapter 16

And I heard a great voice out of the temple saying to the seven angels, Go your ways, and pour out the vials of the wrath of God upon the earth.

2 And the first went, and poured out his vial upon the earth; and there fell a noisome and grievous sore upon the men which had the mark of the beast, and upon them which worshipped his image.

3 And the second angel poured out his vial upon the sea; and it became as the blood of a dead man; and every living soul died in the sea.

4 And the third angel poured out his vial upon the rivers and fountains of waters; and they became blood.

5 And I heard the angel of the waters say, Thou art righteous, O Lord, which art, and wast, and shalt be, because thou hast judged thus.

6 For they have shed the blood of saints and prophets, and thou hast given them blood to drink; for they are worthy.

7 And I heard another out of the altar say, Even so, Lord God Almighty, true and righteous are thy judgments.

8 And the fourth angel poured out his vial upon the sun; and power was given unto him to scorch men with fire.

9 And men were scorched with great heat, and blasphemed the name of God, which hath power over these plagues: and they repented not to give him glory.

10 And the fifth angel poured out his vial upon the seat of the beast; and his kingdom was full of darkness; and they gnawed their tongues for pain,

11 And blasphemed the God of heaven because of their pains and their sores, and repented not of their deeds.

12 And the sixth angel poured out his vial upon the great river Eû-phrā'-tēs; and the water thereof was dried up, that the way of the kings of the east might be prepared.

13 And I saw three unclean spirits like frogs come out of the mouth of the dragon, and out of the mouth of the beast, and out of the mouth of the false prophet.

14 For they are the spirits of devils, working miracles, which go forth unto the kings of the earth and of the whole world, to gather them to the battle of that great day of God Almighty.

15 Behold, I come as a thief. Blessed is he that watcheth, and keepeth his garments, lest he walk naked, and they see his shame.

16 And he gathered them together into a place called in the Hebrew tongue Är-mă-gĕd'-dŏn.

17 And the seventh angel poured out his vial into the air; and there came a great voice out of the temple of heaven, from the throne, saying, It is done.

18 And there were voices, and thunders, and lightnings; and there was a great earthquake, such as was not since men were upon the earth, so mighty an earthquake, and so great.

19 And the great city was divided into three parts, and the cities of the nations fell: and great Babylon came in remembrance before God, to give unto her the cup of the wine of the fierceness of his wrath.

20 And every island fled away, and the mountains were not found.

21 And there fell upon men a great hail out of heaven, every stone about the weight of a talent: and men blasphemed God because of the plague of the hail; for the plague thereof was exceeding great.

Indian: The End of the Kali Age

As seen in the series of sacred texts called the *purānas*, (meaning "stories of the old days"), apocalypse for the Hindu is the natural ending of the world in the fourth age, the Kali Age. It is but one of a series of apocalypses, each of which marks the end of one cycle and the beginning of another creation. The central figure in the story is Vishnu, the preserver god, into whose self the world is absorbed before being born again.

•

Cornelia Dimmitt and J. A. B. van Buitenen, eds. and trans. *Classical Hindu Mythology* (Philadelphia, 1978), pp. 41–43.

The Kali Age

All kings occupying the earth in the Kali Age will be wanting in tranquillity, strong in anger, taking pleasure at all times in lying and dishonesty, inflicting death on women, children and cows, prone to take the paltry possessions of others, with character that is mostly *tamas*, rising to power and soon falling. They will be short-lived, ambitious, of little virtue and greedy. People will follow the customs of others and be adulterated with them; peculiar, undisciplined barbarians will be vigorously supported by the rulers. Because they go on living with perversion, they will be ruined. The destruction of the world will occur because of the departure from virtue and profit, little by little, day by day. Money alone will confer nobility. Power will be the sole definition of virtue. Pleasure will be the only reason for marriage. Lust will be the only reason for womanhood. Falsehood will win out in disputes. Being dry of water will be the only definition of land. The sacred thread alone will distinguish brahmins. Praiseworthiness will be measured by accumulated wealth. Wearing the *linga* will be sufficient cause for religious retreat. Impropriety will be considered good conduct, and only feebleness will be the reason for unemployment. Boldness and arrogance will become equivalent to scholarship. Only those without wealth will show honesty. Just a bath will amount to purification, and charity will be the only virtue. Abduction will be marriage. Simply to be well-dressed will signify propriety. And any water hard to reach will be deemed a pilgrimage site. The pretense of greatness will be the proof of it, and powerful men with many severe faults will rule over all the classes on earth. Oppressed by their excessively greedy rulers, people will hide in valleys between mountains where they will gather honey, vegetables, roots, fruits, birds, flowers and so forth. Suffering from cold, wind, heat and rain, they will put on clothes made of tree-bark and leaves. And no one will live as long as twenty-three years. Thus in the Kali Age humankind will be utterly destroyed.

The Dissolution of the World in Viṣṇu

At the end of a thousand periods of four Ages, when the earth's surface is for the most part wasted, there arises a dreadful drought that lasts for a hundred years. Then all these earthly beings whose strength has declined perish completely through oppression. And so the imperishable lord Viṣṇu, who abides in himself, adopts the form of Rudra, and exerts himself to act in order to destroy all creatures. Permeating the seven rays of the sun, the lord Viṣṇu then drinks up all the waters, O excellent sage. When he has consumed all the waters that had gone to the world of creatures, he dries up the earth's surface. Oceans, rivers and flowing mountain streams as well as whatever water lies in the Pātālas*—all this he leads to dissolution. Then due to his power, those same seven rays become seven suns, invigorated by the absorption of water. These seven blazing suns ignite all three worlds, above and below, along with the surface of the Netherworld, O twice-born. The three worlds, O twice-born one, consumed by these fiery suns, complete with mountains, rivers and the expanse of the ocean, become arid. Then the whole triple world whose water and trees are burned away, and this earth as well, become as bare as a turtle's back. Likewise, when the monstrous fire has burned up these Pātālas, it rises to the earth and utterly devours its surface. And a frightful tornado of flame rolls through the entire Bhuvarloka and Svarloka. The three worlds then blaze like a frying-pan; all things moving and unmoving are consumed by the surrounding flames. The inhabitants of these two worlds, overcome by heat, their duties done, retreat to Maharloka, O great seer. Still seared by the heat they flee again; seeking safety in a different place, they hurry thence to Janaloka. So when Janārdana in Rudra's form has consumed all creation, he produces clouds from the breath of his mouth that look like a herd of elephants, emitting lightning, roaring loudly. Thus do dreadful clouds arise in the sky. Some are dark like the blossom of the blue lotus; some look like the white water-lily; some are the color of smoke; and others are yellow. Some resemble a donkey's hue; others are like red lacquer; some have the appearance of a cat's-eye gem; and some are like sapphire. Still others are white as a conch shell or jasmine, or similar to collyrium; some are like fireflies, while others resemble peacocks. Huge clouds arise resembling red or yellow arsenic, and others look like a bluejay's wing. Some of these clouds are like fine towns, and some like mountains; others resemble houses, and still others, mounds of earth. These dense, elephantine clouds fill up the surface of the sky, roaring loudly. Pouring down rain they completely extinguish this dreadful fire which has overtaken the three worlds. And when the fire is thoroughly quenched, the clouds raining day and night overwhelm the entire world with water, O excellent seer. When they have completely inundated the atmosphere with copious streams of water, then, O twice-born, they flood Bhuvarloka on high. When everything movable and immovable in the world has perished in the watery darkness, these vast clouds pour down rain for another one hundred years. So is it as the end of every Eon, O excellent seer, by the majesty of the eternal Vāsudeva, the supreme lord.

When the waters come to rest, having reached the realm of the seven seers, then this single ocean completely covers the three worlds. Wind blown out of Viṣṇu's mouth makes the clouds disappear in a hundred years. When the eternal lord, fashioner of all creatures, inconceivable, the

*Netherworlds.

condition of creation, the beginning of everything who has no beginning himself, has entirely consumed the wind, then, reposing on Śeṣa in the single ocean, the lord, first creator, rests in the form of Brahmā, praised by Sanaka and others, the seers who went to Janaloka, and also meditated upon by those who went to Brahmaloka seeking freedom. Resting in meditative sleep, in the divine form of his own illusive power, Viṣṇu, destroyer of Madhu, concentrates on the form of himself called Vāsudeva. This is the dissolution called occasional, O Maitreya;* the occasion is that Hari rests in the form of Brahmā. When the soul of all awakens, then the world stirs; when the imperishable one has gone to his bed of illusion, it falls completely asleep. A day of Brahmā, born of from the lotus, lasts a thousand periods of four Ages; a night, when the world is destroyed and made into a vast ocean, is of the same length. At the end of the night, Viṣṇu, unborn, having awakened, takes the form of Brahmā in order to create, as it has already been told to you.

Hopi: Emergence to the Fifth World

This Hopi prophecy resembles other millennial visions of the destruction of the world before the establishment of a new order. It sees the ancient Hopi village of Oraibi as the center of the world and Hopi ceremonies as the repository of life's remaining spiritualism. The Hopis, like the ancient Hebrews, see themselves as surrounded by a world lost in spiritual darkness.

•

The end of all Hopi ceremonialism will come when a *kachina* removes his mask during a dance in the plaza before uninitiated children. For a while there will be no more ceremonies, no more faith. Then Oraibi will be rejuvenated with its faith and ceremonies, marking the start of a new cycle of Hopi life.

World War III will be started by those peoples who first received the light [the divine wisdom or intelligence] in the other old countries [India, China, Egypt, Palestine, Africa].

The United States will be destroyed, land and people, by atomic bombs and radioactivity. Only the Hopis and their homeland will be preserved as an oasis to which refugees will flee. Bomb shelters are a fallacy. "It is only materialistic people who seek to make shelters. Those who are at peace in their hearts already are in the great shelter of life. There is no shelter for evil. Those who take no part in the making of world division by ideology are ready to resume life in another world, be they of the Black, White, Red, or Yellow race. They are all one, brothers."

---

*Sage to whom this text is narrated.

Frank Waters. *Book of the Hopi* (New York, 1963), pp. 408–9.

The war will be "a spiritual conflict with material matters. Material matters will be destroyed by spiritual beings who will remain to create one world and one nation under one power, that of the Creator."

That time is not far off. It will come when the Saquasohuh [Blue Star] Kachina dances in the plaza. He represents a blue star, far off and yet invisible, which will make its appearance soon. The time is also foretold by a song sung during the Wúwuchim ceremony. It was sung in 1914 just before World War I, and again in 1940 before World War II, describing the disunity, corruption, and hatred contaminating Hopi rituals, which were followed by the same evils spreading over the world. This same song was sung in 1961 during the Wúwuchim ceremony.

The Emergence to the future Fifth World has begun. It is being made by the humble people of the little nations, tribes, and racial minorities. "You can read this in the earth itself. Plant forms from previous worlds are beginning to spring up as seeds. This could start a new study of botany if people were wise enough to read them. The same kinds of seeds are being planted in the sky as stars. The same kinds of seeds are being planted in our hearts. All these are the same, depending how you look at them. That is what makes the Emergence to the next, Fifth World.

"These comprise the nine most important prophecies of the Hopis, connected with the creation of the nine worlds: the three previous worlds on which we have lived, the present Fourth World, the future three worlds we have yet to experience, and the world of Taiowa, the Creator, and his nephew, Sótuknang."

Norse: Ragnarök

One of the best known of the apocalyptic stories is the Norse myth of Ragnarök. The gods themselves are doomed in this myth of the end of the world (from the ancient *Voluspa*, the soothsaying of the *volva*, or seeress), movingly retold by the thirteenth-century Icelandic writer Snorri Sturluson in his *Prose Edda*.

Many recognizable events are present here: the earthquakes, the darkening of the sun, the rising of monsters, Armaggedon, the destroying fire followed by the renewal of life.

*

Then Gangleri said: "What is there to relate about Ragnarök? I have never heard tell of this before."

High One said: "There are many and great tidings to tell about it. First will come the winter called Fimbulvetr.[1] Snow will drive from all

---

[1] Terrible Winter.

Snorri Sturluson, *The Prose Edda*, ed. and trans. Jean Young (Berkeley, Calif., 1973), pp. 86–93.

quarters, there will be hard frosts and biting winds; the sun will be no use. There will be three such winters on end with no summer between. Before that, however, three other winters will pass accompanied by great wars throughout the whole world. Brothers will kill each other for the sake of gain, and no one will spare father or son in manslaughter or in incest. As it says in the *Sibyl's Vision:*

> Brothers will fight
> and kill each other,
> siblings
> do incest;
> men will know misery,
> adulteries be multiplied,
> an axe-age, a sword-age,
> shields will be cloven,
> a wind-age, a wolf-age,
> before the world's ruin.

"Then will occur what will seem a great piece of news, the wolf will swallow the sun and that will seem a great disaster to men. Then another wolf will seize the moon and that one too will do great harm. The stars will disappear from heaven. Then this will come to pass, the whole surface of the earth and the mountains will tremble so [violently] that trees will be uprooted from the ground, mountains will crash down, and all fetters and bonds will be snapped and severed. The wolf Fenrir will get loose then. The sea will lash against the land because the Midgard Serpent is writhing in giant fury trying to come ashore. At that time, too, the ship known as Naglfar will become free. It is made of dead men's nails, so it is worth warning you that, if anyone dies with his nails uncut, he will greatly increase the material for that ship which both gods and men devoutly hope will take a long time building. In this tidal wave, however, Naglfar will be launched. The name of the giant steering Naglfar is Hrym. The wolf Fenrir will advance with wide open mouth, his upper jaw against the sky, his lower on the earth (he would gape more widely still if there were room) and his eyes and nostrils will blaze with fire. The Midgard Serpent will blow so much poison that the whole sky and sea will be spattered with it; he is most terrible and will be on the other side of the wolf.

"In this din the sky will be rent asunder and the sons of Muspell ride forth from it. Surt will ride first and with him fire blazing both before and behind. He has a very good sword and it shines more brightly than the sun. When they ride over Bifröst, however—as has been said before—that bridge will break. The sons of Muspell will push forward to the plain called Vígríd and the wolf Fenrir and the Midgard Serpent will go there too. Loki and Hrym with all the frost giants will also be there by then, and all the family of Hel will accompany Loki. The sons of Muspell, however, will form a host in themselves and that a very bright one. The plain Vígríd is a hundred and twenty leagues in every direction.

"When these things are happening, Heimdall will stand up and blow a great blast on the horn Gjöll and awaken all the gods and they will hold an assembly. Then Ódin will ride to Mímir's spring and ask Mímir's advice for himself and his company. The ash Yggdrasil will tremble and nothing in heaven or earth will be free from fear. The Æsir and all the Einherjar will arm themselves and press forward on the plain. Ódin will ride first in a helmet of gold and a beautiful coat of mail and with his spear Gungnir, and he will make for the wolf Fenrir. Thór will advance at his side but will be unable to help him, because he will have his hands full fighting the Midgard Serpent. Frey will fight against Surt and it will be a hard conflict before Frey falls; the loss of the good sword that he gave to Skírnir will bring about his death. Then the hound Garm, which was bound in front of Gnipahellir,[1] will also get free; he is the worst sort of monster. He will battle with Týr and each will kill the other. Thór will slay the Midgard Serpent but stagger back only nine paces before he falls down dead, on account of the poison blown on him by the serpent. The wolf will swallow Ódin and that will be his death. Immediately afterwards, however, Vídar will stride forward and place one foot on the lower jaw of the wolf. On this foot he will be wearing the shoe which has been in the making since the beginning of time; it consists of the strips of leather men pare off at the toes and heels of their shoes, and for this reason people who want to help the Æsir must throw away these strips. Vídar will take the wolf's upper jaw in one hand and tear his throat asunder and that will be the wolf's death. Loki will battle with Heimdall and each will kill the other. Thereupon Surt will fling fire over the earth and burn up the whole world. . . .

Then Gangleri asked: "What will happen afterwards, when heaven and earth and the whole world has been burned and all the gods are dead and all the Einherjar and the whole race of man? Didn't you say before that everyone will go on living for ever in some world or other?"

Then Third answered: "There will be many good dwelling-places then and many bad. The best place to be in at that time will be Gimlé in heaven, for those that like it there is plenty of good drink in the hall called Brimir that is on Ókolnir.[2] There is also an excellent hall on Nidafjöll[3] called Sindri; it is made of red gold. Good and righteous men will live in these halls. On Nástrandir[4] there is a large and horrible hall whose doors face north; it is made of the backs of serpents woven together like wattle-work, with

---

[1]Cliff-cave leading to Hel.
[2]Never Cold.
[3]Dark Mountains.
[4]Corpse-strands.

all their heads turning in to the house and spewing poison so that rivers of it run through the hall. Perjurers and murderers wade these rivers. . . .

Then Gangleri asked: "Will any of the gods be living then? Will there be any earth or heaven then?"

High One said: "At that time earth will rise out of the sea and be green and fair, and fields of corn will grow that were never sown. Vídar and Váli will be living, so neither the sea nor Surt's Fire will have done them injury, and they will inhabit Idavöll where Ásgard used to be. And the sons of Thór, Módi and Magni will come there and possess Mjöllnir. After that Baldr and Höd will come from Hel. They will all sit down together and converse, calling to mind their hidden lore and talking about things that happened in the past, about the Midgard Serpent and the wolf Fenrir. Then they will find there in the grass the golden chessmen the Æsir used to own. . . .

"While the world is being burned by Surt, in a place called Hodd-mímir's Wood, will be concealed two human beings called Líf and Líf-thrasir. Their food will be the morning dews, and from these men will come so great a stock that the whole world will be peopled. . . .

"And you will think this strange, but the sun will have borne a daughter no less lovely than herself, and she will follow the paths of her mother. . . .

"And now, if you have anything more to ask, I can't think how you can manage it, for I've never heard anyone tell more of the story of the world. Make what use of it you can."

The next thing was that Gangleri heard a tremendous noise on all sides and turned about; and when he had looked all round him [he found] that he was standing in the open air on a level plain. He saw neither hall nor stronghold. Then he want on his way and coming home to his kingdom related the tidings he had seen and heard, and after him these stories have been handed down from one man to another.

Modern: Entropy and Heat Death

Modern science provides us with the following picture of the end of the world. This "myth" might best be read in conjunction with the Hindu myths of the destruction of the world at the end of each eon.

•

Whenever scientists begin speculating about the second law, the question ultimately arises as to how broadly it can be applied. For example, does the Entropy Law apply to the macroworld of stars and galaxies that make up the universe? In fact, the Entropy Law is the basis of most cosmological theories. Scientist Benjamin Thompson became the first to draw the cos-

Jeremy Rifkin, *Entropy: A New World View* (New York, 1980), pp. 44–45.

mological implications of the second law back in 1854. According to Thompson, the Entropy Law tells us that

> within a finite period of time past, the earth must have been, and within a finite period of time to come the earth must again be, unfit for the habitation of man as at present constituted, unless operations have been, or are to be performed, which are impossible under the laws to which the known operations going on at present in the material world are subject.

Two years later Helmholtz formulated what has become the standard cosmological theory based on the Entropy Law. His theory of "heat death" stated that the universe is gradually running down and eventually will reach the point of maximum entropy or heat death where all available energy will have been expended and no more activity will occur. The heat death of the universe corresponds to a state of eternal rest.

Today the most widely accepted theory about the origin and development of the universe is the big bang theory. First conceptualized by Canon Georges Lemaître, the big bang theory postulates that the universe began with the explosion of a tremendously dense energy source. As this dense energy expanded outward, it began to slow down, forming galaxies, stars, and planets. As the energy continues to expand and become more diffused, it loses more and more of its order and will eventually reach a point of maximum entropy, or the final equilibrium state of heat death. The big bang theory coincides with the first and second laws. It states that the universe started with complete order and has been moving toward a more and more disordered state ever since. If this theory appears familiar, it should. Both the ancient Greek and the medieval Christian view of history share much in common with the cosmologists' notion of the history of the universe.

Bibliography

The best overall discussion of the end-of-the-world motif is found in Mircea Eliade's *Myth and Reality* (New York, 1963)—especially the fourth chapter ("Eschatology and Cosmogony")—and his *The Myth of the Eternal Return or, Cosmos and History* (New York, 1954). Useful books on the apocalypse in the Old Testament version include Paul D. Hanson's *The Dawn of the Apocalyptic* (Philadelphia, 1975) and D. S. Russell's *Apocalyptic, Ancient and Modern* (Philadelphia, 1978). A great deal has been written about the Book of Revelation in the New Testament. One of the better works, containing a clear interpretation, is Hans Lilje's *The Last Book of the Bible* (Philadelphia, 1975). Another useful work is Bernard McGinn's *Visions of the End: Apocalyptic Traditions in the Middle Ages* (New York, 1979). A more general work, touching on the apocalyptic tradition in many cultures, is a collection of essays called *Apocalypse: The Morphology of a Genre*, published in the journal *Semia* (vol. 14, 1979).

PART II

MYTHS OF THE GODS

World mythology is dominated by an archetypal concept to which we apply the terms "god" and "goddess." Virtually no version of the universal dream that is myth is without the concept of the gods. Whether God or Allah or Brahman or the Great Mother or their many relatives, the gods are seen as immortal; they are personified projections of the human mythmaker's dream of overcoming the inevitable effects of the physical laws that require death and disintegration. Gods are also what Mircea Eliade has called "fecundators" (*Patterns in Comparative Religion*, p. 288) of the universe. They represent the creative force that struggles against the tendency toward the equilibrium of nothing-ness, the force that works to fill the world with life. Furthermore, the gods and goddesses are metaphors for elements of human society. Zeus is a patriarch—a father and a husband, sometimes a philandering one. Hera is a mother and a wife, often a jealous one. Their relationship is a human relationship, their family is a reflection of our families, their hierarchies mirror ours. The gods are also personifications of aspects of nature and of human nature—the sun, the winds, impatience, love.

The existence of the deity fulfills a still more important human need. Gods are symbols of ultimate reality. Their existence provides us with a sense of significance in an otherwise random universe. To say that there are gods or a God is to say that we have meaning, a reason for being. We are made "in the image of God," we are "namers," we are the "guardians" of nature. We are the voice of a meaningful creation. Deity is humankind's metaphor for what Raimundo Pannikar has called "man's effort to discover his identity in confrontation with the limits of his universe" (*The Encyclopedia of Religion*, vol. 4, p. 264). The God archetype in our universal dream is a symbol of the relationship between a meaningful or significant cosmos and our innermost being. Again quoting Pannikar, "Deity is the immanence and transcendence inserted in the heart of every being" (p. 269).

THE PANTHEONS

The officially recognized gods of a culture—its pantheon (Greek pan-theon, all gods)—reflect that culture's value system and view of itself. The Egyptian pantheon speaks directly to that culture's obsession with death and resurrection, which may have arisen from its constant confrontation with the processes of and effects of the passage of the sun and the flooding of the Nile. The Hebrew development of a single patriarchal God concerned with the actions of a "chosen people" suggests a culture with a sense of exclusive identity and mission. The Greek immortal family on Mount Olympos, a family preoccupied with both its own pleasures and the actions of mortals, personifies a realistic if somewhat skeptical view of human nature and the dilemma of a species that revels in life even as it is defined by death.

All pantheons are ontological and teleological; that is, they are metaphors for the human attempt to make sense of existence itself and to assign ultimate cause. To "read" a pantheon is to read a culture's sense of itself and of the nature of the cosmos.

THE PANTHEONIC STORIES

Egyptian

The Egyptian pantheon is marked by a struggle for supremacy among various gods, a struggle that mirrors conflicts among ruling religious and political factions in various parts of Egypt beginning as early as 4000 B.C.E. At one moment in Egyptian history the pantheon of Heliopolis, led by Atum or Re, predominates. At another time Amun in Thebes reigns supreme. The pharaoh Akhenaton even introduced a form of sun god monotheism in the fourteenth century B.C.E. Because of this struggle for religious supremacy and because of the existence of distinct cultural centers, the Egyptian pantheon is marked by inconsistency. The few consistent themes reflect the culture's emphasis on the sun and on death and renewal (probably associated with the passage of the sun and with the seasonal flooding of the Nile). In another consistent motif, the Egyptian immortals are typically depicted as having human bodies and animal heads. If one god emerges as the central figure in the overall Egyptian pantheon, it is Osiris, whose myth, with that of his son Horus, is intricately related to questions of pharoanic legitimacy and the afterlife. A pharaoh dies as Osiris; his successor reigns as Horus.

The Gods of Heliopolis

Summarized below is the Ennead, essentially the pantheon of Heliopolis, which is usually considered to be the most orthodox of Egyptian religious centers. This pantheon was formed by the twenty-eighth century B.C.E. and is found in the Pyramid Texts.

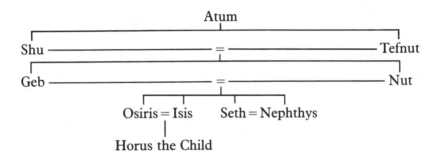

Atum is the sun god. He is at various times and places Ra or Re or Khepri or Amun. As Amun, or Amen-Ra, the sun god of Upper Egypt, He is the great eye of the heavens and of creation.

Shu and his sister Tefnut are the result of Atum's act of masturbation or expectoration. The god embraces his children, bestowing on them his divine essence, or Ka. Shu is the life spirit, while Tefnut is world order or cosmos. Shu and Tefnut produce Geb and Nut.

Geb is the spirit of life; Nut, an Egyptian Great Mother goddess, is the spirit of order. One of the great images of Egyptian mythology is that of Geb and Nut being separated by their father, Shu; Nut becomes the star-filled heavens and Geb becomes Earth, with his erect penis (perhaps represented in Egypt by the ubiquitous obelisk) reaching for his consort.

The children of Geb and Nut complete this most important of Egyptian pantheons:

Osiris is the god of the underworld and of grain. He was the most popular of Egyptian gods, equivalent in spirit to Attis in Phrygia, Adonis in Babylonia, and Dionysos in Greece. He is a god who dies and in one sense or another is revived. (The story of Osiris is told elsewhere in this book.)

Isis, like Demeter in Greece, is a goddess of mysteries. Her cult spread as far as Rome. Isis is the goddess of earth and moon. She is the sister-wife of Osiris and plays the most significant role in his resurrection.

Seth (sometimes spelled Set) is the brother of Osiris and Isis and is their nemesis, a force for evil and darkness in the world. He murders his brother and marries his sister Nephthys.

Nephthys is a goddess of death and dusk. She assists her sister, Isis, in the reviving of the dead Osiris.

Horus, conceived miraculously by Isis and her dead husband, Osiris, has aspects of the sun god; he is the light that defeats the darkness associated with Seth. Horus is the *puer aeternus*, or divine child, of the Egyptian pantheon. He is the spiritual force behind the reigning pharaoh.

The Separation of Geb and Nut

Reprinted here is a portion of the Pyramid Text story of the Egyptian pantheon. By implication, it concerns the separation of Geb and Nut.

(Priest speaks):
   O Nut, spread yourself over your son Osiris,
   and hide him from Seth. Protect him, O Nut!
   Have you come to hide your son? . . .

(Words to be spoken by Geb):
   O Nut! You became a spirit,
   you waxed mighty in the belly of your mother Tefnut
      before you were born.
   How mighty is your heart!

You stirred in the belly of your mother in your name of Nut,
you are indeed a daughter more powerful than her mother . . .
O Great One who has become the sky!
You have the mastery, you have filled every place with your beauty.
the whole earth lies beneath you, you have taken possession thereof,
you have enclosed the whole earth and everything therein within your arms. . . .

R. T. Rundle Clark, *Myth and Symbol in Ancient Egypt* (London, 1959), pp. 48–49.

As Geb shall I impregnate you in your name of sky,
I shall join the whole earth to you in every place.
O high above the earth! You are supported upon your
father Shu,
but you have power over him,
he so loved you that he placed himself—and all things
beside—beneath you
so that you took up into you every god with his heavenly
barque,
and as "a thousand souls is she" did you teach them
that they should not leave you—as the stars.

Greek

Like the Egyptian pantheon, the Greek pantheon emerges in stages. Two
dynasties must be overcome before Zeus and his family can rule the universe. Hesiod's *Theogony*, the epics of Homer, and the *Homeric Hymns* are
among our major sources for the theogonic Greek myths as they emerged
in the ninth through the seventh centuries B.C.E.

The Olympians

More than any other pantheon, the Greek hierarchy of gods and goddesses
is modeled on human families. The official Olympian gods, the family of
Mount Olympus, headed by Zeus, is simply the most powerful of Greek
families. Like other members of the rich and powerful classes, the Olympian family is marred by instances of immorality, arrogance, and stubbornness. In the Greek view, the gods were to be approached warily rather
than in a familiar or loving manner. They were not to be trusted and could
not be counted on for mercy. They were an exaggerated version of what a
human family might become if endowed with infinite power. They were a
mirror of human nature itself. Furthermore, they represented the irrational forces of physical nature.

Other aspects of Greek religion were not so deeply rooted in hierarchy
and in the existing social structure. The cults of Dionysos and Demeter,
for example, have been called earth religions, as opposed to the sky religion
of the Olympians. Their cults were associated with fertility, with deep
emotion, and even with mystery or mysticism, and had a wide following
among the people. The Earth religions were probably well established in
the land we now call Greece or in the lands to the east of Greece long before
the emergence there of the religion of Zeus, which very likely results from
a merging of the religions of various Mediterranean and northern peoples.

The Greek pantheon, as it had developed by the time of Homer, was
made up officially of twelve gods and goddesses, although there is disagreement as to the exact composition of the group. Included in the family tree

below are the usually accepted twelve, with their ancestors (set off by parentheses) and a few alternates or lesser figures [indicated by brackets].

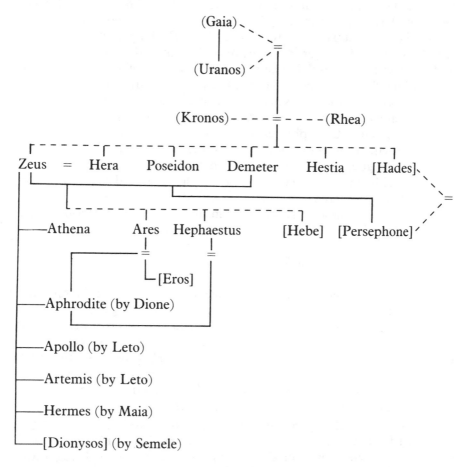

The Originators

The oldest of the Greek gods is the goddess Gaia, or Earth. It is she, the mother of all things, who produces her own mate, Uranos, the sky. This primal couple, like Nut and Geb in Egypt, spawn the first beings. As Earth and the heavens—fertile land and the seed of heaven, often represented by rain—Uranos and Gaia are prototypes for the many Greek stories of the sky god Zeus's liaisons with earthly beings (Semele, Io, and others) and with goddesses in some sense associated with earth (Demeter and even Hera).

The most famous children of Gaia and Uranos are the Titans, who were headed by still another prototypical couple, Kronos and Rhea. Kronos is associated with time, Rhea with fertility. Both Uranos and

Kronos feared being overthrown by their children and both systematically attempted to destroy them at birth, only to be foiled ultimately by alliances between Gaia and her children and Rhea and hers. So it is that Kronos dethrones Uranos, emasculating him with a sickle (it is perhaps of interest to note in this context that Kronos was often called a god of the harvest), and Zeus, after a long war in the heavens, dethrones Kronos (the supreme god overcomes time itself). The reader of this myth will inevitably see it through the filter of the more modern Freudian version, which stresses the struggle between father and son for possession of the mother and of power. We find remnants of the same myth in later stories such as that of Oedipus, especially as retold by Sophocles in *Oedipus Rex*.

The myth of the defeat of the Titans, the "sons of Gaia," by Zeus and the other sky gods is also, of course, a metaphor for the establishment of a patriarchal hierarchy in place of an older, earth-oriented society that was perhaps more matriarchal in its outlook.

The story of these early struggles in heaven is told by Hesiod in the *Theogony* (see this book's section on creation myths).

The Children of Kronos and Rhea

Zeus is the Greek version of the Indo-European chief sky god. He is the patriarch of the Greek pantheon, a pantheon that gives cosmic significance to a patriarchal social system. As a sky god concerned particularly with weather—his standard is the thunderbolt—and as a lover of many, Zeus has links to the older fertility gods. He is the father of Herakles and Helen of Troy by mortal women (Alcmene and Leda). He produces Athena out of his own head. And he is the father of Dionysos by Semele, who herself has earth goddess antecedents. It is generally assumed now that Zeus was himself originally an earth god of ancient Crete.

In one myth, Zeus, in the form of a swan, takes advantage of the mortal Leda. The latter subsequently laid an egg, from which Helen and possibly also Clytemnestra or Castor and Pollux were hatched. Leda was later deified as the goddess Nemesis. This is William Butler Yeats' version of the rape of Leda:

> A sudden blow: the great wings beating still
> Above the staggering girl, her thighs caressed
> By the dark webs, her nape caught in his bill,
> He holds her helpless breast upon his breast.
>
> How can those terrified vague fingers push
> The feathered glory from her loosening thighs?

W. B. Yeats, "Leda and the Swan," in *The Collected Poems of W. B. Yeats*, ed. (New York, 1957), p. 211.

And how can body, laid in that white rush,
But feel the strange heart beating where it lies?

A shudder in the loins engenders there
The broken wall, the burning roof and tower
And Agamemnon dead.
                              Being so caught up,
So mastered by the brute blood of the air,
Did she put on his knowledge with his power
Before the indifferent beak could let her drop?

Poseidon was Zeus's brother and after the defeat of the Titans was made lord of the seas, a role reflected in his tempestuous and often quarrelsome nature. These characteristics would also seem to be appropriate to his role as god of earthquakes, although it is possible that this role refers to an earlier stage of the god's existence when he was associated, as he was at Athens and Troezen even in classical times, with powers of fertility that came from within the earth. Poseidon was also the god of horses and was the father by Medusa of the winged horse, Pegasus. Among his other children, by many women—immortal and mortal—were the great Athenian hero, Theseus, and the cyclops, Polyphemus, the one-eyed monster blinded by Odysseus in the *Odyssey*. Poseidon's revenge on Odysseus for having thus insulted him is the reason for Odysseus' difficulties as described in the Homeric epic. Poseidon's symbol was the trident. Traditionally, bulls were sacrificed to him.

Hestia was the first-born of Kronos and Rhea, a virgin goddess whose name was well known to all Greeks as goddess of the home—specifically, of the hearth or sacred fire. Few stories are told of her, but she was important as a figure to be honored in rituals of sacrifice.

One of the most famous of the Greek myths involves three important members of the Olympian family: Demeter, Persephone, and Hades. Demeter, the sister of Zeus and the mother by him of Persephone (or Kore), spent more time in the world than on Mount Olympos. This is appropriate, as she is the goddess of agriculture, the Greek version of the Great Goddess. Her daughter is identified with young crops and, as the wife of Hades, with death. Demeter's cult, most fully developed in the mysteries of Eleusis, was, with that of Dionysos, pervasive in Greece. The Eleusinian Mysteries grew out of a popular cult that had been strongly influenced by a similar cult centered on the Egyptian goddess Isis. The Eleusinian version was eventually recognized officially in Athens. It was a cult concerned with the earth and with fertility and, like the cult of Dionysos, with the connection between fertility and death—with the burying of the seed in order that it might generate new life. Given this connection, it is not surprising that Demeter came to be associated with the idea of the human soul's immortality.

Hades was, with Zeus and Poseidon, among the most powerful of the gods. When Zeus divided up responsibility for his dominions, he gave Hades control over the underworld, which was also called Hades. Hades is the dark god, the god who carries the two-pronged staff with which to goad people into the lower world. He also carries the keys of Hades and is accompanied by the three-headed dog, Cerberus. Like his brother Poseidon, he is associated with horses.

The myth of Demeter, Persephone, and Hades, originally told in the *Homeric Hymns* and later recounted by Ovid, is retold here by H. J. Rose.

•

As the tale is told, with few important variants, in a number of authors from the writer of the Homeric *Hymn to Demeter* down to Claudian, Kore-Persephone was a virgin goddess of extraordinary beauty [whom her mother kept safe, as she supposed, in Sicily, the island traditionally sacred to the two deities]. But Hades desired a wife, and schemed to carry off Persephone. In this he had his brother Zeus as his confederate; according to Greek, and indeed to most European ideas, his consent would be necessary to a legal marriage, since he was the father and natural guardian of the proposed bride. But Demeter's unwillingness to have so grim a son-in-law had to be reckoned with, and Hades made arrangements to seize his bride by a mixture of force and fraud. As she was gathering flowers [at Henna, a very old seat of the worship of the corn-goddesses], Hades caused a flower of marvellous size and beauty to grow out of the ground. When the goddess plucked it, the earth opened, and Hades appeared in his chariot, for he, like Poseidon, is connected with horses. The reason for this is obscure, but it seems certain that the horse, to the Greeks, was to some extent an uncanny beast, connected with death, although they were from very early times quite well acquainted with its use and able to domesticate it. Seizing Persephone, he carried her off despite her struggles. Demeter grew anxious and came hurrying to look for her. Not finding her, she lit two torches [at the fires of Aitna] and sought for her all over the world. By reason of her mourning, the earth grew desolate and famine-stricken, for without her influence nothing could grow or reach maturity. After nine days the Sun, who had seen everything, told her who had carried off her daughter, and she departed full of indignation against Zeus, Hades and the gods in general for thus wronging her. After further wanderings, she came

H. J. Rose, *A Handbook of Greek Mythology* (London, 1928), pp. 91–93.

to Eleusis, where she took the form of an old woman, and sat down to rest near the well Parthenion, where the daughters of the king of the place, Keleos, found her and spoke courteously to her. She returned home with them, and was employed by their mother, Metaneira, to nurse her young son Demophoon. By this time the goddess was somewhat past the first fury of her grief, having been persuaded to smile by the maiden Iambe's jests; whence ever after jesting and raillery formed part of the Eleusinian Mysteries. She also, though she refused wine, drank *kykeon,* a mixture of water, meal and pennyroyal. Now she proceeded to tend her nursling, whom she rubbed with ambrosia; by night she laid him in the fire to burn away his mortality and make him divine. But one night Metaneira discovered her doing this, and screamed with terror. Demeter cast the child on the ground, took her own form, sternly reproached Metaneira, and commanded that rites should be instituted in her honour at Eleusis, also foretelling that in future a sham-fight should be held yearly in honour of her nursling. On her commands being obeyed, she promised to teach her secret rites, which ever afterwards were practiced at Eleusis, the famous Eleusinian Mysteries.

Meanwhile, negotiations had been set on foot to bring about a reconciliation between Demeter and Hades. The goddess insisted on having her daughter back, but on inquiry found out that Persephone had thoughtlessly eaten food (a seed [or seeds] of a pomegranate) in the lower world. This constituted a bond which there was no breaking, and a compromise had to be agreed to; Persephone was to remain in the house of Hades for a third (or a half) of each year, spending the rest on earth with her mother.

Demeter now fulfilled her promise to the Eleusinians, and also restored the fertility of the ground [making Triptolemos, another son of Keleos and Metaneira, or the son of the hero Eleusis, after whom the town was named, her messenger to carry the art of corn-planting and the seed of corn to lands yet unacquainted with it].

*

The Children of Zeus

Athena, or Pallas Athena, the patroness of Athens, was the goddess of wisdom, and she was concerned with the arts, especially weaving and spinning. She created the olive tree, which was sacred to her. Athena was also associated with war and was depicted carrying a spear and shield and wearing a helmet decorated with griffins. She was one of the great virgin goddesses; the Parthenon (Greek *parthenos,* virgin) on the Acropolis was her temple. Athena was the particular patron of the wily Odysseus in Homer's epic, and she cast the deciding vote in favor of Orestes in his trial for the revenge killing of his mother, Clytemnestra, and her lover, Aighistos.

This ancient goddess in all probability originated as a fertility-oriented patroness of the pre-Greek Mycenean and Minoan rulers and gained her virginal aspect only after the establishment of the patriarchal sky religion during classical times. Her paradoxical nature is reflected in the story of her remarkable birth. In the classical version of her story, as told by Hesiod, Pindar, and Apollodorus, Athena sprang fully armed from the head of her father, Zeus. Thus stripped of her feminine origins and nature, she reflects the patriarchal value system. Athena stands in direct contrast to her sister, Aphrodite, whose exaggerated sexuality and stereotypical femininity is equally revealing of that system.

•

But Athene's own priests tell the following story of her birth. Zeus lusted after Metis the Titaness, who turned into many shapes to escape him until she was caught at last and got with child. An oracle of Mother Earth then declared that this would be a girl-child and that, if Metis conceived again, she would bear a son who was fated to depose Zeus, just as Zeus had deposed Cronus [Kronos], and Cronus had deposed Uranus. Therefore, having coaxed Metis to a couch with honeyed words, Zeus suddenly opened his mouth and swallowed her, and that was the end of Metis, though he claimed afterwards that she gave him counsel from inside his belly. In due process of time, he was seized by a raging headache as he walked by the shores of Lake Triton, so that his skull seemed about to burst, and he howled for rage until the whole firmament echoed. Up ran Hermes, who at once divined the cause of Zeus's discomfort. He persuaded Hephaestus, or some say Prometheus, to fetch his wedge and beetle and make a breach in Zeus's skull, from which Athene sprang, fully armed, with a mighty shout.

•

Zeus had four children by his wife, Hera. Of these, Hebe, the cupbearer for the gods, goddess of youth, and wife of Herakles after he is immortalized on Mount Olympos, and Eileithyia, goddess of childbirth, are not made much of in Greek myth. Two other offspring, the gods Ares and Hephaistos, however, are more important. Ares, the god of war, carries a torch and a spear. Hephaistos, the lame god of fire and crafts, carries a smith's hammer and tongs. Ares and Hephaistos are perhaps best known for their relationships with the goddess Aphrodite. Hephaistos is her husband. Ares is her lover and the father by her of Eros, the god specifically associated with the pangs of love.

According to one story, Aphrodite (Greek, "foam-born"), as the meaning of her name suggests, was born of the foam of the sea. The foam was said to have been caused by the semen from the mutilated genitals of the god Uranos. Aphrodite is often depicted emerging from a seashell. She came

Robert Graves, *The Greek Myths*, vol. 1 (Baltimore, Md., 1955), p. 46.

to land on the island of Cythera, but was also attached to Cyprus. In another birth story, Aphrodite is the child of Zeus by the nymph Dione.

As goddess of love and beauty, Aphrodite is, above all, seductive—an immortal version of the femme fatale. Two of her most famous liaisons are with the youth Adonis, who was killed by a wild boar but was restored to her for six months of each year, and with the mortal Anchises, by whom she became the mother of Aeneas, the hero of Virgil's great Roman epic, the *Aeneid*. Representing the dangers of love, she is partly responsible for the Trojan War, because it is she who tempts Paris to award her the golden apple by promising him the most beautiful woman in the world, Helen.

The following tale of a love triangle is told by Homer about Aphrodite, Ares, and Hephaistos.

·

> Now to his harp the blinded minstrel sang
> of Arês' dalliance with Aphroditê:
> how hidden in Hephaistos' house they played
> at love together, and the gifts of Arês,
> dishonoring Hephaistos' bed—and how
> the word that wounds the heart came to the master
> from Hêlios, who had seen the two embrace;
> and when he learned it, Lord Hephaistos went
> with baleful calculation to his forge.
> There mightily he armed his anvil block
> and hammered out a chain, whose tempered links
> could not be sprung or bent; he meant that they should hold.
> Those shackles fashioned, hot in wrath Hephaistos
> climbed to the bower and the bed of love,
> pooled all his net of chain around the bed posts
> and swung it from the rafters overhead—
> light as a cobweb even gods in bliss
> could not perceive, so wonderful his cunning.
> Seeing his bed now made a snare, he feigned a journey to the
> trim stronghold of Lemnos,
> the dearest of earth's towns to him. And Arês?
> Ah, golden Arês' watch had its reward
> when he beheld the great smith leaving home.
> How promptly to the famous door he came,
> intent on pleasure with sweet Kythereia!
> She, who had left her father's side but now,
> sat in her chamber when her lover entered;
> and tenderly he pressed her hand and said:

Homer, *Odyssey*, VIII, trans. Robert Fitzgerald (New York, 1961), pp. 144–48.

"Come and lie down, my darling, and be happy!
Hephaistos is no longer here, but gone
to see his grunting Sintian friends on Lemnos."

As she, too, thought repose would be most welcome,
the pair went in to bed—into a shower
of clever chains, the netting of Hephaistos.
So trussed, they could not move apart, nor rise,
at last they knew there could be no escape,
they were to see the glorious cripple now—
for Hêlios had spied for him, and told him;
so he turned back, this side of Lemnos Isle,
sick at heart, making his way homeward.
Now in the doorway of the room he stood
while deadly rage took hold of him; his voice,
hoarse and terrible, reached all the gods:

"O Father Zeus, O gods in bliss forever,
here is indecorous entertainment for you,
Aphroditê, Zeus's daughter,
caught in the act, cheating me, her cripple,
with Arês—devastating Arês.
Cleanlimbed beauty is her job, not these
bandylegs I came into the world with:
no one to blame but the two gods who bred me!
Come see this pair entwining here
in my own bed! How hot it makes me burn!
I think they may not care to lie much longer,
pressing on one another, passionate lovers;
they'll have enough of bed together soon.
And yet the chain that bagged them holds them down
till Father sends me back my wedding gifts—
all that I poured out for his damned pigeon,
so lovely, and so wanton."

                                        All the others
were crowding in, now, to the brazen house—
Poseidon who embraces earth, and Hermês
the runner, and Apollo, lord of Distance.
The goddesses stayed home for shame; but these
munifences ranged there in the doorway,
and irrepressible among them all
arose the laughter of the happy gods.
Gazing hard at Hephaistos' handiwork
the gods in turn remarked among themselves:

"No dash in adultery now."

                         "The tortoise tags the hare—
Hephaistos catches Arês—and Arês outran the wind."

"The lame god's craft has pinned him. Now shall he
pay what is due from gods taken in cuckoldry."

They made these improving remarks to one another,
but Apollo leaned aside to say to Hermês:

"Son of Zeus, beneficent Wayfinder,
would you accept a coverlet of chain, if only
you lay by Aphroditê's golden side?"

To this the Wayfinder replied, shining:

"Would I not, though, Apollo of distances!
Wrap me in chains three times the weight of these,
come goddesses and gods to see the fun;
only let me lie beside the pale-golden one!"

The gods gave way again to peals of laughter,
all but Poseidon, and he never smiled,
but urged Hephaistos to unpinion Arês,
saying emphatically, in a loud voice:

                                "Free him;
you will be paid, I swear; ask what you will;
he pays up every jot the gods decree."

To this the Great Gamelegs replied:

                              "Poseidon,
lord of the earth-surrounding sea, I should not
swear to a scoundrel's honor. What have I
as surety from you, if Arês leaves me
empty-handed, with my empty chain?"

The Earth-shaker for answer urged again:

"Hephaistos, let us grant he goes, and leaves
the fine unpaid; I swear, then, I shall pay it."

Then said the Great Gamelegs at last:

                              "No more;
you offer terms I cannot well refuse."

And down the strong god bent to set them free,
till disencumbered of their bond, the chain,

the lovers leapt away—he into Thrace,
while Aphroditê, laughter's darling, fled
to Kypros Isle and Paphos, to her meadow
and altar dim with incense. There the Graces
bathed and anointed her with golden oil—
a bloom that clings upon immortal flesh alone—
and let her folds of mantle fall in glory.

So ran the song the minstrel sang.

Apollo, or Phoibos Apollo, as Homer calls him, is a relative latecomer to
Mount Olympos. His origins are unclear, but it is possible that he was
originally an Asiatic god. His mother was Leto, thought by some to be the
Anatolian goddess Lada from Lycia. The Greeks said that he was born on
the island of Delos and that he was a sacred twin, one of many in mythology. His sister was the great virgin huntress, Artemis. Whether or not he
is Asian in origin, Apollo becomes in Greece a metaphor for the very essence of things Greek. He is the god of what has come to be thought of as
the peculiarly Greek ideal of moderation—in the arts as well as in style of
life. He is the god of law. With Athena, he brings reason to the Greek
world in the trial of Orestes, in which the old earth forces are made sub-
servient to Olympian reason.

To think of Apollo is to think of beauty and order. He has often been
compared to Dionysos. Thus we speak of the necessary and productive
tension between the Apollonian and the Dionysian in the arts—the tension
between orderly discipline and deep emotion—as, for instance, in a
Shakespearean sonnet, with its Apollonian form (its strict meter and its
fourteen lines), which contains and gives particular urgency to the poet's
Dionysian passion.

Apollo's home is Delphi (once Pytho), where he wrested control of
the famous oracle from the dragon or python that guarded it. Again, Pythian Apollo and all that he represents as the protector of the organized
Olympian religion thus takes control of prophecy from the older, more
mysterious earth forces. The mystery is not altogether lost, however. If
Delphi is the home of Apollo, it is also a favorite haunt of Dionysos in the
winter months.

Apollo is the god who reminds us of the necessity of self-control and
self-knowledge. "Know thyself" and "Nothing too much" are his primary
mottoes. By the fifth century B.C.E., the cult of Apollo had taken precedence over that of Zeus himself. The great Sophoclean tragedies make this
abundantly clear. The quest of Oedipus is a quest for self-knowledge on
the personal as well as on the general human level.

Finally, in late classical times, Apollo, as a god of light, was associated with the sun—sometimes with the sun god, Helios. His sister, Artemis, was associated with the moon goddess, Selene.

More often than not, Apollo is depicted in art as a handsome youth, usually nude, with a lyre or a bow and a quiver of arrows.

The goddess Artemis, considered by the Greeks to be the twin sister of Apollo, was the virgin goddess of the hunt and the protector of the young (both animal and human). She was almost certainly Asian—specifically Anatolian—in origin. As Ma in Cappadocia or Cybele in Phrygia, she was the greatest of the Great Mothers, anything but a virgin. In Ephesus, where her cult was strongest, she was Artemis of the many breasts, a mother to all life. Much of this aspect of her character probably blended into the Demeter and Persephone cults in Greece, but remnants of the old Artemis remain in the new Greek version. The Greek Artemis is still the goddess of childbirth, and as a huntress, she is still associated with the wild. Her virginity and the masculine aspect of her nature suggest, as in the case of Pallas Athena, a defeminization of the Great Goddess—an undermining of her powerful matriarchal cult—by the patriarchal Homeric/ Olympian religion.

In the myth that follows we see just how far the Great Goddess of Anatolia—given her Roman name, Diana, by Ovid—has come by the time she is absorbed into the Olympian hierarchy. It seems likely that Artemis, like Ma and Cybele, once had a younger attendant lover. As a virgin in the Greek system, any male attendant had to be chaste or suffer the wrath of the cold-hearted huntress.

*

The scene of this event was a mountain where the ground was stained with the bloodshed of wild beasts of many kinds. The heat of mid-day had shortened the shadows, and the sun was midway between his eastern and his western goal, when the young Actaeon★ called to his comrades, as they roamed the lonely thickets, saying in a gentle tone: "My friends, our nets and swords are dripping with blood from the beasts we have taken—we have had enough success for one day. When tomorrow's dawn, riding in her saffron car, brings us another day, we shall return to our chosen task. But now the sun is at its highest, halfway on its course, cracking open the fields with its heat. For the present, then, put an end to your hunting, and gather in your knotted nets." The men did as he suggested and stopped, for a time their strenuous activities.

★A grandson of King Cadmus of Thebes.

Ovid, *Metamorphoses*, trans. Mary M. Innes (London, 1955), pp. 77–80.

There was a valley, thickly overgrown with pitchpine, and with sharp-needled cypress trees. It was called Gargaphie, and was sacred to Diana, the goddess of the hunt. Far in its depths lay a woodland cave, which no hand of man had wrought: but nature by her own devices had imitated art. She had carved a natural arch from the living stone and the soft tufa rocks. On the right hand was a murmuring spring of clear water, spreading out into a wide pool with grassy banks. Here the goddess, when she was tired with hunting in the woods, used to bathe her fastidious limbs in the pure water. When she entered the grotto she handed her javelin to one of the nymphs, who acted as her armour-bearer, along with her quiver and her bow, unstrung. Another nymph received her cloak and hung it across her arm, while two more took off her sandals. Yet another attendant, more skilled than the rest, Crocale, the daughter of Ismenus, gathered up the tresses which lay scattered on the goddess' shoulders, and bound them into a knot, though her own hair hung loose. Nephele, Hyale, Rhanis, Psecas, and Phiale drew up the water in capacious jars, and poured it over their mistress.

Now while Diana was bathing there in her stream, as usual, the grandson of Cadmus, who had for the present abandoned his hunting, came wandering with hesitant steps through this wood which he had never seen before. He reached the grove—so were the fates directing him—and entered the cave, which was moist with spray. The nymphs, discovered in their nakedness, beat their breasts at the sight of a man, and filled all the grove with their sudden outcry. Crowding round Diana, they sheltered her with their own bodies, but the goddess was taller than they, head and shoulders above them all. When she was caught unclad, a blush mantled her cheeks, as bright as when clouds reflect the sun's rays, as bright as rosy dawn. Though hidden by her comrades, who gathered closely round her, she stood turned aside, looking back over her shoulder. She wished she had her arrows ready to hand: instead, she caught up a handful of the water which she did have, and threw it in the young man's face. As she sprinkled his hair with the vengeful drops she also spoke these words, ominous of coming disaster. "Now, if you can, you may tell how you saw me when I was undressed." She uttered no more threats, but made the horns of a long-lived stag sprout where she had scattered water on his brow. She lengthened his neck, brought the tips of his ears to a point, changed his hands to feet, his arms to long legs, and covered his body with a dappled skin. Then she put panic fear in his heart as well. The hero fled, and even as he ran, marvelled to find himself so swift. When he glimpsed his face and his horns, reflected in the water, he tried to say "Alas!" but no words came. He groaned—that was all the voice he had—and tears ran down his changed cheeks. Only his mind remained the same as before. What was he to do? Return home to the royal palace, or hide in the woods? He was ashamed to do the first, afraid to do the second.

As he hesitated, his hounds caught sight of him. Melampus and the wise Ichnobates were the first to give tongue, Ichnobates of the Cretan breed, and Melampus of the Spartan. Then the others rushed to the chase, swifter than the wind, Pamphagus and Dorceus and Oribasus, all Arcadians, and strong Nebrophonus, fierce Theron and Laelaps too. Pterelas, the swift runner, was there, and keen-scented Agre, Hylaeus who had lately been gored by a wild boar, Nape, offspring of a wolf, Poemenis, the shepherd dog, Harpyia with her two pups, Ladon from Sicyon, slender-flanked, and Dromas and Canace, Sticte and Tigris, Alce, white-coated Leucon, and black-haired Asbolus; with them was Lacon, a dog of outstanding strength, Aello the stout runner, Thous and swift Lycisce with her brother Cyprius, Harpalus, who had a white spot in the middle of his black forehead, and Melaneus and shaggy Lachne, Lebros and Agriodus, both cross-bred of a Cretan mother and a Spartan father, shrill-barking Hylactor, and others whom it would take long to name. The pack, eager for its prey, swept over the rocks and crags, over unapproachable cliffs, through places where the going was difficult, and where there was no way at all. Actaeon fled, where he had himself so often pursued his quarry, fled, alas, before his own faithful hounds. He longed to cry out: "I am Actaeon! Don't you know your own master?" but the words he wanted to utter would not come—the air echoed with barking. First Melanchaetes fastened his teeth in his master's back, then Theridamas and Oresitrophus clung to his shoulder. They had been slow to begin the chase, but had outstripped the others by taking a short cut over the mountains. While they held their master down, the rest of the pack gathered, and sank their teeth in his body, till there was no place left for tearing. Actaeon groaned, uttering a sound which, though not human, was yet such as no stag could produce. The ridges he knew so well were filled with his mournful cries. Falling to his knees, like a suppliant in prayer, he silently swayed his head this way and that, as if stretching out beseeching arms. But his friends, not knowing what they did, urged on the ravening mob with their usual encouragements and looked round for Actaeon, shouted for Actaeon, as if he were not there, each trying to call louder than the other. They lamented that their leader was absent, and that his slowness prevented him from seeing the booty chance had offered. Actaeon turned his head at the sound of his name. Well might he wish to be absent, but he was all too surely present. Well might he wish to see and not to feel the cruel deeds of his hounds. They surrounded him on every side, fastening their jaws on his body, and tore to pieces the seeming stag, which was in fact their master. Only when he had been dispatched by wounds innumerable, so men say, was the anger of Diana, the quiver-bearing goddess, appeased.

*

Among the most popular of Greek gods was Hermes, the son of Zeus by Maia, daughter of the Titan Atlas, who holds the world on his shoulders.

Hermes was probably of Minoan/Mycenean origin. His name in Greek is related to the word for stone cairn. The tradition of Hermes and the cairn took form in the herms—the small posts or pillars with human head and phallus (to represent fertility) that were so prevalent in ancient Greece. The herms had particular functions that were in keeping with qualities associated with the god. They were road markers, and Hermes was the god of the road, of travelers. He was himself a frequent traveler from Mount Olympus, serving as the messenger of Zeus. Herms were often used as grave markers, and Hermes was the god who led people to Hades. Finally, herms were property markers that served to ward off evil from Athenian houses; Hermes was a popular household god.

Hermes was a trickster of sorts, delighting in petty theft and shrewd deals (see stories of him in this book's section on tricksters). Yet Zeus seems to have trusted him above all others with his commands. With his broad hat, his golden caduceus (the staff with writhing snakes later given to the medicine god, Asclepius), and his winged sandals, Hermes is most often depicted skimming the earth on an important mission for his father.

Dionysos is at once the most ambiguous and the most foreign of the Greek gods. His cult became so powerful that the gods and their priests had little choice but to admit him to Mount Olympus. If the theologians and poets of the sixth and fifth centuries B.C.E. were Apollonian by nature, they, like Pentheus in Euripides' the *Bacchae,* were forced to confront the ecstasy that was Dionysos, the ecstasy that complements Apollonian order and discipline and is so necessary to art and religion. So it is that the Greeks recognized this popular Thracian and probably Anatolian god, associated with the strange orgiastic rites of the Phrygian mother goddess Cybele and her son-lover Attis (himself a Dionysos figure), and gave him a respected place with Apollo as a resident of the oracular center at Delphi. Dionysos, in fact, reigned at Delphi in the winter months, when his dances were performed there. Through his association with drama, he was also honored at the great dramatic festivals such as the City Dionysia in Athens. As has been suggested, the reconciliation of Apollo and Dionysos is appropriate to the paradoxical nature of both art and prophecy, in which discipline and possession or inspiration are so closely related.

Dionysos was a god who died and returned to life. His ritual is itself a ritual of death and rebirth in which flesh is consumed and fertility celebrated with drums and dance and the constant presence of ecstatic women or maenads, who may have taken part in mysterious orgies. Dionysos is thus, like Osiris in Egypt, Adonis in Babylonia, Tammuz in Sumer, Attis in Phrygia, and even the early form of Zeus in Crete, associated with crops—specifically, in his case, with the grape (and therefore with wine) and with sexuality (Dionysos was described by Plutarch as the god of all life-giving fluids). Dionysos is a god very much of the earth and, as such, was always an outsider among the gods. Even his birth was odd. Fathered by Zeus on the mortal Semele, he was delivered from Zeus's thigh, where the Supreme Being had hidden the fetus after it was removed from his mother, who had died after foolishly making Zeus promise to reveal himself to her in his true form.

One of Dionysos' most famous escapades is described in the *Homeric Hymns*.

＊

What I remember now
is Dionysus, son of
glorious Semele, how he appeared
by the sand of an empty sea,
how it was far out, on a promontory, how
he was like a young man,
an adolescent

His dark hair
was beautiful, it
blew all around him, and
over his shoulders, the strong
shoulders, he held a purple cloak.

Suddenly,
pirates appeared, Tyrrhenians,
they came on the sea wine
sturdily in their ship
and they came fast.
A wicked fate drove them on.

They saw him,
they nodded to each other,
they leaped out
and grabbed him,
they pulled him
into their boat
jumping for joy!

They thought he was
the son of

Charles Boer, "The Hymn to Dionysos," in *The Homeric Hymns* (Chicago, 1970), pp. 13–17.

one of
Zeus' favorite kings:
they wanted to tie him up
hard.

        The ropes wouldn't hold.
        Willow ropes,
they fell right off him, off
arms and legs.
        He smiled at them,
motionless,
in his dark eyes.
        The helmsman saw this,
he immediately cried out,
he screamed out to his men:
        "You fools!
        What powerful god is this
        whom you've seized,
        whom you've tied up?
        Not even our ship,
        sturdy as it is,
        not even our ship
        can carry him.
        Either this is Zeus,
        or it's Apollo, the silver-bow,
        or else it's Poseidon!
        He doesn't look like
        a human person,
        he's like the gods
        who live on Olympus.
        Come on!
        Let's unload him, right now,
        let's put him
        on the dark land.
        Don't tie his hands
        or he'll be angry, he'll
        draw terrible winds to us,
        he'll bring us a big storm!"
        That's what he said.
The captain, however,
in a bitter voice,
roared back:
        "You fool,

look at the wind!
Grab the ropes,
draw the sail.
We men
will take care of him.
    I think
he'll make it to Egypt,
or Cyprus,
or the the Hyperboreans,
or even further.
In the end
he'll tell
who his friends are,
and his relatives,
and his possessions.
A god sent him to us."
    He said this,
then he fixed the mast
and the sail of the ship.
And a wind began to blow
into the sail. And then
they stretched the rigging.
    Suddenly,
wonderful things
appeared to them.
    First of all,
wine broke out, babbling,
bubbling over their speedy black ship,
it was sweet, it was fragrant,
its odor was divine.
Every sailor who saw it
was terrified.
    Suddenly,
a vine sprang up,
on each side,
to the very top of the sail.
And grapes, all over,
clung to it.
And a dark ivy
coiled the mast,
it blossomed with flowers
and yielded

Suddenly,
all the oar-locks
became garlands.
When they saw this
they cried to the helmsman
then and there
to steer their ship
to land.
    But
the god became a lion,
an awful lion
high up on the ship,
and he roared at them
terribly.
    And then,
in their midst,
he put a bear,
a bear with a furry neck,
and it made gestures.
It threatened,
and the lion,
on the high deck,
scowled down.
    Everybody
fled to the stern,
they panicked, they ran
to the helmsman, because
the head of the helmsman was cool.
    But
the lion, suddenly,
leaped up, it seized
the captain!
They all wanted to escape
such a doom
when they saw it.
They all jumped ship
into the sea, they jumped
into the divine sea.
They became dolphins.
    As for the helmsman,
he was saved:
the god pitied him,
he made him very rich,
and told him this:

"Courage, divine Hecator,
I like you.
I am Dionysus
the ear-splitter.
My mother,
Cadmaean Semele,
had me
when she slept with Zeus."

Farewell,
son of Semele,
who had such a beautiful face.
Without you,
the way to compose a sweet song
is forgotten.

Roman: The Renamed Olympians

The Romans essentially absorbed the Greek gods, primarily through the Etruscans, who were an important presence on the Italian peninsula between 900 and 500 B.C.E. The primary difference between the Greek and the Roman understanding of the gods lay in the Romans' greater emphasis on the gods as personifications of abstractions—love, war, fortune, and so forth. It can also be said that the Roman version was more an official state religion with political ramifications than a religion that spoke to personal or spiritual needs.

In Western literature, the Latin and Greek names for the Olympians have been used almost interchangeably. The list that follows indicates the equivalent names:

Coelus (Heaven) and Terra (Earth) = Uranos and Gaia

Saturn* and Ops (or the Phrygian Cybele) = Kronos and Rhea

Jupiter or Jove = Zeus

Juno = Hera

Neptune = Poseidon

Pluto = Hades

Ceres = Demeter

Proserpina = Persephone

Vesta** = Hestia

*Saturn is associated with the Roman tradition of the Saturnalia, a festival of renewal and fertility marked at times by licentiousness.

**Thus, vestal virgins were priestesses of Vesta.

Apollo = Apollo
Diana = Artemis
Minerva = Athena
Venus = Aphrodite
Cupid = Eros
Mars = Ares
Mercury = Hermes
Vulcan = Hephaistos
Bacchus = Dionysos

Norse (Icelandic): The Aesir

Our source for the Teutonic myths of Northern Europe are Icelandic works, the *Elder* or *Poetic Edda* of the tenth century C.E. and the *Younger* or *Prose Edda* written by Snorri Sturluson in about 1220 C.E.

The Norse gods and goddesses, known as the Aesir, lived in a place called Asgard. As in the case of the Greeks, these gods had gained predominance only at the cost of warfare with another group of gods, called the Vanir. The Aesir were led by Odin and Frigg, the Vanir by Freyr and Freyja, who were children of the god Njord and were associated, like the Vanir in general and the Greek Titans, with forces of the earth. Freyr and Freyja, as brother and sister, remind us of Osiris and Isis, as well. Like the Egyptians, they are, above all, representative of fertility. Eventually the Aesir and the Vanir were reconciled. The end of the gods would come at the apocalyptic Ragnarök.

Odin was the father god. He was also—like Dionysos, Attis, Osiris, and so many others, including Christ—a god who in some sense experiences death. The *Elder Edda*, in a section called the "Havamal," tells of how Odin was pierced by a spear and hanged for having attained the gift of wisdom (see the story in the Dying God section of this book). Odin (Wodan or Wotan, as worshipped by the Germanic peoples) was married to Frigg, who possessed knowledge of the future. But Odin was the father of the thunder god, Thor, by Earth herself. Another son of Odin was Baldr, the most beautiful and best of the gods. Baldr was killed by Hoder with the help of the trickster god, Loki, whose offspring were the wolf Fenrir and the World Serpent (who would fight against the Aesir at the end of the world), and Hel, the ruler of the underworld. The death of Baldr was the occasion of the Norse version of the descent to the underworld.

•

High One replied: "I will tell you about something that seemed far more important to the Æsir. The beginning of this story is that Baldr the Good had some terrible dreams that threatened his life. When he told the

Æsir these dreams, they took counsel together and it was decided to seek protection for Baldr from every kind of peril. Frigg exacted an oath from fire and water, iron and all kinds of metals, stones, earth, trees, ailments, beasts, birds, poison and serpents, that they would not harm Baldr. And when this had been done and put to the test, Baldr and the Æsir used to amuse themselves by making him stand up at their assemblies for some of them to throw darts at, others to strike and the rest to throw stones at. No matter what was done he was never hurt, and everyone thought that a fine thing. When Loki, Laufey's son, saw that, however, he was annoyed that Baldr was not hurt and he went disguised as a woman to Fensalir to visit Frigg. Frigg asked this woman if she knew what the Æsir were doing at assembly. She answered that they were all throwing things at Baldr, moreover that he was not being hurt. Frigg remarked: "Neither weapons nor trees will injure Baldr; I have taken an oath from them all.' The woman asked: 'Has everything sworn you an oath to spare Baldr?' Frigg replied: 'West of Valhalla grows a little bush called mistletoe, I did not exact an oath from it; I thought it too young.' Thereupon the woman disappeared.

"Loki took hold of the mistletoe, pulled it up and went to the assembly. Now Höd was standing on the other edge of the circle of men because he was blind. Loki asked him: 'Why aren't you throwing darts at Baldr?' He replied: 'Because I can't see where Baldr is, and, another thing, I have no weapon.' Then Loki said: 'You go and do as the others are doing and show Baldr honour like other men. I will show you where he is standing: throw this twig at him.' Höd took the mistletoe and aimed at Baldr as directed by Loki. The dart went right through him and he fell dead to the ground. This was the greatest misfortune ever to befall gods and men.

"When Baldr had fallen, the Æsir were struck dumb and not one of them could move a finger to lift him up; each looked at the other, and all were of one mind about the perpetrator of that deed, but no one could take vengeance; the sanctuary there was so holy. When the Æsir did try to speak, weeping came first, so that no one could tell the other his grief in words. Odin, however, was the most affected by this disaster, since he understood best what a loss and bereavement the death of Baldr was for the Æsir. When the gods had recovered from the first shock Frigg spoke. She asked which of the Æsir wished to win her whole affection and favour. Would he ride the road to Hel to try if he could find Baldr, and offer Hel a ransom if she would allow Baldr to come home to Ásgard? The one who undertook this journey was a son of Ódin called Hermód the Bold. Then they caught Ódin's horse, Sleipnir, and led him forward, and Hermód mounted that steed and galloped away.

Snorri Sturluson, *The Prose Edda*, trans. Jean I. Young (Berkeley, Calif., 1954), pp. 80–84.

"The Æsir, however, took Baldr's body and carried it down to the sea. Baldr's ship was called Ringhorn,* it was a very large ship. The gods wanted to launch it and to build Baldr's funeral pyre on it, but they could not move it at all. They sent to Giantland then for the ogress called Hyrrokkin. And when she came—she was riding a wolf with vipers for reins—she jumped off her steed and Ódin called to four berserks to guard it, but they were unable to hold it fast till they struck it down. Then Hyrrokkin went to the prow of the vessel and at the first shove launched it in such a way that the rollers burst into flame and the whole world trembled. Thór became angry then and seizing his hammer would have cracked her skull had not all the gods begged protection for her.

"Then Baldr's body was carried out on to the ship, and when his wife Nanna, daughter of Nep, saw that, her heart broke from grief and she died. She was carried on to the pyre and it was set alight. Thór was standing by and consecrating it with Mjöllnir, when a dwarf called Lit ran in front of his feet. Thór tripped him up and kicked him into the fire, and he was burned to death. All sorts of people came to this cremation. First and foremost, Ódin, accompanied by Frigg and his valkyries and ravens. Frey drove in a chariot drawn by the boar called Gold-bristle or Razor-tooth. Heimdall rode the horse called -old-tuft and Freyja was driving her cats. A great crowd of frost ogres and cliff giants came too. Ódin laid on the pyre the gold ring which is called Draupnir; it had this characteristic afterwards, that every ninth night there dropped from it eight rings of equal value. Baldr's horse with all its harness was led to the pyre.

"Concerning Hermód, however, there is this to tell. For nine nights he rode dales so deep and dark that he saw nothing, until he reached the river Gjöll and rode over its bridge; it is thatched with gleaming gold. The maiden who guards that bridge is called Módgud. She asked him his name and family and said that the day before five troops of dead men had ridden over the bridge, 'but the bridge resounds as much under you alone, and you don't look like a man who has died. Why are you riding here on the road to Hel?' He replied: 'I must ride to Hel to seek for Baldr. Have you seen anything of him on his way there?' She said that Baldr had ridden past over the bridge of the Gjöll, 'but the road to Hel lies downwards and northwards.'

"Hermód rode on then till he came to the gates of Hel. Then he alighted and tightened his stirrups, remounted, and dug in his spurs, and the horse jumped over the gate with such vigour that it came nowhere near it. Then Hermód rode right up to the hall and dismounted. He went inside

*Curved-prow.

and saw his brother Baldr sitting on the high seat there. Hermód stayed there that night. In the morning he asked Hel if Baldr might ride home with him, telling her how much the gods were weeping. Hel said, however, that this test should be made as to whether Baldr was loved as much as people said. 'If everything in the world, both dead or alive, weeps for him, then he shall go back to the Æsir, but he shall remain with Hel if anyone objects or will not weep.' Then Hermód stood up and Baldr led him out of the hall and taking [off] the ring Draupnir sent it to Ódin in remembrance, but Nanna sent Frigg, along with other gifts, linen [for a headdress], and Fulla a gold ring. Hermód rode back again to Ásgard and [when] he arrived [there] related all he had seen and heard.

"Thereupon the Æsir sent messengers throughout the whole world to ask for Baldr to be wept out of Hel; and everything did that—men and beasts, and the earth, and the stones and trees and all metals—just as you will have seen these things weeping when they come out of frost and into the warmth. When the messengers were coming home, having made a good job of their errand, they met with a giantess sitting in a cave; she gave her name as Thökk. They asked her to weep Baldr out of Hel. She answered:

> Thökk will weep
> dry tears
> at Baldr's embarkation;
> the old fellow's son
> was no use to me
> alive or dead,
> let Hel hold what she has.

It is thought that the giantess there was Loki, Laufey's son—who has done most harm amongst the Æsir."

Bibliography

Good, general discussions of the God concept are to be found in *The Encyclopedia of Religion*, ed. Mircea Eliade (New York, 1987). See especially the entries under "God" and "Deity" (IV, pp. 264–76; VI, pp. 1–66). For a valuable discussion of the concept of divinity and the question of sky gods versus earth gods, see Eliade's *Patterns in Comparative Religion* (New York, 1958). For a discussion of the development of the Judeo-Christian God, see Walter Beltz's *God and the Gods: Myths of the Bible* (New York, 1983). Northrop Frye, in *The Great Code: The Bible and Literature* (New York, 1982). presents a useful analysis of the metaphorical aspect of God. Other helpful approaches to the concept of divinity are to be found in E. O. James, *The Concept of Deity* (London, 1950), and Etienne Gilson, *God and Philosophy* (New Haven, Conn., 1941).

W. K.C. Guthrie's *The Greeks and Their Gods* (Boston, 1950) still seems to me to present the most useful discussion of the Greek pantheon, especially as regards its origins. R. T. Rundle Clark's *Myth and Symbol in Ancient Egypt* (London, 1959) serves a similar function in connection with the Egyptian divine family. H. R. Ellis Davidson's *Gods and Myths of Northern Europe* (Harmondsworth, England, 1964) is a good source for stories of the Norse gods.

THE GOD AS ARCHETYPE

In our depictions of divinity, we humans have given form to our sense of the ultimate source of our own significance. When we give form to divinity, we derive that form from our own experience. We make our gods in our own image because our own image marks the physical limits of our being. We cannot know the gods; we can know only our experience of them. Not surprisingly, since the essence of whatever it is to be human is as present in the Indonesian or Nigerian as it is in the Irishman or the Indian, these depictions when seen as a whole—as world mythology—reveal a pattern of archetypal motifs that are as universal as the physical characteristics we humans share. As we study the gods of world mythology, we will encounter, below the surfaces of the many cultural masks they inevitably wear, the constant, universal shadows that we call the Father-Creator, the Great Mother, the trickster, the dying god, the destroyer god, the helper god, the primordial sky-earth, male-female pair, the gods who visit the earth and are shunned, and many other familiar figures.

For the student of mythology, it is important to recognize in any god or goddess or pantheon both the mask, or metaphor, that is worshipped by the culture that created it and the spiritual or psychological source for that mask, the archetype, which is either an aspect of ultimate reality or a creation of what Jung called the collective unconscious—the collective human mind. In either case, the archetypal image is part of our common human heritage. It contains information about our experience as human beings. It is, therefore, of great metaphorical value to the artist, whether he or she be painter, sculptor, or writer. When a Faulkner character called Lena Grove, a product of a particular class of the American South, is depicted in imagery that associates her with the universal Mother Goddess archetype, we recognize her significance whether we are from Atlanta or Madras or Oslo. The same could be said of Hamlet and his association, by way of the tragic hero, with the dying god of myth. The myths

*presented here will serve to illustrate both the cultural diversity and the univer-
sality of our gods.*

STORIES OF ARCHETYPAL GODS

The Supreme Being

The Supreme Being who emerges from the many world myths about the
chief god is one who embodies the prevalent patriarchal arrangement of
society. He is, in short, the embodiment of kingship, of male power, of
the paterfamilias. Frequently a sun god, he is the giver of life-heat and
light and, at the same time, an unapproachable being. Semele dies when
confronted by the revealed Zeus; Dante is nearly overwhelmed by the
"light eternal" in the *Paradiso.*

The word *dios* (god)—and the name Zeus itself—is derived from the
Sanskrit *div*, meaning shine, light, or day. He is a creator—often, as in the
case of the Judeo-Christian-Muslim God, the originator of the universe.
And he is a fecundator—often associated with bulls. This is true of Zeus,
Indra, Thor, the Sumerian Enlil, and many others.

Sometimes the chief sky god is the husband of the Great Earth
Mother, as in the marriage of Gaia and Uranos. This makes sense, as he is
of the sky, nearly always revealed by weather—particularly storms that
produce moisture—and she is of the earth and is the incarnation of fe-
cundity.

Perhaps most important, as the concept of the Supreme Being has
developed in patriarchal society, a god has emerged whose sky home becomes a metaphor for higher values, higher laws. Thus, the god is more
often than not a lawgiver and law preserver, as in the cases of Yahweh,
God, Allah, and the Persian Ahura Mazda. The Supreme Being perhaps
achieves his highest form in the Hindu concept of Brahman, the Ultimate
Reality as idea, of which the great gods Shiva, Vishnu, the Goddess, and
Brahma are mere metaphors. Brahman is the absolute reality out of which
all forms flow. Brahman is beyond definition and, therefore, not limited
or confined by attributes of one gender or the other. As Brahman is never
a personality, there are no Brahman myths; yet, as Brahman informs all
things, as Brahman is at once immanent and transcendent, all myths are
myths of Brahman.

In literature as well as in the other arts, including architecture, the
Supreme Being archetype would seem to inform and provide metaphorical
support for the tendency toward the patriarchal, the authoritarian, or the
monumental. The myth of the Supreme Being is the most universal of
archetypes; it is as common as fatherhood and the idea of God. It is realized
literally everywhere.

Indian: Krishna-Vishnu-Brahman

In the *Bhagavad-Gita*, the philosophical center of the great Hindu epic, the *Mahabharata*, Krishna-Vishnu reveals himself to the warrior Arjuna, as the personal base on which Brahman rests. He is the embodiment of the supreme primal power.

·

Krishna Gives Arjuna a Celestial Eye

The Blessed Lord said:

5. Son of Prithā, behold my forms in their hundreds and their thousands; how various they are, how divine, how many-hued and multiform. . . .
7. Do you today the whole universe behold centred here in One, with all that it contains of moving and unmoving things; [behold it] in my body, and whatever else you fain would see.
8. But never will you be able to see Me with this your [natural] eye. A celestial eye I'll give you, behold my power as Lord!

Krishna's Transfiguration

Sanjaya said:

9. So saying Hari,[1] the great Lord of power-and-the-skilful-use-of-it, revealed to the son of Prithā his highest sovereign form,—
10. [A form] with many a mouth and eye and countless marvellous aspects; many [indeed] were its divine adornments, many the celestial weapons raised on high.
11. Garlands and robes celestial He wore, fragrance divine was his anointing. [Behold this] God whose every [mark] spells wonder, the Infinite, facing every way!
12. If in [bright] heaven together should arise the shining brilliance of a thousand suns, then would that perhaps resemble the brilliance of that [God] so great of Self.
13. Then did the son of Pāndu see the whole [wide] universe in One

[1]"Hari": a name of Vishnu.

From the *Bhagavad Gita*, trans. R. C. Zaehner (Oxford, 1969), pp. 304–19.

converged, there in the body of the God of gods, yet divided out in multiplicity.

14. Then filled with amazement Arjuna, his hair on end, hands joined in reverent greeting, bowing his head before the God, [these words] spake out.

Arjuna said:

15. O God, the gods in your body I behold and all the hosts of every kind of being; Brahmā,[2] the lord, [I see] throned on the lotus-seat, celestial serpents and all the [ancient] seers.

16. Arms, bellies, mouths, and eyes all manifold,—so do I see You wherever I may look,—infinite your form! End, middle, or again beginning I cannot see in You, O Monarch Universal, [manifest] in every form!

17. Yours the crown, the mace, the discus,—a mass of glory shining on all sides,—so do I see You,—yet how hard are You to see,—for on every side there is brilliant light of fire and sun. Oh, who should comprehend it?

18. You are the Imperishable,[3] [You] wisdom's highest goal; You, of this universe the last prop-and-resting-place, You the changeless, [You] the guardian of eternal law,[4] You the primeval Person; [at last] I understand.

19. Beginning, middle, or end You do not know,—how infinite your strength! How numberless your arms,—your eyes the sun and moon! So do I see You,—your mouth a flaming fire, burning up this whole universe with your blazing glory.

20. By You alone is this space between heaven and earth pervaded,— all points of the compass too; gazing on this, your marvellous, frightening form, the three worlds shudder, [All-] Highest Self!

21. Lo! these hosts of gods are entering into You: some, terror-struck, extol You, hands together pressed; great seers and men perfected in serried ranks cry out, "All hail," and praise You with copious hymns of praise.

---

[2]"Brahmā": the creator-god *par excellence.* At the beginning of each world-aeon a lotus emerges from the navel of the recumbent Vishnu and Brahmā is seated on it. He then proceeds to create the universe anew. He must not be confused with the neuter "Brahman."

[3]"The Imperishable" (*neut.*): that is, the "highest Brahman."

[4]"Guardian of eternal law (*dharma*)": the protection of the existing *dharma* is indeed the purpose of Vishnu's incarnations: "for whenever the law of righteousness withers away and lawlessness arises, then do I generate myself [on earth]."

22. Rudras, Ādityas, Vasus, Sādhyas, All-gods, Aśvins, Maruts, and [the ancestors] who quaff the steam, minstrels divine, sprites, demons, and the hosts of perfected saints gaze upon You, all utterly amazed.

23. Gazing upon your mighty form with its myriad mouths, eyes, arms, thighs, feet, bellies, and sharp, gruesome tusks, the worlds [all] shudder [in affright],—how much more I!

24. Ablaze with many-coloured [flames] You touch the sky, your mouths wide open, [gaping,] your eyes distended, blazing: so do I see You and my inmost self is shaken:[5] I cannot bear it, I find no peace, O Vishnu!

25. I see your mouths with jagged, ghastly tusks reminding [me] of Time's [devouring] fire:[6] I cannot find my bearings, I cannot find a refuge; have mercy, God of gods, home of the universe!

26. Lo, all these sons of Dhritarāshtra accompanied by hosts of kings,—Bhīshma, Drona, and [Karna,] son of the charioteer, and those foremost in battle of our party too,

27. Rush [blindly] into your [gaping] mouths that with their horrid tusks strike [them] with terror. Some stick in the gaps between your teeth,—see them!—their heads to powder ground!

28. As many swelling, seething streams rush headlong into the [one] great sea, so do these heroes of the world of men enter into your blazing mouths.

29. As moths in bursting, hurtling haste rush into a lighted blaze to [their own] destruction, so do the worlds, well-trained in hasty violence, pour into your mouths to [their own] undoing!

30. On every side You lick, lick up,—devouring,—worlds, universes, everything,—with burning mouths. Vishnu! your dreadful rays of light fill the whole universe with flames-of-glory, scorching [everywhere].

31. Tell me, who are You, your form so cruel? Homage to You, You best of gods, have mercy! Fain would I know You as You are in the beginning, for what You are set on doing[7] I do not understand.

---

[5]"My inmost self is shaken": . . . *antar-ātman*, the *'inmost* self' which can only be the individual 'self-in-itself,' that 'inmost' self that is at the same time Brahman. This self—the true self of the liberated man—is nevertheless capable either of being absorbed in God or of being terrified by his awful power.

[6]"Time's [devouring] fire": the fire that burns the world up at the end of a world-aeon.

[7]"What You are set on doing": . . . Arjuna does not yet understand the terrible side to his nature displayed by Krishna which is capable even of upsetting the still self that has won liberation. . . . Nothing in Krishna's teaching had prepared him for this. He would sooner know Him "as He is in the beginning," in his eternal rest, rather than his incomprehensible and seemingly savage activity. Krishna now tells him that the reality is quite as fearful as it seems.

Krishna Reveals Himself as Time

The Blessed Lord said:

32. Time am I, wreaker of the world's destruction, matured,—
    [grimly] resolved here to swallow up the worlds. Do what you will,
    all these warriors shall cease to be, drawn up [there] in their op-
    posing ranks.
33. And so stand up, win glory, conquer your enemies and win a pros-
    perous kingdom! Long since have these men in truth been slain
    by Me: yours it is to be the mere occasion. . . .

Sanjaya said:

35. Hearing these words of Krishna, [Arjuna,] wearer of the crown,
    hands joined in veneration, trembling, bowed down to Krishna
    and spake again with stammering voice, as terrified he did obeis-
    ance.

Arjuna's Hymn of Praise

Arjuna said:

36. Full just is it that in praise of You the world should find its plea-
    sure and its joy, that monsters struck with terror should scatter in
    all directions, and that all the hosts of men perfected should do
    You homage.
37. And why should they not revere You, great [as is your] Self, more
    to be prized even than Brahman, first Creator, Infinite, Lord of
    the gods, home of the universe? You are the Imperishable, what
    IS and what is not and what surpasses both.
38. You are the Primal God, Primeval Person, You of this universe the
    last prop-and-resting-place, You the knower and what is to be
    known, [You our] highest home, O You whose forms are infinite,
    by You the whole universe was spun. . . .
40. All hail [to You] when I stand before You, [all hail] when I stand
    behind You, all hail to You wherever I may be, [all hail to You,]
    the All! How infinite your strength, how limitless your prowess!
    All things You bring to their consummation: hence You are All.
41. How rashly have I called You comrade, for so I thought of You,
    [how rashly said,] "Hey Krishna, hey Yādava, hey comrade!" Lit-

tle did I know of this your majesty; distraught was I . . . or was it that I loved You?

42. Sometimes in jest I showed You disrespect as we played or rested or sat or ate at table, sometimes together, sometimes in sight of others: I crave your pardon, O [Lord,] unfathomable, unfallen!

43. You are the father of the world of moving and unmoving things, You their venerable teacher, most highly prized; none is there like You,—how could there be another greater?—in the three worlds, Oh, matchless is your power.

44. And so I bow to You, prostrate my body, crave grace of You, [my] Lord adorable: bear with me, I beg You, as father [bears] with son, or friend with friend, or lover with the one he loves, O God!

45. Things never seen before I have seen, and ecstatic is my joy; yet fear-and-trembling perturb my mind. Show me, then, God, that [same human] form [I knew]; have mercy, Lord of gods, home of the universe!

46. Fain would I see You with [your familiar] crown and mace, discus in hand, just as You used to be; take up again your four-armed form, O thousand-armed, to whom every form belongs.

The Blessed Lord said:

47. Because I desired to show you favour, Arjuna, by my Self's own power I have shown you my highest form,—glorious, all-embracing, infinite, primeval, which none but you has ever seen before.

48. Not by the Vedas, not by sacrifice, not by [much] study or the giving of alms, not by rituals or grim ascetic practice can I be seen in such a form in the world of men: to you alone [have I revealed it,] champion of the Kurus.

49. You need not tremble nor need your spirit be perplexed though you have seen this form of mine, so awful, grim. Banish all fear, be glad at heart: behold again that [same familiar] form [you knew].

Krishna Assumes His Human Form Again

Sanjaya said:

50. Thus speaking did the son of Vasudeva show his [human] form to Arjuna again, comforting him in his fear. For once again the great-souled [Krishna] assumed the body of a friend.

Hebrew: Yahweh

The Yahweh of the Book of Job reveals himself to Job "out of the tempest," which is the appropriate element of the sky-storm god, of whom he is a particular embodiment.

•

Chapter 38

Then the Lord answered Job out of the whirlwind, and said,

2 Who is this that darkeneth counsel by words without knowledge?

3 Gird up now thy loins like a man; for I will demand of thee, and answer thou me.

4 Where wast thou when I laid the foundations of the earth? declare, if thou hast understanding.

5 Who hath laid the measures thereof, if thou knowest? or who hath stretched the line upon it?

6 Whereupon are the foundations thereof fastened? or who laid the corner stone thereof;

7 When the morning stars sang together, and all the sons of God shouted for joy?

8 Or *who* shut up the sea with doors, when it brake forth, *as if* it had issued out of the womb?

9 When I made the cloud the garment thereof, and thick darkness a swaddlingband for it,

10 And brake up for it my decreed *place*, and set bars and doors,

11 And said, Hitherto shalt thou come, but no further: and here shall thy proud waves be stayed?

12 Hast thou commanded the morning since thy days; *and* caused the dayspring to know his place;

13 That it might take hold of the ends of the earth, that the wicked might be shaken out of it?

14 It is turned as clay *to* the seal; and they stand as a garment.

15 And from the wicked their light is withholden, and the high arm shall be broken.

16 Hast thou entered into the springs of the sea? or hast thou walked in the search of the depth?

17 Have the gates of death been opened unto thee? or hast thou seen the doors of the shadow of death?

18 Hast thou perceived the breadth of the earth? declare if thou knowest it all.

Job 38–39.

19 Where *is* the way *where* light dwelleth? and *as for* darkness, where is the place thereof,

20 That thou shouldest take it to the bound thereof, and that thou shouldest know the paths *to* the house thereof?

21 Knowest thou *it,* because thou wast then born? or *because* the number of thy days *is* great?

22 Hast thou entered into the treasures of the snow? or hast thou seen the treasures of the hail,

23 Which I have reserved against the time of trouble, against the day of battle and war?

24 By what way is the light parted, *which* scattereth the east wind upon the earth?

25 Who hath divided a water-course for the overflowing of waters, or a way for the lightning of thunder;

26 To cause it to rain on the earth, *where* no man *is; on* the wilderness, wherein *there is* no man;

27 To satisfy the desolate and waste *ground;* and to cause the bud of the tender herb to spring forth?

28 Hath the rain a father? or who hath begotten the drops of dew?

29 Out of whose womb came the ice? and the hoary frost of heaven, who hath gendered it?

30 The waters are hid as *with* a stone, and the face of the deep is frozen.

31 Canst thou bind the sweet influences of Plei'-ă-dēs, or loose the bands of Ō-rī'-on?

32 Canst thou bring forth Măzz'-ă-rōth in his season? or canst thou guide Ärc-tū'-rŭs with his sons?

33 Knowest thou the ordinances of heaven? canst thou set the dominion thereof in the earth?

34 Canst thou lift up thy voice to the clouds, that abundance of waters may cover thee?

35 Canst thou send lightnings, that they may go, and say unto thee, Here we *are?*

36 Who hath put wisdom in the inward parts? or who hath given understanding to the heart?

37 Who can number the clouds in wisdom? or who can stay the bottles of heaven,

38 When the dust groweth into hardness, and the clods cleave fast together?

39 Wilt thou hunt the prey for the lion? or fill the appetite of the young lions,

40 When they couch in *their* dens, *and* abide in the covert to lie in wait?

41 Who provideth for the raven his food? when his young ones cry unto God, they wander for lack of meat.

Chapter 39

Knowest thou the time when the wild goats of the rock bring forth? *or* canst thou mark when the hinds do calve?

2 Canst thou number the months *that* they fulfil? or knowest thou the time when they bring forth?

3 They bow themselves, they bring forth their young ones, they cast out their sorrows.

4 Their young ones are in good liking, they grow up with corn; they go forth, and return not unto them.

5 Who hath sent out the wild ass free? or who hath loosed the bands of the wild ass?

6 Whose house I have made the wilderness, and the barren land his dwellings.

7 He scorneth the multitude of the city, neither regardeth he the crying of the driver.

8 The range of the mountains *is* his pasture, and he searcheth after every green thing.

9 Will the unicorn be willing to serve thee, or abide by thy crib?

10 Canst thou bind the unicorn with his band in the furrow? or will he harrow the valleys after thee?

11 Wilt thou trust him, because his strength *is* great? or wilt thou leave thy labour to him?

12 Wilt thou believe him, that he will bring home thy seed, and gather *it into* thy barn?

13 *Gavest thou* the goodly wings unto the peacocks? or wings and feathers unto the ostrich?

14 Which leaveth her eggs in the earth, and warmeth them in dust,

15 And forgetteth that the foot may crush them, or that the wild beast may break them.

16 She is hardened against her young ones, as though *they were* not hers: her labour is in vain without fear;

17 Because God hath deprived her of wisdom, neither hath he imparted to her understanding.

18 What time she lifteth up herself on high, she scorneth the horse and his rider.

19 Hast thou given the horse strength? hast thou clothed his neck with thunder?

20 Canst thou make him afraid as a grasshopper? the glory of his nostrils *is* terrible.

21 He paweth in the valley, and rejoiceth in *his* strength: he goeth on to meet the armed men.

22 He mocketh at fear, and is not affrighted; neither turneth he back from the sword.

23 The quiver rattleth against him, the glittering spear and the shield.

24 He swalloweth the ground with fierceness and rage: neither believeth he that *it is* the sound of the trumpet.

25 He saith among the trumpets, Ha, ha; and he smelleth the battle afar off, the thunder of the captains, and the shouting.

26 Doth the hawk fly by thy wisdom *and* stretch her wings toward the south?

27 Doth the eagle mount up at thy command, and make her nest on high?

28 She dwelleth and abideth on the rock, upon the crag of the rock, and the strong place.

29 From thence she seeketh the prey, *and* her eyes behold afar off.

30 Her young ones also suck up blood: and where the slain are, there is she.

Modern: Immanent Mind

The modern scientific mind has continued to consider and be fascinated by the idea of a Supreme Being, at least as a metaphor for a transcendent, immanent, and unifying ultimate reality. Gregory Bateson was a philosopher-scientist who postulated a universal Mind of which our individual minds are in some sense the image. Are we, after all, made in the image of God? Is Mind, separate from our individual minds, a reality in itself?

*

The individual mind is immanent but not only in the body. It is immanent also in pathways and messages outside the body; and there is a larger Mind of which the individual mind is only a subsystem. This larger Mind is comparable to God and is perhaps what some people mean by "God," but it is still immanent in the total interconnected social system and planetary ecology.

Freudian psychology expanded the concept of mind inwards to include the whole communication system within the body—the autonomic, the habitual, and the vast range of unconscious process. What I am saying

Gregory Bateson, *Steps to an Ecology of Mind* (New York, 1972), pp. 461–62.

expands mind outwards. And both of these changes reduce the scope of the conscious self. A certain humility becomes appropriate, tempered by the dignity or joy of being part of something much bigger. A part—if you will—of God.

The Great Mother

In ancient times the archetype that we refer to as the Great Mother seems likely to have been primarily an earth mother—that is, a personification of Earth itself. With the Earth Mother we associate ideas of nourishment and creation. Gaia in Greece existed before any other immortal; it was she who gave birth to her own mate, Uranos. (See the Creation section of this book.) Frequently the Earth Mother is important in connection with an equal or dominant mate, usually a representation of the sky or heaven. Heaven and Earth then become the primal couple, united in the act of creation. This couple is one of the most prevalent motifs in myth: Papa and Rangi among the Maori, Sky Man and Earth Woman among the Navajo, the Sun God and Spider Woman among the Hopi, Izanagi and Izanami among the Japanese, and Geb and Nut among the ancient Egyptians, to mention only a few. The Earth Mother was worshipped as the source of life; out of her body came the necessary nourishment, and she had the capability of giving new birth to objects that had seemed dead. She gave life even as she caused life to wither up and return to her. She was the guardian of the dead and the agent of birth and rebirth. In early societies her importance was rivaled only by that of the sun, the source of heat and light which was identified with the supreme sky god.

As agricultural practices began to supersede gathering as a means of obtaining plant food, the Earth Mother gradually lost importance or developed into the Corn Mother, the Great Goddess, whose concern is planting and harvesting. Demeter, who supplanted Gaia in importance in Greece, is the best known of the Great Goddesses, but she has counterparts in such figures as the Roman Ceres, the many-breasted Artemis at Ephesus, Cybele, the *Magna Mater* of Phrygia, the Devi in her various forms in India, Isis in Egypt, and Inanna-Ishtar in Mesopotamia.

The Great Goddess, like the Earth Mother before her, and like nature itself and the mysteries of the unconscious (which she may be said to represent), is often ambiguous, often capable of doing great harm. Her folkloric expressions are at once the wise old woman–fairy godmother and the witch. In her Christian form—that of the Madonna—she has lost the dark side, just as the old Hebrew Yahweh—whose treatment of Job and of Abraham and Isaac, for example, is at least morally questionable—gives way in Christianity to a God who contains no evil.

If the Christian Madonna is a Great Mother unblemished by evil, however, the Great Goddess of the East remains realistically ambiguous. In India, for instance, Devi—the Goddess—is more often worshipped as the fierce Durga or the dark Kali than she is as Lakshmi and Parvati, the more nurturing spouses of Vishnu and Shiva. This is not to say that the positive side of the Goddess is not stressed. The depictions of Shiva in union with his spouse or Vishnu with his—the union with the *shakti*, the animating soul embodied in the female, as in the case of the Greek Psyche or the Byzantine Sophia—represent the same kind of spiritual and psychic wholeness or balance that is represented by the ancient Chinese combination of *yin* and *yang*, masculine and feminine, light and dark, even good and evil. We can think of *yin* as the Great Mother, the *prima materia*, the matrix of forms, the mystery of the unconscious world; and we can think of *yang* as the primal energy that impregnates that matrix and allows forms to be realized, the representative of consciousness and the ego's role in our psychic lives. The Great Mother and that energy are meaningless without each other. Form—life itself—is death-defined and is thus the proper province of the ambiguous Great Mother who contains in herself both life and death. For divinity to enter this world, the full mystery of the Great Mother must be experienced. So it is that the hero—the son-lover—dies and is reunited with the Goddess in her underworld-womb, from which he can, like the flowers of spring, be reborn. Or, to use the psychological "myth" of our own age, so it is that the ego must fully explore the mysteries of the unconscious before it can emerge into wholeness or individuation.

In the stories of the Great Goddess, a pattern emerges in which the Goddess figure mourns the loss of a loved one, goes on a search, and in bringing about a form of resurrection—clearly associated with the planting and harvesting of crops—establishes new religious practices or mysteries for her followers. These mysteries are inevitably concerned with the connection between death, planting, sexuality, and resurrection or immortality, on the one hand, and physical as well as spiritual renewal, on the other. The best known of these mystery-fertility cults are the Eleusinian (associated with Demeter), the Egyptian (associated with Isis), and the Phrygian (associated with Cybele). Aspects of these cults also exist in the ritual of Dionysos, whose phallus was carried in procession by the Mother Goddess, and in the story of Jesus, whose rebirth as the Christ or "Son of Man" from the maternal tomb is in a sense presided over by representatives of the two sides of the Great Goddess—the Virgin Mary, or Madonna, and the worldly prostitute, Mary Magdalene.

One of the most striking Goddess myths is that of the Hopi creator, Spider Woman in which the hero, Tiyo, is placed in a coffinlike object, which is sent by way of various forms of water—the element of birth—to the depths of the Earth, where Spider woman waits. The symbols of planting, of sexual penetration, and of death and rebirth are all present corroborated by references to the Hopi *kiva*, the underground sacred space which is itself, like the underworld to which her initiates must often go, representative of the Great Mother's womb and is the place in which the Hopi men weave the sacred stoles used in the Hopi religious ceremonies.

Modern literary embodiments of the Great Goddess are William Faulkner's Lena Grove in *Light in August*, Molly Bloom in James Joyce's *Ulysses*, and Mrs. Ramsay in Virginia Woolf's *To the Lighthouse*.

Mesopotamian: Inanna-Ishtar

In this ancient myth, the Great Goddess Inanna-Ishtar journeys to the underworld, perhaps to retrieve her lover, the shepherd king, Dumuzi-Tammuz, from her sister or dark other half. The myth reminds us of similar journeys undertaken by Isis in search of Osiris (see the story of Isis and Osiris in the Dying God section of this book) and by Demeter in search of Persephone (see the story of Demeter in the Pantheon section).

●

From the "great above" she set her mind toward the "great
   below,"
The *goddess*, from the "great above" she set her mind toward
   the "great below,"
Inanna, from the "great above" she set her mind toward the
   "great below."

My lady abandoned heaven, abandoned earth,
   To the nether world she descended,
Inanna abandoned heaven, abandoned earth,
   To the nether world she descended,
Abandoned lordship, abandoned ladyship,
   To the nether world she descended.

In Erech she abandoned Eanna,
   To the nether world she descended,
In Badtibira she abandoned Emushkalamma,
   To the nether world she descended,
In Zabalam she abandoned Giguna,
   To the nether world she descended,
In Adab she abandoned Esharra,
   To the nether world she descended,

S. N. Kramer, *Sumerian Mythology* (New York, 1961), pp. 88–96.

In Nippur she abandoned Baratushgarra,
To the nether world she descended,
In Kish she abandoned Hursagkalamma,
   To the nether world she descended,
In Agade she abandoned Eulmash,
   To the nether world she descended.

The seven divine decrees she fastened at the side,
She sought out the divine decrees, placed them at her hand,
All the decrees she set up at (her) waiting foot,
The *shugurra*, the crown of the plain, she put upon her head,
Radiance she placed upon her countenance,
The . . . rod of lapis lazuli she gripped in (her) hand,
Small lapis lazuli stones she tied about her neck,
Sparkling . . . stones she fastened to her breast,
A gold ring she gripped in her hand,
A . . . breastplate she bound about her breast,
All the garments of ladyship she *arranged* about her body,
. . . *ointment* she put on her face.

Inanna walked toward the nether world,
Her messenger Ninshubur walked at her *side*,
The pure Inanna says to Ninshubur:
"O (thou who art) my constant support,
My messenger of favorable words,
My carrier of supporting words,
I am now descending to the nether world.

"When I shall have come to the nether world,
Fill heaven *with complaints for me*,
In the assembly shrine *cry out* for me,
In the house of the gods *rush about* for me,
Lower thy eye for me, *lower* thy mouth for me,
With . . . *lower* thy great . . . for me,
Like a pauper in a single garment dress for me,
To the Ekur, the house of Enlil, all alone direct thy step.

"Upon thy entering the Ekur, the house of Enlil,
Weep before Enlil:
'O father Enlil, let not thy daughter be *put to death* in the nether
   world,
Let not thy good metal be *ground up* into the dust of the nether
   world,
Let not thy good lapis lazuli be *broken up* into the stone of the
   stone-worker,

Let not thy *boxwood* be *cut up* into the wood of the wood-
   worker,
Let not the maid Inanna be *put to death* in the nether world,'

"If Enlil stands not by thee in this matter, go to Ur.

"In Ur upon thy entering the house of the . . . of the land,
The Ekishshirgal, the house of Nanna,
Weep before Nanna:
'O Father Nanna, let not thy daughter be *put to death* in the
   nether world,
Let not thy good metal be *ground up* into the dust of the nether
   world,
Let not thy good lapis lazuli be *broken up* into the stone of the
   stone-worker,
Let not thy *boxwood* be *cut up* into the wood of the wood-
   worker,
Let not the maid Inanna be put to death in the nether world.'

"If Nanna stands not by thee in this matter, go to Eridu.

"In Eridu upon thy entering the house of Enki,
Weep before Enki:
'O father Enki, let not thy daughter be *put to death* in the
   nether world,
Let not thy good metal be *ground up* into the dust of the nether
   world,
Let not thy good lapis lazuli be *broken up* into the stone of the
   stone-worker,
Let not thy *boxwood* be *cut up* into the wood of the wood-
   worker,
Let not the maid Inanna be *put to death* in the nether world.'

"Father Enki, the lord of wisdom,
Who knows the food of life, who knows the water of life,
He will surely bring me to life."

Inanna walked toward the nether world,
To her messenger Ninshubur she says:
"Go, Ninshubur,
The word which I have commanded thee . . ."

When Inanna had arrived at the lapis lazuli palace of the
   nether world,
At the door of the nether world she acted evilly,
In the palace of the nether world she spoke evilly:

"Open the house, gatekeeper, open the house,
Open the house, Neti, open the house, all alone I would enter."

Neti, the chief gatekeeper of the nether world,
Answers the pure Inanna:
"Who pray art thou?"

"I am the queen of heaven, the place where the sun rises."

"If thou art the queen of heaven, the place where the sun rises,
Why pray hast thou come to the land of no return?
On the road whose traveller returns not how has thy heart led
    thee?"

The pure Inanna answers him:
"My elder sister Ereshkigal,
Because her husband, the lord Gugalanna, had been killed,
To witness the funeral rites,
. . .; so be it."

Neti, the chief gatekeeper of the nether world,
Answers the pure Inanna:
"*Stay*, Inanna, to my queen let me speak,
To my queen Ereshkigal let me speak . . . let me speak."

Neti, the chief gatekeeper of the nether world,
Enters the house of his queen Ereshkigal and says to her:
"O my queen, a maid,
Like a god . . .,
The door . . .,

. . .,
In Eanna . . .,
The seven divine decrees she has fastened at the side,
She has sought out the divine decrees, has placed them at her
    hand,
All the decrees she has set up at (her) waiting foot,
The *shugurra*, the crown of the plain, she has put upon her
    head,
Radiance she has placed upon her countenance,
The . . . rod of lapis lazuli she has gripped in (her) hand,
Small lapis lazuli stones she has tied about her neck,
Sparkling . . . stones she has fastened to her breast,
A gold ring she has gripped in her hand,
A . . . breastplate she has bound about her breast,
All her garments of ladyship she has *arranged* about her body,
. . . *ointment* she has put on her face."

Then Ereshkigal . . .,
Answers Neti, her chief gatekeeper:
"Come, Neti, chief gatekeeper of the nether world,
Unto the word which I command thee, give ear.
Of the seven gates of the nether world, open their locks,
Of the gate Ganzir, the 'face' of the nether world, define its
    rules;
Upon her (Inanna's) entering,
Bowed low . . . let her . . ."

Neti, the chief gatekeeper of the nether world,
Honored the word of his queen,
Of the seven gates of the nether world, he opened their locks,
Of the gate Ganzir, the 'face' of the nether world, he defined
    its rules.
To the pure Inanna he says:
"Come, Inanna, enter."

Upon her entering the first gate,
The *shugurra*, the "crown of the plain" of her head, was re-
    moved.
"What, pray, is this?"
"Extraordinarily, O Inanna, have the decrees of the nether world
    been perfected,
O Inanna, *do not question* the rites of the nether world."

Upon her entering the second gate,
The . . . rod of lapis lazuli was removed.
"What, pray, is this?"
"Extraordinarily, O Inanna, have the decrees of the nether world
    been perfected,
O Inanna, *do not question* the rites of the nether world."

Upon her entering the third gate,
The small lapis lazuli stones of her neck were removed.
"What, pray, is this?"
"Extraordinarily, O Inanna, have the decrees of the nether world
    been perfected,
O Inanna, *do not question* the rites of the nether world,"

Upon her entering the fourth gate,
The sparkling . . . stones of her breast were removed.
What, pray, is this?"
"Extraordinarily, O Inanna, have the decrees of the nether world
    been perfected,
O Inanna, *do not question* the rites of the nether world."

Upon her entering the fifth gate,
The gold ring of her hand was removed.
What, pray, is this?"
"Extraordinarily, O Inanna, have the decrees of the nether world
    been perfected,
O Inanna, *do not question* the rites of the nether world."

Upon her entering the sixth gate,
The . . . breastplate of her breast was removed.
What, pray, is this?"
"Extraordinarily, O Inanna, have the decrees of the nether world
    been perfected,
O Inanna, *do not question* the rites of the nether world."

Upon her entering the seventh gate,
All the garments of ladyship of her body were removed.
"What, pray, is this?"
"Extraordinarily, O Inanna, have the decrees of the nether world
    been perfected,
O Inanna, *do not question* the rites of the nether world."

Bowed low . . .

The pure Ereshkigal seated herself upon her throne,
The Anunnaki, the seven judges, pronounced judgment before
    her,
They fastened (their) eyes upon her, the eyes of death,
At their word, the word which tortures the spirit,
. . .,
The sick woman was turned into a *corpse*,
The *corpse* was hung from a *stake*.

After three days and three nights had passed,
Her messenger Ninshubur,
Her messenger of favorable words,
Her carrier of supporting words,
Fills the heaven *with complaints for her,*
Cried for her in the assembly shrine,
Rushed about for her in the house of the gods,
Lowered his eye for her, *lowered* his mouth for her,
With . . . he *lowered* his great . . . for her,
Like a pauper in a single garment he dressed for her,
To the Ekur, the house of Enlil, all alone he directed his step.

Upon his entering the Ekur, the house of Enlil,
Before Enlil he weeps:

"O father Enlil, let not thy daughter be *put to death* in the nether
    world,
Let not thy good metal be *ground up* into the dust of the nether
    world,
Let not thy good lapis lazuli be *broken up* into the stone of the
    stone-worker,
Let not thy *boxwood* be *cut up* into the wood of the wood-
    worker,
Let not the maid Inanna be *put to death* in the nether world."

Father Enlil answers Ninshubur:
"My daughter, in the 'great above' . . ., in the 'great below'
    . . .,
Inanna, in the 'great above' . . ., in the 'great below' . . .,
The decrees of the nether world, the . . . decrees, to their
    place . . .,
Who, pray, *to* their place . . .?"

Father Enlil stood not by him in this matter, he went to Ur.

In Ur upon his entering the house of the . . . of the land,
The Ekishshirgal, the house of Nanna,
Before Nanna he weeps:
"O father Nanna, let not thy daughter be *put to death* in the
    nether world,
Let not thy good metal be *ground up* into the dust of the nether
    world,
Let not thy good lapis lazuli be *broken up* into the stone of the
    stone-worker,
Let not thy *boxwood* be *cut up* into the wood of the wood-
    worker,
Let not the maid Inanna be *put to death* in the nether world."

Father Nanna answers Ninshubur:
"My daughter in the 'great above' . . ., in the 'great below'
    . . .,
Inanna, in the 'great above' . . ., in the 'great below' . . .,
The decrees of the nether world, the . . . decrees, to their
    place . . .,
Who, pray, *to* their place . . .?"

Father Nanna stood not by him in this matter, he went to Eridu.

In Eridu upon his entering the house of Enki,
Before Enki he weeps:
"O father Enki, let not thy daughter be *put to death* in the
    nether world,

Let not thy good metal be *ground up* into the dust of the nether
    world,
Let not thy good lapis lazuli be *broken up* into the stone of the
    stone-worker,
Let not thy *boxwood* be *cut up* into the wood of the wood-
    worker,
Let not the maid Inanna be *put to death* in the nether world."

Father Enki answers Ninshubur:
"What now has my daughter done! I am troubled,
What now has Inanna done! I am troubled,
What now has the queen of all the lands done! I am troubled,
What now has the heirodule of heaven done! I am troubled."

. . . *he brought forth dirt* (and) fashioned the *kurgarru*,
. . . *he brought forth dirt* (and) fashioned the *kalaturru*,
To the *kurgarru* he gave the food of life,
To the *kalaturru* he gave the water of life,
Father Enki says to the *kalaturru* and *kurgarru*:
. . . (nineteen lines destroyed)
"*Upon the corpse hung from a stake direct the fear of the rays*
    of fire,
Sixty times the food of life, *sixty times* the water of life,
    sprinkle upon it,
Verily Inanna will arise."

. . . (twenty-four (?) lines destroyed)

Upon the corpse hung from a stake they directed the fear of
    the rays of fire,
Sixty times the food of life, *sixty times* the water of life, they
    sprinkled upon it,
Inanna arose.

Inanna ascends from the nether world,
The Anunnaki fled,
(And) whoever of the nether world that had descended peace-
    fully to the nether world;
When Inanna ascends from the nether world,
Verily the dead *hasten ahead of her*.

Inanna ascends from the nether world,
The small *demons* like . . . reeds,
The large demons like tablet styluses,
Walked at her side.
Who walked in front of her, being without . . ., held a staff
    in the hand,

Who walked at her side, being without . . ., carried a weapon
  on the loin.
They who *preceded* her,
They who *preceded* Inanna,
(Were beings who) know not food, who know not water,
Who eat not sprinkled flour,
Who drink not libated *wine*,
Who take away the wife from the loins of man,
Who take away the child from the breast of the nursing mother.

Inanna ascends from the nether world;
Her messenger Ninshubur threw himself at her feet,
Sat in the dust, dressed in *dirt*.
The demons say to the pure Inanna:
"O Inanna, *wait before* thy city, *we would bring him to thee.*"

The pure Inanna answers the demons:
"(He is) my messenger of favorable words,
My carrier of supporting words,
He *fails* not my directions,
He delays not my commanded word,
He *fills* heaven *with complaints for me*,
In the assembly shrine he cried out for me,
In the house of the gods he rushed about for me,
He *lowered* his eye for me, he *lowered* his mouth for me,
With . . . he *lowered* his great . . . for me,
Like a pauper in a single garment he dressed for me,
To the Ekur, the house of Enlil,
In Ur, to the house of Nanna,
In Eridu, to the house of Enki (he directed his step),
He brought me to life."

"Let us *precede* her, in Umma to the Sigkurshagga let us precede
  her."

In Umma, from the Sigkurshagga,
Shara threw himself at her feet,
Sat in the dust, dressed in *dirt*.
The demons say to the pure Inanna:
"O Inanna, *wait before* thy city, we would bring him to thee."

The pure Inanna answers the demons:
  (Inanna's answer is destroyed)

"Let us *precede* her, in Badtibira to the Emushkalamma let us
  precede her."

In Badtibira from the Emushkalamma,
. . . threw themselves at her feet,
Sat in the dust, dressed in *dirt*.
The demons say to the pure Inanna:
"O Inanna, *wait before* thy city, we would bring them to thee."

The pure Inanna answers the demons:
  (Inanna's answer destroyed; the end of the poem is wanting).

Modern: Gaia as Earth

In recent years the theory of British scientist James Lovelock has suggested
that Earth—"a planet-sized entity . . . with properties which could not be
predicted from the sum of its parts"—can best be seen as a living organism
with the capability of organizing its own biosphere. This theory is now
seriously discussed by scientists who study Earth's ecology. Lovelock and
others have given their newly discovered giant organism a name, which
they have taken from an earlier mythological version of the theory: Mother
Earth, or Gaia.

•

The concept of Mother Earth or, as the Greeks called her long ago, Gaia,
has been widely held throughout history and has been the basis of a belief
which still coexists with the great religions. As a result of the accumulation
of evidence about the natural environment and the growth of the science
of ecology, there have recently been speculations that the biosphere may
have been more than just the complete range of all living things within
their natural habitat of soil, sea, and air. Ancient belief and modern knowledge have fused emotionally in the awe with which astronauts with their
own eyes and we by indirect vision have seen the Earth revealed in all its
shining beauty against the deep darkness of space. Yet this feeling, however strong, does not prove that Mother Earth lives. Like a religious belief,
it is scientifically untestable and therefore incapable in its own context of
further rationalization.

Journeys into space did more than present the Earth in a new perspective. They also sent back information about its atmosphere and its
surface which provided a new insight into the interactions between the
living and the inorganic parts of the planet. From this has arisen the hypothesis, the model, in which the Earth's living matter, air, oceans, and
land surface form a complex system which can be seen as a single organism
and which has the capacity to keep our planet a fit place for life.

. . .

James E. Lovelock. *Gaia: A New Look at Life on Earth* (Oxford, 1979), pp. ix–x, 11–12.

We have since defined Gaia as a complex entity involving the Earth's biosphere, atmosphere, oceans, and soil; the totality constituting a feedback or cybernetic system which seeks an optimal physical and chemical environment for life on this planet. The maintenance of relatively constant conditions by active control may be conveniently described by the term "homoeostasis."

Gaia has remained a hypothesis but, like other useful hypotheses, she has already proved her theoretical value, if not her existence, by giving rise to experimental questions and answers which were profitable exercises in themselves. If, for example, the atmosphere is, among other things, a device for conveying raw materials to and from the biosphere, it would be reasonable to assume the presence of carrier compounds for elements essential in all biological systems, for example, iodine and sulphur. It was rewarding to find evidence that both were conveyed from the oceans, where they are abundant, through the air to the land surface, where they are in short supply. The carrier compounds, methyl iodide and dimethyl sulphide respectively, are directly produced by marine life. Scientific curiosity being unquenchable, the presence of these interesting compounds in the atmosphere would no doubt have been discovered in the end and their importance discussed without the stimulus of the Gaia hypothesis. But they were actively sought as a result of the hypothesis and their presence was consistent with it.

If Gaia exists, the relationship between her and man, a dominant animal species in the complex living system, and the possibly shifting balance of power between them, are questions of obvious importance. . . . The Gaia hypothesis is for those who like to walk or simply stand and stare, to wonder about the Earth and the life it bears, and to speculate about the consequences of our own presence here. It is an alternative to that pessimistic view which sees nature as a primitive force to be subdued and conquered. It is also an alternative to that equally depressing picture of our planet as a demented spaceship, forever travelling, driverless and purposeless, around an inner circle of the sun.

The Dying God

As should already be evident, the dying god motif is closely related to the myth of the Great Goddess. In this motif, a god-king dies and is in some sense revived if not actually brought back to the living world. Traditionally, scholars have associated this mythological pattern, so prevalent in the fertile Middle East, with the cycle of vegetation, a cycle also associated with the Great Goddess. The dead god becomes the seed planted in the Mother. Perhaps for this reason, he is sometimes hanged on a tree (Attis, Odin, Jesus—"Were you there when they nailed him to the tree?") or in some other way associated with trees (Adonis, Osiris, Dionysos). The emphasis on genitals or their loss (Osiris, Dionysos, Attis) is perhaps also suggestive of the god's seed-bearing vegetable role. As has been suggested in connection with the Great Goddess archetype, the descent into death can also be seen as a metaphor for a psychological descent into the unconscious. Any rebirth or resurrection, then, would seem to speak not only to the question of physical fertility but also to the hope of overcoming the brokenness of the ordinary life in favor of the achievement of full individuation.

In *The Golden Bough* (1911–15), Sir James Frazer first suggested the pattern of the dying god in connection with sacrificial rites in which a sacred king or a surrogate king was sacrificed to ensure the renewed fertility of a given tribe. The mythological evidence supports this theory only partially, in that the myths usually involve a symbolic rather than an actual resurrection (Jesus being a notable exception). The dead hero becomes a flower (Adonis) or he becomes king of the dead (Osiris) or a renewal is only ambiguously hinted at (Tammuz-Dumuzi—see the Inanna story, above). The dying god model has been most useful to the postmythological writer as a source for metaphors that can suggest psychic, spiritual, or emotional rebirth or the lack of it. Writers of elegies find it especially useful. Milton's *Lycidas* and Eliot's *The Waste Land* are both poems that make concrete use of the dying god archetype.

The rebirth process can also have a social aspect. In both its original ritual and mythic forms as well as in its later metaphorical masks, the dying god or his literary surrogate is often a "scapegoat," one who dies for the good of a society, who somehow takes on the burden of his society's shortcomings or sins: "And the goat shall bear upon him all their iniquities unto a land not inhabited" (Leviticus). The stories of Jesus, Attis, Osiris, Dionysos, and the other dying gods all have scapegoat elements. The most obvious literary descendant of the scapegoat gods (and scapegoat heroes) is the tragic hero, be he Oedipus, Lear, Hamlet, or Hedda Gabler. The tragic hero must die before the society that he or she represents can turn from rottenness to normality.

The sources for the metaphorical or literary use of the archetype are evident in the stories that follow.

Egyptian: Osiris and Isis

The story of Osiris, the god of maize and of the underworld, and his sister-wife, Isis, is rooted in or closely associated with mummification practices in ancient Egypt. Whether the myth was created to justify the ritual or vice versa is open to question. What is important is the expression the myth gives to the human hope for some kind of permanent existence. In this version of the story, told by Sir James Frazer and based on Plutarch in the early second century C.E., we have an elaboration of the basic story line, which can be found in the much earlier Pyramid Texts. Present are the tree, the scattering of the god-seed, the loss of genitalia, the return of the god to the Mother (underworld, Earth), the emphasis on immortality, the Earth Goddess as mourner and as midwife for the rebirth. Note the similarity between the story of Demeter's attempt to bestow immortality on the child of which she is a nursemaid (see the Demeter story in the Pantheon section of this book) and the events that take place in this story.

•

Osiris was the offspring of an intrigue between the earth-god Geb and the sky-goddess Nut. When the sun-god Ra perceived that his wife Nut has been unfaithful to him, he declared with a curse that she should be delivered of the child in no month and no year. But the goddess had another lover, the god Thoth, and he, playing at draughts with the moon, won from her a seventy-second part of every day, and having thus compounded five whole days he added them to the Egyptian year of three hundred and sixty days. On these five days, regarded as outside the year of twelve months—that is, as "epagomenal"—the curse of the sun-god did not rest, and accordingly Osiris was born on the first of them. But he was not the only child of his mother. On the second of the supplementary days she gave birth to the elder Horus, on the third to the god Set, on the fourth to the goddess Isis, and on the fifth to the goddess Nephthys. Afterwards Set married his sister Nephthys, and Osiris his sister Isis.

Reigning as a king on earth, Osiris reclaimed the Egyptians from savagery, gave them laws, and taught them to worship the gods. Before his time the Egyptians had been cannibals. But Isis, the sister and wife of Osiris, discovered wheat and barley growing wild, and Osiris introduced the cultivation of these grains amongst his people, who forthwith took kindly to a corn diet. Moreover, Osiris is said to have been the first to gather fruit from trees, to train the vine to poles, and to tread the grapes. Eager to communicate these beneficent discoveries to all mankind, he committed the whole government of Egypt to his wife Isis, and travelled over the world, diffusing the blessings of civilization and agriculture wherever he went. In countries where a harsh climate or niggardly soil forbade the cultivation of the vine, he taught the inhabitants to console themselves for the want of wine by brewing beer from barley. Loaded with the wealth that had been showered upon him by grateful nations, he returned to Egypt, and on account of the benefits he had conferred on mankind he was unanimously hailed and worshipped as a deity. But his brother Set

Sir James Frazer, *The New Golden Bough*, ed. Theodor H. Gaster (New York, 1959), pp. 384–90.

with seventy-two others plotted against him. Having taken the measure of his good brother's body by stealth, the bad brother fashioned and highly decorated a coffer of the same size, and once when they were all drinking and making merry he brought in the coffer and jestingly promised to give it to the one whom it should fit exactly. They all tried one after the other, but it fitted none of them. Last of all Osiris stepped into it and lay down. On that the conspirators ran and slammed the lid down on him, nailed it fast, soldered it with molten lead, and flung the coffer into the Nile. This happened on the seventeenth day of the month Athyr, when the sun is in the sign of the Scorpion, and in the eight-and-twentieth year of the reign or the life of Osiris. When Isis heard of it she sheared off a lock of her hair, put on mourning attire, and wandered disconsolately up and down, seeking the body.

By the advice of the god of wisdom she took refuge in the papyrus swamps of the Delta. There she conceived a son while she fluttered in the form of a hawk over the corpse of her dead husband. The infant was the younger Horus, who in his youth bore the name of Harpocrates, that is, the child Horus. Him Buto, the goddess of the north, hid from the wrath of his wicked uncle Set. Yet she could not guard him from all mishap; for one day when Isis came to her little son's hiding-place she found him stretched lifeless and rigid on the ground: a scorpion had stung him. Then Isis prayed to the sun-god Ra for help. The god hearkened to her and staid his bark in the sky, and sent down Thoth to teach her the spell by which she might restore her son to life. She uttered the words of power, and straightway the poison flowed from the body of Horus, air passed into him and he lived. Then Thoth ascended up into the sky and took his place once more in the bark of the sun, and the bright pomp passed onward jubilant.

Meantime the coffer containing the body of Osiris had floated down the river and away out to sea, till at last it drifted ashore at Byblus, on the coast of Syria. Here a fine *erica*-tree shot up suddenly and enclosed the chest in its trunk. The king of the country, admiring the growth of the tree, had it cut down and made into a pillar of his house; but he did not know that the coffer with the dead Osiris was in it. Word of this came to Isis and she journeyed to Byblus, and sat down by the well, in humble guise, her face wet with tears. To none would she speak till the king's handmaidens came, and them she greeted kindly, and braided their hair, and breathed on them from her own divine body a wondrous perfume. When the queen beheld the braids of her handmaidens' hair and smelt the sweet smell that emanated from them, she sent for the stranger woman and took her into her house and made her the nurse of her child. Isis gave the babe her finger instead of her breast to suck, and at night she began to burn all that was mortal of him away, while she herself in the likeness of a swallow fluttered round the pillar that contained her dead brother, twittering mournfully. The queen spied what she was doing and shrieked out when she saw her child in flames, and thereby she hindered him from becoming immortal. Then the goddess revealed herself and begged for the pillar of the roof, and they gave it her, and she cut the coffer out of it, and fell upon it and embraced it and lamented so loud that the younger of the king's children died of fright on the spot. But the trunk of the tree she wrapped in fine linen, and poured ointment on it, and gave it to the king and queen, and the wood stands in a temple of Isis and is worshipped by the people of Byblus to this day. And Isis put the coffer in a boat and took the eldest of the king's children with her and sailed away. As soon as they were alone, she opened the chest, and laying her face on the face of her brother she kissed him and wept. But the child came behind her softly and saw what she was about, and she turned and looked at him in anger, and the child could not bear her look and died; but some say that it was not so, but that he fell into the sea and was drowned. It is he whom the Egyptians sing of at their banquets under the name of Maneros.

But Isis put the coffer by and went to see her son Horus at the city of Buto, and Set found the coffer as he was hunting a boar one night by the light of a full moon. And he knew the body, and rent it into fourteen pieces, and scattered them abroad. But Isis sailed up and down the marshes in a shallop made of papyrus, looking for the pieces; and that is why when people sail in shallops made of papyrus, the crocodiles do not hurt them, for they fear or respect the goddess. And that is the reason, too, why there are many graves of Osiris in Egypt, for she buried each limb as she found it. But others will have it that she buried an image of him in every city, pretending it was his body, in order that Osiris might be worshipped in many places, and that if Set searched for the real grave he might not be able to find it. However, the genital member of Osiris had been eaten by the fishes, so Isis made an image of it instead, and the image is used by the Egyptians at their festivals to this day. "Isis," writes the historian Diodorus Siculus, "recovered all the parts of the body except the genitals; and because she wished that her husband's grave should be unknown and honoured by all who dwell in the land of Egypt, she resorted to the following device. She moulded human images out of wax and spices, corresponding to the stature of Osiris, round each one of the parts of his body. Then she called in the priests according to their families and took an oath of them all that they would reveal to no man the trust she was about to repose in them. So to each of them privately she said that to them alone she entrusted the burial of the body, and reminding them of the benefits they had received she exhorted them to bury the body in their own land and to honour Osiris as a god. She also besought them to dedicate one of the animals of their country, whichever they chose, and to honour it in life as they had formerly honoured Osiris, and when it died to grant it obsequies like his. And because she would encourage the priests in their own interest to bestow the aforesaid honours, she gave them a third part of the land to be used by them in the service and worship of the gods. Accordingly it is said that the priests, mindful of the benefits of Osiris, desirous of gratifying the queen, and moved by the prospect of gain, carried out all the injunctions of Isis. Wherefore to this day each of the priests imagines that Osiris is buried in his country, and they honour the beasts that were consecrated in the beginning, and when the animals die the priests renew at their burial the mourning for Osiris. But the sacred bulls, the one called Apis and the other Mnevis, were dedicated to Osiris, and it was ordained that they should be worshipped as gods in common by all the Egyptians; since these animals above all others had helped the discoverers of corn in sowing the seed and procuring the universal benefits of agriculture."

Such is the myth or legend of Osiris, as told by Greek writers and eked out by more or less fragmentary notices or allusions in native Egyptian literature. A long inscription in the temple at Denderah has preserved a list of the god's graves, and other texts mention the parts of his body which were treasured as holy relics in each of the sanctuaries. Thus his heart was at Athribis, his backbone at Busiris, his neck at Letopolis, and his head at Memphis. As often happens in such cases, some of his divine limbs were miraculously multiplied. His head, for example, was at Abydos as well as at Memphis, and his legs, which were remarkably numerous, would have sufficed for several ordinary mortals.

According to native Egyptian accounts, which supplement that of Plutarch, when Isis had found the corpse of her husband Osiris, she and her sister Nephthys sat down beside it and uttered a lament which in after ages became the type of all Egyptian lamentations for the dead. "Come to thy house," they wailed, "Come to thy house. O god On! come to thy house, thou who hast no foes. O fair youth, come to thy house, that thou mayest see me. I am thy sister, whom thou lovest; thou shalt not part from me. O fair boy, come to thy house. . . . I see thee not, yet doth my heart yearn after thee and mine eyes desire thee. Come to her who loves thee, who loves thee, Unnefer, thou blessed one! Come to thy sister, come to thy wife, to thy wife, thou whose heart stands still. Come to thy housewife. I am thy sister by the same mother, thou shalt not be far from me. Gods and men have turned their faces towards thee and weep for thee together. . . . I call after thee and weep, so that my cry is heard to heaven, but thou hearest not my voice; yet am I thy sister, whom thou didst love on earth; thou didst love none but me, my brother! my brother!" This lament for the fair youth cut off in his prime reminds us of the laments for Adonis. The title of Unnefer or "the Good Being" bestowed on him marks the beneficence which tradition universally ascribed to Osiris; it was at once his commonest title and one of his names as king.

The lamentations of the two sad sisters were not in vain. In pity for her sorrow the sun-god Ra sent down from heaven the jackal-headed god Anubis, who, with the aid of Isis and Nephthys, of Thoth and Horus, pieced together the broken body of the murdered god, swathed it in linen bandages, and observed all the other rites which the Egyptians were wont to perform over the bodies of the departed. Then Isis fanned the cold clay with her wings: Osiris revived, and thenceforth reigned as king over the dead in the other world. There he bore the titles of Lord of the Underworld, Lord of Eternity, Ruler of the Dead. There, too, in the great Hall of the Two Truths, assisted by forty-two assessors, one from each of the principal districts of Egypt, he presided as judge at the trial of the souls of the departed, who made their solemn confession before him, and, their heart having been weighed in the balance of justice, received the reward of virtue in a life eternal or the appropriate punishment of their sins.

In the resurrection of Osiris the Egyptians saw the pledge of a life everlasting for themselves beyond the grave. They believed that every man would live eternal in the other world if only his surviving friends did for his body what the gods had done for the body of Osiris. Hence the ceremonies observed by the Egyptians over the human dead were an exact copy of those which Anubis, Horus, and the rest had performed over the dead god. "At every burial there was enacted a representation of the divine mystery which had been performed of old over Osiris, when his son, his sisters, his friends were gathered round his mangled remains and succeeded by their spells and manipulations in converting his broken body into the first mummy, which they afterwards reanimated and furnished with the means of entering on a new individual life beyond the grave. The mummy of the deceased was Osiris; the professional female mourners were his two sisters Isis and Nephthys; Anubis, Horus, all the gods of the Osirian legend gathered about the corpse."

Thus every dead Egyptian was identified with Osiris and bore his name. From the Middle Kingdom onwards it was the regular practice to address the deceased as "Osiris So-and-So," as if he were the god himself, and to add the standing epithet "true of speech," because true speech was characteristic of Osiris. The thousands of inscribed and pictured tombs that have been opened in the valley of the Nile prove that the mystery of the resurrection was performed for the benefit of every dead Egyptian; as Osiris died and rose again from the dead, so all men hoped to arise like him from dead to life eternal. In an Egyptian text it is said of the departed that "as surely as Osiris lives, so shall he live also; as surely as Osiris did not die, so shall he not die; as surely as Osiris is not annihilated, so shall he too not be annihilated." The dead man, conceived to be lying, like Osiris, with mangled body, was comforted by being told that the heavenly goddess Nut, the mother of Osiris, was coming to gather up his poor scattered limbs and mould them with her own hands into a form immortal and divine. "She gives thee thy head, she brings thee thy bones, she sets thy limbs together and puts thy heart in thy body." Thus the resurrection of the dead was conceived, like that of Osiris, not merely as spiritual but also as bodily. "They possess their heart, they possess their senses, they possess their mouth, they possess their feet, they possess their arms, they possess all their limbs."

Babylonian–Greco-Roman: Adonis and Aphrodite

Adonis was a Greco-Roman version of a Semitic god of Mesopotamia who at various times was identified with Osiris and Tammuz as well as with Jesus. Adonis' Semitic name, Adonai, means "the Lord." In some versions of his story he was born of a virgin (Myrrha), and some versions say that at his death he was castrated. After his death the red anemone sprang in symbolic resurrection from the earth. Early Christian writers—Origen, Jerome, and others—report joyous celebrations of resurrection on the third day after his birth. The version here is the most famous and literary one; it is taken from *The Metamorphoses* of Ovid. It stresses the Aphrodite (Venus) relationship, which itself seems to point back to an earlier emphasis on the return of the sacrificed savior and god-king to the Great Mother, his castration or wound in the loins being a literal reaping of the seed-bearing crop.

•

The infant that Myrrha had conceived in sin had grown inside the tree,* and was now seeking some way by which it might leave its mother, and thrust itself into the outer world. Within the tree trunk, Myrrha's womb was swollen and distended with the burden she carried, but her agony found no expression in words, nor could she, in her labour, summon Lucina by her cries. Yet she had all the appearance of a woman struggling to be delivered: the tree bent over, uttered constant moans, and was moist with falling tears. Gentle Lucina stood by the suffering branches and, laying her hand upon them, spoke the words of deliverance. At this, the trunk split open and, through the fissure in the bark, gave up its living burden. The wailing cry of a baby boy was heard. The nymphs laid him on the soft turf, and washed him in his mother's tears. Even Jealousy personified would have praised his beauty, for he looked like one of the naked Cupids painted in pictures, differing from them only in his attire: for to make them alike, the one would have to be given a light quiver, or the others would have to relinquish theirs.

The fleeting years glide on unnoticed, and nothing is swifter than time. This baby, offspring of his sister and his grandfather, so recently enclosed in the tree-trunk, born but yesterday, soon grew into a lovely child, soon became a young man, and then a man full-grown, surpassing

---

*Myrrha had been turned into a tree by the gods. She had conceived Adonis by her father.

Ovid, *The Metamorphoses*, trans. Mary M. Innes (London, 1955), pp. 238–39, 244–45.

even himself in handsomeness. He now became the darling of Venus, and
avenged the passion which had assailed his mother. For, while her son
Cupid was kissing Venus, with his quiver on his shoulders, he unwittingly
grazed her breast with an arrow which was projecting from the sheath.
The injured goddess pushed her son away. The wound was deeper than it
seemed, deeper than she herself at first realized. The goddess of Cythera,
captivated by the beauty of a mortal, cared no more for her sea shores,
ceased to visit seagirt Paphos, Cnidos rich in fishes, or Amathis with its
valuable ores. She even stayed away from heaven, preferring Adonis to the
sky.

She used to hold him in her arms, and became his constant companion. Though she had always before been accustomed to idle in the shade,
devoting all her attention to enhancing her beauty, now she roamed the
ridges and woods and tree-clad rocks, her garments caught up as high as
her knees, just as Diana wears hers, shouting encouragement to the dogs,
and pursuing such animals as it is safe to hunt—fleeing hares, deer, or stags
with lofty antlers. She kept clear of sturdy wild boars, and did not not risk
any encounter with thieving wolves, bears armed with claws, or lions that
glut themselves on slain cattle. Hoping that her warnings might be of some
avail, she advised Adonis, too, to beware of such creatures. "Show yourself
bold when your quarry flees," she told him. "It is not safe to be daring
when the animal you are hunting is daring too. Do not be rash, dear boy,
when I may be the one to suffer. Do not provoke wild animals which nature has armed against you, lest your desire for glory should cost me dear.
Your youth and beauty, and the charms which make Venus love you, have
no effect upon lions or bristling boars, or on the eyes and minds of other
wild beasts. The fierce boar deals a blow with his fangs, as swift as a lightning flash, and tawny lions, filled with boundless rage, are ever ready to
attack—I hate their whole tribe! . . .

. . . Now they haunt the woods, the forest is their only home.
Changed into lions, they strike terror into the hearts of others, but have
themselves been tamed by Cybele, and their mouths champ the harness of
her car. You must avoid them, my dear one, and with them every kind of
wild beast which does not turn tail and flee, but faces up to battle. Otherwise your valour may be the ruin of us both.

With these words, she yoked her swans, and drove off through the
air. But, though she had warned Adonis, his natural courage ran contrary
to her advice. By chance, his hounds came upon a well-marked trail and,
following the scent, roused a wild boar from its lair. As it was about to
emerge from the woods, the young grandson of Cinyras pierced its side
with a slanting blow. Immediately the fierce boar dislodged the blood-
stained spear, with the help of its crooked snout, and then pursued the
panic-stricken huntsman, as he was making for safety. It sank its teeth

deep in his groin, bringing him down, mortally wounded, on the yellow sand.

Venus, as she drove through the air in her light chariot drawn by winged swans, had not yet reached Cyprus. She recognized the groans of the dying Adonis from afar, and turned her white birds in his direction. As she looked down from on high she saw him, lying lifeless, his limbs still writhing in his own blood. Leaping down from her car, she tore at her bosom and at her hair, beat her breast with hands never meant for such a use, and reproached the fates. "But still," she cried, "you will not have everything under your absolute sway! There will be an everlasting token of my grief, Adonis. Every year, the scene of your death will be staged anew, and lamented with the wailing cries, in imitation of those cries of mine. But your blood will be changed into a flower. Persephone was once allowed to change a woman's body into fragrant mint, and shall I be grudged the right to transform Cinyras' brave grandson?"

With these words, she sprinkled Adonis' blood with sweet-smelling nectar and, at the touch of the liquid, the blood swelled up, just as clear bubbles rise in yellow mud. Within an hour, a flower sprang up, the colour of blood, and in appearance like that of the pomegranate, the fruit which conceals its seeds under a leathery skin. But the enjoyment of this flower is of brief duration: for it is so fragile, its petals so lightly attached, that it quickly falls, shaken from its stem by those same winds that give it its name, anemone.

Phrygian: Attis

Attis, too, is often identified with Jesus, because his death and renewal ritual includes a "Day of Blood" and a "Day of Joy," both in the early spring. Attis is hanged on a tree, and as in so many dying-god myths, the loss of genitals is an important theme, as is the death-union with the Great Goddess, represented in Phrygian myth by Cybele. (On this topic see Sir James Frazer, *The New Golden Bough*, ed. Theodor H. Gaster [New York, 1959], pp. 369–73.) An interesting aspect of this myth is the fact that Cybele is also—in her form as the virgin Nana—the mother of Attis. The son-lover theme underlies many of the dying god stories. The objective observer might well find it in the Jesus story. The Virgin Mary is made pregnant by God (the Holy Spirit), is the "mother of God" (Jesus, the Son), and is the "queen of heaven" (God the father is king of heaven).

A literary remnant of the son-lover motif occurs in the story of Oedipus and Jocasta, and, of course, the motif is a central element in the modern psychological "myth" propounded by Freud.

Greek: Dionysos

The complicated myth of Dionysos is retold here by Sir James Frazer. In
this prototype of the Christ figure we find many of the elements already
outlined in connection with the myth of the dying god in general.

•

Like the other gods of vegetation whom we have considered, Dionysus was
believed to have died a violent death, but to have been brought to life
again; and his sufferings, death, and resurrection were enacted in his sacred rites. His tragic story is thus told by the poet Nonnus. Zeus in the
form of a serpent visited Persephone, and she bore him Zagreus, that is,
Dionysus, a horned infant. Scarcely was he born, when the babe mounted
the throne of his father Zeus and mimicked the great god by brandishing
the lightning in his tiny hand. But he did not occupy the throne long; for
the treacherous Titans, their faces whitened with chalk, attacked him with
knives while he was looking at himself in a mirror. For a time he evaded
their assaults by turning himself into various shapes, assuming the likeness
successively of Zeus and Cronus [Kronos], of a young man, of a lion, a
horse, and a serpent. Finally, in the form of a bull, he was cut to pieces
by the murderous knives of his enemies. His Cretan myth, as related by
Firmicus Maternus, ran thus. He was said to have been the bastard son of
Jupiter, a Cretan king. Going abroad, Jupiter transferred the throne and
sceptre to the youthful Dionysus, but, knowing that his wife Juno cherished a jealous dislike of the child, he entrusted Dionysus to the care of
guards upon whose fidelity he believed he could rely. Juno, however,
bribed the guards, and amusing the child with rattles and a cunningly-
wrought looking-glass lured him into an ambush, where her satellites, the
Titans, rushed upon him, cut him limb from limb, boiled his body with
various herbs, and ate it. But his sister Minerva, who had shared in the
deed, kept his heart and gave it to Jupiter on his return, revealing to him
the whole history of the crime. In his rage, Jupiter put the Titans to death
by torture, and, to soothe his grief for the loss of his son, made an image
in which he enclosed the child's heart, and then built a temple in his honour. In this version a Euhemeristic turn has been given to the myth by
representing Jupiter and Juno (Zeus and Hera) as a king and queen of
Crete. The guards referred to are the mythical Curetes who danced a war-
dance round the infant Dionysus, as they are said to have done round the
infant Zeus. Very noteworthy is the legend, recorded both by Nonnus and
Firmicus, that in his infancy Dionysus occupied for a short time the throne
of his father Zeus. So Proclus tells us that "Dionysus was the last king of
the gods appointed by Zeus. For his father set him on the kingly throne,
and placed in his hand the sceptre, and made him king of all the gods of

Sir James Frazer, *The New Golden Bough*, ed. Theodor H. Gaster (New York, 1959), pp. 418–20.

the world." Such traditions point to a custom of temporarily investing the king's son with the royal dignity as a preliminary to sacrificing him instead of his father. Pomegranates were supposed to have sprung from the blood of Dionysus, as anemones from the blood of Adonis and violets from the blood of Attis: hence women refrain from eating seeds of pomegranates at the festival of the Thesmophoria. According to some, the severed limbs of Dionysus were pieced together, at the command of Zeus, by Apollo, who buried them on Parnassus. The grave of Dionysus was shewn in the Delphic temple beside a golden statue of Apollo. However, according to another account, the grave of Dionysus was at Thebes, where he is said to have been torn in pieces. Thus far the resurrection of the slain god is not mentioned, but in other versions of the myth it is variously related. According to one version, which represented Dionysus as a son of Zeus and Demeter, his mother pieced together his mangled limbs and made him young again. In others it is simply said that shortly after his burial he rose from the dead and ascended up to heaven; or that Zeus raised him up as he lay mortally wounded; or that Zeus swallowed the heart of Dionysus and then begat him afresh by Semele, who in the common legend figures as mother of Dionysus. Or, again, the heart was pounded up and given in a potion to Semele, who thereby conceived him.

Aztec-Toltec:Quetzalcoatl

Quetzalcoatl, the helper god and savior-King of the Aztecs, was conceived by a virgin and was, like Osiris, a god of corn. He was known as the Feathered Serpent, combining attributes of a sky god and an earth god, of eternity and of the death-defined world. As he is often considered a hero rather than a god, his story is told later in this book, in the section on hero myths.

Christian: Jesus

The familiar story of Christ's Passion has been the most popular subject of Western painting, music, sculpture, and even architecture, during the past 2,000 years. It is a full blossoming (with, for some, a historical aspect) of the dying god myth. However, it is a version of the myth that reflects the particular values of the early Christians. The "pagan" sexual elements are gone, the planted seed and the resurrection of the savior king-god results for his followers not so much in the vegetation of spring (though this is a constant Easter theme in ritual if not in myth) as in a spiritual renewal or possibility of returning through Christ—the "New Adam"—to the original state of Adam and Eve before the Fall. Ultimately, immortality is celebrated in this story and in its ritual as it is in the other dying-god tales and ceremonies.

The following is the evangelist Matthew's version of the Passion, in the King James translation. The dressing up of Jesus as a mock king of the Jews suggests the scapegoat element so important in the theology of Jesus in particular and in the tradition of the dying god in general. It has been suggested by Frazer and others that an ancient tradition of sacrificing a true king in the hope of renewing a tribe was eventually replaced by the tradition of sacrificing a criminal or ordinary citizen who dresses up as a sacrificial "king for a day."

•

Chapter 27

When the morning was come, all the chief priests and elders of the people took counsel against Jesus to put him to death:

2 And when they had bound him, they led him away, and delivered him to Pontius Pilate the governor.

3 Then Judas, which had betrayed him, when he saw that he was condemned, repented himself, and brought again the thirty pieces of silver to the chief priests and elders,

4 Saying, I have sinned in that I have betrayed the innocent blood. And they said, What is that to us? see thou to that.

5 And he cast down the pieces of silver in the temple, and departed, and went and hanged himself.

6 And the chief priests took the silver pieces, and said, It is not lawful for to put them into the treasury, because it is the price of blood.

7 And they took counsel, and bought with them the potter's field, to bury strangers in.

8 Wherefore that field was called, The field of blood, unto this day.

9 Then was fulfilled that which was spoken by Jeremy the prophet, saying, And they took the thirty pieces of silver, the price of him that was valued, whom they of the children of Israel did value;

10 And gave them for the potter's field, as the Lord appointed me.

11 And Jesus stood before the governor: and the governor asked him, saying, Art thou the King of the Jews? And Jesus said unto him, Thou sayest.

12 And when he was accused of the chief priests and elders, he answered nothing.

13 Then said Pilate unto him, Hearest thou not how many things they witness against thee?

14 And he answered him to never a word; insomuch that the governor marvelled greatly.

Matthew 27–28:8.

15 Now at that feast the governor was wont to release unto the people a prisoner, whom they would.

16 And they had then a notable prisoner, called Barabbas.

17 Therefore when they were gathered together, Pilate said unto them, Whom will ye that I release unto you? Barabbas, or Jesus which is called Christ?

18 For he knew that for envy they had delivered him.

19 When he was set down on the judgment seat, his wife sent unto him, saying, Have thou nothing to do with that just man: for I have suffered many things this day in a dream because of him.

20 But the chief priests and elders persuaded the multitude that they should ask Barabbas, and destroy Jesus.

21 The governor answered and said unto them, Whether of the twain will ye that I release unto you? They said, Barabbas.

22 Pilate saith unto them, What shall I do then with Jesus which is called Christ? They all say unto him, Let him be crucified.

23 And the governor said, Why, what evil hath he done? But they cried out the more, saying, Let him be crucified.

24 When Pilate saw that he could prevail nothing, but that rather a tumult was made, he took water, and washed his hands before the multitude, saying, I am innocent of the blood of this just person: see ye to it.

25 Then answered all the people, and said, His blood be on us, and on our children.

26 Then released he Barabbas unto them: and when he had scourged Jesus, he delivered him to be crucified.

27 Then the soldiers of the governor took Jesus into the common hall, and gathered unto him the whole band of soldiers.

28 And they stripped him, and put on him a scarlet robe.

29 And when they had platted a crown of thorns, they put it upon his head, and a reed in his right hand: and they bowed the knee before him, and mocked him, saying, Hail, King of the Jews!

30 And they spit upon him, and took the reed, and smote him on the head.

31 And after that they had mocked him, they took the robe off from him, and put his own raiment on him, and led him away to crucify him.

32 And as they came out, they found a man of Cȳ-rē'-nē, Simon by name: him they compelled to bear his cross.

33 And when they were come unto a place called Golgotha, that is to say, a place of a skull,

34 They gave him vinegar to drink mingled with gall: and when he has tasted thereof, he would not drink.

35 And they crucified him, and parted his garments, casting lots: that it might be fulfilled which was spoken by the prophet, They parted my garments among them, and upon my vesture did they cast lots.

36 And sitting down they watched him there;

37 And set up over his head his accusation written, THIS IS JESUS THE KING OF THE JEWS.

38 Then were there two thieves crucified with him, one on the right hand, and another on the left.

39 And they that passed by reviled him, wagging their heads,

40 And saying, Thou that destroyest the temple, and buildest it in three days, save thyself. If thou be the Son of God, come down from the cross.

41 Likewise also the chief priests mocking him, with the scribes and elders, said,

42 He saved others; himself he cannot save. If he be the King of Israel, let him now come down from the cross, and we will believe him.

43 He trusted in God; let him deliver him now, if he will have him: for he said, I am the Son of God.

44 The thieves also, which were crucified with him, cast the same in his teeth.

45 Now from the sixth hour there was darkness over all the land unto the ninth hour.

46 And about the ninth hour Jesus cried with a loud voice, saying, Eli, Eli, lä'-mä să-băch'-thă-nī? that is to say, My God, my God, why hast thou forsaken me?

47 Some of them that stood there, when they heard that, said, This man calleth for Ē-lī'-ăs.

48 And straightway one of them ran, and took a sponge, and filled it with vinegar, and put it on a reed, and gave him to drink.

49 The rest said, Let be, let us see whether Ē-lī'-ăs will come to save him.

50 Jesus, when he had cried again with a loud voice, yielded up the ghost.

51 And, behold, the veil of the temple was rent in twain from the top to the bottom; and the earth did quake, and the rocks rent;

52 And the graves were opened; and many bodies of the saints which slept arose,

53 And came out of the graves after his resurrection, and went into the holy city, and appeared unto many.

54 Now when the centurion, and they that were with him, watching Jesus, saw the earthquake, and those things that were done, they feared greatly, saying, Truly this was the Son of God.

55 And many women were there beholding afar off, which followed Jesus from Galilee, ministering unto him:

56 Among which was Mary Magdalene, and Mary the mother of James and Joses, and the mother of Zebedee's children.

57 When the even was come, there came a rich man of Ăr-im-ă-thāē'-ă, named Joseph, who also himself was Jesus' disciple:

58 He went to Pilate, and begged the body of Jesus. Then Pilate commanded the body to be delivered.

59 And when Joseph had taken the body, he wrapped it in a clean linen cloth,

60 And laid it in his own new tomb, which he had hewn out in the rock: and he rolled a great stone to the door of the sepulchre, and departed.

61 And there was Mary Magdalene, and the other Mary, sitting over against the sepulchre.

62 Now the next day, that followed the day of the preparation, the chief priests and Pharisees came together unto Pilate,

63 Saying, Sir, we remember that that deceiver said, while he was yet alive, After three days I will rise again.

64 Command therefore that the sepulchre be made sure until the third day, lest his disciples come by night, and steal him away, and say unto the people, He is risen from the dead: so the last error shall be worse than the first.

65 Pilate said unto them, Ye have a watch: go your way, make it as sure as ye can.

66 So they went, and made the sepulchre sure, sealing the stone, and setting a watch.

Chapter 28

In the end of the sabbath, as it began to dawn toward the first day of the week, came Mary Magdalene and the other Mary to see the sepulchre.

2 And, behold, there was a great earthquake: for the angel of the Lord descended from heaven, and came and rolled back the stone from the door, and sat upon it.

3 His countenance was like lightning, and his raiment white as snow:

4 And for fear of him the keepers did shake, and became as dead men.

5 And the angel answered and said unto the women, Fear not ye: for I know that ye seek Jesus, which was crucified.

6 He is not here: for he is risen, as he said. Come, see the place where the Lord lay.

7 And go quickly, and tell his disciples that he is risen from the dead; and, behold, he goest before you into Galilee; there shall ye see him: lo, I have told you.

8 And they departed quickly from the sepulchre with fear and great joy; and did run to bring his disciples word.

Norse (Icelandic): Odin

In Norse mythology as recorded originally in the ancient *Elder Edda* and as retold by Snorri Sturleson in the *Prose Edda* (c. 1220 C.E.), we find two stories that at least suggest the dying-god motif. One concerns the great god Odin's hanging on a tree, and the other concerns the death of the god Baldr. Baldr, like Attis, Adonis, and Dionysos, is known as the "beautiful god." After his death he travels to the underworld, the womb of Mother Hel. He would return to Earth at the time of the great apocalypse, Ragnarök (for Baldr's story, see this book's section on the pantheonic myths). The following selection recounts the story of Odin, found in *Havamal*, a poem of the *Elder Edda*. Odin's "death" upon the tree is really more of a shamanic ritual descent to discover magic runes than an actual death. But the tree, the sword piercing, and the sense of gaining knowledge through suffering recall the Christian story, for example, and suggest the Dying God motif.

•

I know that I hung
on the windswept tree
for nine full nights,
wounded with a spear
and given to Odin,
myself to myself;
on that tree
of which none know
from what roots it rises.

They did not comfort me with bread,
and not with the drinking horn;
I peered downward,
I grasped the "runes,"
screeching I grasped them;
I fell back from there.

I learned nine mighty songs
from the famous son
of Bolthor, father of Bestla,
and I got a drink
of the precious mead,
I was sprinkled with Odrerir.

Havamal, in E. O. G. Turville-Petre, *Myth and Religion of the North: The Religion of Ancient Scandinavia* (New York, 1964), p. 42.

> Then I began to be fruitful
> and to be fertile,
> to grow and to prosper;
> one word sought
> another word from me;
> one deed sought
> another deed from me.

The Trickster

One of the most popular archetypal motifs in myth and literature is that of the trickster. Whether he be Hermes in Greece, Krishna in India, Loki in Northern Europe, Coyote or Raven among the Native Americans, or related popular figures such as Aesop's and La Fontaine's fable animals, Davy Crockett on the American frontier, Brer Rabbit in the American South, Inspector Clouseau in the film, "The Pink Panther," or any number of animated-cartoon characters, the trickster is at once wise and foolish, the perpetrator of tricks and the butt of his own jokes. Always male, he is promiscuous and amoral; he is outrageous in his actions; he emphasizes the "lower" bodily functions; he often takes animal form. Yet the trickster is profoundly inventive, creative by nature, and in some ways a helper to humanity. Jung sees in him a hint of the later savior figure (*Four Archetypes*, p. 151).

The trickster, then, speaks to our animal nature, to our physical as opposed to our spiritual side, and reflects what Jung calls "an earlier, rudimentary stage of consciousness" (*Four Archetypes*, p. 141). He has the charming if sometimes dangerous appetites of the child, as yet untamed by the larger social conscience. And, of course, he is almost always funny.

Greek: Hermes

Hermes, who is best known as the messenger of the gods, was also a trickster. In this story, based on the *Homeric Hymns* and several other ancient sources and retold here by Robert Graves, Hermes has the trickster qualities of deceitfulness, trickery, childishness, amorality, humor, extreme inventiveness, and great charm. He also has the proper sexual credentials. Graves suggests that Hermes evolved from an earlier fertility cult that represented its god by means of stone phalli (*The Greek Myths*, vol. 1, p. 66). As has been noted, the *herm*, a marking stone with a human head and an erect phallus, was in common use in classical Greece.

•

When Hermes was born on Mount Cyllene his mother Maia laid him in swaddling bands on a winnowing fan, but he grew with astonishing quickness into a little boy, and as soon as her back was turned, slipped off and went looking for adventure. Arrived at Pieria, where Apollo was tending a fine herd of cows, he decided to steal them. But, fearing to be betrayed by their tracks, he quickly made a number of shoes from the bark of a fallen oak and tied them with plaited grass to the feet of the cows, which he then drove off by night along the road. Apollo discovered the loss, but Hermes's trick deceived him, and though he went as far as Pylus in his westward search, and to Onchestus in his eastern, he was forced, in the end, to offer a reward for the apprehension of the thief. Silenus and his satyrs, greedy of reward, spread out in different directions to track him down but, for a long while, without success. At last, as a party of them passed through Arcadia, they heard the muffled sound of music such as they had never heard before, and the nymph Cyllene, from the mouth of a cave, told them that a most gifted child had recently been born there, to whom she was acting as nurse: he had constructed an ingenious musical toy from the shell of a tortoise and some cow-gut, with which he had lulled his mother to sleep.

"And from whom did he get the cow-gut?" asked the alert satyrs, noticing two hides stretched outside the cave. "Do you charge the poor child with theft?" asked Cyllene. Harsh words were exchanged.

At that moment Apollo came up, having discovered the thief's identity by observing the suspicious behaviour of a long-winged bird. Entering the cave, he awakened Maia and told her severely that Hermes must restore the stolen cows. Maia pointed to the child, still wrapped in his swaddling bands and feigning sleep. "What an absurd charge!" she cried. But Apollo had already recognized the hides. He picked up Hermes, carried him to Olympus, and there formally accused him of theft, offering the hides as evidence. Zeus, loth to believe that his own new-born son was a thief, encouraged him to plead not guilty, but Apollo would not be put off and Hermes, at last, weakened and confessed.

"Very well, come with me," he said, "and you may have your herd. I slaughtered only two, and those I cut up into twelve equal portions as a sacrifice to the twelve gods."

"*Twelve* gods?" asked Apollo. "Who is the twelfth?"

"Your servant, sir," replied Hermes modestly. "I ate no more than my share, though I was very hungry, and duly burned the rest."

Now, this was the first flesh-sacrifice ever made.

The two gods returned to Mount Cyllene, where Hermes greeted his mother and retrieved something that he had hidden underneath a sheepskin.

Robert Graves, *The Greek Myths*, vol. 1 (Baltimore, Md., 1955), pp. 63–65.

"What have you there?" asked Apollo.

In answer, Hermes showed his newly-invented tortoise-shell lyre, and played such a ravishing tune on it with the plectrum he had also invented, at the same time singing in praise of Apollo's nobility, intelligence, and generosity, that he was forgiven at once. He led the surprised and delighted Apollo to Pylus, playing all the way, and there gave him the remainder of the cattle, which he had hidden in a cave.

"A bargain!" cried Apollo. "You keep the cows, and I take the lyre."

"Agreed," said Hermes, and they shook hands on it.

While the hungry cows were grazing, Hermes cut reeds, made them into a shepherd's pipe, and played another tune. Apollo, again delighted, cried: "A bargain! If you give me that pipe, I will give you this golden staff with which I herd my cattle; in future you shall be the god of all herdsmen and shepherds."

"My pipe is worth more than your staff," replied Hermes. "But I will make the exchange, if you teach me augury too, because it seems to be a most useful art."

"I cannot do that," Apollo said, "but if you go to my old nurses, the Thriae who live on Parnassus, they will teach you how to divine from pebbles."

They again shook hands and Apollo, taking the child back to Olympus, told Zeus all that had happened. Zeus warned Hermes that henceforth he must respect the rights of property and refrain from telling downright lies; but he could not help being amused. "You seem to be a very ingenious, eloquent, and persuasive godling," he said.

"Then make me your herald, Father," Hermes answered, "and I will be responsible for the safety of all divine property, and never tell lies, though I cannot promise always to tell the whole truth."

"That would not be expected of you," said Zeus, with a smile. "But your duties would include the making of treaties, the promotion of commerce, and the maintenance of free rights of way for travellers on any road in the world." When Hermes agreed to these conditions, Zeus gave him a herald's staff with white ribbons, which everyone was ordered to respect; a round hat against the rain, and winged golden sandals which carried him about with the swiftness of wind. He was at once welcomed into the Olympian family, whom he taught the art of making fire by the rapid twirling of the fire-stick. . . .

Indian: Krishna

The lord Krishna, one of the most important of the avatars of the god Vishnu, has many trickster characteristics, as these two stories from the tenth-century *Bhagavata Purana* will demonstrate. It should be noted, however, that Krishna's trickery has a moral purpose that transcends its apparent amorality.

•

After a little while, Rāma[1] and Keśava began to play in the village, crawling on their hands and knees. They slithered about quickly, dragging their feet in the muddy pastures, delighting in the tinkling sound.[2] They would follow someone and then, suddenly bewildered and frightened, they would hasten back to their mothers. Their mothers' breasts would flow with milk out of tenderness for their own sons, whose bodies were beautifully covered with mud, and they would embrace them in their arms and give them their breasts to suck, and as they gazed at the faces with their innocent smiles and tiny teeth they would rejoice. Then the children began to play in the village at those boyish games that women love to see. They would grab hold of the tails of calves and be dragged back and forth in the pasture, and the women would look at them and forget their housework and laugh merrily. But the mothers, trying to keep the two very active and playful little boys from the horned animals, fire, animals with teeth and tusks, and knives, water, birds, and thorns, were unable to do their housework, and they were rather uneasy.

After a little while, Rāma and Kṛṣṇa stopped crawling on their hands and knees and began to walk about the pastures quickly on their feet. Then the lord Kṛṣṇa began to play with Rāma and with the village boys of their age, giving great pleasure to the village women. When the wives of the cow-herds saw the charming boyish pranks of Kṛṣṇa, they would go in a group to tell his mother, saying, "Kṛṣṇa unties the calves when it is not the proper time, and he laughs at everyone's angry shouts. He devises ways to steal and eat curds and milk and thinks food sweet only if he steals it. He distributes the food among the monkeys; if he doesn't eat the food, he breaks the pot. If he cannot find anything, he becomes angry at the house and makes the children cry before he runs away. If something is beyond his reach, he fashions some expedient by piling up pillows, mortars, and so on; or if he knows that the milk and curds have been placed in pots suspended in netting, he makes holes in the pots. When the wives of the cow-herds are busy with household duties, he will steal things in a dark room, making his own body with its masses of jewels serve as a lamp. This is the sort of impudent act which he commits; and he pees and so forth in clean houses. These are the thieving tricks that he contrives, but he behaves in the opposite way and is good when you are near." When his mother heard this report from the women who were looking at Kṛṣṇa's frightened eyes and beautiful face, she laughed and did not wish to scold him.

Wendy Doniger O'Flaherty, ed., *Hindu Myths* (London, 1975), pp. 218–21, 228–31.

One day when Rāma and the other little sons of the cow-herds were playing, they reported to his mother, Kṛṣṇa has eaten dirt." Yaśodā took Kṛṣṇa by the hand and scolded him, for his own good, and she said to him, seeing that his eyes were bewildered with fear, "Naughty boy, why have you secretly eaten dirt? These boys, your friends, and your elder brother say so." Kṛṣṇa said, "Mother, I have not eaten. They are all lying. If you think they speak the truth, look at my mouth yourself." "If that is the case, then open your mouth," she said to the lord Hari, the god of unchallenged sovereignty who had in sport taken the form of a human child, and he opened his mouth.

She then saw in his mouth the whole eternal universe, and heaven, and the regions of the sky, and the orb of the earth with its mountains, islands, and oceans; she saw the wind, and lightning, and the moon and stars, and the zodiac; and water and fire and air and space itself; she saw the vacillating senses, the mind, the elements, and the three strands of matter. She saw within the body of her son, in his gaping mouth, the whole universe in all its variety, with all the forms of life and time and nature and action and hopes, and her own village, and herself. Then she became afraid and confused, thinking, "Is this a dream or an illusion wrought by a god? Or is it a delusion of my own perception? Or is it some portent of the natural powers of this little boy, my son? I bow down to the feet of the god, whose nature cannot be imagined or grasped by mind, heart, acts, or speech; he in whom all of this universe is inherent, impossible to fathom. The god is my refuge, he through whose power of delusion there arise in me such false beliefs as 'I,' 'This is my husband,' 'This is my son,' 'I am the wife of the village chieftain and all his wealth is mine, including these cow-herds and their wives and their wealth of cattle.'"

When the cow-herd's wife had come to understand the true essence in this way, the lord spread his magic illusion in the form of maternal affection. Instantly the cow-herd's wife lost her memory of what had occurred and took her son on her lap. She was as she had been before, her heart flooded with even greater love. She considered Hari—whose greatness is extolled by the three Vedas and the Upaniṣads and the philosophies of Sāṅkhya and yoga and all the Sātvata texts—she considered him to be her son.

. . .

In the first month of winter, the girls of Nanda's village performed a certain vow to the goddess Kātyāyanī. They ate rice cooked with clarified butter; they bathed in the water of the Kālindī river at sunrise; they made an image of the goddess out of sand and worshipped it with fragrant perfumes and garlands, with offerings and incense and lamps, and with bouquets of flowers, fresh sprigs of leaves, fruits, and rice. And they prayed: "Goddess Kātyāyanī, great mistress of yoga, empress of great deluding magic, make the son of the cow-herd Nanda my husband. I bow to you."

Saying this prayer, the girls would worship her, and having set their hearts on Kṛṣṇa, the girls performed this vow for a month; they worshipped Bhadrakālī so that the son of Nanda would be their husband. Arising at dawn, calling one another by name, they would join hands and go to bathe in the Kālindī every day, singing loudly about Kṛṣṇa as they went.

One day, when they had gone to the river and taken off their clothes on the bank as usual, they were playing joyfully in the water, singing about Kṛṣṇa. The lord Kṛṣṇa, lord of all masters of yoga, came there with his friends of the same age in order to grant them the object of their rites. He took their clothes and quickly climbed a Nīpa tree, and laughing with the laughing boys he told what the joke was: "Girls, let each one of you come here and take her own clothes as she wishes. I promise you, this is no jest, for you have been exhausted by your vows. I have never before told an untruth, and these boys know this. Slender-waisted ones, come one by one or all together and take your clothes." When the cow-herd girls saw what his game was, they were overwhelmed with love, but they looked at one another in shame, and they smiled, but they did not come out. Flustered and embarrassed by Govinda's words and by his jest, they sank down up to their necks in the icy water, and, shivering, they said to him, "You should not have played such a wicked trick. We know you as our beloved, son of the cow-herd Nanda, the pride of the village. Give us our clothes, for we are trembling. O darkly handsome one, we are your slaves and will do as you command, but you know *dharma:* give us our clothes or we will tell your father, the chieftain."[3]

The lord said to them, "If you are my slaves and will do as I command, then come here and take back your clothes, O brightly smiling ones." Then all the girls, shivering and smarting with cold, came out of the water, covering their crotches with their hands. The lord was pleased and gratified by their chaste actions, and he looked at them and placed their clothes on his shoulder and smiled and said, "Since you swam in the water without clothes while you were under a vow, this was an insult to the divinity.[4] Therefore you must fold your hands and place them on your heads and bow low in expiation of your sin, and then you may take your clothes." When the village girls heard what the infallible one said, they thought that bathing naked had been a violation of their vows, and they bowed down to Kṛṣṇa, the very embodiment of all their rituals, who had thus fulfilled their desires and wiped out their disgrace and sin. Then the lord, the son of Devakī, gave their clothes to them, for he felt pity when he saw them bowed down in this way and he was satisfied with them.

Though they were greatly deceived and robbed of their modesty, though they were mocked and treated like toys and stripped of their clothes, yet they held no grudge against him, for they were happy to be together with their beloved. Rejoicing in the closeness of their lover, they put on their clothes; their bashful glances, in the thrall of their hearts, did not move from him. Knowing that the girls had taken a vow because they desired to touch his feet, the lord with a rope around his waist said to the girls, "Good ladies, I know that your desire is to worship me. I rejoice in this vow, which deserves to be fulfilled. The desire of those whose hearts have been placed in me does not give rise to further desire, just as seed corn that has been boiled or fried does not give rise to seed. You have achieved your aim. Now, girls, go back to the village and you will enjoy your nights with me, for it was for this that you fine ladies undertook your vow and worship." When the girls heard this from Kṛṣṇa, they had obtained what they desired; and, meditating upon his lotus feet, they forced themselves to go away from him to the village.

Notes

1. Rāma in the *Bhāgavata Purāna* stories of Kṛṣṇa always refers to Balarāma, Samkarsana, the brother of Kṛṣṇa, and has nothing to do with the Rāma of the *Rāmāyana*.
2. The commentator says that this is the sound of their own anklets and bangles.
3. *dharma:* social order, morality, social duty and law.
4. Because they had exposed their naked bodies to Varuna, god of the waters.

Shoshoni: Old Man Coyote

In this Shoshoni Indian tale, Old Man Coyote behaves according to trickster form.

•

Old Man Coyote was sitting out on a hillside, resting. He was just too tired to go anywhere else. He looked at himself. His skin was patchy and wrinkled, and his claws were worn down to the bone, and he could feel that there were almost no teeth left in his mouth.

"What am I going to do with myself?" Old Man wondered. "I can't hunt anymore, because I get short of breath when I run. If I did catch something I couldn't eat it, because I can't chew. What's going to happen to me? I used to have grandchildren I could depend on, but they've all run away and started families of their own."

He looked out across the prairies, and there stood a young, strong buffalo bull, with the sun shining on him and his head in the air, all proud and strong.

Alice Marriott and Carol K. Rachlin, *Plains Indian Mythology* (New York, 1975), pp. 64–66.

"My," Old Man thought, "I used to be just like that; I wish I could be again. Maybe he can help me."

He got up and hobbled down the hillside, and the buffalo just stood and watched, because he knew Old Man couldn't hurt him if he wanted to.

"What do you want?" the buffalo asked, when Old Man got pretty close to him.

"Huh? What you say?" Old Man Coyote said, putting his paw behind his ear so he could hear better.

"I said, what do you want?" the buffalo bull bellowed.

"Oh," said Old Man, "I don't want much. I just want to be young and strong again, like you. Buffaloes have all the power. They are everything for the poor Indians: food, shelter, clothes . . ."

"I know that," roared the buffalo. "Is that what you want? You want to be young and strong and beautiful?"

"Yes," answered Old Man, "and if anybody can do it for me, I know you can."

"I can do it," the buffalo told him, "but remember. If I do it, I am not giving you my power. You will look like a young strong buffalo, but you will still be Old Man Coyote inside. Don't ever forget that."

"I won't," Old Man promised.

"Then sit down there on the side of the mountain, and close your eyes," the buffalo directed. "Whatever you do, keep them closed until I tell you to open them."

"All right," said Old Man. He sat down on the south slope of the mountain and shut his eyes. The buffalo came running at him, and then he ran around Old Man. The first time Old Man kept his eyes shut tight, but the second time the buffalo stirred up so much dust, he sneezed and opened them.

"You've just about wrecked it," the buffalo complained. "I really was going to give you some power the fourth time around, but now you've spoiled things. Shut your eyes again, and I'll do what I can."

Old Man shut his eyes and put his paws over them. The buffalo ran around him again, and the fourth time he hit Old Man in the back, hard. They both tumbled down the side of the mountain, and when they got to the bottom, the buffalo said, "Now you can open your eyes."

Old Man opened them and looked at himself. He was a young, springy buffalo calf, all full of life.

"Thank you, my friend," he said to the buffalo, but the buffalo just snorted, and turned away. "I haven't got any time to play with youngsters," he said.

Well, for the next four years, Old Man really had himself a time. He was a young bull buffalo, growing up, and he felt wonderful. He ran and he wallowed in the shallow ponds, and he met a young buffalo woman, and made love to her. My, he was happy!

When the Calf-Coyote was full grown, he was running across the prairie, when he met a poor, old ragged coyote.

"Oh, help me, my friend," the old coyote said. "You have everything. Make me young and strong again, like you."

Calf-Coyote thought how sad the other one looked, and he forgot what the buffalo had told him when he became young again himself. "All right," he said. "I know how to do it. Come on to the Bear Butte with me."

So they went to the Bear Butte, very slowly, because the poor old coyote was just limping along. Sometimes Calf-Coyote got impatient and ran ahead, but the old coyote always called him back and asked for help, so he would slow down again because the other was so pitiful.

When they got to the Bear Butte, Calf-Coyote showed the other just where to sit and told him to close his eyes. And he ran around and around him, twice, raising the biggest cloud of dust he could, until the other sneezed and opened his eyes.

"Now you've spoiled it," Calf-Coyote said, "but I'll try again and see what I can do."

So he ran around him twice more, and hit him in the back. They rolled down the side of Bear Butte, and when they got to the foot, there were two old hungry, poor Coyotes. You see Old Man had forgotten that the buffalo hadn't given him any power.

So always remember, don't start anything unless you know you can finish it.

Fon (Dahomey): Legba

The Fon tribe of West Africa possesses a myth about a trickster called Legba, whose *herm*-like phallic symbol stands outside all tribal dwellings. Like most African tricksters, Legba has all the traditional components of the archetype but is most notably an articulator of the divine.

*

. . . In the beginning Legba lived on earth with God and only acted on his orders. Sometimes God told Legba to do something harmful and then people blamed Legba for it and came to hate him: They never gave him credit for his good deeds but thanked God instead. Legba got tired of this and went to ask God why he should always be blamed, since he was only doing the divine will. God replied that the ruler of a kingdom ought to be thanked for good things and his servants blamed for evil.

Now God had a garden in which fine yams were growing, and Legba told him that thieves were planning to plunder it. Therefore God called all

Geoffrey Parinder, *African Mythology* (London, 1967), p. 91.

men together and warned them that whoever stole his yams would be killed. During the night Legba crept into God's house and stole his sandals, put them on and went into the garden. He took away all the yams. It had rained not long before and the footprints were clearly seen. In the morning Legba reported the theft, saying that it would be easy to find the thief from the prints. All the people were called but nobody's feet fitted the prints since they were too big. Then Legba suggested that perhaps God had taken the yams in his sleep. God denied this and accused Legba of his usual mischief, but when he consented to put his foot down it matched the prints exactly. The people cried out that God had stolen from himself, but God replied that his son had tricked him. So God left the world, and told Legba to come to the sky every night to give an account of what went on below.

A variant, giving another version of the stories of God retiring to heaven, says that when God and Legba lived near the earth Legba was always being reprimanded for his mischief. He did not like this and persuaded an old woman to throw her dirty water into the sky after washing. God was annoyed at the water being constantly thrown into his face and he gradually moved away to his present distance. But Legba was left behind and that is why he has a shrine in every house and village, to report on human doings to God.

Legba is closely associated in Fon story and ritual with the oracle Fa. One myth says that Fa had sixteen eyes, the nuts of divination. He lived on a palm tree in the sky. From this height Fa could see all that went on in the world. Every morning Legba climbed the palm tree to open Fa's eyes. Fa did not wish to convey his wishes by speaking out loud, so he put one palm nut in Legba's hand if he wanted two eyes open, and two palm nuts to have one eye open. Then he looked round to see what was happening. And so today one palm nut thrown by the diviner is a sign for two marks to be made on the divining board, and two nuts make one mark.

Later God gave Fa the keys to the doors of the future, for the future is a house of sixteen doors. If men used the palm nuts correctly they opened the eyes of Fa and showed the right door of the future. Legba worked with Fa, and when there was a great war on earth which threatened to destroy everything God sent Legba to teach the method of the Fa divination so that men could consult the oracle and know the proper way of conduct.

Bibliography

For treatment of the concept of the archetype, the works of Carl Jung are indispensable. See especially his *Symbols of Transformation* (Princeton, 1967) and his *The Archetypes and the Collective Unconscious* (Princeton, N.J., 1971). For an explanation of

Jung's theories of the archetype and the collective unconscious, see Jolande Jacobi's *Complex, Archetype, Symbol in the Psychology of C. G. Jung* (Princeton, N.J., 1959). For another definition of archetype—as a model or paradigm—see the works of Mircea Eliade, especially his *Patterns in Comparative Religion* (New York, 1958) and the first chapter of his *The Myth of the Eternal Return or, Cosmos and History* (New York, 1954). For a brief overview of the subject, see the entry "Archetypes" by Beverly Moon in *The Encyclopedia of Religion* (vol. 1, pp. 379–82). Joseph Campbell's works are much influenced by Jung's theories and are among the most stimulating treatments of myth available to us. See especially his four-volume *The Masks of God* (New York, 1962–68).

Numerous works of literary criticism make use of an archetypal approach to literature. Maud Bodkin's *Archetypal Patterns in Poetry* (Oxford, 1934) is a pioneering book in the field. The most prestigious of the archetypal or "myth critics" is Northrop Frye. See his *Anatomy of Criticism* (Princeton, N.J., 1957) for his general theory of a scientific approach to literature by way of myth. His *Fables of Identity* (New York, 1963) contains theoretical essays, including one titled "The Archetypes of Literature" and several applications of the theory to specific works. Frye's *The Great Code* (New York, 1982) applies the theory to the Bible.

For treatments of the Supreme Being, see Chapter 2 of Eliade's *Patterns in Comparative Religion;* Raffaele Pettazzoni's "The Supreme Being: Phenomenological Structure and Historical Development," in *The History of Religions: Essays in Methodology,* edited by Eliade and Joseph M. Kitagawa (Chicago, 1959): and Lawrence E. Sullivan's comprehensive article, "Supreme Beings," in *The Encyclopedia of Religion* (vol. 14, pp. 166–81).

The classic work on the Great Goddess is Eric Neumann's *The Great Mother: An Analysis of the Archetype* (Princeton, N.J., 1963). Neumann's approach is Jungian, as is Joseph Campbell's treatment of the subject in *The Masks of God,* especially in volumes 1 and 2. Jung has much to say about the Great Mother archetype in *The Archetypes and the Collective Unconscious;* his comments are also collected in *Four Archetypes* (Princeton, N.J., 1970). Useful articles on the Great Goddess by Merlin Stone, Momolina Marconi, and James Preston are to be found in *The Encyclopedia of Religion* (vol. 6, pp. 35–59). Preston's "Overview" and his "Theoretical Perspectives" in that volume are written from the point of view of anthropology and are particularly valuable. Robert Graves is always provocative on the question of the Goddess. The classic work is his *The White Goddess* (New York, 1966). His theories of the feminine principle in myth also pervade his two-volume *The Greek Myths* (Baltimore, Md., 1955).

As outdated as it may be, Sir James Frazer's *The Golden Bough* (12 vols., London, 1907–15)—especially volume 4, "The Dying and Reviving Gods," in which he has much to say about Attis, Osiris, Adonis, and the Mother Goddess—remains one of the great anthropological treatments of myth, particularly the myth of the dying god. Jung's essay on rebirth in *The Archetypes and the Collective Unconscious* and in *Four Archetypes* is also useful. See also Chapters 8 and 9 of Eliade's *Patterns in Comparative Religion.* For a somewhat skeptical view of the dying-god archetype, see Jonathan Z. Smith's entry under "Dying and Rising Gods" in *The Encyclopedia of Religion* (vol. 4, pp. 521–27).

The classic archetypal consideration of the trickster is Paul Radin's *The Trickster: A Study in American Indian Mythology* (New York, 1956). Jung's comments on the subject appear in both *The Archetypes and the Collective Unconscious* and *Four Archetypes*. For further bibliographical information on the trickster and for a useful survey of the subject, see Lawrence E. Sullivan's overview and consideration by others of particular cultural manifestations of the archetype in *The Encyclopedia of Religion* (vol. 15, pp. 45–53). See also the trickster issue of *Parabola* (vol. 4, no. 1, Feb. 1979).

GODS, GODDESSES, AND LESSER SPIRITS

The stories included in this section are primarily of Greek origin and are relatively familiar to us because they are so frequently alluded to by our writers and other artists. Also included, however, is a sampling of less familiar myths of great importance to other cultures. Many of the stories in this section have religious significance, and many can be read in the light of the archetypal categories treated earlier. Some of them appear to be intended primarily for entertainment. All of them are part of the general vocabulary of the cultures from which they come, and all of them transcend these cultures as masks of the universal dream— part wish fulfillment, part nightmare—that is world mythology.

STORIES OF GODS, GODDESSES, AND LESSER SPIRITS

Greco-Roman

Prometheus
Prometheus is the archetype of the god who helps humankind. Other versions of this myth of the helper god are those of the Aztec god Quetzalcoatl and the Hittite Telipinu. In this case, the helper god incurs the wrath of the Supreme Being himself. This is Robert Graves's retelling of a story that has fascinated writers since the days of Homer and Hesiod. Included in this story are the popular tales of Atlas and Pandora.

•

Prometheus, the creator of mankind, whom some include among the seven Titans, was the son either of the Titan Eurymedon, or of Iapetus by the nymph Clymene; and his brothers were Epimetheus, Atlas, and Menoetius.

Gigantic Atlas, eldest of the brothers, knew all the depths of the sea; he ruled over a kingdom with a precipitous coastline, larger than Africa and Asia put together. This land of Atlantis lay beyond the Pillars of Heracles, and a chain of fruit-bearing islands separated it from a farther continent, unconnected with ours. Atlas's people canalized and cultivated an enormous central plain, fed by water from the hills which ringed it completely, except for a seaward gap. They also built palaces, baths, racecourses, great harbour works, and temples; and carried war not only westwards as far as the other continent, but eastward as far as Egypt and Italy. The Egyptians say that Atlas was the son of Poseidon, whose five pairs of male twins all swore allegiance to their brother by the blood of a bull sacrificed at the pillar-top; and that at first they were extremely virtuous, bearing with fortitude the burden of their great wealth in gold and silver. But one day greed and cruelty overcame them and, with Zeus's permission, the Athenians defeated them single-handed and destroyed their power. At the same time, the gods sent a deluge which, in one day and one night, overwhelmed all Atlantis, so that the harbour works and temples were buried beneath a waste of mud and the sea became unnavigable.

Atlas and Menoetius, who escaped, then joined Cronus [Kronos] and the Titans in their unsuccessful war against the Olympian gods. Zeus killed Menoetius with a thunderbolt and sent him down to Tartarus, but spared Atlas, whom he condemned to support Heaven on his shoulders for all eternity.

Atlas was the father of the Pleiades, the Hyades, and the Hesperides; and has held up the Heavens ever since, except on one occasion, when Heracles temporarily relieved him of the task. Some say that Perseus petrified Atlas into Mount Atlas by showing him the Gorgon's head; but they forget that Perseus was reputedly a distant ancestor of Heracles.

Prometheus, being wiser than Atlas, foresaw the issue of the rebellion against Cronus, and therefore preferred to fight on Zeus's side, persuading Epimetheus to do the same. He was, indeed, the wisest of his race, and Athene, at whose birth from Zeus's head he had assisted, taught him architecture, astronomy, mathematics, navigation, medicine, metallurgy, and other useful arts, which he passed on to mankind. But Zeus, who had decided to extirpate the whole race of man, and spared them only at Prometheus's urgent plea, grew angry at their increasing powers and talents.

One day, when a dispute took place at Sicyon, as to which portions of a sacrificial bull should be offered to the gods, and which should be reserved for men, Prometheus was invited to act as arbiter. He therefore flayed and jointed a bull, and sewed its hide to form two open-mouthed bags, filling these with what he had cut up. One bag contained all the flesh,

Robert Graves, *The Greek Myths*, vol. 1 (Baltimore, Md., 1955), pp. 143–45.

but this he concealed beneath the stomach, which is the least tempting part of any animal; and the other contained the bones, hidden beneath a rich layer of fat. When he offered Zeus the choice of either, Zeus, easily deceived, chose the bag containing the bones and fat (which are still the divine portion); but punished Prometheus, who was laughing at him behind his back, by withholding fire from mankind. 'Let them eat their flesh raw!' he cried.

Prometheus at once went to Athene, with a plea for a backstairs admittance to Olympus, and this she granted. On his arrival, he lighted a torch at the fiery chariot of the Sun and presently broke from it a fragment of glowing charcoal, which he thrust into the pithy hollow of a giant fennel-stalk. Then, extinguishing his torch, he stole away undiscovered, and gave fire to mankind.

Zeus swore revenge. He ordered Hephaestus to make a clay woman, and the four Winds to breathe life into her, and all the goddesses of Olympus to adorn her. This woman, Pandora, the most beautiful ever created, Zeus sent as a gift to Epimetheus, under Hermes's escort. But Epimetheus, having been warned by his brother to accept no gift from Zeus, respectfully excused himself. Now angrier even than before, Zeus had Prometheus chained naked to a pillar in the Caucasian mountains, where a greedy vulture tore at his liver all day, year in, year out; and there was no end to the pain, because every night (during which Prometheus was exposed to cruel frost and cold) his liver grew whole again.

But Zeus, loth to confess that he had been vindictive, excused his savagery by circulating a falsehood: Athene, he said, had invited Prometheus to Olympus for a secret love affair.

Epimetheus, alarmed by his brother's fate, hastened to marry Pandora, whom Zeus had made as foolish, mischievous, and idle as she was beautiful—the first of a long line of such women. Presently she opened a box, which Prometheus had warned Epimetheus to keep closed, and in which he had been at pains to imprison all the Spites that might plague mankind: such as Old Age, Labour, Sickness, Insanity, Vice, and Passion. Out these flew in a cloud, stung Epimetheus and Pandora in every part of their bodies, and then attacked the race of mortals. Delusive Hope, however, whom Prometheus had also shut in the box, discouraged them by her lies from a general suicide.

Pandora

Hesiod was perhaps the first to tell the story we have just read of the woman who, like Eve, was said to be the source of all human misery. Angry at Prometheus for having stolen fire from the gods to give to humanity, Zeus decides to punish the human species by creating one of the earliest examples of the archetypal femme fatale. It has been suggested by Jane Harrison (*Prolegomena to the Study of Greek Religion*, pp. 284–85) that this myth is a patriarchal perversion of a story that must originally have reflected the meaning of Pandora's name, the "All-Giver," a title that also belonged to the Earth Goddess, Rhea, and suggests that Pandora was in reality an earth goddess as well. Here the myth is rewritten by Charlene Spretnak and Pandora's earlier nature restored to her.

•

Earth-Mother had given the mortals life. This puzzled them greatly. They would stare curiously at one another, then turn away to forage for food. Slowly they found that hunger has many forms.

One morning the humans followed an unusually plump bear cub to a hillside covered with bushes that hung heavy with red berries. They began to feast at once, hardly aware of the tremors beginning beneath their feet. As the quaking increased, a chasm gaped at the crest of the hill. From it arose Pandora with Her earthen *pithos*. The mortals were paralyzed with fear but the Goddess drew them into Her aura.

"I am Pandora, Giver of All Gifts." She lifted the lid from the large jar. From it She took a pomegranate, which became an apple, which became a lemon, which became a pear. "I bring you flowering trees that bear fruit, gnarled trees hung with olives and, this, the grapevine that will sustain you." She reached into the jar for a handful of seeds and sprinkled them over the hillside. "I bring you plants for hunger and illness, for weaving and dyeing. Hidden beneath My surface you will find minerals, ore, and clay of endless form." She took from the jar two flat stones. "Attend with care My plainest gift: I bring you flint."

Then Pandora turned the jar on its side, inundating the hillside with Her flowing grace. The mortals were bathed in the changing colors of Her aura. "I bring you wonder, curiosity, memory. I bring you wisdom. I bring you justice with mercy. I bring you caring and communal bonds. I bring you courage, strength, endurance. I bring you loving kindness for all beings. I bring you the seeds of peace."

Tiresias, Echo, and Narcissus

The seer Tiresias predicted that Narcissus would live to an old age "provided that he never knows himself." Ovid tells the story of the seer and then the one of this fated youth, who became the first of many narcissists to carry the law of Apollo ("Know thyself") into the realm of absurdity.

•

. . . Jupiter put aside his weighty cares; mellowed by deep draughts of nectar, he indulged in idle banter with Juno, who shared his leisure, and teased her, saying: "Of course, you women get far more pleasure out of

Charlene Spretnak, *Lost Goddesses of Early Greece* (Boston, 1981), pp. 55–57.

love than men do." Juno denied that this was true. They decided to ask
the opinion of the wise Tiresias, for he had experienced love both as a man
and as a woman.

Once, when two huge serpents were intertwining themselves in the
depths of the green wood, he had struck them with his staff; from being a
man he was miraculously changed into a woman, and had lived as such for
seven years. In the eighth year he saw the same serpents again and said:
"If there is such potent magic in the act of striking you that it changes the
striker to the opposite sex, I shall now strike you again." So, by striking
the same snakes, he was restored to his former shape, and the nature with
which he was born returned.

He, then, was chosen to give his verdict in this playful argument, and
he confirmed what Jupiter had said. Then, they say, Juno was more indignant than she had any right to be, more so than the case demanded, and
she condemned the judge to eternal blindness. It is not possible for any
god to undo the actions of another god, but in return for his loss of sight,
the omnipotent father granted Tiresias the power to know the future and
softened his punishment by conferring this honour upon him.

His fame spread throughout the Aonian cities, and when the people
consulted him he gave replies with which none could find fault.

The dark river nymph, Liriope, was the first to test this reliability
and truthfulness. She was the nymph whom Cephisus once embraced with
his curving stream, imprisoned in his waves, and forcefully ravished.
When her time was come, that nymph most fair brought forth a child with
whom one could have fallen in love even in his cradle, and she called him
Narcissus. When the prophetic seer was asked whether this boy would live
to a ripe old age, he replied: "Yes, if he does not come to know himself."
For a long time this pronouncement seemed to be nothing but empty
words: however it was justified by the outcome of events: the strange madness which afflicted the boy and the nature of his death proved its truth.

Cephisus' child had reached his sixteenth year, and could be counted
as at once boy and man. Many lads and many girls fell in love with him,
but his soft young body housed a pride so unyielding that none of those
boys or girls dared to touch him. One day, as he was driving timid deer
into his nets, he was seen by that talkative nymph who cannot stay silent
when another speaks, but yet has not learned to speak first herself. Her
name is Echo, and she always answers back.

Echo still had a body then, she was not just a voice: but although she
was always chattering, her power of speech was no different from what it
is now. All she could do was to repeat the last words of the many phrases

Ovid, *The Metamorphoses*, trans. Mary M. Innes (London, 1955), pp. 82–87.

that she heard. Juno had brought this about because often, when she could have caught the nymphs lying with her Jupiter on the mountainside, Echo, knowing well what she did, used to detain the goddess with an endless flow of talk, until the nymphs could flee. When Juno realized what was happening, she said: "I shall curtail the powers of that tongue which has tricked me: you will have only the briefest possible use of your voice." And in fact she carried out her threats. Echo still repeats the last words spoken, and gives back the sounds she has heard.

So, when she saw Narcissus wandering through the lonely country-side, Echo fell in love with him, and followed secretly in his steps. The more closely she followed, the nearer was the fire which scorched her: just as sulphur, smeared round the tops of torches, is quickly kindled when a flame is brought near it. How often she wished to make flattering overtures to him, to approach him with tender pleas! But her handicap prevented this, and would not allow her to speak first; she was ready to do what it would allow, to wait for sounds which she might re-echo with her own voice.

The boy, by chance, had wandered away from his faithful band of comrades, and he called out: "Is there anybody here?" Echo answered: "Here!" Narcissus stood still in astonishment, looking round in every di-rection, and cried at the pitch of his voice: "Come!" As he called, she called in reply. He looked behind him, and when no one appeared, cried again: "Why are you avoiding me?" But all he heard were his own words echoed back. Still he persisted, deceived by what he took to be another's voice, and said, "Come here, and let us meet!" Echo answered: "Let us meet!" Never again would she reply more willingly to any sound. To make good her words she came out of the wood and made to throw her arms round the neck she loved: but he fled from her, crying as he did so, "Away with these embraces! I would die before I would have you touch me!" Her only answer was: "I would have you touch me!" Thus scorned, she concealed herself in the woods, hiding her shamed face in the shelter of the leaves, and ever since that day, she dwells in lonely caves. Yet still her love re-mained firmly rooted in her heart, and was increased by the pain of having been rejected. Her anxious thoughts kept her awake, and made her piti-fully thin. She became wrinkled and wasted; all the freshness of her beauty withered into the air. Only her voice and her bones were left, till finally her voice alone remained; for her bones, they say, were turned to stone. Since then, she hides in the woods, and, though never seen on the moun-tains, is heard there by all: for her voice is the only part of her that still lives.

Narcissus had played with her affections, treating her as he had pre-viously treated other spirits of the waters and the woods, and his male admirers too. Then one of those he had scorned raised up his hands to heaven and prayed: "May he himself fall in love with another, as we have done with him! May he too be unable to gain his loved one!" Nemesis heard and granted his righteous prayer.

There was a clear pool, with shining silvery waters, where shepherds had never made their way; no goats that pasture on the mountains, no cattle had ever come there. Its peace was undisturbed by bird or beast or falling branches. Around it was a grassy sward, kept ever green by the nearby waters; encircling woods sheltered the spot from the fierce sun, and made it always cool.

Narcissus, wearied with hunting in the heat of the day, lay down here: for he was attracted by the beauty of the place, and by the spring. While he sought to quench his thirst, another thirst grew in him, and as he drank, he was enchanted by the beautiful reflection that he saw. He fell in love with an insubstantial hope, mistaking a mere shadow for a real body. Spellbound by his own self, he remained there motionless, with fixed gaze, like a statue carved from Parian marble. As he lay on the bank, he gazed at the twin stars that were his eyes, at his flowing locks, worthy of Bacchus or Apollo, his smooth cheeks, his ivory neck, his lovely face where a rosy flush stained the snowy whiteness of his complexion, admiring all the features for which he was himself admired. Unwittingly, he desired himself, and was himself the object of his own approval, at once seeking and sought, himself kindling the flame with which he burned. How often did he vainly kiss the treacherous pool, how often plunge his arms deep in the waters, as he tried to clasp the neck he saw! But he could not lay hold upon himself. He did not know what he was looking at, but was fired by the sight, and excited by the very illusion that deceived his eyes. Poor foolish boy, why vainly grasp at the fleeting image that eludes you? The thing you are seeing does not exist: only turn aside and you will lose what you love. What you see is but the shadow cast by your reflection; in itself it is nothing. It comes with you, and lasts while you are there; it will go when you go, if go you can.

No thought of food or sleep could draw him from the spot. Stretched on the shady grass, he gazed at the shape that was no true shape with eyes that could never have their fill, and by his own eyes he was undone. Finally he raised himself a little. Holding out his arms to the surrounding woods: "Oh you woods," he cried, "has anyone ever felt a love more cruel? You surely know, for many lovers have found you an ideal haunt for secret meetings. You who have lived so many centuries, do you remember anyone, in all your long years, who has pined away as I do? I am in love, and see my loved one, but that form which I see and love, I cannot reach: so far am I deluded by my love. My distress is all the greater because it is not a mighty ocean that separates us, nor yet highways or mountains, or city walls with close-barred gates. Only a little water keeps us apart. My love himself desires to be embraced: for whenever I lean forward to kiss the clear waters he lifts up his face to mine and strives to reach me. You would think he could be reached—it is such a small thing that hinders our love. Whoever you are, come out to me! Oh boy beyond compare, why do you elude me? Where do you go, when I try to reach you? Certainly it is not my looks or my years which you shun, for I am one of those the nymphs have loved. With friendly looks you proffer me some hope. When I stretch out my arms to you, you stretch yours towards me in return: you laugh when I do, and often I have marked your tears when I was weeping. You answer my signs with nods, and, as far as I can guess from the movement of your lovely lips, reply to me in words that never reach my ears. Alas! I am myself the boy I see. I know it: my own reflection does not deceive me. I am on fire with love for my own self. It is I who kindle the flames which I must endure. What should I do? Woo or be wooed? But what then shall I seek by my wooing? What I desire, I have. My very plenty makes me poor. How I wish I could separate myself from my body! A new prayer this, for a lover, to wish the thing he loves away! Now grief is sapping my strength; little of life remains for me—I am cut off in the flower of my youth. I have no quarrel with death, for in death I shall forget my pain: but I could wish that the object of my love might outlive me: as it is, both of us will perish together, when this one life is destroyed."

When he had finished speaking, he returned to gazing distractedly at that same face. His tears disturbed the water, so that the pool rippled, and the image grew dim. He saw it disappearing, and cried aloud: "Where are you fleeing? Cruel creature, stay, do not desert one who loves you! Let me look upon you, if I cannot touch you. Let me, by looking, feed my ill-starred love." In his grief, he tore away the upper portion of his tunic, and beat his bared breast with hands as white as marble. His breast flushed rosily where he struck it, just as apples often shine red in part, while part gleams whitely, or as grapes, ripening in variegated clusters, are tinged with purple. When Narcissus saw this reflected in the water—for the pool had returned to its former calm—he could bear it no longer. As golden wax melts with gentle heat, as morning frosts are thawed by the warmth of the sun, so he was worn and wasted away with love, and slowly consumed by its hidden fire. His fair complexion with its rosy flush faded away, gone was his youthful strength, and all the beauties which lately charmed his eyes. Nothing remained of that body which Echo once had loved.

The nymph saw what had happened, and although she remembered her own treatment, and was angry at it, still she grieved for him. As often as the unhappy boy sighed "Alas," she took up his sigh, and repeated "Alas!" When he beat his hands against his shoulders she too gave back the same sound of mourning. His last words as he gazed into the familiar waters were: "Woe is me for the boy I loved in vain!" and the spot re-echoed the same words. When he said his last farewell, "Farewell!" said Echo too. He laid down his weary head on the green grass, and death closed the eyes which so admired their owner's beauty. Even then, when he was received into the abode of the dead, he kept looking at himself in the waters of the Styx. His sisters, the nymphs of the spring, mourned for him, and cut off their hair in tribute to their brother. The wood nymphs mourned him too, and Echo sang her refrain to their lament.

The pyre, the tossing torches, and the bier, were now being prepared, but his body was nowhere to be found. Instead of his corpse, they discovered a flower with a circle of white petals round a yellow centre.

When this story became known, it brought well-deserved fame to the seer Tiresias. It was told throughout all the cities of Greece, and his reputation was boundless.

Hyacinthus

Ovid's tale of another dying youth is a rare myth in that it places the god Apollo in a homosexual context. Sung by Orpheus, the myth of Hyacinthus is immediately preceded by the story of Zeus's illicit love for the boy Ganymede. Conceivably, both the Narcissus and Hyacinth stories have their origins in earlier fertility rites or in the dying-god myth, or both. As in the case of such figures as Adonis and Attis, spring flowers result directly from their deaths.

•

The king of the gods was once fired with love for Phrygian Ganymede, and when that happened Jupiter found another shape preferable to his own. Wishing to turn himself into a bird, he none the less scorned to change into any save that which can carry his thunderbolts. Then without delay, beating the air on borrowed pinions, he snatched away the shepherd of Ilium, who even now mixes the winecups, and supplies Jove with nectar, to the annoyance of Juno.

Hyacinthus too, the boy from Amyclae, would have been given a place in heaven by Phoebus, had cruel destiny allowed the god time to set him there. Still, he was made immortal in such fashion as was possible, and whenever spring drives winter off, and the Ram succeeds the watery sign of Pisces, every year he comes to life again, and grows as a flower in the green turf. My father, Phoebus, loved Hyacinthus beyond all other mortals, and Delphi, the centre of the earth, lost its presiding deity, while the god haunted Eurotas and Sparta's unwalled city, neglecting his harp and

Ovid, *The Metamorphoses*, trans. Mary M. Innes (London, 1955), pp. 229–30.

his arrows. Heedless of his old habits, Apollo was willing to carry hunting nets, or direct a pack of hounds, as he accompanied Hyacinthus over the rough mountain ridges and, by constant companionship, added fuel to the fire of his love.

One day, when the sun was halfway between the night that was over and the night that was to come, equally far from both, the god and the boy stripped off their garments, rubbed their bodies, till they gleamed, with rich olive oil, and began to compete with one another in throwing the broad discus. Phoebus threw first: he poised the discus, then flung it through the air. Its weight scattered the clouds in its path and then, after a long time, it fell back again to its natural element, the earth. It was a throw which showed skill and strength combined. Immediately the young Spartan, in his eagerness for the game, ran forward without stopping to think, in a hurry to pick up the discus, but it bounced back off the hard ground, and rose into the air, striking him full in the face. The god grew as pale as the boy himself: he caught up Hyacinthus' limp frame, and tried to staunch the grim wound, rubbing warmth into the limbs, and applying herbs to stay the fleeting spirit. But Apollo's art was of no avail—the wound was beyond any cure. Just as violets in a garden, or stiff poppies or lilies with clustering yellow stamens, once their stems are broken, no longer stand erect but, drooping, let their withered tops hang down and, with lowered heads, gaze upon the ground, so did the head of the dying Hyacinthus droop. His neck, drained of its strength, was a burden to itself, and sank down upon his shoulders. "You are slipping away from me, Hyacinthus, robbed of the flower of your youth," said Phoebus. "Here before my eyes I see the wound that killed you and reproaches me. You are the cause of my grief, as of my guilt, for your death must be ascribed to my hand. I am responsible for killing you. Yet how was I at fault, unless taking part in a game can be called a fault, unless I can be blamed for loving you? I wish that I might give my life in exchange for yours, as you so well deserve, or die along with you! But, since I am bound by the laws of fate, that cannot be. Still you will always be with me, your name constantly upon my lips, never forgotten. When I strike the chords of my lyre, and when I sing, my songs and music will tell of you. You will be changed into a new kind of flower and will show markings that imitate my sobs. Further, a time will come when the bravest of heroes will be connected with this flower, and his name will be read on these same petals."

While Apollo, who cannot lie, was uttering these words, the blood which had flowed to the ground, and stained the grass, ceased to be blood, and a flower brighter than Tyrian purple grew up and took on the shape of a lily: it was purple in colour, where lilies are silvery white. Phoebus was responsible for so honouring Hyacinthus, by changing him into a flower; not content with that, he himself inscribed his own grief upon the petals, and the hyacinth bears the mournful letters AI AI marked upon it. Nor was Sparta ashamed of having produced Hyacinthus, for he is honoured there to this very day, and every year the Hyacinthian games are celebrated with festive displays, in accordance with ancient usage.

Eros and Psyche

The story of Eros (Cupid) and Psyche is a late one, told by Apuleius in *The Golden Ass*. It has been a favorite of poets, perhaps because of its allegorical implications, Eros standing for passion and the body, *psyche* being the Greek word for feminine soul or spirit.

Eros (Cupid) fell in love with the mortal Psyche and she with him. The lovers met under cover of darkness each night until, urged on by her jealous sisters, Psyche shone a lamp on the sleeping Eros one night, causing him to awaken and depart while scolding her for her mistrust. After a period of aimless wandering in search of her lover, Psyche begged Aphrodite for assistance, and the lovers were eventually reunited.

Daphne and Apollo

As Daphne means laurel in Greek, this is an origin story, but it is also a celebration of the powers of Mother Earth, to whom Daphne prays for help in the myth as told by Apollodorus. A similar situation occurred in connection with the Pleiades, daughters of the world-bearing Titan Atlas and virgin companions of Artemis. They are saved from an unwanted lover, Orion, by being turned into doves and then into a constellation of stars that still carries their name.

•

Daphne, the daughter of Peneus, was Phoebus' first love, and it was not blind chance which brought this about, but Cupid's savage spite. Not long before, the Delian god, still exultant over his slaying of the serpent, had seen Cupid bending his taut bow, and had said: "You naughty boy, what have you to do with a warrior's arms? Weapons such as these are suited to my shoulders: for I can aim my shafts unerringly, to wound wild beast or human foe, as I lately slew the bloated Python with my countless arrows, though it covered so many acres with its pestilential coils. You be content with your torch to excite love, whatever that may be, and do not aspire to praises that are my prerogative." But Venus' son replied: "Your bow may pierce everything else, Phoebus, but mine will pierce *you:* and as all animals are inferior to the gods, your glory is to that extent less than mine."

With these words he swiftly winged his way through the air, till he

Ovid, *The Metamorphoses*, trans. Mary M. Innes (London, 1955), pp. 41–44.

alighted on the shady summit of Parnassus. From his quiver, full of arrows, he drew two darts, with different properties. The one puts love to flight, the other kindles it. That which kindles love is golden, and shining, sharp-tipped; but that which puts it to flight is blunt, its shaft tipped with lead. With this arrow the god pierced the nymph, Peneus' daughter, but Apollo he wounded with the other, shooting it into the marrow of his bones. Immediately the one fell in love; the other, fleeing the very word "lover," took her delight in woodland haunts and in the spoils of captured beasts, emulating Diana, the maiden goddess, with her hair carelessly caught back by a single ribbon.

Many a suitor wooed her but, turning away from their entreaties, she roamed the pathless woods, knowing nothing of men, and caring nothing for them, heedless of what marriage or love or wedded life might be. Again and again her father said: "It is your duty to marry and give me a son-in-law, my child." Often he repeated, "My child, it is your duty to give me grandchildren." But she blushed, hating the thought of marriage as if it were some crime. The modest colour crimsoned her fair face and, throwing her arms round her father's neck, she cried imploringly: "My dear, dear father, let me enjoy this state of maiden bliss for ever! Diana's father granted her such a boon in days gone by!" Her father did, indeed, yield to her request, but her very loveliness prevented her from being what she desired, and her beauty defeated her own wishes.

As soon as Phoebus saw Daphne, he fell in love with her, and wanted to marry her. His own prophetic powers deceived him and he hoped to achieve his desire. As the light stubble blazes up in a harvested field, or as the hedge is set alight, if a traveller chance to kindle a fire too close, or leaves one smouldering when he goes off at daybreak, so the god was all on fire, his whole heart was aflame, and he nourished his fruitless love on hope. He eyed her hair as it hung carelessly about her neck, and sighed: "What if it were properly arranged!" He looked at her eyes, sparkling bright as stars, he looked at her lips, and wanted to do more than look at them. He praised her fingers, her hands and arms, bare almost to the shoulder. Her hidden charms he imagined lovelier still.

But Daphne ran off, swifter than the wind's breath, and did not stop to hear his words, though he called her back: "I implore you, nymph, daughter of Peneus, do not run away! Though I pursue you, I am no enemy. Stay, sweet nymph! You flee as the lamb flees the wolf, or the deer the lion, as doves on fluttering wings fly from an eagle, as all creatures flee their natural foes! But it is love that drives me to follow you. Alas, how I fear lest you trip and fall, lest briars scratch your innocent legs, and I be the cause of your hurting yourself. These are rough places through which you are running—go less swiftly, I beg of you, slow your flight, and I in turn shall pursue less swiftly!

"Yet stay to inquire whose heart you have charmed. I am no peasant, living in a mountain hut, nor am I a shepherd or boorish herdsman who tends his flocks and cattle in these regions. Silly girl, you do not know from whom you are fleeing: indeed, you do not, or else you would not flee. I am lord of Delphi, Claros, and Tenedos, and of the realms of Patara too. I am the son of Jupiter. By my skill, the past, the present, and the future are revealed; thanks to me, the lyre strings thrill with music. My arrow is sure, though there is one surer still, which has wounded my carefree heart. The art of medicine is my invention, and men the world over give me the name of healer. All the properties of herbs are known to me: but alas, there are no herbs to cure love, and the skill which helps others cannot help its master."

He would have said more, but the frightened maiden fled from him, leaving him with his words unfinished; even then, she was graceful to see, as the wind bared her limbs and its gusts stirred her garments, blowing them out behind her. Her hair streamed in the light breeze, and her beauty was enhanced by her flight. But the youthful god could not endure to waste his time on further blandishments and, as love itself prompted, sped swiftly after her. Even so, when a Gallic hound spies a hare in some open meadow he tries by his swiftness to secure his prey, while the hare, by her swiftness, seeks safety: the dog, seeming just about to fasten on his quarry, hopes at every moment that he has her, and grazes her hind quarters with outstretched muzzle, but the hare, uncertain whether she has not already been caught, snatches herself out of his very jaws, and escapes the teeth which almost touch her.

Thus the god and the nymph sped on, one made swift by hope and one by fear; but he who pursued was swifter, for he was assisted by love's wings. He gave the fleeing maiden no respite, but followed close on her heels, and his breath touched the locks that lay scattered on her neck, till Daphne's strength was spent, and she grew pale and weary with the effort of her swift flight. Then she saw the waters of the Peneus: "O father," she cried, "help me! If you rivers really have divine powers, work some transformation, and destroy this beauty which makes me please all to well!" Her prayer was scarcely ended when a deep languor took hold on her limbs, her soft breast was enclosed in thin bark, her hair grew into leaves, her arms into branches, and her feet that were lately so swift were held fast by sluggish roots, while her face became the treetop. Nothing of her was left, except her shining loveliness.

Even as a tree, Phoebus loved her. He placed his hand against the trunk, and felt her heart still beating under the new bark. Embracing the branches as if they were limbs he kissed the wood: but, even as a tree, she shrank from his kisses. Then the god said: "Since you cannot be my bride, surely you will at least be my tree. My hair, my lyre, my quivers will always display the laurel. You will accompany the generals of Rome, when the Capitol beholds their long triumphal processions, when joyful voices raise the song of victory. You will stand by Augustus' gateposts too, faithfully guarding his doors, and keeping watch from either side over the wreath of oak leaves that will hang there. Further, as my head is ever young, my tresses never shorn, so do you also, at all times, wear the crowning glory of never-fading foliage." Paean, the healer, had done: the laurel tree inclined her newmade branches, and seemed to nod her leafy top, as if it were a head, in consent.

Pan

Pan has much in common with Dionysos in that he is associated with wine, sex, and passion in general. He was a popular god, though never part of the official Olympian pantheon. Complete with horns, a goat's beard, and goat legs, he personifies humanity's animal nature. This is the *Homeric Hymn* to Pan.

●

Tell me about that dear son of Hermes,
　　　Muse,
　　with the goat-feet,
　　　and the two horns,
　　the one who loves noise,
　　　　who goes around
　　　　　　　in meadows
　　with dancing nymphs
　　　that tramp even on
　　　　　　rocky peaks
　　　that goats can't reach
　　　　　　calling for

Pan,
　　the pastoral god
　　　with magnificent hair,
　　　　　unwashed,
　　who's got
　　　all the snow crests
　　　　　and mountain ridges
　　　　　　and all the rocky roads

Charles Boer, trans., "The Hymn to Pan" in *The Homeric Hymns* (Chicago, 1970), pp. 67–71.

He goes about
    here and there
        in the thick shrubbery
and sometimes
    he is drawn down to
        gentle streams
and sometimes
    he just wanders about
        on steep rocks
climbing up
    to the highest peak
        to watch his sheep
and often
    he runs across
        a great white mountain range
and often
    he comes down
        the side of mountains
killing animals.
    He has a very sharp eye.

And sometimes—
    but only in the evening—
        relaxing from the hunt,
    he makes music,
        playing a song
            on his flute—
                it's sweet
and no bird
        weeping a lament,
no bird crying
        the song of its honeyed voice
    in the leaves
        of Spring's many flowers
            could outrun him,
            Pan,
                in song

And the mountain nymphs
    with clear voices
        go along with him,
            their feet excited,
    they sing too,
        by the springs of dark water—

Echo wailing
                on the mountain-top

And the god
            on this side
        on that side
                        of the chorus
                                enters the dance
                speeding his feet
                        into their midst, dancing
the red skin of a lynx
            on his back
                    for covering,
        his head delights in
            the piercing songs
in a soft meadow
        where crocus and hyacinth
            with their sweet fragrance
            mix in with the grass
                        any-old-where

They sing about
            the blessed gods and great Olympos—

            for example,
        they sing about Hermes
                the helper,
            above all others,
                how he is a quick messenger
                for all the gods,
        how he came to Arcadia
            with its many springs,
                    the mother of sheep,
        where his precinct,
                Cyllene, is
                And there,
        though he was a god,
            he had tended sheep,
                with their rough fleece,
            for a mortal man,
        because he,
                Hermes,
            felt a sensual wave
                coming over him
                to make love with

a nymph with beautiful hair,
the daughter of Dryops

It ended
in happy marriage,
and, in their rooms,
she produced for Hermes
a dear son—
fantastic to look at,
with goat-feet,
and two horns,
very noisy
but laughing
sweetly

Its mother
jumped up and fled—
instead of nursing it
she abandoned the child—
she was scared
as she looked at
its brutal face!
its heavy beard!

But Hermes,
the helper,
was overjoyed
in his mind
and he took it in his hands
and received it.

And he hid the boy
in the thick skin
of a mountain rabbit
and he went immediately
to the home
of the immortal gods.
He set him down
next to Zeus
and the other immortal gods
and he showed them
his boy.
And all the immortal gods
were delighted
in their hearts
and more than anyone else even

Dionysos,
> Bacchos

And they decided to call him
> Pan
because he had delighted the minds of
all.

And so, lord,
> I greet you,
>> and with this song
>> I would please you.
> I will remember you
>> in my other songs.

The Muses
The Muses, of whom Hesiod said there were nine, presided over the arts and sciences. They were the daughters of Zeus and Mnemosyne (Memory).

The Eumenides
The Eumenidies (or Erinnyes or Furies) are disgusting flying crones who harass people for breaking social codes or taboos. Homer knew of them, and the playwright Aeschylus treats them in the third play of his Orestes trilogy (the *Eumenides*). Orestes is hounded by the Furies for having committed matricide in order to avenge his mother Clytemnestra's murder of his father, King Agamemnon. The ordeal of Orestes ends at his famous trial at Athens, during which Apollo argues for Orestes against the Furies and Athena acts as judge and in which the ancient power of the earth-oriented Furies gives way to the rational power of the two great sky gods. The trial itself can be seen as a metaphor for this important change in Greek religion.

Zeus and Io
Io is perhaps the most famous object of Zeus's predilection for mortal women. As a result of Hera's jealousy, Io is chased around the world in the form of a white cow, in which Zeus had attempted to conceal her identity. In Aeschylus's *Prometheus Bound*, Io tells her sad tale to Prometheus, and he predicts her future.

•

IO
I do not know how to distrust you.
You shall hear all. And yet—

I am ashamed to speak,
to tell of that god-driven storm
that struck me, changed me, ruined me.
How shall I tell you who it was?
How ever to my maiden chamber
visions came by night,
persuading me with gentle words:
"Oh happy, happy girl,
Why are you all too long a maid
when you might marry with the highest?
The arrow of desire has pierced Zeus.
For you he is on fire.
With you it is his will to capture love.
Would you, child, fly from Zeus' bed?
Go forth to Lerna, to the meadows deep in grass.
There is a sheep-fold there,
an ox-stall, too, that holds your father's oxen—
so shall Zeus find release from his desire.'
Always, each night, such dreams possessed me.
I was unhappy and at last I dared
to tell my father of these visions.
He sent to Pytho and far Dodona
man after man to ask the oracle
what he must say to do to please the gods.
But all brought answers back of shifting meaning,
hard to discern, like golden coins unmarked.
At last a clear word came. It fell upon him
like lightning from the sky. It told him
to thrust me from his house and from his country,
to wander to the farthest bounds of earth
like some poor dumb beast set apart
for sacrifice, whom no man will restrain.
And if my father would not, Zeus would send
his thunder-bolt with eyes of flame to end
his race, all, everyone.
He could not but obey such words
from the dark oracle. He drove me out.
He shut his doors to me—against his will
as against mine. Zeus had him bridled.
He drove him as he would.

Aeschylus, *Prometheus Bound*, in *Three Greek Plays*, trans. Edith Hamilton (New York, 1937, 1965), pp. 124–28.

Straightway I was distorted, mind and body.
A beast—with horns—look at me—
stung by a fly, who madly leaps and bounds.
And so I ran and found myself beside
the waters, sweet to drink, of Kerchneia
and Lerna's well-spring.
Beside me went the herdsman Argus,
the violent of heart, the earth-born,
watching my footsteps with his hundred eyes.
But death came to him, swift and unforeseen.
Plagued by a gadfly then, the scourge of God,
I am driven on from land to land.
So for what has been. But what still remains
of anguish for me, tell me.
Do not in pity soothe me with false tales.
Words strung together by a lie
are like a foul disease.

LEADER

Oh, shame. Oh, tale of shame.
Never, oh never, would I have believed that my ears
would hear words such as these, of strange meaning.
Evil to see and evil to hear,
misery, defilement, and terror.
They pierce my heart with a two-edged sword.
A fate like that—
I shudder to look upon Io.

PROMETHEUS

You are too ready with your tears and fears.
Wait for the end.

LEADER

Speak. Tell us, for when one lies sick,
to face with clear eyes all the pain to come
is sweet.

PROMETHEUS

What first you asked was granted easily,
to hear from her own lips her trials.
But for the rest, learn now the sufferings
she still must suffer, this young creature,
at Hera's hands. Child of Inachus,
keep in your heart my words, so you shall know
where the road ends. First to the sunrise,

over furrows never plowed, where wandering
    Scythians
live in huts of wattles made, raised high
on wheels smooth-rolling. Bows they have,
and they shoot far. Turn from them.
Keep to the shore washed by the moaning sea.
Off to the left live the Chalybians,
workers of iron. There be on your guard.
A rough people they, who like not strangers.
Here rolls a river called the Insolent,
true to its name. You cannot find a ford
until you reach the Caucasus itself,
highest of mountains. From beneath its brow
the mighty river rushes. You must cross
the summit, neighbor to the stars.
Then by the southward road, until you reach
the warring Amazons, men-haters, who one day
will found a city by the Thermodon,
where Salmydessus thrusts
a fierce jaw out into the sea that sailors hate,
stepmother of ships.
And they will bring you on your way right gladly
to the Cimmerian isthmus, by a shallow lake,
Maeotis, at the narrows.
Here you must cross with courage.
And men shall tell forever of your passing.
The strait shall be named for you, Bosporus,
Ford of the Cow. There leave the plains of Europe,
and enter Asia, the great Continent.
—Now does he seem to you, this ruler of the gods,
evil, to all, in all things?
A god desired a mortal—drove her forth
to wander thus.
A bitter lover you have found, O girl,
for all that I have told you is not yet
the prelude even.

IO

Oh, wretched, wretched.

PROMETHEUS

You cry aloud for this? What then
when you have learned the rest?

LEADER
You will not tell her of more trouble?

PROMETHEUS
A storm-swept sea of grief and ruin.

IO
What gain to me is life? Oh, now to fling myself
down from this rock peak to the earth below,
and find release there from my trouble.
Better to die once than to suffer
through all the days of life.

Zeus and Europa
Ovid tells this bizarre tale of another of Zeus's philandering escapades.
Zeus takes the form of a bull to carry away Europa, the daughter of Age-
nor.

•

Majesty and love go ill together, nor can they long share one abode. Aban-
doning the dignity of his sceptre, the father and ruler of the gods, whose
hand wields the flaming three-forked bolt, whose nod shakes the universe,
adopted the guise of a bull; and, mingling with the other bullocks, joined
in their lowing and ambled in the tender grass, a fair sight to see. His hide
was white as untrodden snow, snow not yet melted by the rainy South
wind. The muscles stood out on his neck, and deep folds of skin hung
along his flanks. His horns were small, it is true, but so beautifully made
that you would swear they were the work of an artist, more polished and
shining than any jewel. There was no menace in the set of his head or in
his eyes; he looked completely placid.

Agenor's daughter was filled with admiration for one so handsome and
so friendly. But, gentle though he seemed, she was afraid at first to touch
him; then she went closer, and held out flowers to his shining lips. The
lover was delighted and, until he could achieve his hoped-for pleasure,
kissed her hands. He could scarcely wait for the rest, only with great difficulty did he restrain himself.

Now he frolicked and played on the green turf, now lay down, all
snowy white on the yellow sand. Gradually the princess lost her fear, and
with her innocent hands she stroked his breast when he offered it for her
caress, and hung fresh garlands on his horns: till finally she even ventured
to mount the bull, little knowing on whose back she was resting. Then the
god drew away from the shore by easy stages, first planting the hooves that

Ovid, *The Metamorphoses*, trans. Mary M. Innes (London, 1955), pp. 72–73.

were part of his disguise in the surf at the water's edge, and then proceeding farther out to sea, till he bore his booty away over the wide stretches of mid ocean. The girl was sorely frightened, and looked back at the sands behind her, from which she had been carried away. Her right hand grasped the bull's horn, the other rested on his back, and her fluttering garments floated in the breeze.

Non-Greek

Persian: Mithras

The god Mithras (or Mithra) was a major influence on Christianity until the fourth century C.E. In this version of his story, by Barbara Walker, the parallels between the two cults are emphasized.

•

Mithra [was the] Persian savior, whose cult was the leading rival of Christianity in Rome, and more successful than Christianity for the first four centuries of the "Christian" era. In 307 A.D. the emperor officially designated Mithra "Protector of the Empire."

Christians copied many details of the Mithraic mystery-religion, explaining the resemblance later with their favorite argument, that the devil had anticipated the true faith by imitating it before Christ's birth. Some resemblances between Christianity and Mithraism were so close that even St. Augustine declared the priests of Mithra worshipped the same deity as he did.

Mithra was born on the 25th of December, called "Birthday of the Unconquered Sun," which was finally taken over by Christians in the 4th century A.D. as the birthday of Christ. Some said Mithra sprang from an incestuous union between the sun god and his own mother, just as Jesus, who was God, was born of the Mother of God. Some claimed Mithra's mother was a mortal virgin. Others said Mithra had no mother, but was miraculously born of a female Rock, the *petra genetrix*, fertilized by the Heavenly Father's phallic lightning.

Mithra's birth was witnessed by shepherds and by Magi who brought gifts to his sacred birth-cave of the Rock. Mithra performed the usual assortment of miracles: raising the dead, healing the sick, making the blind see and the lame walk, casting out devils. As a Peter, son of the *petra*, he carried the keys of the kingdom of heaven. His triumph and ascension to heaven were celebrated at the spring equinox (Easter), when the sun rises toward its apogee.

Before returning to heaven, Mithra celebrated a Last Supper with his twelve disciples, who represented the twelve signs of the zodiac. In mem-

Barbara Walker, *The Woman's Encyclopedia of Myths and Secrets* (New York, 1983), pp. 663–65.

ory of this, his worshippers partook of a sacramental meal of bread marked with a cross. This was one of seven Mithraic sacraments, the models for the Christians' seven sacraments. It was called *mizd*, Latin *missa*, English *mass*. Mithra's image was buried in a rock tomb, the same sacred cave that represented his Mother's womb. He was withdrawn from it and said to live again.

Like early Christianity, Mithraism was an ascetic, anti-female religion. Its priesthood consisted of celibate men only. Women were forbidden to enter Mithraic temples. The women of Mithraic families had nothing to do with the men's cult, but attended services of the Great Mother in their own temples of Isis, Diana, or Juno.

To eliminate the female principle from their creation myth, Mithraists replaced the Mother of All Living in the primal garden of paradise (Pairidaeza) with the bull named Sole-Created. Instead of Eve, this bull was the partner of the first man. All creatures were born from the bull's blood. Yet the bull's birth-giving was oddly female-imitative. The animal was castrated and sacrificed, and its blood was delivered to the moon for magical fructification, the moon being the source of women's magic lunar "blood of life" that produced real children on earth.

Persians have been called the Puritans of the heathen world. They developed Mithraism out of an earlier Aryan religion that was not so puritanical or so exclusively male-oriented. Mithra seems to have been the Indo-Iranian sun god Mitra, or Mitravaruna, one of the twelve zodiacal sons of the Infinity-goddess Aditi. Another of Aditi's sons was Aryaman, eponymous ancestor of "Aryans," whom the Persians transformed into Ahriman, the Great Serpent of Darkness, Mithra's enemy.

Early on, there seems to have been a feminine Mithra. Herodotus said the Persians used to have a sky-goddess Mitra, the same as Mylitta, Assyria's Great Mother. Lydians combined Mithra with his archaic spouse Anahita as an androgynous Mithra-Anahita, identified with Sabazius-Anaitis, the Serpent and Dove of Anatolian mystery cults.

Anahita was the Mother of Waters, traditional spouse of the solar god whom she bore, loved, and swallowed up. She was identified with the Anatolian Great Goddess Ma. Mithra was naturally coupled with her, as her opposite, a spirit of fire, light, and the sun. Her "element," water, overwhelmed the world in the primordial flood, when one man built an ark and saved himself, together with his cattle, according to Mithraic myth. The story seems to have been based on the Hindu Flood of Manu, transmitted through Persian and Babylonian scriptures to appear in a late, rather corrupt version in the Old Testament.

What began in water would end in fire, according to Mithraic eschatology. The great battle between the forces of light and darkness in the Last Days would destroy the earth with its upheavals and burnings. Virtuous ones who followed the teachings of the Mithraic priesthood would join the spirits of light and be saved. Sinful ones who followed other teachings would be cast into hell with Ahriman and the fallen angels. The Christian notion of salvation was almost wholly a product of this Persian eschatology, adopted by Semitic eremites and sun-cultists like the Essenes, and by Roman military men who thought the rigid discipline and vivid battle-imagery of Mithraism appropriate for warriors. Under emperors like Julian and Commodus, Mithra became the supreme patron of Roman armies.

After extensive contact with Mithraism, Christians also began to describe themselves as soldiers for Christ; to call their savior Light of the World, Helios the Rising Sun, and Sun of Righteousness; to celebrate their feasts on Sun-day rather than the Jewish sabbath; to claim their savior's death was marked by an eclipse of the sun; and to adopt the seven Mithraic sacraments. Like Mithraists, Christians practiced baptism to ascend after death through the planetary spheres to the highest heaven, while the wicked (unbaptized) would be dragged down to darkness.

Mithra's cave-temple on the Vatican Hill was seized by Christians in 376 A.D. Christian bishops of Rome pre-empted even the Mithraic high priest's title of Pater Patrum, which became Papa, or Pope. Mithraism entered into many doctrines of Manichean Christianity and continued to influence its old rival for over a thousand years. The Mithraic festival of Epiphany, marking the arrival of sun-priests or Magi at the Savior's birthplace, was adopted by the Christian church only as late as 813 A.D.

Japanese: Amaterasu and Susanowo

The following is the story of the sun goddess Amaterasu, whom the followers of the Shinto cult consider to be the ancestor of the Japanese emperors. The motif of the struggle between the male and female creator gods is common. It occurs again in Japanese mythology between other creator gods, Izanagi and Izanami. Padraic Colum retells the Amaterasu tale.

•

That lady, the resplendent Sun Goddess, was born out of the left eye of the august Father creator, and her brother, the powerful Storm God, was born out of his nostrils. To her was given the Plain of High Heaven for dwelling with the Earth for dominion, and to him the Sea was given for dwelling and dominion.

But between Ama-terasu, the Sun Goddess, and Susa-no-wo, the Storm God, there was strife. The resplendent Goddess was beneficently careful of things that grew upon the earth; she strove against the evil spirits

Padraic Colum, *Myths of the World* (New York, 1930, 1972), pp. 245–48.

that were abroad on the earth, and she was especially careful of the temples
that men built for their celebrations of the harvest rites. Her powerful
brother had no care for these things. He would leave his own realm and
go clamorously upon the earth. He would strip off branches and level trees,
and tear out of the ground the crops that his beneficent sister had cared
for. He would break down all that guarded men from the evil spirits that
were abroad upon the earth. He would make turmoil in the temples and
prevent the harvest rites from being celebrated. All the work whose beginnings on earth were helped by Ama-terasu, that shining and beneficent
lady, were destroyed by Susa-no-wo, the bearded and impetuous Storm
God.

Once he ascended into High Heaven. He came before the Heavenly
River, the Yasu. The Goddess cried out, "You who would destroy all I
have given growth to upon earth, have you come to darken and lay waste
the Plain of High Heaven?" The Storm God declared that he had come to
establish peace and trust between himself and his resplendent sister.

Then on the bank of the Heavenly River, the Yasu, the powerful
Storm God and the resplendent Sun Goddess exchanged tokens of their
trust in one another. To the Storm God the Sun Goddess gave her jewels;
to the Sun Goddess the Storm God gave his sword. Then, from the spring
whence rose the Heavenly River, the Yasu, Ama-terasu, the Sun Goddess,
and Susa-no-wo, the Storm God, drank. They put into their mouths the
tokens they had received from each other: from the sword that the Goddess
put into hers was born a beautiful and courageous boy; from the jewels
that the Storm God put into his, were born shining Gods of growth and
power.

Thereafter the cocks, the long-singing birds of the Eternal Land,
crowed everywhere upon the earth, prophesying the flourishing of all
growing things and the checking of all the evil spirits that went abroad
upon the earth. Men gathered full crops in and celebrated the harvest rites
in temples that were blown upon no more. The beneficent lady, Ama-
terasu, had her way upon earth, and the powerful God, Susa-no-wo, stayed
in his own realm, the sea.

Out of the sea he went once more. He went clamorously upon the
earth, destroying growing things, and breaking down the guards put up
against the evil spirits that went abroad upon the earth. He threw down
the temples and scattered the people who had come to celebrate the harvest
rites. Then Ama-terasu would look no more upon the earth that her
brother had wasted. She went within a cavern and would not come forth.
Confusion came upon the eight million Gods, and the spirits of evil
wrought havoc through the whole of creation.

She came forth again. The Gods seized upon Susa-no-wo, cut off his
great beard, and took from him all his possessions. Then he went wander-

ing upon the earth, but he was no longer able to work havoc upon it. He came to the mountains by the side of the ocean; he planted the mountains with the hairs of his beard, and the hairs became the Forest of Kii. The forest was his dominion; men gave homage to him as Lord of the Forest. It was he who slew the dragon of that land. Once, with its eight heads rearing up, the dragon stood in his way. Susa-no-wo slew it and cut it to pieces. In the dragon's tail there was a sword—a sword that would be ever victorious—and that sword Susa-no-wo sent to Ama-terasu as his tribute to her and to her descendants.

Many were the dragons that were in the land that Susa-no-wo had come to. Once when he was on his way from his forest to the sea he came upon an old man and woman who were weeping upon the bank of a river. They told him the reason of their grief. Every year a maiden was given to the dragon of the place, and this time their daughter was being given him. The fury of the Storm God was aroused when he heard this: he went to where the dragon waited by the river, and he destroyed him, cutting him to pieces. Susa-no-wo then took the maiden for his wife. They lived in that land of Izumo, and they and their children after them had the lordship of that place.

Another God came to woo his daughter. He came within his house when Susa-no-wo was lying in slumber on his mat. He tied the hairs of his head to the beams of the roof, and he took in his hands the things that were Susa-no-wo's most cherished possessions—his sword, his bow and arrows, and his harp. He lifted the maiden up and carried her off with the treasures. But the harp cried out as it was taken in the hand of the younger God. Susa-no-wo awakened. He could not even move his head since his hair was tied to the beams of the roof, and he had to loosen each strand of hair before he could go in pursuit of the one who had carried off his daughter and his treasures. At last he freed himself; led by the sound of the harp that still played of itself he followed that one. But when he came to where Oh-kuni-nushi was with the maiden whom he had carried off, Susa-no-wo said, "You have great craft, and because you have I will give you this maiden and all my possessions; I will take you for my son-in-law."

Together Susa-no-wo and Oh-kuni-nushi ruled the Izumo, and, through his daughter, the descendants of Susa-no-wo peopled that land. But Susa-no-wo knew, and Oh-kuni-nushi knew, that their children would have to give place to the children of the resplendent Sun Goddess who were destined to be the rulers of the Eight Islands.

When Ama-terasu, on account of the destructiveness which her brother had wrought, had hidden herself in the cavern, the Gods had come together and had consulted as to how Ama-terasu's beneficence might be brought into the world once more. They had brought the cocks, the long-singing birds of the Eternal Land, and had placed them outside the cavern;

they had lighted fires that made such a brightness before the cavern that the cocks crowed perpetually. They had the Goddess Uzume dance for all their company. On an upturned tub she had danced, and her dancing and her laughter had made all the Gods laugh loudly. Their laughter and merriment and the sound of the cocks crowing had filled the air and had made the earth shake. Ama-terasu, within the cavern, had heard the merry din. She had wondered what merriment could be in the world while she was within the cavern. She had put a finger out and had made a little hole in the rock that closed her in. She had looked out at the crowd of the Gods, and she had seen the dancing and laughing Goddess. Then Ama-terasu had laughed. One of the strong-armed Gods had put his hand where the hole was in the rock and had made a wider opening. Then a long-armed God had put his hands within and had drawn the resplendent Goddess to the wide opening. Light immediately had filled the world. The cocks had crowed louder, and the evil spirits had drawn away. The Gods were made joyful, and the din of their merriment had filled all creation.

So the resplendent Sun Goddess had come back to the world. Then it was that the Storm God, banished, had gone forth and founded a new realm for himself. And the realm he had founded, he knew, was to pass to the descendants of the resplendent Goddess.

After the coming-forth of the Goddess from her cavern the growing plants flourished upon the earth, and the evil spirits were kept away. The cocks crew. The harvests were brought in, and the harvest rites celebrated. The temples stood unshaken and unbroken. The banished Storm God went back to his own realm, and his descendants bore rule in the Eight Islands. Then the resplendent Goddess willed to have her grandson take possession of the Islands. He came; he faced the rulers of the land armed with the sword that must always be victorious. They gave him the land and they gave him power over all that was visible. But they kept for themselves the hidden world and all the powers of divination and sorcery. And since that time the children of the Sun Goddess bear rule in our land.

Polynesian: Pele and Hiiaka'

The tale of the goddesses Pele and Hiiaka' is at once a typical quest narrative and a story of resurrection.

•

At one time Pele fell in love with a mortal; and this is the story of the fiery wooing. Pele, her brothers, and sisters one day, to amuse themselves with a taste of mortal enjoyments, left their lurid caves in the crater of Kilauea, and went down to the coast of Puna to bathe, surf-ride, sport in the sands,

Johannes Andersen, *Myths and Legends of the Polynesians* (Rutland and Tokyo, 1969), pp. 268–74.

and gather squid, limpets, edible seaweed, and like delicacies. As they had assumed human forms for the time, so for the time they experienced human appetites.

While the others were amusing themselves in various ways Pele, in the guise of an old woman, sought repose and sleep in the shade of a *hala*-tree. Her favourite sister was Hiiaka', her full name being Hiiaka-i-ka-pali-o-Pele. She was younger than Pele, and they frequently occupied the same grotto under the burning lake of Kilauea.

Hiiaka' accompanied her sister, and, sitting beside her, kept her cool with a *kahili* (feather plume). Her eyelids growing heavy, Pele settled herself to sleep, instructing Hiiaka' to allow her under no circumstances to be disturbed, no matter how long she might sleep, be it for hours or be it for days; she then fell into a sound sleep.

Hardly was she lapped in the silence of forgetfulness when the sound of a beaten drum fell on her ear; a distant beating, but regular as if to the impulse of music. Before leaving the crater she had heard the same sound, but had paid little attention to it. Now in her dreams, however, her curiosity was awakened, and assuming her spiritual form she set off in the direction from which the sound seemed to come. Leaving her slumbering body in the care of Hiiaka', Pele followed the sound all over Hawaii; and always it seemed just before her, but never there, so that she could not overtake it. At Upolu it came to her from over the sea, and she followed it to the island of Maui. It was still beyond, and she followed to Molokai; still beyond, and she followed to Oahu; still beyond, and she followed to Kauai. She stood on the peak of Haupu, when she saw at last that the sound came from the beach at Kaena.

Hovering unseen over the place, she observed that the sound she had so long followed was that of the *pahu-hula*, or *hula* drum, beaten by Lohiau, the young and handsome Prince of Kauai, who was noted not only for the splendour of his *hula* entertainments, where danced the most beautiful women of the island, but also for his own personal graces as dancer and musician. The favourite deity of Lohiau was Laka-kane, the god of the *hula* and similar sport, and it was this god who, in a spirit of mischief, had conveyed the sound to Pele, awaking in her the curiosity that urged her on and on.

The beach was thronged with dancers, musicians, and spectators, all enjoying themselves under the shade of the *hala*- and coconut-trees, with the Prince as leader and the centre of attraction. Assuming the form of a beautiful woman, Pele suddenly appeared among them. Displaying every imaginable charm of form and feature, her presence was at once noted; and, a way being opened for her to the Prince, he received her graciously and invited her to a seat near him, where she could best witness the entertainment.

Glancing at the beautiful stranger from time to time in the midst of his performances, Lohiau at length became so fascinated that he failed to follow the music, when he yielded the instrument to another, and seated himself beside the enchantress. In answer to his inquiry she informed the Prince that she was a stranger in Kauai, and had come from the direction of the rising sun.

"You are most welcome," said Lohiau, adding, after a pause, "but I cannot rejoice that you have come."

"And why, since I do not come as your enemy?" asked Pele, increasing, with her glances, the turmoil within him.

"Because until now," answered the Prince, "my thought has been that there are beautiful women in Kauai."

"I see you know how to shape your speech to suit the fancies of women," said Pele provocatively.

"Not better than I know how to love them," answered Lohiau. "Would you be convinced?"

"Lohiau is in his own kingdom, and has but to command," was her reply; and her play of modesty completed the enthralment of the Prince.

Thus Pele became the wife of Lohiau. He knew nothing of her but what delighted him, nor did he care to inquire about that which he could not discover without inquiry. He saw that she was beautiful above all women, and for a few days they lived so happily together that life seemed a dream to him, as it was a dream to her. But the time had to come when she must return to Hawaii; and, pledging him to remain true to her, she left him with protestations of affection and the promise of a speedy return; and on the wings of the wind she was wafted back to the shores of Puna, where her sister was still patiently watching and waiting in the shade of the *hala*.

Lohiau was inconsolable. As each day passed, he thought she would be with him the next, until more than a month went by, when he refused food, and died in grief at her absence. The strange death of the Prince caused much comment, for he was physically strong, and suffered from no malady. Some declared that he had been prayed to death by enemies; some that he had been poisoned; but an old *kaula* (prophet), who had seen Pele at Kaena and noted her actions, advised against further inquiry concerning the cause of death, offering as a reason the opinion that the strangely beautiful and unknown woman he had taken as wife was an immortal, who had become attached to her earthly husband and called his spirit to her.

The Prince was much loved by his people; and his body, wrapped in many folds of *tapa*, was kept in state for some time in the royal house. It was guarded by the high chiefs of the kingdom, and every night funeral hymns were chanted round it, and *mele* recited of the deeds of the dead prince and his ancestors.

Let us return now to Pele. Her body had been carefully watched by her brothers and sisters, who had not dared to disturb it; and her return was greeted with joy, for the fires of Kilauea had almost died out with neglect. Pele rose to her feet in the form of the old woman she had assumed when falling asleep in the care of Hiiaka'; and without referring to her adventures in Kauai, or to the cause of her long slumber, she returned with the others to Kilauea, and with a breath renewed the dying fires of the crater. Hiiaka' asked and received from Pele permission to remain for a few days at the beach with her loved friend Hopoe, a young woman of Puna, who had lost both her parents in an eruption of Kilauea.

It is probable that Pele, on leaving Kauai, notwithstanding her fervent words to the contrary, never expected, or particularly desired, to see Lohiau again; but he had so endeared himself to her during their brief union that she found it difficult to forget him; and, after struggling against the feeling for some time, she resolved to send for him. But to whom could she entrust the important mission? She applied to her sisters at the crater one after another; but the way was beset with evil spirits, and one after another refused to go.

In this dilemma Pele sent her brother Lono-i-ka-onolii to bring Hiiaka' from the beach, well knowing that she would not refuse to undertake the journey, however hazardous. Hiiaka' accepted the mission, with the understanding that during her absence her friend Hopoe should remain in the guardianship of Pele.

Arrangements were made for her immediate departure. Pele conferred upon her some of her own powers, and for a companion servant gave her Pauo-palae, a woman of proved sagacity and prudence.

With a farewell from the relatives of Hiiaka' and many an admonition from Pele they took their departure; and, travelling as mortals, they were subject to the fatigues and perils of mortals. They met a woman, whose name was Omeo, and who was leading a hog to the volcano as a sacrifice to Pele. She desired to accompany them; and, they agreeing, she hastened to the crater with her offering, returned, and followed Hiiaka' and her companion. Proceeding through the forests toward the coast of Hilo, they were impeded by a hideous demon, who threw himself across their path in a narrow defile and attempted to destroy them; but Pele was aware of their danger, and ordered her brothers to protect them with a rain of fire and thunder, which drove the monster to his den and enabled them to escape.

The forests abounded in mischievous gnomes and fairies, nymphs and monsters guarded the streams; the air was peopled with spirits, for a thin veil only separated the living from the dead, the natural from the supernatural.

Again they had not gone far when they encountered a man of fierce appearance who was either insane or possessed of demons; but he lacked the power or the disposition to injure them, and they passed on unharmed. Coming to a small stream, they found the waters dammed by a huge *mo'o*, or lizard (*moko*), lying in the bed. He was more than a hundred paces in length, with eyes the size of great calabashes. He glared viciously, and opened his mouth as if to devour the travellers; but Hiiaka' tossed a stone into his mouth which on touching his throat became red-hot, and with a roar of pain that made the trees tremble he disappeared down the stream.

After many adventures with monsters and evil spirits they reached the coast at Honoipo, where they found a number of men and women engaged in the sport of surf-riding. As they were about to start on another trial Hiiaka' in a spirit of mischief turned their surf-boards into stone, and they fled from the beach in terror, fearing that some sea-god was preparing to devour them.

Observing a fisherman drawing in a line, Hiiaka' caused a human head to be fastened to the submerged hook. The man raised it to the surface, stared at it in horror for a moment, then dropped the line and paddled swiftly away, to the great amusement of Hiiaka' and her companions.

Embarking in a canoe, the travellers reached Maui, crossed it with further adventures, then sailed with a fisherman for Oahu. They landed at Maka-puu, journeyed overland to Kou—now Honolulu—and from Haena made sail for Kauai. Arriving at Kaena, Hiiaka' saw the spirit hand of Lohiau beckoning to her from the mouth of a cave up in the cliffs. Turning to her companion she said, "We have failed; the lover of Pele is dead! I see his spirit beckoning from the *pali* [cliff] where it is held and hidden by the lizard-women Kilioa and Kalamainu."

Instructing her companions to proceed to the *puoa* where the body of Lohiau was lying in state, Hiiaka' started at once up the *pali*, to give battle to the demons and rescue the spirit of the dead prince. Ascending the cliff and entering the cave, she waved her *pau*, and with angry hisses the demons disappeared. She searched for the spirit of Lohiau, and at last found it in a niche of the rocks where it had been imprisoned by a moonbeam. Taking it tenderly in her hand, she folded it in her *pau* and in an invisible form floated down with it to the *puoa*.

Waiting until after nightfall, Hiiaka' entered the chamber of death unseen, and restored the spirit to the body of Lohiau. Recovering life and consciousness, the bewildered Prince looked about him. The guards were filled with fear when he raised his head, and would have fled in alarm had they not been prevented by Hiiaka', who that instant appeared before them in mortal form. Holding up her hand to command obedience, she said, "Fear nothing; say nothing of this to anyone living, and do nothing except as you may be ordered. The Prince has returned to life, and may recover if properly cared for. His body is weak and wasted. Let him at once be secretly removed to the seashore. The night is dark, and this may be done without observation."

Not doubting that these instructions were from the gods, the guards obeyed, and Lohiau was soon comfortably resting in a hut by the seashore, with Hiiaka' and her companion attending to his wants.

The return of the Prince to health and strength was rapid, and in a few days he reappeared among his friends, to their amazement and great joy. In answer to their inquiries he told them that he owed to the gods his restoration to life. This did not altogether satisfy them, but no other explanation was offered.

Indian: Indra and the Parade of Ants

One thing mythologies attempt to do is to provide humans with a sense of their relative importance in the universe, a sense of proportion. We need such a perspective, such an understanding of our significance or lack of it on the cosmic scale. In this famous tale of the parade of ants from the *Brahmavaivarta Purana,* retold by Heinrich Zimmer, we find the god Indra himself in need of this understanding.

•

Indra slew the dragon, a giant titan that had been couching on the mountains in the limbless shape of a cloud serpent, holding the waters of heaven captive in its belly. The god flung his thunderbolt into the midst of the ungainly coils; the monster shattered like a stack of withered rushes. The waters burst free and streamed in ribbons across the land, to circulate once more through the body of the world.

This flood is the flood if life and belongs to all. It is the sap of field and forest, the blood coursing in the veins. The monster had appropriated the common benefit, massing his ambitious, selfish hulk between heaven and earth, but now was slain. The juices again were pouring. The titans were retreating to the underworlds; the gods were returning to the summit of the central mountain of the earth, there to reign from on high.

During the period of the supremacy of the dragon, the majestic mansions of the lofty city of the gods had cracked and crumbled. The first act of Indra was to rebuild them. All the divinities of the heavens were acclaiming him their savior. Greatly elated in his triumph and in the knowledge of his strength, he summoned Vishvakarman, the god of arts and crafts, and commanded him to erect such a palace as should befit the unequaled splendor of the king of the gods.

The miraculous genius, Vishvakarman, succeeded in constructing in a single year a shining residence, marvelous with palaces and gardens, lakes and towers. But as the work progressed, the demands of Indra became even more exacting and his unfolding visions vaster. He required additional terraces and pavilions, more ponds, groves, and pleasure grounds. Whenever Indra arrived to appraise the work, he developed vi-

Heinrich Zimmer, Myths and Symbols in Indian Art and Civilization (Princeton, N.J., 1946, 1972), pp. 3–11.

sion beyond vision of marvels remaining to be contrived. Presently the divine craftsman, brought to despair, decided to seek succor from above. He would turn to the demiurgic creator, Brahmā, the pristine embodiment of the Universal Spirit, who abides far above the troubled Olympian sphere of ambition, strife, and glory.

When Vishvakarman secretly resorted to the higher throne and presented his case, Brahmā comforted the petitioner. "You will soon be relieved of your burden," he said. "Go home in peace." Then, while Vishvakarman was hurrying down again to the city of Indra, Brahmā himself ascended to a still higher sphere. He came before Vishnu, the Supreme Being, of whom he himself, the Creator, was but an agent. In beatific silence Vishnu gave ear, and by a mere nod of the head let it be known that the request of Vishvakarman would be fulfilled.

Early next morning a brahmin boy, carrying the staff of a pilgrim, made his appearance at the gate of Indra, bidding the porter announce his visit to the king. The gate-man hurried to the master, and the master hastened to the entrance to welcome in person the auspicious guest. The boy was slender, some ten years old, radiant with the luster of wisdom. Indra discovered him amidst a cluster of enraptured, staring children. The boy greeted the host with a gentle glance of his dark and brilliant eyes. The king bowed to the holy child and the boy cheerfully gave his blessing. The two retired to the hall of Indra, where the god ceremoniously proffered welcome to his guest with oblations of honey, milk, and fruits, then said: "O Venerable Boy, tell me of the purpose of your coming."

The beautiful child replied with a voice that was as deep and soft as the slow thundering of auspicious rain clouds. "O King of Gods, I have heard of the mighty palace you are building, and have come to refer to you the questions in my mind. How many years will it require to complete this rich and extensive residence? What further feats of engineering will Vishvakarman be expected to accomplish? O Highest of the Gods,"—the boy's luminous features moved with a gentle, scarcely perceptible smile—"no Indra before you has ever succeeded in completing such a palace as yours is to be."

Full of the wine of triumph, the king of the gods was entertained by this mere boy's pretension to a knowledge of Indras earlier than himself. With a fatherly smile he put the question: "Tell me, Child! Are they then so very many, the Indras and Vishvakarmans whom you have seen—or at least, whom you have heard of?"

The wonderful guest calmly nodded. "Yes, indeed, many have I seen." The voice was as warm and sweet as milk fresh from the cow, but the words sent a slow chill through Indra's veins. "My dear child," the boy continued, "I knew your father, Kashyapa, the Old Tortoise Man, lord and progenitor of all the creatures of the earth. And I knew your grandfather, Marīchi, Beam of Celestial Light, who was the son of Brahā. Marīchi was begotten of the god Brahmā's pure spirit; his only wealth and glory were his sanctity and devotion. Also, I know Brahmā, brought forth by Vishnu from the lotus calix growing from Vishnu's navel. And Vishnu himself—the Supreme Being, supporting Brahmā in his creative endeavor—him too I know.

"O King of Gods, I have known the dreadful dissolution of the universe. I have seen all perish, again and again, at the end of every cycle. At that terrible time, every single atom dissolves into the primal, pure waters of eternity, whence originally all arose. Everything then goes back into the fathomless, wild infinity of the ocean, which is covered with utter darkness and is empty of every sign of animate being. Ah, who will count the universes that have passed away, or the creations that have risen afresh, again and again, from the formless abyss of the vast waters? Who will number the passing ages of the world, as they follow each other endlessly? And who will search through the wide infinities of space to count the universes side by side, each containing its Brahmā, its Vishnu, its Shiva? Who will count the Indras in them all—those Indras side by side, who reign at once in all the innumerable worlds; those others who passed away before them; or even the Indras who succeed each other in any given line, ascending to godly kingship, one by one, and, one by one, passing away? King of Gods, there are among your servants certain who maintain that it may be possible to number the grains of sand on earth and the drops of rain that fall from the sky, but no one will ever number all those Indras. This is what the Knowers know.

"The life and kingship of an Indra endure seventy-one eons, and when twenty-eight Indras have expired, one Day and Night of Brahmā has elapsed. But the existence of one Brahmā, measured in such Brahmā Days and Nights, is only one hundred and eight years. Brahmā follows Brahmā; one sinks, the next arises; the endless series cannot be told. There is no end to the number of those Brahmās—to say nothing of Indras.

"But the universes side by side at any given moment, each harboring a Brahmā and an Indra: who will estimate the number of these? Beyond the farthest vision, crowding outer space, the universes come and go, an innumerable host. Like delicate boats they float on the fathomless, pure waters that form the body of Vishnu. Out of every hair-pore of that body a universe bubbles and breaks. Will you presume to count them? Will you number the gods in all those worlds—the worlds present and the worlds past?"

A procession of ants had made its appearance in the hall during the discourse of the boy. In military array, in a column four yards wide, the tribe paraded across the floor. The boy noted them, paused, and stared, then suddenly laughed with an astonishing peal, but immediately subsided into a profoundly indrawn and thoughtful silence.

"Why do you laugh?" stammered Indra. "Who are you, mysterious being, under this deceiving guise of a boy?" The proud king's throat and lips had gone dry, and his voice continually broke. "Who are you, Ocean of Virtues, enshrouded in deluding mist?"

The magnificent boy resumed: "I laughed because of the ants. The reason is not to be told. Do not ask me to disclose it. The seed of woe and the fruit of wisdom are enclosed within this secret. It is the secret that smites with an ax the tree of worldly vanity, hews away its roots, and scatters its crown. This secret is a lamp to those groping in ignorance. This secret lies buried in the wisdom of the ages, and is rarely revealed even to saints. This secret is the living air of those ascetics who renounce and transcend mortal existence; but worldlings, deluded by desire and pride, it destroys."

The boy smiled and sank into silence. Indra regarded him, unable to move. "O Son of a Brahmin," the king pleaded presently, with a new and visible humility, "I do not know who you are. You would seem to be Wisdom Incarnate. Reveal to me this secret of the ages, this light that dispels the dark."

Thus requested to teach, the boy opened to the god the hidden wisdom. "I saw the ants, O Indra, filing in long parade. Each was once an Indra. Like you, each by virtue of pious deeds once ascended to the rank of a king of gods. But now, through many rebirths, each has become again an ant. This army is an army of former Indras.

"Piety and high deeds elevate the inhabitants of the world to the glorious realm of the celestial mansions, or to the higher domains of Brahmā and Shiva and to the highest sphere of Vishnu; but wicked acts sink them into the worlds beneath, into pits of pain and sorrow, involving reincarnation among birds and vermin, or out of the wombs of pigs and animals of the wild, or among trees, or among insects. It is by deeds that one merits happiness or anguish, and becomes a master or a serf. It is by deeds that one attains to the rank of a king or brahmin, or of some god, or of an Indra or a Brahmā. And through deeds again, one contracts disease, acquires beauty and deformity, or is reborn in the condition of a monster.

"This is the whole substance of the secret. This wisdom is the ferry to beatitude across the ocean of hell.

"Life in the cycle of the countless rebirths is like a vision in a dream. The gods on high, the mute trees and the stones, are alike apparitions in this phantasy. But Death administers the law of time. Ordained by time, Death is the master of all. Perishable as bubbles are the good and the evil of the beings of the dream. In unending cycles the good and evil alternate. Hence, the wise are attached to neither, neither the evil nor the good. The wise are not attached to anything at all."

The boy concluded the appalling lesson and quietly regarded his host.

The king of gods, for all his celestial splendor, had been reduced in his own regard to insignificance. Meanwhile, another amazing apparition had entered the hall.

The newcomer had the appearance of a kind of hermit. His head was piled with matted hair; he wore a black deerskin around his loins; on his forehead was painted a white mark; his head was shaded by a paltry parasol of grass; and a quaint, circular cluster of hair grew on his chest: it was intact at the circumference, but from the center many of the hairs, it seemed, had disappeared. This saintly figure strode directly to Indra and the boy, squatted between them on the floor, and there remained, motionless as a rock. The kingly Indra, somewhat recovering his hostly role, bowed and paid obeisance, offering sour milk with honey and other refreshments; then he inquired, falteringly but reverently, after the welfare of the stern guest, and bade him welcome. Whereupon the boy addressed the holy man, asking the very questions Indra himself would have proposed.

"Whence do you come, O Holy Man? What is your name and what brings you to this place? Where is your present home, and what is the meaning of this grass parasol? What is the portent of that circular hair-tuft on your chest: why is it dense at the circumference but at the center almost bare? Be kind enough, O Holy Man, to answer, in brief, these questions. I am anxious to understand."

Patiently the old saint smiled, and slowly began his reply. "I am a brahmin. Hairy is my name. And I have come here to behold Indra. Since I know that I am short-lived, I have decided to possess no home, to build no house, and neither to marry nor to seek a livelihood. I exist by begging alms. To shield myself from sun and rain I carry over my head this parasol of grass.

"As to the circle of hair on my chest, it is a source of grief to the children of the world. Nevertheless, it teaches wisdom. With the fall of an Indra, one hair drops. That is why, in the center all the hairs have gone. When the other half of the period allotted to the present Brahmā will have expired, I myself shall die. O Brahmin Boy, it follows that I am somewhat short of days; what, therefore, is the use of a wife and a son, or of a house?

"Each flicker of the eyelids of the great Vishnu registers the passing of a Brahmā. Everything below that sphere of Brahmā is as insubstantial as a cloud taking shape and again dissolving. That is why I devote myself exclusively to meditating on the incomparable lotus-feet of highest Vishnu. Faith in Vishnu is more than the bliss of redemption; for every joy, even the heavenly, is as fragile as a dream, and only interferes with the one-pointedness of our faith in Him Supreme.

"Shiva, the peace-bestowing, the highest spiritual guide, taught me this wonderful wisdom. I do not crave to experience the various blissful forms of redemption: to share the highest god's supernal mansions and enjoy his eternal presence, or to be like him in body and apparel, or to become a part of his august substance, or even to be absorbed wholly in his ineffable essence."

Abruptly, the holy man ceased and immediately vanished. It had been the god Shiva himself; he had now returned to his supramundane abode. Simultaneously, the brahmin boy, who had been Vishnu, disappeared as well. The king was alone, baffled and amazed.

The king, Indra, pondered; and the events seemed to him to have been a dream. But he no longer felt any desire to magnify his heavenly splendor or to go on with the construction of his palace. He summoned Visvakarman. Graciously greeting the craftsman with honeyed words, he heaped on him jewels and precious gifts, then with a sumptuous celebration sent him home.

The king, Indra, now desired redemption. He had acquired wisdom, and wished only to be free. He entrusted the pomp and burden of his office to his son, and prepared to retire to the hermit life of the wilderness. Whereupon his beautiful and passionate queen, Shachi, was overcome with grief.

Weeping, in sorrow and utter despair, Shachi resorted to Indra's ingenious house-priest and spiritual advisor, the Lord of Magic Wisdom, Brihaspati. Bowing at his feet, she implored him to divert her husband's mind from its stern resolve. The resourceful counselor of the gods, who by his spells and devices had helped the heavenly powers wrest the government of the universe from the hands of their titan rivals, listened thoughtfully to the complaint of the voluptuous, disconsolate goddess, and knowingly nodded assent. With a wizard's smile, he took her hand and conducted her to the presence of her spouse. In the role, then, of spiritual teacher, he discoursed sagely on the virtues of the spiritual life, but on the virtues also, of the secular. He gave to each its due. Very skillfully he developed his theme. The royal pupil was persuaded to relent in his extreme resolve. The queen was restored to radiant joy.

This Lord of Magic Wisdom, Brihaspati, once had composed a treatise on government, in order to teach Indra how to rule the world. He now issued a second work, a treatise on the polity and stratagems of married love. Demonstrating the sweet art of wooing ever anew, and of enchaining the beloved with enduring bonds, this priceless book established on sound foundations the married life of the reunited pair.

Thus concludes the marvelous story of how the king of gods was humiliated in his boundless pride, cured of an excessive ambition, and through wisdom, both spiritual and secular, brought to a knowledge of his proper role in the wheeling play of unending life.

Bibliography

Only a few of the many good collections of mythological tales can be mentioned here. For the Greek myths, Edith Hamilton's *Mythology* (New York, 1969) is useful if somewhat dated in approach. The same can be said of the other great standard collection, a nineteenth-century work by Thomas Bulfinch, *Bulfinch's Mythology* (New York, 1962), which includes a volume on medieval myths. Robert Graves's two-volume *The Greek Myths* (Baltimore, Md., 1955) is still the liveliest interpretation of the myths—with special emphasis on the struggle between the patriarchal and the feminine in myth. His work is also the best source for the origins and derivations of the myths, even if his accuracy is sometimes questionable. Mark Morford and Robert Lenardon present thorough interpretations of many of the classical myths in their *Classical Mythology* (New York, 1971). Lively retellings of small selections of myths from other parts of the world are to be found in *The Oldest Stories in the World* (Boston, 1952) by Theodor Gaster and in *Myths of the World* (New York, 1932, 1972) by Padraic Colum. Of course, numerous encyclopedia-like works on world mythology can be found in any library or bookstore.

PART III

HERO

MYTHS

Mythology comes alive for us most clearly in the stories of heroes, for the hero, wherever he comes from—the "hero with a thousand faces" as Joseph Campbell calls him—is our persona, our representative in the world dream that is myth. Campbell tells us that the universal hero pattern or "monomyth" (here he uses a word coined by James Joyce) involves a process by which the hero leaves the ordinary world of waking consciousness, enters the dark world of the supernatural, overcomes those who would destroy him there, and then returns to the ordinary, possessed of powers and new knowledge for his people (*The Hero with a Thousand Faces*, p. 30).

When the hero, be he the Jewish Jesus or the Irish Cuchulainn or the Greek Herakles, journeys on his quest into the world of mysteries, he resembles the shamans of certain cultures who journey into the spirit world to retrieve lost or sick tribe members. Some heroes are, in fact, perhaps shamanic in origin or are metaphors for shamanic rituals and beliefs. We feel this especially in the hero stories that involve a literal descent into the underworld to retrieve a lost lover or relative. The myths of Dionysos, Orpheus, Isis, and Jesus contain examples of this kind of descent. But whoever the hero may be, he or she journeys for us, carries us metaphorically into our darker side, into the unconscious realm that we tentatively explore in our own dreams—into the world where our nightmares become real, where the monsters inside of us take on terrifyingly real forms, where our deepest wishes sometimes are fulfilled.

The myth that emerges from the many cultural versions of the hero, then, must be seen as a universal metaphor for the human search for self-knowledge, for what Teilhard de Chardin might have called the evolutionary path to full consciousness. And, of course, on the individual level it speaks to our attempts to achieve individuation. To follow the hero is to lose ourselves in order to find ourselves, to recognize our true selves in what Campbell calls "the wonderful song of the soul's high adventure" (*The Hero with a Thousand Faces*, p. 6).

The monomyth contains many elements. This is not to say that every hero acts out each element. Many heroes have miraculous conceptions and births, while some do not. Some descend to the underworld, and others do not. But a comparison of mythical heroes from all over the world reveals the common identity behind their highly differentiated cultural masks: they all experience the majority of the ritual acts—the *rites of passage*—outlined below.

More often than not the hero is miraculously conceived and born under unusual circumstances. Jesus and Quetzalcoatl and many others are born of virgins, the Buddha conceives himself in his mother's dream, the Native American Kutoyis is conceived by a clot of blood, Adonis is born of a tree. Heroes are born when they are needed, during a culture's dark period, often symbolized by the winter solstice. The pure or virgin birth provides a special status for the hero and announces the primordial hope for a new beginning. Mithras was born of a rock on December 25 and was attended by shepherds. The founders of the early Christian church arrived at the same date for the birth of Jesus in a stable and report that shepherds attended him there.

The darkest time of the year, the darkest period in a culture's history, can be for us metaphors for a psychological reality and need. The hero's conception and birth represent the birth of the hero process within us—that is, of the process of individuation by which we agree to a shamanic journey into our own unknown in order eventually to discover our relationship with the overall significance of things, what in myth is called the Supreme Being or, in patriarchal cultures, the Father. So it is that one of the important leitmotifs of myth and literature is the hero's search for his father. This is the real father, the universal source, the agent of conception that transcends even the biological father.

By the same token, the virgin who gives birth to the hero is the Great Goddess herself—the Mother of us all, the provider of the physical existence in which we must carry the divine energy. The hero may be fathered by that intangible energy, but to be truly human, truly us, he must enter the element of flesh and blood by the only doorway available. As a metaphor for our psychological journey within, therefore, the hero story gains strength from the fact that the hero's birth often takes place in a hidden place—a cave, a rock, a stable, a grove, a water pot—which may be seen as a symbolic Mother Earth womb that prefigures the tomb. The body of the Mother and our reality on earth are, after all, death-defined.

A further dimension is added by the threat to the young

hero's life. If one side—the heroic side—of the individual or the society desires a new beginning, the other, more ordinary side prefers the status quo and struggles against the birth. The Herods, the demons, the jealous or angry fathers—all are only too willing to murder the hero, to leave him unattended in the wilderness, or to place him in a basket and leave him to his fate on a river's current. In psychological terms a part of us, representing everything we have been taught about safety and the nest, resists this dangerous journey within. Perhaps this is why heroes so often must separate themselves from or be separated from their human families in order to go about "my father's business."

The quest itself is the predominant aspect of the hero myth. It usually begins with a call to adventure: the voice of God calls Moses from the burning bush, the appearance of the Holy Grail calls Arthur's knights, the young Buddha is called by the "Four Signs" that appear to him as he rides about with his charioteer. Often the hero refuses the summons. We all resist radical change, and the hero, as our persona in the universal dream, is no exception. "Who am I" to perform such a task, asks Moses. In effect, Jonah asks the same question, as does Jesus in the Garden of Gethsemane.

The quest is marked by trials, by confrontations with and the defeat of our inner monsters. These monsters appear, as they would in dreams, in forms that reflect the social beliefs and concerns of the particular cultures that give them life. For instance, the patriarchal cultures out of which most of our extant myths emerge nearly always see the hero as being threatened by a femme fatale or temptress—Circe, the Sirens, Samson's Delilah. Cultures that stress the division of nature into good and evil place the hero against some epitome of evil, a satanic figure.

However, the monsters of the inner world are balanced by sources of strength. Heroes are often guided—Aeneas by the Sibyl, countless fairy tale heroes and heroines by a spirit who takes the form of a fairy godmother, a wise old man, or a wise fool (the last perhaps a remnant of our trickster god).

At some point in the hero's journey quest he or she must confront the ultimate nemesis, death itself, and must undertake a journey to the Land of the Dead. Through this descent, the hero takes us to the very depths of the unconscious world where individual destiny and human destiny lie. In the death motif we confront the essence of what we are. In facing our death-defined nature, we rob death of "dominion" and emerge in rebirth from the womb of the earth into a new individuated existence, a new wisdom or wholeness. It remains only for the hero to return to the Supreme Being in an act of apotheosis or ascension signifying that wholeness. In many of the myths the hero, like the dying god, descends into death and in returning brings great boons to his or her culture. Often the gift is a new crop—corn or wheat— or some new spiritual knowledge. The hero's descent into the Mother is, as in the dying-god motif, a form of planting associated with the Great Goddess, and even in the myths of patriarchal cultures we find in this aspect of the hero cycle an important female presence, signifying the psyche or spiritual energy—what Jung called the *anima*—without which the hero cannot achieve wholeness or full individuation.

Each of these heroic rites becomes for the literary artist an archetypal form that speaks to our common human experience and lends power and reality to the creative work. When we read that the hero of Henry Fielding's novel *Tom Jones* is a foundling, we associate him in our minds with all those heroes who are abandoned in the wilderness, and Tom's actions take on added significance in light of the lives of those heroes who, like him, go on to be questers in their cultures and metaphors for our own individual quests for wholeness, for the union with wisdom symbolized by Tom's eventual marriage with Sophia (Greek, "wisdom"), by Jesus' ascension into heaven, and by the mysterious apotheosis of Oedipus at the end of *Oedipus at Colonus*. The characters these heroes confront—the guides such as Dante's Beatrice or Lambert Strether's Maria Gostrey or the enchantresses such as Henry James's Madame Merle or John Keats's "belle dame sans merci" or the satanic figures such as William Shakespeare's Iago or Nathaniel Hawthorne's Chillingworth—take their power to communicate with our psyches from the archetypal guides, *femmes fatales*, and satanic characters of myth. When we read William Faulkner's *The Bear* or James Joyce's *A Portrait of the Artist as a Young Man*, the very images chosen by the two authors lead us to myths and rituals of childhood initiation; as a result, these stories, which on the surface seem to be about hunting in the American South and growing up a Catholic in Ireland, become clear and moving metaphors for our own initiations into adulthood and into the mysteries of our own "other" selves. In the same way, Fyodor Dostoevsky turns Raskolnikov's wanderings in Petersburg in *Crime and Punishment* into a modern anti-hero's pilgrimage through a modern hell. Raskolnikov's situation takes its irony from the presence in our mythic heritage of all those heroes who descend to the underworld to discover a father, a lover, or themselves. And when we realize that Shakespeare's Lear and Hamlet must die before their nations can rediscover normality under their much more ordinary successors, we realize that we are experiencing anew the sacred mythic ritual of the scapegoat, that, like dying gods and heroes, Lear and Hamlet speak to the psychological process by which we die to the old and are reborn to the new in the path toward individuation.

The hero stories collected here are from various parts of the world, with some emphasis on myths that have been most important to the imagery and subject matter of the arts in Western culture. Some of the figures treated as heroes can and have been treated as gods as well. Jesus, the Buddha, and Quetzalcoatl, for example, are seen sometimes as primarily human, sometimes as primarily divine. The stories here are meant to illustrate the existence of that "hero with a thousand faces" who lives within us all. They are loosely arranged according to the archetypal themes that make up the hero biography.

THE HERO STORIES

The Conception, Birth, and Childhood of the Hero

Native American (Tewa): Water Jar Boy

Divinity finds many paths to the doorway to human life. The Aztec Quetzalcoatl was conceived when his mother, Chimalman, was breathed upon by the Supreme Being in his form as the morning; the Phrygian Nana conceived Attis by losing a pomegranate in her lap. Many heroes, while not actually born of virgins, are miraculously conceived. The Blackfoot Indian Kutoyis was born of a clot of blood; Isaac, the Virgin Mary, and John the Baptist were all born to women who were barren or postmenopausal. Water Jar Boy is a wonderfully unusual representation of the classic myth of the virgin birth, and his story also contains the motif of the search for the Father.

*

The people were living at Sikyatki. There was a fine looking girl who refused to get married. Her mother made water jars all the time. One day as she was using her foot to mix some clay, she told her daughter to go on with this while she went for water. The girl tried to mix the clay on a flat stone by stepping on it. Somehow some of it entered her. This made her pregnant, and after a time she gave birth. The mother was angry about this, but when she looked she saw it was not a baby that had been born, but a little jar. When the mother asked where it came from the girl just cried. Then the father came in. He said he was very glad his daughter had a baby. When he found out that it was a water jar, he became very fond of it.

He watched it and saw it move. It grew, and in twenty days it had become big. It could go about with the other children and was able to talk. The children also became fond of it. They found out from his talk that he was Water Jar Boy. His mother cried, because he had no legs or arms or eyes. But they were able to feed him through the jar mouth.

When snow came the boy begged his grandfather to take him along with the men to hunt rabbits. "My poor grandson, you can't hunt rabbits; you have no arms or legs."

"Take me anyway," said the boy. "You are so old, you can't kill anything." His grandfather took him down under the mesa where he rolled along. Pretty soon he saw a rabbit track and followed it. Then a rabbit ran out, and he began to chase it. He hit himself against a rock. The jar broke, and up jumped a boy.

He was very glad his skin had been broken and that he was a big boy. He had lots of beads around his neck, earstrings of turquoise, a dance kilt and moccasins, and a buckskin shirt. He was fine-looking and handsomely dressed. He killed four jackrabbits before sunset, because he was a good runner.

His grandfather was waiting for him at the foot of the mesa, but did not know him. He asked the fine looking boy, "Did you see my grandson anywhere?"

"No, I did not see him."

"That's too bad; he's late."

"I didn't see anyone anywhere," said the boy. Then he said, "I am your grandson." He said this because his grandfather looked so disappointed.

"No, you are not my grandson."

"Yes, I am."

T. P. Coffin, ed., *Indian Tales of North America* (Philadelphia, 1961), pp. 99–101.

"You are only teasing me. My grandson is a round jar and has no arms and legs."

Then the boy said, "I am telling you the truth. I am your grandson. This morning you carried me down here. I looked for rabbits and chased one, just rolling along. Pretty soon I hit myself on a rock. My skin was broken, and I came out of it. I am the very one who is your grandson. You must believe me." Then the old man believed him, and they went home together.

When the grandfather came to the house with a fine looking man, the girl was ashamed, thinking the man was a suitor. The old man said, "This is Water Jar Boy, my grandson." The grandmother then asked how the water jar became a boy, and the two men told her. Finally, the women were convinced.

The boy went about with the other boys of the village. One day he said to his mother, "Who is my father?"

"I don't know," she replied. He kept on asking, but it just made her cry. Finally he said, "I am going to find my father, tomorrow."

"You can't find him. I have never been with any man so there is no place for you to look for a father," she said.

"But I know I have one," the boy said. "I know where he lives. I am going to see him."

The mother begged him not to go, but he insisted. The next day she fixed food for him, and he went off toward the southwest to a place called Horse Mesa Point. There was a spring at this place. As he approached he saw a man walking a little way from the spring. He said to the boy, "Where are you going?"

"To the spring," the boy answered.

"Why are you going there?"

"I want to see my father."

"Who is your father?"

"He lives in this spring."

"Well, you will never find your father," said the man.

"Well, I want to go to the spring. My father is living in it," said the boy.

"Who is your father?" asked the man again.

"Well, I think you are my father."

"How do you know that?"

"I just know, that's all."

Then the man stared hard at the boy, trying to scare him. The boy just kept on saying, "You are my father." At last the man said, "Yes, I am your father. I came out of the spring to meet you." He put his arms around the boy's neck. He was very glad his boy had come, and he took him down to the spring.

There were many people living there. The women and the girls ran up to the boy and put their arms around him, because they were glad he had come. This way he found his father and his father's relatives. He stayed there one night. The next day he went to his own home and told his mother he had found his father.

Soon his mother got sick and died. The boy thought to himself, "It's no use for me to stay with these people," so he went to the spring. There he found his mother among the other women. He learned that his father was Red Water Snake. He told his boy that he could not live over at Sik-yatki, so he had made the boy's mother sick so she would die and come to live with him. After that they all lived together.

Greek: Theseus

In the case of Theseus, as with so many other heroes—for example, Jesus, Herakles, Helen of Troy—the father-god chooses a mortal woman to be the hero's vessel.

•

Now, while Pittheus was still living at Pisa, Bellerophon had asked to marry his daughter Aethra, but had been sent away to Caria in disgrace before the marriage could be celebrated; though still contracted to Beller-ophon, she had little hope of his return. Pittheus, therefore, grieving at her enforced virginity, and influenced by the spell which Medea was casting on all of them from afar, made Aegeus drunk, and sent him to bed with Aethra. Later in the same night, Poseidon also enjoyed her. For, in obedience to a dream sent by Athene, she left the drunken Aegeus, and waded across to the island of Sphaeria, which lies close to the mainland of Troezen, carrying libations to pour at the tomb of Sphaerus, Pelops's char-ioteer. There, with Athene's connivance, Poseidon overpowered her, and Aethra subsequently changed the name of the island from Sphaeria to Hiera, and founded on it a temple of Apaturian Athene, establishing a rule that every Trozenian girl should henceforth dedicate her girdle to the god-dess before marriage. Poseidon, however, generously conceded to Aegeus the paternity of any child born to Aethra in the course of the next four months.

Aegeus, when he awoke and found himself in Aethra's bed, told her that if a son were born to them he must not be exposed or sent away, but secretly reared in Troezen. Then he sailed back to Athens, to celebrate the All-Athenian Festival, after hiding his sword and his sandals under a hol-low rock, known as the Altar of Strong Zeus, which stood on the road from Troezen to Hermium. If, when the boy grew up, he could move this rock and

Robert Graves, *The Greek Myths*, vol. 1 (Baltimore, Md., 1955), pp. 324–25.

recover the tokens, he was to be sent with them to Athens. Meanwhile, Aethra must keep silence, lest Aegeus's nephews, the fifty children of Pallas, plotted against her life. The sword was an heirloom from Cecrops.

At a place now called Genethlium, on the way from the city to the harbour of Troezen, Aethra gave birth to a boy. Some say that she at once named him Theseus, because the tokens had been *deposited* for him; others, that he afterwards won this name at Athens. He was brought up in Troezen, where his guardian Pittheus discreetly spread the rumour that Poseidon had been his father; and one Connidas, to whom the Athenians still sacrifice a ram on the day before the Thesean Feasts, acted as his pedagogue. But some say that Theseus grew up at Marathon.

Indian: Krishna

Krishna, as an incarnation of Vishnu, is properly considered a god, but as Krishna son of Devaki, he is often seen as a human hero. His birth and childhood, recorded in the *Vishnu Purana*, the *Bhagavata Purana*, and the *Prem Sagara*, are those of the world hero.

•

Vasudev was a descendant of Yadu, of the Lunar dynasty; he was married to Rohinī, daughter of King Rohan, and to him Kans also gave his own sister Devakī. Immediately after the marriage a heavenly voice was heard announcing: "O Kans, thy death will come to pass at the hand of her eighth son." Kans therefore resolved to slay Vasudev at once, and dissuaded from this, he did actually slay the sons one by one till six were dead. In Devakī's seventh pregnancy the serpent Shesh, or Ananta, on whom Nārāyana rests, took on a human birth. To save this child from Kans, Vishnu created a thought-form of himself and sent it to Mathurā. It took the babe from Devakī's womb and gave it to Rohinī, who had taken refuge with the herdsmen at Gokula, and was cared for by Nand and Yasodā, good people dwelling there, who had as yet no son of their own. The child born of Rohinī was afterwards called Balarāma. After transferring the child, the Sending of Vishnu returned to Devakī and revealed the matter in a dream, and Vasudev and Devakī gave Kans to understand that the child had miscarried.

Then Shrī Krishna himself took birth in Devakī's womb, and the Sending of Vishnu in Yasodā's, so that both were with child. Kans, when he learnt that Devakī was again pregnant, set a strong guard about the house of Vasudev to slay the child the moment it was born; for, much as he feared the prophecy, he dared not incur the sin of slaying a woman. At

Ananda K. Coomaraswamy and The Sister Nivedita, *Myths of the Hindus and Buddhists* (New York, 1967), pp. 219–21.

last Krishna was born, and all the heavens and earth were filled with signs of gladness—trees and forests blossomed and fruited, pools were filled, the gods rained down flowers, and gandharvas played on drums and pipes. But Krishna stood up before his father and mother, and this was the likeness of him—cloudy grey, moon-faced, lotus-eyed, wearing a crown and jewels and a robe of yellow silk, with four arms holding conch and disc and mace and lotus-flower. Vasudev and Devakī bowed down to him, and Shrī Krishna said to them: "Do not fear, for I have come to put away your fear. Take me to Yasodā, and bring her daughter and deliver her to Kans." Then he became again a human child, and the memory of his Godhead left both father and mother, and they thought only, "We have a son," and how they might save him from Kans.

Devakī, with folded palms, said to her husband: "Let us take him to Gokula, where dwell our friends Nand and Yasodā and your wife Rohinī." At that very moment the fetters fell from their limbs, the gateways opened, and the guards fell fast asleep. Then Vasudev placed Krishna in a basket on his head and set out for Gokula. He knew not how to cross the Jamna, but with thought intent on Vishnu he entered the water. It rose higher and higher till it reached his nose; but then Krishna saw his distress and stretched down his foot, and the water sank. So Vasudeva crossed the river and came to Nand's house, where a girl had been born to Yasodā; but Devī had put forgetfulness upon her so that she remembered nothing of it. Vasudeva exchanged the children and returned to Mathurā; and when he was back again with Devakī the fetters and the doors closed, the guards awoke, and the baby cried. Word was sent to Kans, and he went in terror, sword in hand, to his sister's house. A voice announced to him: "Thy enemy is born, and thy death is certain"; but finding that a girl had been born, he released Vasudeva and Devakī, and prayed their pardon for the past slayings and treated them well. But Kans was more than ever enraged against the gods forasmuch as they had deceived him and his guarding of Devakī had been in vain, and especially he longed to slay Nārāyana—that is, Vishnu. To this end his ministers counselled him to slay all those who served Vishnu, Brāhmans, yogīs, sannyāsis, and all holy men. Kans gave orders accordingly, and sent forth his rākshasas to kill cows and Brāhmans and all worshippers of Hari.

Indian: Karna

Karna is one of the heroes of the ancient Indian epic entitled the *Mahabharata*. Karna's early biography includes his miraculous conception, a renewal of his mother's virginity after birth (a motif common to several cultures), his abandonment in a river, his adoption by (as is most usual) a member of a lower class, and a divine sign. The motifs of the child's abandonment in water and adoption are particularly interesting; they are repeated in the stories of distantly separated heroes: Moses, who was hidden in a basket in the bulrushes and adopted by the pharaoh's daughter; the German Siegfried, who was left in a glass vessel in the river and adopted first by a doe and then by a blacksmith; the Polynesian demigod Maui, who was thrown into the sea and adopted by sea spirits; and the Greek Oedipus, who was left to die in the wilderness but was saved by a shepherd.

The emergent myth seems to say that the world child—the *puer aeternus,* the hope for a new beginning—must be reborn of the waters of the universal Earth Mother, that he can belong to no single mortal family.

•

The princess Pritha, also known as Kunti, bore as a virgin the boy Karna, whose father was the sun-god Surya. The young Karna was born with the golden ear ornaments of his father and with an unbreakable coat of mail. The mother in her distress concealed and exposed the boy. In the adaptation of the myth by A. Holtzmann, verse 1458 reads: "Then my nurse and I made a large basket of rushes, placed a lid thereon, and lined it with wax; into this basket I laid the boy and carried him down to the river Acva." Floating on the waves, the basket reaches the river Ganges and travels as far as the city of Campa. "There was passing along the bank of the river, the charioteer, the noble friend of Dhritarashtra, and with him was Radha, his beautiful and pious spouse. She was wrapt in deep sorrow, because no son had been given to her. On the river she saw the basket, which the waves carried close to her on the shore; she showed it to Azirath, who went and drew it forth from the waves." The two take care of the boy and raise him as their own child.

Kunti later on marries King Pandu, who is forced to refrain from conjugal intercourse by the curse that he is to die in the arms of his spouse. But Kunti bears three sons, again through divine conception, one of the children being born in the cave of a wolf. One day Pandu dies in the embrace of his second wife. The sons grow up, and at a tournament which they arrange, Karna appears to measure his strength against the best fighter, Arjuna, the son of Kunti. Arjuna scoffingly refuses to fight the charioteer's son. In order to make him a worthy opponent, one of those present anoints him as king. Meanwhile Kunti has recognized Karna as her son, by the divine mark, and prays him to desist from the contest with his brother, revealing to him the secret of his birth. But he considers her revelation as a fantastic tale, and insists implacably upon satisfaction. He falls in the combat, struck by Arjuna's arrow.

Otto Rank, *The Myth of the Birth of the Hero* (New York, 1959), pp. 18–19.

Greek: Herakles

Herakles, the illegitimate son of Zeus, is one of the greatest and most complex of Greek heroes—at once unbelievably powerful and surprisingly unintelligent. His conception and birth, and especially the threat to his life, follow the pattern of the hero's childhood. Other great heroes who overcome early threats to their lives include the Persian Zoroaster (Zarathustra), Siegfried, and Jesus, who are threatened by demons, a dragon, and a wicked king, respectively.

•

Alcmene, fearing Hera's jealousy, exposed her newly-born child in a field outside the walls of Thebes; and here, at Zeus's instigation, Athene took Hera for a casual stroll. "Look, my dear! What a wonderfully robust child!" said Athene, pretending surprise as she stopped to pick him up. "His mother must have been out of her mind to abandon him in a stony field! Come, you have milk. Give the poor little creature suck!" Thoughtlessly Hera took him and bared her breast, at which Herakles drew with such force that she flung him down in pain, and a spurt of milk flew across the sky and became the Milky Way. "The young monster!" Hera cried. But Herakles was now immortal, and Athene returned him to Alcmene with a smile, telling her to guard and rear him well. The Thebans still show the place where this trick was played on Hera; it is called "The Plain of Herakles."

Some, however, say that Hermes carried the infant Herakles to Olympus; that Zeus himself laid him at Hera's breast while she slept; and that the Milky Way was formed when she awoke and pushed him away, or when he greedily sucked more milk than his mouth would hold, and coughed it up. At all events, Hera was Herakles's foster-mother, if only for a short while; and the Thebans therefore style him her son, and say that he had been Alcaeus before she gave him suck, but was renamed in her honour.

One evening, when Herakles had reached the age of eight or ten months or, as others say, one year, and was still unweaned, Alcmene having washed and suckled her twins, laid them to rest under a lamb-fleece coverlet, on the broad brazen shield which Amphitryon had won from Pterelaus. At midnight, Hera sent two prodigious azure-scaled serpents to Amphitryon's house, with strict orders to destroy Herakles. The gates opened as they approached; they glided through, and over the marble floors to the nursery—their eyes shooting flames, and poison dripping from their fangs.

Robert Graves, *The Greek Myths*, vol. 2 (Baltimore, Md., 1955), pp. 90–91.

The twins awoke, to see the serpents writhed above them, with dart-
ing, forked tongues; for Zeus again divinely illumined the chamber. Iphicles screamed, kicked off the coverlet and, in an attempt to escape, rolled
from the shield to the floor. His frightened cries, and the strange light
shining under the nursery door, roused Alcmene. "Up with you, Amphitryon!" she cried. Without waiting to put on his sandals, Amphitryon
leaped from the cedar-wood bed, seized his sword which hung close by on
the wall, and drew it from its polished sheath. At that moment the light in
the nursery went out. Shouting to his drowsy slaves for lamps and torches,
Amphitryon rushed in; and Herakles, who had not uttered so much as a
whimper, proudly displayed the serpents, which he was in the act of stran-
gling, one in either hand. As they died, he laughed, bounced joyfully up
and down, and threw them at Amphitryon's feet.

While Alcmene comforted the terror-stricken Iphicles, Amphitryon
spread the coverlet over Herakles again, and returned to bed. At dawn,
when the cock had crowed three times, Alcmene summoned the aged Teiresias and told him of the prodigy. Teiresias, after foretelling Herakles's
future glories, advised her to strew a broad hearth with dry faggots of
gorse, thorn and brambles, and burn the serpents upon them at midnight.
In the morning, a maid-servant must collect their ashes, take them to the
rock where the Sphinx had perched, scatter them to the winds, and run
away without looking back. On her return, the palace must be purged with
fumes of sulphur and salted spring water; and its roof crowned with wild
olive. Finally, a boar must be sacrificed at Zeus's high altar. All this Alcmene did. But some hold that the serpents were harmless, and placed in
the cradle by Amphitryon himself; he had wished to discover which of the
twins was his son, and now he knew well.

Indian: The Buddha

Siddhartha Gautama, the Buddha, was said to have been miraculously conceived and born, like so many other heroes, without any impurity. His
mother, Maya—the embodiment of tangible reality—dies soon after the
hero's birth (again, like the mothers of other heroes—for example, the
mothers of Quetzalcoatl and of Water Jar Boy). The boy, in the tradition
of Quetzalcoatl, Water Jar Boy, Kutoyis, Siegfried, the Bantu hero Lituolone, and others, is possessed of adult qualities almost at birth. These two
motifs indicate the Buddha's special status as the *puer aeternus*.

•

It is related that at that time the midsummer festival had been proclaimed
in the city of Kapilavatthu, and the multitude were enjoying the feast. And
queen Maha-Maya, abstaining from strong drink, and brilliant with garlands and perfumes, took part in the festivities for the six days previous to

the day of full moon. And when it came to be the day of full moon, she rose early, bathed in perfumed water, and dispensed four hundred thousand pieces of money in great largess. And decked in full gala attire, she ate of the choicest food; after which she took the eight vows, and entered her elegantly furnished chamber of state. And lying down on the royal couch, she fell asleep and dreamed the following dream:

The four guardian angels came and lifted her up, together with her couch, and took her away to the Himalaya Mountains. There, in the Manosila table-land, which is sixty leagues in extent, they laid her under a prodigious sal-tree, seven leagues in height, and took up their positions respectfully at one side. Then came the wives of these guardian angels, and conducted her to Anotatta Lake, and bathed her, to remove every human stain. And after clothing her with divine garments, they anointed her with perfumes and decked her with divine flowers. Not far off was Silver Hill, and in it a golden mansion. There they spread a divine couch with its head toward the east, and laid her down upon it. Now the future Buddha had become a superb white elephant, and was wandering about at no great distance, on Gold Hill. Descending thence, he ascended Silver Hill, and approaching from the north, he plucked a white lotus with his silvery trunk, and trumpeting loudly, went into the golden mansion. And three times he walked round his mother's couch, with his right side towards it, and striking her on her right side, he seemed to enter her womb. Thus the conception took place in the midsummer festival.

On the next day the queen awoke, and told the dream to the king. And the king caused sixty-four eminent Brahmanas to be summoned, and spread costly seats for them on ground festively prepared with green leaves, dalbergia flowers, and so forth. The Brahmanas being seated, he filled gold and silver dishes with the best of milk-porridge compounded with ghee, honey, and treacle; and covering these dishes with others, made likewise of gold and silver, he gave the Brahmanas to eat. And not only with food, but with other gifts, such as new garments, tawny cows, and so forth, he satisfied them completely. And when their every desire had been satisfied, he told them the dream and asked them what would come of it.

"Be not anxious, great king!" said the Brahmanas; "a child has planted itself in the womb of your queen, and it is a male child and not a female. You will have a son. And he, if he continue to live the household life, will become a universal monarch; but if he leave the household life and retire from the world, he will become a Buddha, and roll back the clouds of sin and folly of this world." . . .

Henry Clarke Warren, Introduction to the *Jataka* in *Buddhism in Translations* (Cambridge, Mass., 1896), pp. 183–87.

Now the instant the future Buddha was conceived in the womb of his mother, all the ten thousand worlds suddenly quaked, quivered, and shook. And the thirty-two prognostics appeared, as follows: an immeasurable light spread through ten thousand worlds; the blind recovered their sight, as if from desire to see this his glory; the deaf received their hearing; the dumb talked; the hunchbacked became straight of body; the lame recovered the power to walk; all those in bonds were freed from their bonds and chains; the fires went out in all the hells; the hunger and thirst of the departed ancestors were stilled; wild animals lost their timidity; diseases ceased among men; all mortals became mild-spoken; horses neighed and elephants trumpeted in a manner sweet to the ear; all musical instruments gave forth their notes without being played upon; bracelets and other ornaments jingled; in all quarters of the heavens the weather became fair; a mild, cool breeze began to blow, very refreshing to men; rain fell out of season; water burst forth from the earth and flowed in streams; the birds ceased flying through the air; the rivers checked their flowing; in the mighty ocean the water became sweet; the ground became everywhere covered with lotuses of the five different colours; all flowers bloomed, both those on land and those that grow in the water; trunk-lotuses bloomed on the trunks of trees, branch-lotuses on the branches, and vine-lotuses on the vines; on the ground, stalk-lotuses, as they are called, burst through the overlying rocks and came up by sevens; in the sky were produced others, called hanging-lotuses; a shower of flowers fell all about; celestial music was heard to play in the sky; and the whole ten thousand worlds became one mass of garlands of the utmost possible magnificence, with waving chowries, and saturated with the incenselike fragrance of flowers, and resembled a bouquet of flowers sent whirling through the air, or a closely woven wreath, or a superbly decorated altar of flowers.

From the time the future Buddha was thus conceived, four angels with swords in their hands kept guard, to ward off all harm from both the future Buddha and the future Buddha's mother. No lustful thought sprang up in the mind of the future Buddha's mother; having reached the pinnacle of good fortune and of glory, she felt comfortable and well, and experienced no exhaustion of body. And within her womb she could distinguish the future Buddha, like a white thread passed through a transparent jewel. And whereas a womb that has been occupied by a future Buddha is like the shrine of a temple, and can never be occupied or used again, therefore it was that the mother of the future Buddha died when he was seven days old, and was reborn in the Tusita heaven.

Now other women sometimes fall short of and sometimes run over the term of ten lunar months, and bring forth either sitting or lying down; but not so the mother of a future Buddha. She carries the future Buddha in her womb for just ten months, and then brings forth while standing up.

This is a characteristic of the mother of a future Buddha. So also queen Maha-Maya carried the future Buddha in her womb, as it were oil in a vessel, for ten months; and being then far gone with child, she grew desirous of going home to her relatives, and said to king Suddhodana,

"Sire, I should like to visit my kinsfolk in their city Devadaha."

"So be it," said the king; and from Kapilavatthu to the city of Devadaha he had the road made even, and garnished it with plantain-trees set in pots, and with banners, and streamers; and, seating the queen in a golden palanquin borne by a thousand of his courtiers, he sent her away in great pomp.

Now between the two cities, and belonging to the inhabitants of both, there was a pleasure-grove of sal-trees, called Lumbini Grove. And at this particular time this grove was one mass of flowers from the ground to the topmost branches, while amongst the branches and flowers hummed swarms of bees of the five different colours, and blocks of various kinds of birds flew about warbling sweetly. Throughout the whole of Lumbini Grove the scene resembled the Chittalata Grove in Indra's paradise, or the magnificently decorated banqueting pavilion of some potent king.

When the queen beheld it she became desirous of disporting herself therein, and the courtiers therefore took her into it. And going to the foot of the monarch sal-tree of the grove, she wished to take hold of one of its branches. And the sal-tree branch, like the tip of a well-stemmed reed, bent itself down within reach of the queen's hand. Then she reached out her hand, and seized hold of the branch, and immediately her pains came upon her. Thereupon the people hung a curtain about her, and retired. So her delivery took place while she was standing up, and keeping fast hold of the sal-tree branch.

At that very moment came four pure-minded Maha-Bramha angels bearing a golden net; and, receiving the future Buddha on this golden net, they placed him before his mother and said,

"Rejoice, O queen! A mighty son has been born to you."

Now other mortals on issuing from the maternal womb are smeared with disagreeable, impure matter; but not so the future Buddha. He issued from his mother's womb like a preacher descending from his preaching-seat, or a man coming down a stair, stretching out both hands and both feet, unsmeared by any impurity from his mother's womb, and flashing pure and spotless, like a jewel thrown upon a vesture of Benares cloth. Notwithstanding this, for the sake of honouring the future Buddha and his mother, there came two streams of water from the sky, and refreshed the future Buddha and his mother.

Then the Brahma angels, after receiving him on their golden net, delivered him to the four guardian angels, who received him from their hands on a rug which was made of the skins of black antelopes, and was soft to the touch, being such as is used on state occasions; and the guardian angels delivered him to men who received him on a coil of fine cloth; and the men let him out of their hands on the ground, where he stood and faced the east. There, before him, lay many thousands of worlds, like a great open court; and in them, gods and men, making offerings to him of perfumes, garlands, and so on, were saying,

"Great Being! There is none your equal, much less your superior."

When he had in this manner surveyed the four cardinal points, and the four intermediate ones, and the zenith, and the nadir, in short, all the ten directions in order, and had nowhere discovered his equal, he exclaimed, "This is the best direction," and strode forward seven paces, followed by Maha-Brahma holding over him the white umbrella, Suyama bearing the fan, and other divinities having the other symbols of royalty in their hands. Then, at the seventh stride, he halted, and with a noble voice he shouted the shout of victory, beginning,

"The chief am I in all the world."

Now at the very time that our future Buddha was born in Lumbini Grove there also came into existence the mother of Rahula, and Channa the courtier, Kaludayi the courtier, Kanthaka the king of horses, the great Bo-tree, and the four urns full of treasure. Of these last, one was a quarter of a league in extent, another a half-league, the third three-quarters of a league, and the fourth a league. These seven are called the connate ones.

Then the inhabitants of both cities took the future Buddha, and carried him to Kapilavatthu.

Irish: Cuchulainn

Cuchulainn resembles Krishna, Herakles, and Theseus. As a child he already possesses the powers of the world hero.

•

Before his fifth year, when already possessed of man's strength, he heard of the "boy corps" of his uncle Conchobar and went to test them, taking his club, ball, spear, and javelin, playing with these as he went. At Emain he joined the boys at play without permission; but this was an insult, and they set upon him, throwing at him clubs, spears, and balls, all of which he fended off, besides knocking down fifty of the boys, while his "contortion" seized him—the first reference to this curious phenomenon. Conchobar now interfered, but Cuchulainn would not desist until all the boys came under his protection and guarantee.

At Conchobar's court he performed extraordinary feats and expelled

Louis Gray, ed., *The Mythology of All Races*, vol. 3, *Celtic* (Boston, 1916–32), pp. 141–43.

a band of invaders when the Ulstermen were in their yearly weakness. He was first known as Setanta, and was called Cuchulainn in the following way. Culann the smith had prepared a banquet for Conchobar, who, on his way to it, saw the youth holding the field at ball against three hundred and fifty others; and though he bade him follow, Setanta refused to come until the play was over. While the banquet was progressing, Culann let loose his great watch-dog, which had the strength of a hundred, and when Setanta reached the fort, the beast attacked him, whereupon he thrust his ball into its mouth, and seizing its hind legs, battered it against a rock. Culann complained that the safe-guard of his flocks and herds was destroyed, but the boy said that he would act as watch-dog until a whelp of its breed was ready; and Cathbad the Druid now gave him a name—Cu Chulainn, or "Culann's Dog." This adventure took place before he was seven years old. Baudis suggests that as Cuchulainn was not the hero's birth-name, a dog may have been his *manito*, his name being given him in some ceremonial way at puberty, a circumstance afterward explained by the mythical story of Culann's Hound.

One day Cuchulainn overheard Cathbad saying that whatever stripling assumed arms on that day would have a short life, but would be the greatest of warriors. He now demanded arms from Conchobar, but broke every set of weapons given him until he received Conchobar's own sword and shield; and he also destroyed seventeen chariots, so that nothing but Conchobar's own chariot sufficed him. Cuchulainn made the charioteer drive fast and far until they reached the *dun* of the sons of Nechtan, each of whom he fought and slew, cutting off their heads; while on his return he killed two huge stags and then captured twenty-four wild swans, fastening all these to the chariot. From afar Levarcham the prophetess saw the strange cavalcade approaching Emain and bade all be on their guard, else the warrior would slay them; but Conchobar alone knew who he was and recognized the danger from a youth whose appetite for slaughter had been whetted. A stratagem was adopted, based upon Cuchulainn's well-known modesty. A hundred and fifty women with uncovered breasts were sent to meet him, and while he averted his face, he was seized and plunged into vessels of cold water. The first burst asunder; the water of the second boiled with the heat from his body; that of the third became warm; and thus his rage was calmed.

Bantu: Lituolone

In this Bantu myth, the hero is born miraculously of an old woman and achieves adulthood and the power to fight evil almost at birth.

•

There is a Sesuto tale that tells of a monster that used to devour humans; eventually the only person left on earth was an old woman who had gone

into hiding, and who, without the aid of a man, gave birth to a child be-
decked with amulets, to whom she gave the name of the god Lituolone.
On the very day he was born, the child attained adult stature. He asked
his mother where other men were, and, being told of the monster Kammapa, he took hold of a knife and prepared to fight it. He was swallowed
by the fabulous animal, and this allowed him to tear the beast's entrails to
pieces and bring forth from its stomach thousands of human beings.

The Journey Quest of the Hero

French: Joan of Arc

The quest of Joan of Arc, the Maid of Orléans, is a saintly mission; she is
driven by a power within, which takes the form of her famous "voices,"
the vehicle for the first stage of the hero quest, the call to adventure.

•

St Joan was in her fourteenth year when she experienced the earliest of
those supernatural manifestations which were to lead her through the path
of patriotism to death at the stake. At first it was a single voice addressing
her apparently from near by, and accompanied by a blaze of light: afterwards, as the voices increased in number, she was able to see her interlo-
cutors whom she identified as St Michael, St Catherine, St Margaret and
others. Only very gradually did they unfold her mission: it was a mission
which might well appal her: she, a simple peasant girl, was to save France!
She never spoke about these Voices in Domrémy; she was too much afraid
of her stern father. By May 1428 they had become insistent and explicit.
She must present herself at once to Robert Baudricourt, who commanded
the king's forces in the neighbouring town of Vaucouleurs. Joan succeeded
in persuading an uncle who lived near Vaucouleurs to take her to him, but
Baudricourt only laughed and dismissed her, saying that her father ought
to give her a good hiding.

   At this time the military position was well-nigh desperate, for Orleans, the last remaining stronghold, had been invested by the English and
was in danger of falling. After Joan's return to Domrémy her voices gave
her no rest. When she protested that she was a poor girl who could neither
ride nor fight, they replied; "It is God who commands it." Unable to resist
such a call she secretly left home and went back to Vaucouleurs. Baudri-

Pierre Grimal, ed., *Larousse World Mythology* (London, 1965), p. 522.

Thurston, Herbert, and Donald Attwater, eds. *Butler's Lives of the Saints*, vol. 2 (New York, 1963),
pp. 427–29.

court's scepticism as to her mission was somewhat shaken when official confirmation reached him of a serious defeat of the French which Joan had previously announced to him. He now not only consented to send her to the king but gave her an escort of three men-at-arms. At her own request she travelled in male dress to protect herself. Although the little party reached Chinon, where the king was residing, on March 6, 1429, it was not till two days later that Joan was admitted to his presence. Charles had purposely disguised himself, but she identified him at once and, by a secret sign communicated to her by her Voices and imparted by her to him alone, she obliged him to believe in the supernatural nature of her mission. She then asked for soldiers whom she might lead to the relief of Orleans. This request was opposed by La Trémouille, the king's favourite, and by a large section of the court, who regarded the girl as a crazy visionary or a scheming impostor. To settle the matter it was decided to send her to be examined by a learned body of theologians at Poitiers.

After a searching interrogatory extending over three weeks this council decided that they found nothing to disapprove of, and advised Charles to make prudent use of her services. Accordingly after her return to Chinon arrangements were pushed forward to equip her to lead an expeditionary force. A special standard was made for her bearing the words "Jesus: Maria," together with a representation of the Eternal Father to whom two kneeling angels were presenting a fleur-de-lis. On April 27 the army left Bois with Joan at its head clad in white armour, and in spite of some contretemps she entered Orleans on April 29. Her presence in the beleaguered city wrought marvels. By May 8, the English forts which surrounded Orleans had been captured and the siege raised, after she herself had been wounded in the breast by an arrow. All these events with their approximate dates she had prophesied before starting the campaign. She would fain have followed up these successes, for her Voices had told her that she would not last for long; but La Trémouille and the archbishop of Rheims were in favour of negotiating with the enemy. They persisted in regarding the relief of Orleans merely as a piece of good luck. However, the Maid was allowed to undertake a short campaign on the Loire with the Duc d'Alençon, one of her best friends. It was completely successful and ended with a victory at Patay in which the English forces under Sir John Fastolf suffered a crushing defeat. Joan now pressed for the immediate coronation of the Dauphin. The road to Rheims had practically been cleared and the last obstacle was removed by the unexpected surrender of Troyes.

But the French leaders dallied, and only very reluctantly did they consent to follow her to Rheims where, on July 17, 1429, Charles VII was solemnly crowned, Joan standing at his side with her standard. That event, which completed the mission originally entrusted to her by the Voices, marked also the close of her military successes.

Greek: Oedipus

Sophocles' tragedy *Oedipus the King* is concerned with a quest that is the most important event in the hero-king's life. It is a quest for identity (albeit ironic, since at first he is not even aware that he is the object of his quest), for self, and therefore for the father. It is an acceptance of a call from the oracle to remove the moral pollution that is destroying Thebes, and it is a quest that will confirm the king's eventual fear that he has killed his father and married his mother. In this speech King Oedipus reveals his fear to his mother-wife, Jocasta.

•

OEDIPUS

It shall not be kept from you, since my mind
has gone so far with its forebodings. Whom
should I confide in rather than you, who is there
of more importance to me who have passed
through such a fortune?
Polybus was my father, king of Corinth,
and Merope, the Dorian, my mother.
I was held greatest of the citizens
in Corinth till a curious chance befell me
as I shall tell you—curious, indeed,
but hardly worth the store I set upon it.
There was a dinner and at it a man,
a drunken man, accuscd mc in his drink
of being bastard. I was furious
but held my temper under for that day.
Next day I went and taxed my parents with it;
they took the insult very ill from him,
the drunken fellow who had uttered it.
So I was comforted for their part, but
still this thing rankled always, for the story
crept about widely. And I went at last
to Pytho, though my parents did not know.
But Phoebus sent me home again unhonoured
in what I came to learn, but he foretold
other and desperate horrors to befall me,
that I was fated to lie with my mother,
and show to daylight an accursed breed
which men would not endure, and I was doomed
to be murderer of the father that begot me.
When I heard this I fled, and in the days

Sophocles, *Oedipus the King*, in *Sophocles I*, trans. David Grene (New York, 1967), pp. 45–47.

that followed I would measure from the stars
the whereabouts of Corinth—yes, I fled
to somewhere where I should not see fulfilled
the infamies told in that dreadful oracle.
And as I journeyed I came to the place
where, as you say, this king met with his death.
Jocasta, I will tell you the whole truth.
When I was near the branching of the crossroads,
going on foot, I was encountered by
a herald and a carriage with a man in it,
just as you tell me. He that led the way
and the old man himself wanted to thrust me
out of the road by force. I became angry
and struck the coachman who was pushing me.
When the old man saw this he watched his moment,
and as I passed he struck me from his carriage,
full on the head with his two pointed goad.
But he was paid in full and presently
my stick had struck him backwards from the car
and he rolled out of it. And then I killed them
all. If it happened there was any tie
of kinship twixt this man and Laius,
who is then now more miserable than I,
what man on earth so hated by the Gods,
since neither citizen nor foreigner
may welcome me at home or even greet me,
but drive me out of doors? And it is I,
I and no other have so cursed myself.
And I pollute the bed of him I killed
by the hands that killed him. Was I not born evil?
Am I not utterly unclean? I had to fly
and in my banishment not even see
my kindred nor set foot in my own country,
or otherwise my fate was to be yoked
in marriage with my mother and kill my father,
Polybus who begot me and had reared me.
Would not one rightly judge and say that on me
these things were sent by some malignant God?
O no, no, no—O holy majesty
of God on high, may I not see that day!
May I be gone out of men's sight before
I see the deadly taint of this disaster
come upon me.

Greek: Antigone

Antigone, the brave daughter of King Oedipus, answers the call that comes to her through her reverence for religious codes and her sense of the irrationality of the male-dominated society in which she must live. In the excerpt from Sophocles' *Antigone* that follows, the heroine argues her point with her uncle, King Creon, the representative of the patriarchal arbitrariness that refuses the call. As a result of her defiance Antigone will die, but Creon (like the stubborn Pentheus, who refuses the call of Dionysos in Euripides' *Bacchae*) will pay a high price for his moral blindness.

Antigone is brought before her uncle to be charged with having broken the edict that denied burial to her treasonous brother, one of the unfortunate sons of the even more unfortunate Oedipus.

•

CREON
Explain the circumstance of the arrest.

GUARD
She was burying the man. You have it all.

CREON
Is this the truth? And do you grasp its meaning?

GUARD
I saw her burying the very corpse
you had forbidden. Is this adequate?

CREON
How was she caught and taken in the act?

GUARD
It was like this: when we got back again
struck with those dreadful threatenings of yours,
we swept away the dust that hid the corpse.
We stripped it back to slimy nakedness.
And then we sat to windward on the hill
so as to dodge the smell.
We poked each other up with growling threats
if anyone was careless of his work.

Sophocles, *Antigone*, in *Sophocles I*, trans. Elizabeth Wyckoff (New York, 1967), pp. 176–81.

For some time this went on, till it was noon.
The sun was high and hot. Then from the earth
up rose a dusty whirlwind to the sky,
filling the plain, smearing the forest-leaves,
clogging the upper air. We shut our eyes,
sat and endured the plague the gods had sent.
So the storm left us after a long time.
We saw the girl. She cried the sharp and shrill
cry of a bitter bird which sees the nest
bare where the young birds lay.
So this same girl, seeing the body stripped,
cried with great groanings, cried a dreadful curse
upon the people who had done the deed.
Soon in her hands she brought the thirsty dust,
and holding high a pitcher of wrought bronze
she poured the three libations for the dead.
We saw this and surged down. We trapped her fast;
and she was calm. We taxed her with the deeds
both past and present. Nothing was denied.
And I was glad, and yet I took it hard.
One's own escape from trouble makes one glad;
but bringing friends to trouble is hard grief.
Still, I care less for all these second thoughts
than for the fact that I myself am safe.

CREON
You there, whose head is drooping to the ground,
do you admit this, or deny you did it?

ANTIGONE
I say I did it and I don't deny it.

CREON (*to the guard*)
Take yourself off wherever you wish to go
free of a heavy charge.

CREON (*to Antigone*)
You—tell me not at length but in a word.
You knew the order not to do this thing?

ANTIGONE
I knew, of course I knew. The word was plain.

CREON
And still you dared to overstep these laws?

ANTIGONE

For me it was not Zeus who made that order.
Nor did that Justice who lives with the gods below
mark out such laws to hold among mankind.
Nor did I think your orders were so strong
that you, a mortal man, could over-run
the gods' unwritten and unfailing laws.
Not now, nor yesterday's, they always live,
and no one knows their origin in time.
So not through fear of any man's proud spirit
would I be likely to neglect these laws,
draw on myself the gods' sure punishment.
I knew that I must die; how could I not?
even without your warning. If I die
before my time, I say it is a gain.
Who lives in sorrows many as are mine
how shall he not be glad to gain his death?
And so, for me to meet this fate, no grief.
But if I left that corpse, my mother's son,
dead and unburied I'd have cause to grieve
as now I grieve not.
And if you think my acts are foolishness
the foolishness may be in a fool's eye.

CHORUS

The girl is bitter. She's her father's child.
She cannot yield to trouble; nor could he.

CREON

These rigid spirits are the first to fall.
The strongest iron, hardened in the fire,
most often ends in scraps and shatterings.
Small curbs bring raging horses back to terms.
Slave to his neighbor, who can think of pride?
This girl was expert in her insolence
when she broke bounds beyond established law.
Once she had done it, insolence the second,
to boast her doing, and to laugh in it.
I am no man and she the man instead
if she can have this conquest without pain.
She is my sister's child, but were she child
of closer kin than any at my hearth,
she and her sister should not so escape

their death and doom. I charge Ismene too.
She shared the planning of this burial.
Call her outside. I saw her in the house,
maddened, no longer mistress of herself.
The sly intent betrays itself sometimes
before the secret plotters work their wrong.
I hate it too when someone caught in crime
then wants to make it seem a lovely thing.

ANTIGONE
Do you want more than my arrest and death?

CREON
No more than that. For that is all I need.

ANTIGONE
Why are you waiting? Nothing that you say
fits with my thought. I pray it never will.
Nor will you ever like to hear my words.
And yet what greater glory could I find
than giving my own brother funeral?
All these would say that they approved my act
did fear not mute them.
(A king is fortunate in many ways,
and most, that he can act and speak at will.)

CREON
None of these others see the case this way.

ANTIGONE
They see, and do not say. You have them cowed.

CREON
And you are not ashamed to think alone?

ANTIGONE
No, I am not ashamed. When was it shame
to serve the children of my mother's womb?

CREON
It was not your brother who died against him,
then?

ANTIGONE
Full brother, on both sides, my parents' child.

CREON
Your act of grace, in this regard, is crime.

ANTIGONE
The corpse below would never say it was.

CREON
When you honor him and the criminal just alike?

ANTIGONE
It was a brother, not a slave, who died.

CREON
Died to destroy this land the other guarded.

ANTIGONE
Death yearns for equal law for all the dead.

CREON
Not that the good and bad draw equal shares.

ANTIGONE
Who knows that this is holiness below?

CREON
Never the enemy, even in death, a friend.

ANTIGONE
I cannot share in hatred, but in love.

CREON
Then go down there, if you must love, and love
the dead. No woman rules me while I live.

Celtic: King Arthur

King Arthur is called to adventure by the existence of a magic sword in a
rock, the removal of which is possible only for the true king. Eventually,
Arthur's quest will be for unity and renewal, represented by the Holy
Grail. Arthur's birth is marked by mysterious circumstances, and he and
his knights must face such familiar obstacles as the femme fatale in the
persons of Morgan le Fay, Viviane, the Lady of the Lake, and Queen Guinevere herself, whose attraction to Sir Lancelot was the cause of much pain
in Arthur's realm.

•

Arthur, though only fifteen years old at his father's death, was elected king
at a general meeting of the nobles. It was not done without opposition, for

Thomas Bulfinch, *Bulfinch's Mythology: The Age of Chivalry* (New York, 1962), pp. 72–73.

there were many ambitious competitors; but Bishop Brice, a person of great sanctity, on Christmas eve addressed the assembly and represented that it would well become them, at that solemn season, to put up their prayers for some token which should manifest the intentions of Providence respecting their future sovereign. This was done, and with such success, that the service was scarcely ended when a miraculous stone was discovered, before the church door, and in the stone was firmly fixed a sword, with the following words engraven on its hilt:

> I am hight Escalibore,
> Unto a king fair tresore.

Bishop Brice, after exhorting the assembly to offer up their thanksgivings for this signal miracle, proposed a law that, whoever should be able to draw out the sword from the stone, should be acknowledged as sovereign of the Britons; and his proposal was decreed by general acclamation. The tributary kings of Uther and the most famous knights successively put their strength to the proof, but the miraculous sword resisted all their efforts. It stood till Candlemas; it stood till Easter, and till Pentecost, when the best knights in the kingdom usually assembled for the annual tournament. Arthur, who was at that time serving in the capacity of squire to his foster-brother, Sir Kay, attended his master to the lists. Sir Kay fought with great valor and success, but had the misfortune to break his sword, and sent Arthur to his mother for a new one. Arthur hastened home, but did not find the lady; but having observed near the church a sword, sticking in a stone, he galloped to the place, drew out the sword with great ease, and delivered it to his master. Sir Kay would willingly have assumed to himself the distinction conferred by the possession of the sword; but when, to confirm the doubters, the sword was replaced in the stone, he was utterly unable to withdraw it, and it would yield a second time to no hand but Arthur's. Thus decisively pointed out by Heaven as their king, Arthur was by general consent proclaimed as such, and an early day appointed for his solemn coronation.

Greek: Theseus

Theseus' call to a life of adventure, which will fulfill his destiny as the son of a god and as a great hero, is represented by the existence of his foster father's sword and sandals under a magic rock. He goes on to participate in many of the ritual deeds of the world hero—for example, the search for his father (a motif repeated by many great heroes, including Aeneas, Water Jar Boy, and, in a metaphysical sense, Jesus); the confrontation with a monster (the Minotaur); and the descent into the underworld.

At the age of sixteen years he visited Delphi, and offered his first manly hair-clippings to Apollo. He shaved, however, only the fore-part of his head, like the Arabians and Mysians, or like the war-like Abantes of Euboea, who thereby deny their enemies any advantage in close combat. This kind of tonsure, and the precinct where he performed the ceremony, are both still called Thesean. He was now a strong, intelligent and prudent youth; and Aethra, leading him to the rock underneath which Aegeus had hidden the sword and sandals, told him the story of his birth. He had no difficulty in moving the rock, since called the "Rock of Theseus," and recovered the tokens. Yet, despite Pittheus's warnings and his mother's entreaties, he would not visit Athens by the safe sea route, but insisted on travelling overland; impelled by a desire to emulate the feats of his cousin-german Herakles, whom he greatly admired. . . .

Theseus in Crete

It is a matter of dispute whether Medea persuaded Aegeus to send Theseus against Poseidon's ferocious white bull, or whether it was after her expulsion from Athens that he undertook the destruction of this fire-breathing monster, hoping thereby to ingratiate himself further with the Athenians. Brought by Herakles from Crete, let loose on the plain of Argos, and driven thence across the Isthmus to Marathon, the bull had killed men by the hundred between the cities of Probalinthus and Tricorynthus, including (some say) Minos's son Androgeus. Yet Theseus boldly seized those murderous horns and dragged the bull in triumph through the streets of Athens, and up the steep slope of the Acropolis, where he sacrificed it to Athene, or to Apollo.

As he approached Marathon, Theseus had been hospitably entertained by a needy old spinster named Hecale, or Hecalene, who vowed a ram to Zeus if he came back safely. But she died before his return, and he instituted the Hecalesian Rites, to honour her and Zeus Hecaleius, which are still performed today. Because Theseus was no more than a boy at this time, Hecale had caressed him with childish endearments, and is therefore commonly called by the diminutive Hecalene, rather than Hecale.

In requital for the death of Androgeus, Minos gave orders that the Athenians should send seven youths and seven maidens every ninth year—namely at the close of every Great Year—to the Cretan Labyrinth, where the Minotaur waited to devour them. This Minotaur, whose name was Asterius, or Asterion, was the bull-headed monster which Pasiphaë had

Robert Graves, *The Greek Myths*, vol. 1 (Baltimore, Md., 1955), pp. 325, 336–43.

borne to the white bull. Soon after Theseus's arrival at Athens the tribute fell due for the third time, and he so deeply pitied those parents whose children were liable to be chosen by lot, that he offered himself as one of the victims, despite Aegeus's earnest attempts at dissuasion. But some say that the lot had fallen on him. According to others, King Minos came in person with a large fleet to choose the victims; his eye lighted on Theseus who, though a native of Troezen, not Athens, volunteered to come on the understanding that if he conquered the Minotaur with his bare hands the tribute would be remitted.

On the two previous occasions, the ship which conveyed the fourteen victims had carried black sails, but Theseus was confident that the gods were on his side, and Aegeus therefore gave him a white sail to hoist on return, in signal of success; though some say that it was a red sail, dyed in juice of the kerm-oak berry.

When the lots had been cast at the Law Courts, Theseus led his companions to the Dolphin Temple where, on their behalf, he offered Apollo a branch of consecrated olive, bound with white wool. The fourteen mothers brought provisions for the voyage, and told their children fables and heroic tales to hearten them. Theseus, however, replaced two of the maiden victims with a pair of effeminate youths, possessed of unusual courage and presence of mind. These he commanded to take warm baths, avoid the rays of the sun, perfume their hair and bodies with unguent oils, and practise how to talk, gesture, and walk like women. He was thus able to deceive Minos by passing them off as maidens.

Phaeax, the ancestor of the Phaeacians, among whom Odysseus fell, stood as pilot at the prow of the thirty-oared ship in which they sailed, because no Athenian as yet knew anything about navigation. Some say that the helmsman was Phereclus; but those who name him Nausitheus are likely to be right, since Theseus on his return raised monuments to Nausitheus and Phaeax at Phalerum, the port of departure; and the local Pilots' Festival is held in their joint honour.

The Delphic Oracle had advised Theseus to take Aphrodite for his guide and companion on the voyage. He therefore sacrificed to her on the strand; and lo! the victim, a she-goat, became a he-goat in its death-throes. This prodigy won Aphrodite her title of Epitragia.

Theseus sailed on the sixth day of Munychion [April]. Every year on this date the Athenians still send virgins to the Dolphin Temple in propitiation of Apollo, because Theseus had omitted to do so before taking his leave. The god's displeasure was shown in a storm, which forced him to take shelter at Delphi and there offer belated sacrifices.

When the ship reached Crete some days afterwards, Minos rode down to the harbour to count the victims. Falling in love with one of the Athenian maidens—whether it was Periboea (who became the mother of Ajax) or Eriboea, or Phereboea, is not agreed, for these three bore confusingly similar names—he would have ravished her then and there, had Theseus not protested that it was his duty as Poseidon's son to defend virgins against outrage by tyrants. Minos, laughing lewdly, replied that Poseidon had never been known to show delicate respect for any virgins who took his fancy.

"Ha!" he cried, "prove yourself a son of Poseidon, by retrieving this bauble for me!" So saying, he flung his golden signet ring into the sea.

"First prove that you are a son of Zeus!" retorted Theseus.

This Minos did. His prayer: "Father Zeus, hear me!" was at once answered by lightning and a clap of thunder. Without more ado, Theseus dived into the sea, where a large school of dolphins escorted him honourably down to the palace of the Nereids. Some say that Thetis the Nereid then gave him the jewelled crown, her wedding gift from Aphrodite, which Ariadne afterwards wore; others, that Amphitrite the Sea-goddess did so herself, and that she sent the Nereids swimming in every direction to find the golden ring. At all events, when Theseus emerged from the sea, he was carrying both the ring and the crown, as Micon has recorded in his painting on the third wall of Theseus's sanctuary.

Aphrodite had indeed accompanied Theseus: for not only did both Periboea and Phereboea invite the chivalrous Theseus to their couches, and were not spurned, but Minos's own daughter Ariadne fell in love with him at first sight. "I will help you to kill my half-brother, the Minotaur," she secretly promised him, "if I may return to Athens with you as your wife." This offer Theseus gladly accepted, and swore to marry her. Now, before Daedalus left Crete, he had given Ariadne a magic ball of thread, and instructed her how to enter and leave the Labyrinth. She must open the entrance door and tie the loose end of the thread to the lintel; the ball would then roll along, diminishing as it went and making, with devious turns and twists, for the innermost recess where the Minotaur was lodged. This ball Ariadne gave to Theseus, and instructed him to follow it until he reached the sleeping monster, whom he must seize by the hair and sacrifice to Poseidon. He could then find his way back by rolling up the thread into a ball again.

That same night Theseus did as he was told; but whether he killed the Minotaur with a sword given him by Ariadne, or with his bare hands, or with his celebrated club, is much disputed. A sculptured frieze at Amyclae shows the Minotaur bound and led in triumph by Theseus to Athens; but this is not the generally-accepted story.

When Theseus emerged from the Labyrinth, spotted with blood, Ariadne embraced him passionately, and guided the whole Athenian party to the harbour. For, in the meantime, the two effeminate-looking youths had killed the guards of the women's quarters, and released the maiden victims. They all stole aboard their ship, where Nausitheus and Phaeax were expecting them, and rowed hastily away. But although Theseus had first stove in the hulls of several Cretan ships, to prevent pursuit, the alarm sounded and he was forced to fight a sea-battle in the harbour, before escaping, fortunately without loss, under cover of darkness.

Some days later, after disembarking on the island then named Dia, but now known as Naxos, Theseus left Ariadne asleep on the shore, and sailed away. Why he did so must remain a mystery. Some say that he deserted her in favour of a new mistress, Aegle, daughter of Panopeus; others that, while wind-bound on Dia, he reflected on the scandal which Ariadne's arrival at Athens would cause. Others again, that Dionysus, appearing to Theseus in a dream, threateningly demanded Ariadne for himself, and that, when Theseus awoke to see Dionysus's fleet bearing down on Dia, he weighed anchor in sudden terror; Dionysus having cast a spell which made him forget his promise to Ariadne and even her very existence.

Whatever the truth of the matter may be, Dionysus's priests at Athens affirm that when Ariadne found herself alone on the deserted shore, she broke into bitter laments, remembering how she had trembled while Theseus set out to kill her monstrous half-brother; how she had offered silent vows for his success; and how, through love of him, she had deserted her parents and motherland. She now invoked the whole universe for vengeance, and Father Zeus nodded assent. Then, gently and sweetly, Dionysus with his merry train of satyrs and maenads came to Ariadne's rescue. He married her without delay, setting Thetis's crown upon her head, and she bore him many children. Of these only Thoas and Oenopion are sometimes called Theseus's sons. The crown, which Dionysus later set among the stars as the Corona Borealis, was made by Hephaestus of fiery gold and red Indian gems, set in the shape of roses. . . .

Ariadne was soon revenged on Theseus. Whether in grief for her loss, or in joy at the sight of the Attic coast, from which he had been kept by prolonged winds, he forgot his promise to hoist the white sail. Aegeus, who stood watching for him on the Acropolis, where the Temple of the Wingless Victory now stands, sighted the black sail, swooned, and fell headlong to his death into the valley below. But some say that he deliberately cast himself into the sea, which was thenceforth named the Aegean.

Hebrew: Moses

Moses' call to lead his people on a quest for the Promised Land comes from Yahweh in the form of an angel in a burning bush. Like so many heroes, he initially refuses the call, only to be quickly converted to an acceptance of it. Even Jesus in the Garden of Gethsemane asks God if he might be relieved of his task.

•

Chapter 3

Now Moses kept the flock of Jethro his father in law, the priest of Midian: and he led the flock to the backside of the desert, and came to the mountain of God, even to Horeb.

2 And the angel of the Lord appeared unto him in a flame of fire out of the midst of a bush: and he looked, and, behold, the bush burned with fire, and the bush was not consumed.

3 And Moses said, I will now turn aside, and see this great sight, why the bush is not burnt.

4 And when the Lord saw that he turned aside to see, God called unto him out of the midst of the bush, and said, Moses, Moses. And he said, Here am I.

5 And he said, Draw not nigh hither: put off thy shoes from off thy feet, for the place whereon thou standest is holy ground.

6 Moreover he said, I am the God of thy father, the God of Abraham, the God of Isaac, and the God of Jacob. And Moses hid his face; for he was afraid to look upon God.

7 And the Lord said, I have surely seen the affliction of my people which are in Egypt, and have heard their cry by reason of their taskmasters; for I know their sorrows;

8 And I am come down to deliver them out of the hand of the Egyptians, and to bring them up out of that land unto a good land and a large, unto a land flowing with milk and honey; unto the place of the Cā'-nă-ăn-ītes, and the Hittites, and the Amorites, and the Pĕ-riz'-zītes, and the Hivites, and the Jĕb'-ū-śites.

9 Now therefore, behold, the cry of the children of Israel is come unto me: and I have also seen the oppression wherewith the Egyptians oppress them.

10 Come now therefore, and I will send thee unto Phâr'-aōh, that thou mayest bring forth my people the children of Israel out of Egypt.

11 And Moses said unto God, Who am I, that I should go unto Phâr'-aōh, and that I should bring forth the children of Israel out of Egypt?

12 And he said, Certainly I will be with thee; and this shall be a token unto thee, that I have sent thee: When thou has brought forth the people out of Egypt, ye shall serve God upon this mountain.

13 And Moses said unto God, Behold, when I come unto the children of Israel, and shall say unto them, The God of your fathers hath sent me

Exodus 3–4

unto you; and they shall say to me, What is his name? what shall I say unto them?

14 And God said unto Moses, I AM THAT I AM: and he said, Thus shalt thou say unto the children of Israel, I AM hath sent me unto you.

15 And God said moreover unto Moses, Thus shalt thou say unto the children of Israel, The Lord God of your fathers, the God of Abraham, the God of Isaac, and the God of Jacob, hath sent me unto you: this is my name for ever, and this is my memorial unto all generations.

16 Go, and gather the elders of Israel together, and say unto them, The Lord God of your fathers, the God of Abraham, of Isaac, and of Jacob, appeared unto me, saying, I have surely visited you, and seen that which is done to you in Egypt:

17 And I have said, I will bring you up out of the affliction of Egypt unto the land of the Cā'-nă-ăn-îtes, and the Hittites, and the Amorites, and the Pĕ-riz'-zîtes, and the Hivites, and the Jĕb'-ū-sîtes, unto a land flowing with milk and honey.

18 And they shall hearken to thy voice: and thou shalt come, thou and the elders of Israel, unto the king of Egypt, and ye shall say unto him, The Lord God of the Hebrews hath met with us: and now let us go, we beseech thee, three days' journey into the wilderness, that we may sacrifice to the Lord our God.

19 And I am sure that the king of Egypt will not let you go, no, not by a mighty hand.

20 And I will stretch out my hand, and smite Egypt with all my wonders which I will do in the midst thereof: and after that he will let you go.

21 And I will give this people favour in the sight of the Egyptians: and it shall come to pass, that, when ye go, ye shall not go empty:

22 But every woman shall borrow of her neighbour, and of her that sojourneth in her house, jewels of silver, and jewels of gold, and raiment: and ye shall put them upon your sons, and upon your daughters; and ye shall spoil the Egyptians.

Chapter 4

And Moses answered and said, But, behold, they will not believe me, nor hearken unto my voice: for they will say, The Lord hath not appeared unto thee.

2 And the Lord said unto him, What is that in thine hand? And he said, A rod.

3 And he said, Cast it on the ground. And he cast it on the ground, and it became a serpent; and Moses fled from before it.

4 And the Lord said unto Moses, Put forth thine hand, and take it by the tail. And he put forth his hand, and caught it, and it became a rod in his hand:

5 That they may believe that the Lord God of their fathers, the God of Abraham, the God of Isaac, and the God of Jacob, hath appeared unto thee.

6 And the Lord said furthermore unto him, Put now thine hand into thy bosom. And he put his hand into his bosom: and when he took it out, his hand was leprous as snow.

7 And he said, Put thine hand into thy bosom again. And he put his hand into his bosom again; and plucked it out of his bosom, and, behold, it was turned again as his other flesh.

8 And it shall come to pass, if they will not believe thee, neither hearken to the voice of the first sign, that they will believe the voice of the latter sign.

9 And it shall come to pass, if they will not believe also these two signs, neither hearken unto thy voice, that thou shalt take of the water of the river, and pour it upon the dry land: and the water which thou takest out of the river shall become blood upon the dry land.

10 And Moses said unto the Lord, O my Lord, I am not eloquent, neither heretofore, nor since thou hast spoken unto thy servant: but I am slow of speech, and of a slow tongue.

11 And the Lord said unto him, Who hath made man's mouth? or who maketh the dumb, or deaf, or the seeing, or the blind? have not I the Lord?

12 Now therefore go, and I will be with thy mouth, and teach thee what thou shalt say.

13 And he said, O my Lord, send, I pray thee, by the hand of him whom thou wilt send.

14 And the anger of the Lord was kindled against Moses, and he said, Is not Aaron the Levite thy brother? I know that he can speak well. And also, behold, he cometh forth to meet thee: and when he seeth thee, he will be glad in his heart.

15 And thou shalt speak unto him, and put words in his mouth: and I will be with thy mouth, and with his mouth, and will teach you what ye shall do.

16 And he shall be thy spokesman unto the people: and he shall be, even he shall be to thee instead of a mouth, and thou shalt be to him instead of God.

17 And thou shalt take this rod in thine hand, wherewith thou shalt do signs.

18 And Moses went and returned to Jethro his father in law, and said unto him, Let me go, I pray thee, and return unto my brethren which are

in Egypt, and see whether they be yet alive. And Jethro said to Moses, Go in peace.

19 And the Lord said unto Moses in Midian, Go, return into Egypt: for all the men are dead which sought thy life.

20 And Moses took his wife and his sons, and set them upon an ass, and he returned to the land of Egypt: and Moses took the rod of God in his hand.

21 And the Lord said unto Moses, When thou goest to return into Egypt, see that thou do all those wonders before Phâr'-āoh, which I have put in thine hand: but I will harden his heart, that he shall not let the people go.

22 And thou shalt say unto Phâr'-āoh, Thus saith the Lord, Israel is my son, even my firstborn:

23 And I say unto thee, Let my son go, that he may serve me: and if thou refuse to let him go, behold, I will slay thy son, even thy first-born.

24 And it came to pass by the way in the inn, that the Lord met him, and sought to kill him.

25 Then Zip'-pŏ-răh took a sharp stone, and cut off the foreskin of her son, and cast it at his feet, and said, Surely a bloody husband art thou to me.

26 So he let him go: then she said, A bloody husband thou art, because of the circumcision.

27 And the Lord said to Aaron, Go into the wilderness to meet Moses. And he went, and met him in the mount of God, and kissed him.

28 And Moses told Aaron all the words of the Lord who had sent him, and all the signs which he had commanded him.

29 And Moses and Aaron went and gathered together all the elders of the children of Israel:

30 And Aaron spake all the words which the Lord had spoken unto Moses, and did the signs in the sight of the people.

31 And the people believed: and when they heard that the Lord had visited the children of Israel, and that he had looked upon their affliction, then they bowed their heads and worshipped.

Celtic: Parcival

Parcival (or Percival), one of the greatest knights of King Arthur's Round Table, goes on a quest for the Holy Grail. His initial failure is a particularly poignant example of the quest hero's refusal of the call.

•

The Sangreal [or Holy Grail] was the cup from which our Saviour drank at his last supper. He was supposed to have given it to Joseph of Arimathea, who carried it to Europe, together with the spear with which the soldier pierced the Saviour's side. From generation to generation, one of the descendants of Joseph of Arimathea had been devoted to the guardianship of these precious relics; but on the sole condition of leading a life of purity in thought, word, and deed. For a long time the Sangreal was visible to all pilgrims, and its presence conferred blessings upon the land in which it was preserved. But, at length, one of those holy men to whom its guardianship had descended so far forgot the obligation of his sacred office as to look with unhallowed eye upon a young female pilgrim whose robe was accidentally loosened as she knelt before him. The sacred lance instantly punished his frailty, spontaneously falling upon him and inflicting a deep wound. The marvellous wound could by no means be healed, and the guardian of the Sangreal was ever after called "Le Roi Pecheur"—the Sinner King [the Fisher King]. The Sangreal withdrew its visible presence from the crowds who came to worship, and an iron age succeeded to the happiness which its presence had diffused among the tribes of Britain.

. . . Merlin, . . . that great prophet and enchanter, sent a message to King Arthur by Sir Gawain, directing him to undertake the recovery of the Sangreal, informing him at the same time that the knight who should accomplish that sacred quest was already born, and of a suitable age to enter upon it. Sir Gawain delivered his message, and the king was anxiously revolving in his mind how best to achieve the enterprise when, at the vigil of Pentecost, all the fellowship of the Round Table being met together at Camelot, as they sat at meat, suddenly there was heard a clap of thunder, and then a bright light burst forth, and every knight, as he looked on his fellow, saw him, in seeming, fairer than ever before. All the hall was filled with sweet odors, and every knight had such meat and drink as he best loved. Then there entered into the hall the Holy Grail, covered with white samite, so that none could see it, and it passed through the hall suddenly, and disappeared. During this time no one spoke a word, but when they had recovered breath to speak, King Arthur said, "Certainly we ought greatly to thank the Lord for what he hath showed us this day." Then Sir Gawain rose up and made a vow that for twelve months and a day he would seek the Sangreal, and not return till he had seen it, if so he might speed. When they of the Round Table heard Sir Gawain say so, they arose, the most part of them, and vowed the same. When King Arthur heard this, he was greatly displeased, for he knew well that they might not gainsay their vows. "Alas!" said he to Sir Gawain, "you have nigh slain me with the vow and promise that ye have made, for ye have bereft me of the fairest fellowship that ever were seen together in any realm of the world;

Thomas Bulfinch, *Bulfinch's Mythology: The Age of Chivalry* (New York, 1962), pp. 157–59; and W. Wagner, *Romances and Epics of Our Northern Ancestors* (London, 1907), pp. 302–05.

for when they shall depart hence, I am sure that all shall never meet more in this world."

One day [Percival] came to a great lake which he had never seen before. He saw a man seated in a boat, fishing. The man was richly dressed, but pale and sad. Percival asked if he could get food and shelter anywhere about for himself and his tired horse, and was told that if he went straight on, and did not lose his way, he would come to a castle, where he would be kindly received. He started in the direction indicated by the fisherman, and reached the castle at nightfall, after a long and toilsome search. There he met with so much kindness and consideration, garments even being provided for him "by Queen Repanse's orders," that he was filled with amazement. When freshly attired he was taken into the hall, which was brilliantly lighted. Four hundred knights were seated on softly-cushioned seats at small tables, each of which was laid for four. They all sat grave and silent, as though in expectation. When Percival entered, they rose and bowed, and a ray of joy passed over each woeful countenance.

The master of the house, who much resembled the fisherman Percival had seen on the lake, sat in an armchair near the fire, wrapped in sables, and was apparently suffering from some wasting disease.

The deep silence that reigned in the hall was at length broken by the host, who invited Percival, in a low, weak voice, to sit down beside him, telling him that he had been long expected and, at the same time, giving him a sword of exquisite workmanship. The young knight was filled with astonishment. A servant now entered carrying the head of a lance stained with blood, with which he walked round the room in silence. Percival would much have liked to ask the meaning of this strange ceremony and also how his arrival had come to be expected, but he feared lest he should be deemed unwarrantably curious. While thus thinking, the door opened again and a number of beautiful blue-eyed maidens came in, two and two, with a velvet cushion embroidered with pearls, an ebony stand, and various other articles. Last of all came Queen Repanse bearing a costly vessel, whose radiance was more than the human eye could steadfastly gaze upon.

"The holy Grail," Percival heard whispered by one voice after another. He longed to question some one; but felt too much awed by the strangeness and solemnity of all he saw.

The maidens withdrew, and the squires and pages of the knights came forward. Then from the shining vessel streamed an endless supply of the costliest dishes and wines, which they set before their masters. The lord of the castle, however, only ate of one dish, and but a small quantity of that. Percival glanced round the great hall. What could this strange stillness and sadness mean?

When the meal was at an end, the lord of the castle dragged himself to his feet, leaning on two servants. He looked eagerly at his guest, and then retired with a deep sigh. Servants now came to conduct Percival to his sleeping apartment. Before leaving the hall they opened the door of a room in which a venerable old man slept on a low couch. His still handsome face was framed in a coronal of white curls. His sleep was uneasy, and his lips quivered as though he were trying to speak. The servants closed the door again, and led Percival to his chamber.

When he entered the room he looked about him, and at once became aware of a picture embroidered on the silken tapestry, that arrested his attention. It was the picture of a battle, in which the most prominent figure, a knight strangely like the lord of the castle in appearance, was sinking to the ground, wounded by a spear of the same kind as the broken weapon that had been carried round the hall. Much as he desired to know the meaning of this, he determined to ask no questions till the following morning, though the servants told him that his coming had been long expected, and deliverance was looked for at his hands; and they went away, sighing deeply.

His sleep was disturbed by bad dreams, and he awoke next morning unrefreshed. He found his own clothes and armour beside his bed; but no one came to help him. He got up and dressed. All the doors in the castle were locked except those that led out to the ramparts, where his horse stood saddled and bridled at the drawbridge. No sooner had he crossed the bridge than it was drawn up behind him, and a voice called from the battlements:

"Accursed of God, thou that wast chosen to do a great work, and hast not done it. Go, and return no more. Walk they evil way till it leads thee down to hell."

Hebrew: Jonah

One of the better-known biblical stories of the refusal of the call is that of Jonah. Perhaps Jonah and others, such as the Greek Pentheus, who refused the call of Dionysos and paid the full price for denying the god in one's life, are not properly called heroes. By definition, the hero is the one who finally accepts the call and confronts his destiny, his true being.

•

Chapter 1

Now the word of the Lord came unto Jonah the son of A-mĭt′ta-ī, saying,

2 Arise, go to Nĭn′-ĕ-vēh, that great city, and cry against it; for their wickedness is come up before me.

Jonah 1–3:5.

3 But Jonah rose up to flee unto Tar-shish from the presence of the Lord, and went down to Joppa; and he found a ship going to Tarshish: so he paid the fare thereof, and went down into it, to go with them unto Tarshish from the presence of the Lord.

4 ¶ But the Lord sent out a great wind into the sea, and there was a mighty tempest in the sea, so that the ship was like to be broken.

5 Then the mariners were afraid, and cried every man unto his god, and cast forth the wares that were in the ship into the sea, to lighten it of them. But Jonah was gone down into the sides of the ship; and he lay, and was fast asleep.

6 So the shipmaster came to him, and said unto him, What meanest thou, O sleeper? arise, call upon thy God, if so be that God will think upon us, that we perish not.

7 and they said every one to his fellow, Come, and let us cast lots, that we may know for whose cause this evil is upon us. So they cast lots, and the lot fell upon Jonah.

8 Then said they unto him, Tell us, we pray thee, for whose cause this evil is upon us; What is thine occupation? and whence comest thou? what is thy country? and of what people art thou?

9 And he said unto them, I am an Hebrew; and I fear the Lord, the God of heaven, which hath made the sea and the dry land.

10 Then were the men exceedingly afraid, and said unto him, Why hast thou done this? For the men knew that he fled from the presence of the Lord, because he had told them.

11 Then said they unto him, What shall we do unto thee, that the sea may be calm unto us? for the sea wrought, and was tempestuous.

12 And he said unto them, Take me up, and cast me forth into the sea; so shall the sea be calm unto you: for I know that for my sake this great tempest is upon you.

13 Nevertheless the men rowed hard to bring it to the land; but they could not: for the sea wrought, and was tempestuous against them.

14 Wherefore they cried unto the Lord, and said, We beseech thee, O Lord, we beseech thee, let us not perish for this man's life, and lay not upon us innocent blood: for thou, O Lord, hast done as it pleased thee.

15 So they took up Jonah, and cast him forth into the sea: and the sea ceased from her raging.

16 Then the men feared the Lord exceedingly, and offered a sacrifice unto the Lord, and made vows.

17 Now the Lord had prepared a great fish to swallow up Jonah. And Jonah was in the belly of the fish three days and three nights.

Chapter 2

Then Jonah prayed unto the Lord his God out of the fish's belly,

2 And said, I cried by reason of mine affliction unto the Lord, and he heard me; out of the belly of hell cried I, and thou heardest my voice.

3 For thou hadst cast me into the deep, in the midst of the seas; and the floods compassed me about: all thy billows and thy waves passed over me.

4 Then I said, I am cast out of thy sight; yet I will look again toward thy holy temple.

5 The waters compassed me about, even to the soul: the depth closed me round about, the weeds were wrapped about my head.

6 I went down to the bottoms of the mountains; the earth with her bars was about me for ever; yet hast thou brought up my life from corruption, O Lord my God.

7 When my soul fainted within me I remembered the Lord: and my prayer came in unto thee, into thine holy temple.

8 They that observe lying vanities forsake their own mercy.

9 But I will sacrifice unto thee with the voice of thanksgiving; I will pay that that I have vowed. Salvation is of the Lord.

10 And the Lord spake upon the fish, and it vomited out Jonah upon the dry land.

Chapter 3

And the word of the Lord came unto Jonah the second time, saying,

2 Arise, go unto Nĭn'-e-vēh, that great city, and preach unto it the preaching that I bid thee.

3 So Jonah arose, and went unto Nĭn'-ĕ-vēh, according to the word of the Lord. Now Nineveh was an exceeding great city of three days' journey.

4 And Jonah began to enter into the city a day's journey, and he cried, and said, Yet forty days, and Nĭn'-ĕ-vēh shall be overthrown.

5 So the people of Nĭn'-ĕ-vēh believed God, and proclaimed a fast, and put on sackcloth, from the greatest of them even to the least of them.

Greek: Jason

In the quest that is central to the hero's life, he or she searches for a particular person, object, or concept. The Buddha searches for enlightenment under the Bodhi Tree; Aeneas looks for Rome, the new Troy; Odysseus strives to return home; Rama searches for his wife, Sita in the Indian epic the *Ramayana;* Tristan waits for his Isolde.

One of the most famous quest stories is that of Jason and the Golden Fleece. Like so many heroes of the patriarchal tradition, Jason becomes involved with a woman who might in earlier times have been a guiding goddess but is now a femme fatale. This pattern is present as well in the story of Helen of Troy, who in the *Odyssey* is a wise woman with prophetic powers (reminiscent of the priestly role permitted for some women in pre-classical societies), but who in the more patriarchal *Iliad* is a wanton woman whose sexual attraction is the cause of the Trojan War. Similar origins may exist in the story of Clytemnestra, who, with her lover, killed her husband, Agamemnon, when he returned from the Trojan War, and was killed in turn by her son Orestes at the urging of her daughter Elektra. The story as told by Aeschylus in the *Oresteia* trilogy is a patriarchal condemnation of what in earlier times might have been a ritual sacrificing of the old king for the sake of renewal in the person of a new mate for the matriarch.

The story of Jason and Medea is told by Apollonius of Rhodes in the third-century B.C.E. epic the *Argonauts,* by Pindar in the fourth *Pythian Ode* of the fifth century B.C.E., and by Euripides in the fifth-century B.C.E. tragedy *Medea.*

Roman: Aeneas

The femme fatale figure is by no means always evil. As in the case of Dido, with whom the Trojan-Roman hero Aeneas falls in love in Carthage during his quest for the new Troy, she can be the representation of true love or honest passion. Nevertheless, this love can prevent the hero from doing his patriarchal "duty." The story of Dido and Aeneas was first told by Virgil in Book IV of the *Aeneid.*

•

Carthage, where the exiles had now arrived, was a spot on the coast of Africa opposite Sicily, where at that time a Tyrian colony under Dido, their queen, was laying the foundations of a state destined in later ages to be the rival of Rome itself. Dido was the daughter of Belus, King of Tyre, and sister of Pygmalion, who succeeded his father on the throne. Her husband was Sichæus, a man of immense wealth, but Pygmalion, who coveted his treasures, caused him to be put to death. Dido, with a numerous body of friends and followers, both men and women, succeeded in effecting their

Thomas Bulfinch, *Bulfinch's Mythology: The Age of Fable* (New York, 1962), pp. 302–03.

escape from Tyre, in several vessels, carrying with them the treasures of Sichæus. On arriving at the spot which they selected as the seat of their future home, they asked of the natives only so much land as they could enclose with a bull's hide. When this was readily granted, she caused the hide to be cut into strips, and with them enclosed a spot on which she built a citadel, and called it Byrsa (a hide). Around this fort, the city of Carthage rose and soon became a powerful and flourishing place.

Such was the state of affairs when Aeneas with his Trojans arrived there. Dido received the illustrious exiles with friendliness and hospitality. "Not unacquainted with distress," she said, "I have learned to succor the unfortunate." The queen's hospitality displayed itself in festivities at which games of strength and skill were exhibited. The strangers contended for the palm with her own subjects, on equal terms, the queen declaring that whether the victor were "Trojan or Tyrian should make no difference to her." At the feast which followed the games, Aeneas gave at her request a recital of the closing events of the Trojan history and his own adventures after the fall of the city. Dido was charmed with his discourse and filled with admiration of his exploits. She conceived an ardent passion for him, and he for his part seemed well content to accept the fortunate chance which appeared to offer him at once a happy termination of his wanderings, a home, a kingdom, and a bride. Months rolled away in the enjoyment of pleasant intercourse, and it seemed as if Italy and the empire destined to be founded on its shores were alike forgotten. Seeing which, Jupiter despatched Mercury with a message to Aeneas, recalling him to a sense of his high destiny and commanding him to resume his voyage.

Aeneas parted from Dido, though she tried every allurement and persuasion to detain him. The blow to her affection and her pride was too much for her to endure, and when she found that he was gone, she mounted a funeral pile which she had caused to be prepared, and, having stabbed herself, was consumed with the pile. The flames rising over the city were seen by the departing Trojans, and though the cause was unknown, gave to Aeneas some intimation of the fatal event.

The following epigram we find in Elegant Extracts:

From the Latin

Unhappy, Dido, was thy fate
In first and second married state!
One husband caused thy flight by dying,
Thy death the other caused by flying.

Hebrew: Samson and Delilah

A biblical version of the patriarchal femme fatale motif is the well-known story of Samson and Delilah, in which the emasculating power of women is expressed through the metaphor of the cutting of a man's hair.

•

Then went Samson to Gaza, and saw there an harlot, and went in unto her.

2 And it was told the Gazites, saying, Samson is come hither. And they compassed him in, and laid wait for him all night in the gate of the city, and were quiet all the night, saying, In the morning, when it is day, we shall kill him.

3 And Samson lay till midnight, and arose at midnight, and took the doors of the gate of the city, and the two posts, and went away with them, bar and all, and put them upon his shoulders, and carried them up to the top of an hill that is before Hebron.

4 And it came to pass afterward, that he loved a woman in the valley of Sorek, whose name was Delilah.

5 And the lords of the Philistines came up unto her, and said unto her, Entice him, and see wherein his great strength lieth, and by what means we may prevail against him, that we may bind him to afflict him: and we will give thee every one of us eleven hundred pieces of silver.

6 And Delilah said to Samson, Tell me, I pray thee, wherein thy great strength lieth, and wherewith thou mightest be bound to afflict thee.

7 And Samson said unto her, If they bind me with seven green withs that were never dried, then shall I be weak, and be as another man.

8 Then the lords of the Philistines brought up to her seven green withs which had not been dried, and she bound him with them.

9 Now there were men lying in wait, abiding with her in the chamber. And she said unto him, The Philistines be upon thee, Samson. And he brake the withs, as a thread of tow is broken when it toucheth the fire. So his strength was not known.

10 And Delilah said unto Samson, Behold, thou hast mocked me, and told me lies: now tell me, I pray thee, wherewith thou mightest be bound.

11 And he said unto her, If they bind me fast with new ropes that never were occupied, then shall I be weak, and be as another man.

12 Delilah therefore took new ropes, and bound him therewith, and said unto him, The Philistine be upon thee, Samson. And there were liers in wait abiding in the chamber. And he brake them from off his arms like a thread.

13 And Delilah said unto Samson, Hitherto thou has mocked me, and

Judges 16.

told me lies: tell me wherewith thou mightest be bound. And he said unto her, If thou weavest the seven locks of my head with the web.

14 And she fastened it with the pin, and said unto him, The Philistines be upon thee, Samson. And he awaked out of his sleep, and went away with the pin of the beam, and with the web.

15 And she said unto him, How canst thou say, I love thee, when thine heart is not with me? thou hast mocked me these three times, and hast not told me wherein thy great strength lieth.

16 And it came to pass, when she pressed him daily with her words, and urged him, so that his soul was vexed unto death;

17 That he told her all his heart, and said unto her, There hath not come a razor upon mine head; for I have been a Nazarite unto God from my mother's womb: if I be shaven, then my strength will go from me, and I shall become weak, and be like any other man.

18 And when Delilah saw that he had told her all his heart, she sent and called for the lords of the Philistines, saying, Come up this once, for he hath shewed me all his heart. Then the lords of the Philistines came up unto her, and brought money in their hand.

19 And she made him sleep upon her knees; and she called for a man, and she caused him to shave off the seven locks of his head; and she began to afflict him, and his strength went from him.

20 And she said, The Philistines be upon thee, Samson. And he awoke out of his sleep, and said, I will go out as at other times before, and shake myself. And he wist not that the Lord was departed from him.

21 But the Philistines took him, and put out his eyes, and brought him down to Gaza, and bound him with fetters of brass; and he did grind in the prison house.

22 Howbeit the hair of his head began to grow again after he was shaven.

23 Then the lords of the Philistines gathered them together for to offer a great sacrifice unto Dagon their god, and to rejoice: for they said, Our god hath delivered Samson our enemy into our hand.

24 And when the people saw him, they praised their god: for they said, Our god hath delivered into our hands our enemy, and the destroyer of our country, which slew many of us.

25 And it came to pass, when their hearts were merry, that they said, Call for Samson, that he may make us sport. And they called for Samson out of the prison house; and he made them sport: and they set him between the pillars.

26 And Samson said unto the lad that held him by the hand, Suffer me that I may feel the pillars whereupon the house standeth, that I may lean upon them.

27 Now the house was full of men and women; and all the lords of

the Philistines were there; and there were upon the roof about three thousand men and women, that beheld while Samson made sport.

28 And Samson called unto the Lord, and said, O Lord God, remember me, I pray thee, and strengthen me, I pray thee, only this once, O God, that I may be at once avenged of the Philistines for my two eyes.

29 And Samson took hold of the two middle pillars upon which the house stood, and on which it was borne up, of the one with his right hand, and of the other with his left.

30 And Samson said, Let me die with the Philistines. And he bowed himself with all his might; and the house fell upon the lords, and upon all the people that were therein. So the dead which he slew at his death were more than they which he slew in his life.

31 Then his brethren and all the house of his father came down, and took him, and brought him up, and buried him between Zorah and Ěsh'-tă-ŏl in the buryingplace of Mă-nō-ăh his father. And he judged Israel twenty years.

Indian: The Buddha

The story of the Buddha under the Bodhi, or Bo, Tree is as central to the mythology and philosophy of Buddhism as the Crucifixion and Resurrection are to those of Christianity. The story itself bears a strong resemblance to the story of Jesus' temptation by the Devil in the wilderness (Luke 4).

•

Now during the time that Gautama had been dwelling in the forest near by Uruvela, the daughter of the village headman, by name Sujata, had been accustomed to make a daily offering of food to eight hundred Brahmans, making the prayer—"May the Bodhisatta at length, receive an offering of food from me, attain enlightenment, and become a Buddha!" And now that the time had come when he desired to receive nourishing food, a Deva appeared in the night to Sujata and announced that the Bodhisatta had put aside his austerities and desired to partake of good and nourishing food, "and now shall your prayer be accomplished." Then Sujata with all speed arose early and went to her father's herd. Now for a long time she had been accustomed to take the milk of a thousand cows and to feed therewith five hundred, and again with their milk to feed two hundred and fifty, and so on until eight only were fed with the milk of the rest, and this she called "working the milk in and in." It was the full-moon day of the month of May when she received the message of the gods, and rose early, and milked the eight cows, and took the milk and boiled it in new pans,

Ananda Coomaraswamy, *Buddha and the Gospel of Buddhism* (London, 1928), pp. 30–38.

and prepared milk-rice. At the same time she sent her maid Punna to the foot of the great tree where she had been wont to lay her daily offerings. Now the Bodhisatta knowing that he would that day attain Supreme Enlightenment, was sitting at the foot of the tree, awaiting the house for going forth to beg his food; and such was his glory that all the region of the East was lit up. The girl thought that it was the spirit of the tree who would deign to receive the offering with his own hands. When she returned to Sujata and reported this, Sujata embraced her and bestowed on her the jewels of a daughter, and exclaimed, "Henceforth thou shalt be to me in the place of an elder daughter!" And sending for a golden vessel she put the well-cooked food therein, and covered it with a pure white cloth, and bore it with dignity to the foot of the great Nigrodha-tree; and there she too saw the Bodhisatta, and believed him to be the spirit of the tree. Sujata approached him, and placed the vessel in his hand, and she met his gaze and said: "My lord, accept what I have offered thee," and she added "May there arise to thee as much of joy as has come to me!" and so she departed.

The Bodhisatta took the golden bowl, and went down to the bank of the river and bathed, and then dressing himself in the garb of an Arahat, he again took his seat, with his face towards the East. He divided the rice into forty-nine portions, and this food sufficed for his nourishment during the forty-nine days following the Enlightenment. When he had finished eating the milk rice, he took the golden vessel and cast it into the stream, saying, "If I am able to attain Enlightenment to-day, let this pot go up stream, but if not, may it go down stream." And he threw it into the water, and it went swiftly up the river until it reached the whirlpool of the Black Snake King, and there it sank.

The Bodhisatta spent the heat of the day in a grove of Saltrees beside the stream. But in the evening he made his way to the foot of the tree of wisdom, and there, making the resolution: "Though my skin, my nerves and my bones should waste away and my life-blood dry, I will not leave this seat until I have attained Supreme Enlightenment," he took his seat with his face towards the East.

At this moment Mara the Fiend became aware that the Bodhisatta had taken his seat with a view to attaining Perfect Enlightenment; and thereupon, summoning the hosts of the demons, and mounting his elephant of war, he advanced towards the Tree of Wisdom. And there stood Maha Brahma holding above the Bodhisatta a white canopy of state, and Sakka, blowing the great trumpet, and with them were all the companies of gods and angels. But so terrible was the array of Mara that there was not one of all this host of the Devas that dared to remain to face him. The Great Being was left alone.

First of all, however, Mara assumed the form of a messenger, with disordered garments, and panting in haste, bearing a letter from the Sakya princes. And in the letter it was written that Devadatta had usurped the kingdom of Kapilavatthu and entered the Bodhisatta's palace, taken his goods and his wife, and cast Suddhodana into prison and they prayed him to return to restore peace and order. But the Bodhisatta reflected lust it was that had caused Devadatta thus to misuse the women, malice had made him imprison Suddhodana, while the Sakyas neutralized by cowardice failed to defend their King: and so reflecting on the folly and weakness of the natural heart, his own resolve to attain a higher and better state was strengthened and confirmed.

Failing in this device, Mara now advanced to the assault with all his hosts, striving to overcome the Bodhisatta first by a terrible whirlwind, then by a storm of rain, causing a mighty flood: but the hem of the Bodhisatta's robe was not stirred, nor did a single drop of water reach him. Then Mara cast down upon him showers of rocks, and a storm of deadly and poisoned weapons, burning ashes and coals, and a storm of scorching sand and flaming mud; but all these missiles only fell at the Bodhisatta's feet as a rain of heavenly flowers, or hung in the air like a canopy above his head. Nor could he be moved by an onset of thick and fourfold darkness. Then finding all these means to fail, he addressed the Bodhisatta and said: "Arise, Siddhattha, from that seat, for it is not thine, but mine!" The Bodhisatta replied, "Mara! thou hast not accomplished the Ten Perfections, nor even the minor virtues. Thou hast not sought for knowledge, nor for the salvation of the world. The seat is mine." Then Mara was enraged, and cast at the Bodhisatta his Sceptre-javelin, which cleaves asunder a pillar of solid rock like a tender shoot of cane: and all the demon hosts hurled masses of rock. But the javelin hung in the air like a canopy, and the masses of rock fell down as garlands of flowers.

Then the Great Being said to Mara: "Mara, who is the witness that thou hast given alms?" Mara stretched forth his hand, and a shout arose from the demon hosts, of a thousand voices crying: "I am his witness!" Then the Fiend addressed the Bodhisatta, and enquired: "Siddhattha! who is the witness that thou has given alms?" and the Great Being answered: "Mara, thou hast many and living witnesses that thou hast given alms, and no such witnesses have I. But apart from the alms I have given in other births, I call upon this solid earth to witness to my supernatural generosity when I was born as Vessantara." And drawing his right hand from his robe, he stretched it forth to touch the earth, and said: "Do you or do you not witness to my supernatural generosity when I was born as Vessantara?" And the great Earth replied with a voice of thunder: "I am witness of that." And thereat the great elephant of Mara bowed down in adoration, and the demon hosts fled far away in dread.

Then Mara was abashed. But he did not withdraw, for he hoped to accomplish by another means what he could not effect by force: he summoned his three daughters, Tanha, Rati, and Raga, and they danced before the Bodhisatta like the swaying branches of a young leafy tree, using all the arts of seduction known to beautiful women. Again they offered him the lordship of the earth, and the companionship of beautiful girls: they appealed to him with songs of the season of spring, and exhibited their supernatural beauty and grace. But the Bodhisatta's heart was not in the least moved, and he answered:

> Pleasure is brief as a flash of lightning
> Or like an Autumn shower, only for a moment . . .
> Why should I then covet the pleasures you speak of?
> I see your bodies are full of all impurity:
> Birth and death, sickness and age are yours.
> I seek the highest prize, hard to attain by men—
> The true and constant wisdom of the wise.

And when they could not shake the Bodhisatta's calm, they were filled with shame, and abashed: and they made a prayer to the Bodhisatta, wishing him the fruition of his labour:

> That which your heart desires, may you attain,
> And finding for yourself deliverance, deliver all!

And now the hosts of heaven, seeing the army of Mara defeated, and the wiles of the daughters of Mara vain, assembled to honour the Conqueror, they came to the foot of the Tree of Wisdom and cried for joy:

> The Blessed Buddha—he hath prevailed!
> And the Tempter is overthrown!

The victory was achieved while the sun was yet above the horizon. The Bodhisatta sank into ever deeper and deeper thought. In the first watch of the night he reached the Knowledge of Former States of being, in the middle watch he obtained the heavenly eye of Omniscient Vision, and in the third watch he grasped the perfect understanding of the Chain of Causation which is the Origin of Evil, and thus at break of day he attained to Perfect Enlightenment. Therewith there broke from his lips the song of triumph:

> Through many divers births I passed
> Seeking in vain the builder of the house.[1]

---

[1] The house is, of course, the house—or rather the prison—of individual existence: the builder of the house is desire (*tankā*)—the will to enjoy and possess [Coomaraswamy's note].

But O framer of houses, thou art found—
Never again shalt thou fashion a house for me!
Broken are all they beams,
The king-post shattered!
My mind has passed into the stillness of Nibbana
The ending of desire has been attained at last!

Innumerable wonders were manifest at this supreme hour. The earth quaked six times, and the whole universe was illuminated by the supernatural splendour of the sixfold rays that proceeded from the body of the seated Buddha. Resentment faded from the hearts of all men, all lack was supplied, the sick were healed, the chains of hell were loosed, and every creature of whatsoever sort found peace and rest.

Gautama, who was now Buddha, the Enlightened, remained seated and motionless for seven days, realizing the bliss of Nibbana; and thereafter rising, he remained standing for seven days more, steadfastly regarding the spot where had been won the fruit of countless deeds of heroic virtue performed in past births: then for seven days more he paced to and fro along a cloistered path from West to East, extending from the throne beneath the Wisdom Tree to the place of the Steadfast Gazing; and again for seven days he remained seated in a god-wrought pavilion near to the same place, and there reviewed in detail, book by book, all that is taught in the *Abhidhamma Pitaka*, as well as the whole doctrine of causality; then for seven days more he sat beneath the Nigrodha tree of Sujata's offering, meditating on the doctrine and the sweetness of Nibbana—and according to some books it was at this time the temptation by the daughters of Mara took place; and then for seven days more while a terrible storm was raging, the snake king Mucalinda sheltered him with his sevenfold hood; and for seven days more he sat beneath a Rajayatana tree, still enjoying the sweetness of liberation.

And so passed away seven weeks, during which the Buddha experienced no bodily wants, but fed on the joy of contemplation, the joy of the Eightfold Path, and the joy of its fruit, Nibbana.

Only upon the last day of the seven weeks he desired to bathe and eat, and receiving water and a tooth-stick from the god Sakka, the Buddha bathed his face and seated himself at the foot of a tree. Now at that time two Brahman merchants were travelling with a caravan from Orissa to the middle country, and a Deva, who had been a blood relation of the merchants' in a former life, stopped the carts, and moved their hearts to make an offering of rice and honey cakes to the Lord. They went up to him accordingly, saying: "O Blessed One, have mercy upon us, and accept this food." Now the Buddha no longer possessed a bowl, and as the Buddhas never receive an offering in their hands, he reflected how he should take

it. Immediately the Four Great Kings, the Regents of the Quarters appeared before him, each of them with a bowl; and in order that none of
them should be disappointed, the Buddha received the four bowls, and
placing them one above the other made them to be one, showing only the
four lines round the mouth, and in this bowl the Blessed One received
the food, and ate it, and gave thanks. The two merchants took refuge in
the Buddha, the Norm, and the Order, and became professed disciples.
Then the Buddha rose up and returned again to the tree of Sujata's offering
and there took his seat. And there, reflecting upon the depth of truth
which he had found, a doubt arose in his mind whether it would be possible to make it known to others: and this doubt is experienced by every
Buddha when he becomes aware of the Truth. But Maha Brahma exclaiming: "Alas! the world will be altogether lost!" came thither in haste, with
all the Deva hosts, and besought the Master to proclaim the Truth; and he
granted their prayer.[2]

Native American: Wunzh, or Hiawatha

The quest hero often has to struggle with monsters or superhuman beings.
The result is sometimes a boon for humanity. The following is a Native
American story of the discovery of corn (Mondamin) by the hero Wunzh,
who in Longfellow's famous version of the story is called Hiawatha. As in
the Buddha's story, Wunzh's quest involves fasting and self-denial.

•

> You shall hear how Hiawatha
> Prayed and fasted in the forest,
> Not for greater skill in hunting,
> Not for greater craft in fishing,
> Not for triumphs in the battle,
> And renown among the warriors,
> But for profit of the people,
> For advantage of the nations.
>   First he built a lodge for fasting,
> Built a wigwam in the forest,

---

[2]"Great truths do not take hold of the hearts of the masses. . . . And now, as all the world is in error,
I, though I know the true path—how shall I, how shall I guide? If I know that I cannot succeed and yet try
to force success, this would be but another source of error. Better, then, to desist and strive no more. But
if I strive not, who will?"—Chuang Tzu. It is highly characteristic of the psychology of genius that when
this doubt assails the Buddha he nevertheless immediately responds to a definite request for guidance; the
moment the pupil puts the right questions, the teacher's doubts are resolved [Coomaraswamy's note].

Henry Wadsworth Longfellow, "Hiawatha's Fasting," section V of *The Song of Hiawatha,* in *Longfellow's
Poems* (Cambridge, Mass., 1899), pp. 153–56.

By the shining Big-Sea-Water,
In the blithe and pleasant springtime,
In the Moon of Leaves he built it,
And, with dreams and visions many,
Seven whole days and nights he fasted.
  On the first day of his fasting
Through the leafy woods he wandered;
Saw the deer start from the thicket,
Saw the rabbit in his burrow,
Heard the pheasant, Bena, drumming,
Heard the squirrel, Adjidaumo,
Rattling in his hoard of acorns,
Saw the pigeon, the Omeme,
Building nests among the pine-trees,
And in flocks the wild-goose, Wawa,
Flying to the fen-lands northward,
Whirring, wailing far above him.
"Master of Life!" he cried, desponding,
"Must our lives depend on these things?"
  On the next day of his fasting
By the river's brink he wandered,
Through the Muskoday, the meadow,
Saw the wild rice, Mahnomonee,
Saw the blueberry, Meenahga,
And the strawberry, Odahmin,
And the gooseberry, Shahbomin,
And the grape-vine, the Bemahgut,
Trailing o'er the alder-branches,
Filling all the air with fragrance!
"Master of Life!" he cried, desponding,
"Must our lives depend on these things?"
  On the third day of his fasting
By the lake he sat and pondered,
By the still, transparent water;
Saw the sturgeon, Nahma, leaping,
Scattering drops like beads of wampum,
Saw the yellow perch, the Sahwa,
Like a sunbeam in the water,
Saw the pike, the Maskenozha,
And the herring, Okahahwis,
And the Shawgashee, the crawfish!
"Master of Life!" he cried, desponding,
"Must our lives depend on these things?"

On the fourth day of his fasting
In his lodge he lay exhausted;
From his couch of leaves and branches
Gazing with half-open eyelids,
Full of shadowy dreams and visions,
On the dizzy, swimming landscape,
On the gleaming of the water,
On the splendor of the sunset.

And he saw a youth approaching,
Dressed in garments green and yellow,
Coming through the purple twilight,
Through the splendor of the sunset;
Plumes of green bent o'er his forehead,
And his hair was soft and golden.

Standing at the open doorway,
Long he looked at Hiawatha,
Looked with pity and compassion
On his wasted form and features,
And, in accents like the sighing
Of the South Wind in the tree-tops,
Said he, "O my Hiawatha!
All your prayers are heard in heaven,
For you pray not like the others;
Not for greater skill in hunting,
Not for greater craft in fishing,
Not for triumph in the battle,
Nor renown among the warriors,
But for profit of the people,
For advantage of the nations.

"From the Master of Life descending,
I, the friend of man, Mondamin,
Come to warn you and instruct you,
How by struggle and by labor
You shall gain what you have prayed for.
Rise up from your bed of branches,
Rise, O youth, and wrestle with me!"

Faint with famine, Hiawatha
Started from his bed of branches.
From the twilight of his wigwam
Forth into the flush of sunset
Came, and wrestled with Mondamin;
At his touch he felt new courage
Throbbing in his brain and bosom,

Felt new life and hope and vigor
Run through every nerve and fibre.
    So they wrestled there together
In the glory of the sunset,
And the more they strove and struggled,
Stronger still grew Hiawatha;
Till the darkness fell around them,
And the heron, the Shuh-shuh-gah,
From her nest among the pine-trees,
Gave a cry of lamentation,
Gave a scream of pain and famine.
    " 'T is enough!" then said Mondamin,
Smiling upon Hiawatha,
"But to-morrow, when the sun sets,
I will come again to try you."
And he vanished, and was seen not;
Whether sinking as the rain sinks,
Whether rising as the mists rise,
Hiawatha saw not, knew not,
Only saw that he had vanished,
Leaving him alone and fainting,
With the misty lake below him,
And the reeling stars above him.
    On the morrow and the next day,
When the sun through heaven descending,
Like a red and burning cinder
From the hearth of the Great Spirit,
Fell into the western waters,
Came Mondamin for the trial,
For the strife with Hiawatha;
Came as silent as the dew comes,
From the empty air appearing,
Into empty air returning,
Taking shape when earth it touches,
But invisible to all men
In its coming and its going.
    Thrice they wrestled there together
In the glory of the sunset,
Till the darkness fell around them,
Till the heron, the Shuh-shuh-gah,
From her nest among the pine-trees,
Uttered her loud cry of famine,
And Mondamin paused to listen.

Tall and beautiful he stood there,
In his garments green and yellow;
To and fro his plumes above him
Waved and nodded with his breathing,
And the sweat of the encounter
Stood like drops of dew upon him.
And he cried, "O Hiawatha!
Bravely have you wrestled with me,
Thrice have wrestled stoutly with me,
And the Master of Life, who sees us,
He will give to you the triumph!"
Then he smiled, and said: "Tomorrow
Is the last day of your conflict,
Is the last day of your fasting.
You will conquer and o'ercome me;
Make a bed for me to lie in,
Where the rain may fall upon me,
Where the sun may come and warm me;
Strip these garments, green and yellow,
Strip this nodding plumage from me,
Lay me in the earth, and make it
Soft and loose and light above me.
"Let no hand disturb my slumber,
Let no weed nor worm molest me,
Let not Kahgahgee, the raven,
Come to haunt me and molest me,
Only come yourself to watch me,
Till I wake, and start, and quicken,
Till I leap into the sunshine."
And thus saying, he departed;
Peacefully slept Hiawatha,
But he heard the Wawonaissa,
Heard the whippoorwill complaining,
Perched upon his lonely wigwam;
Heard the rushing Sebowisha,
Heard the rivulet rippling near him,
Talking to the darksome forest;
Heard the sighing of the branches,
As they lifted and subsided
At the passing of the night-wind,
Heard them, as one hears in slumber
Far-off murmurs, dreamy whispers:
Peacefully slept Hiawatha.

On the morrow came Nokomis,
On the seventh day of his fasting,
Came with food for Hiawatha,
Came imploring and bewailing,
Lest his hunger should o'ercome him,
Lest his fasting should be fatal.

But he tasted not, and touched not,
Only said to her, "Nokomis,
Wait until the sun is setting,
Till the darkness falls around us,
Till the heron, the Shuh-shuh-gah,
Crying from the desolate marches,
Tells us that the day is ended."

Homeward weeping went Nokomis,
Sorrowing for her Hiawatha,
Fearing lest his strength should fail him,
Lest his fasting should be fatal.
He meanwhile sat weary waiting
For the coming of Mondamin,
Till the shadows, pointing eastward,
Lengthened over field and forest,
Till the sun dropped from the heaven,
Floating on the waters westward,
As a red leaf in the Autumn
Falls and floats upon the water,
Falls and sinks into its bosom.

And behold! the young Mondamin,
With his soft and shining tresses,
With his garments green and yellow,
With his long and glossy plumage,
Stood and beckoned at the doorway.
And as one in slumber walking,
Pale and haggard, but undaunted,
From the wigwam Hiawatha
Came and wrestled with Mondamin.

Round about him spun the landscape,
Sky and forest reeled together,
And his strong heart leaped within him,
As the sturgeon leaps and struggles
In a net to break its meshes.
Like a ring of fire around him
Blazed and flared the red horizon,
And a hundred suns seemed looking

At the combat of the wrestlers.
   Suddenly upon the greensward
All alone stood Hiawatha,
Panting with his wild exertion,
Palpitating with the struggle;
And before him breathless, lifeless,
Lay the youth, with hair dishevelled,
Plumage torn, and garments tattered,
Dead he lay there in the sunset.
   And victorious Hiawatha
Made the grave as he commanded,
Stripped the garments from Mondamin,
Stripped his tattered plumage from him,
Laid him in the earth, and made it
Soft and loose and light above him;
And the heron, the Shuh-shuh-gah,
From the melancholy moorlands,
Gave a cry of lamentation,
Gave a cry of pain and anguish!
   Homeward then went Hiawatha
To the lodge of old Nokomis,
And the seven days of his fasting
Were accomplished and completed.
But the place was not forgotten
Where he wrestled with Mondamin;
Nor forgotten nor neglected
Was the grave where lay Mondamin,
Sleeping in the rain and sunshine,
Where his scattered plumes and garments
Faded in the rain and sunshine.
   Day by day did Hiawatha
Go to wait and watch beside it;
Kept the dark mould soft above it,
Kept it clean from weeds and insects,
Drove away, with scoffs and shoutings,
Kahgahgee, the king of ravens.
   Till at length a small green feather
From the earth shot slowly upward,
Then another and another,
And before the Summer ended
Stood the maize in all its beauty,
With its shining robes about it,
And its long, soft, yellow tresses;

And in rapture Hiawatha
Cried aloud, "It is Mondamin!
Yes, the friend of man, Mondamin!"
    Then he called to old Nokomis
and Iagoo, the great boaster,
Showed them where the maize was growing,
Told them of his wondrous vision,
Of his wrestling and his triumph,
Of this new gift to the nations,
Which should be their food forever.
    And still later, when the Autumn
Changed the long, green leaves to yellow,
And the soft and juicy kernels
Grew like wampum hard and yellow,
Then the ripened ears he gathered,
Stripped the withered husks from off them,
As he once had stripped the wrestler,
Gave the first Feast of Mondamin,
And made known unto the people
This new gift of the Great Spirit.

Greek: Herakles

In the Greek tradition especially, the hero must often prove himself by
accomplishing an impossible series of tasks. The twelve labors of Herakles
(or Hercules), which include a descent into the underworld, have echoes
in the only slightly less onerous labors of Perseus, who struggled against
and killed the monstrous Gorgon (Medusa), and of Bellerophon, who, with
the help of the winged horse Pegasus, killed the horrible Chimaera. Heroes
of all traditions must confront monsters of the collective nightmare. Oedipus must destroy the Sphinx before he can enter Thebes. Saint George
and many other medieval heroes must kill the dragon. The Buddha, Jesus,
and other heroes whose adventures are as much spiritual as physical must
confront the monsters within.

•

Before he was eighteen he had done many famous deeds in the country of
Thebes, and Creon, the king, gave him his daughter in marriage. But he
could not long escape the anger of Juno, who afflicted him with a sudden
madness, so that he did not know what he was doing and in a fit of frenzy
killed both his wife and his children. When he came to his senses, in horror

Rex Warner, *The Stories of the Greeks* (New York, 1967), pp. 94–102.

and shame at what he had done, he visited the great cliffs of Delphi, where the eagles circle all day and where Apollo's oracle is. There he asked how he could be purified of his sin and he was told by the oracle that he must go to Mycenae and for twelve years obey all the commands of the cowardly king Eurystheus, his kinsman. It seemed a hard and cruel sentence, but the oracle told him also, that at the end of many labours he would be received among the gods.

Hercules therefore departed to the rocky citadel of Mycenae that looks down upon the blue water of the bay of Argos. He was skilled in the use of every weapon, having been educated, like Jason was, by the wise centaur Chiron. He was tall and immensely powerful. When Eurystheus saw him he was both terrified of him and jealous of his great powers. He began to devise labours that would seem impossible, yet Hercules accomplished them all.

First he was ordered to destroy and to bring back to Mycenae the lion of Nemea which for long had ravaged all the countryside to the north. Hercules took his bow and arrows, and, in the forest of Memea, cut himself a great club, so heavy that a man nowadays could hardly lift it. This club he carried ever afterwards as his chief weapon.

He found that his arrows had no effect on the tough skin of the lion, but, as the beast sprang at him, he half-stunned it with his club, then closing in with it, he seized it by the throat and killed it with his bare hands. They say that when he carried back on his shoulders to Mycenae the body of the huge beast, Eurystheus fled in terror and ordered Hercules never again to enter the gates of the city, but to wait outside until he was told to come in . Eurystheus also built for himself a special strong room of brass into which he would retire if he was ever again frightened by the power and valiance of Hercules. Hercules himself took the skin of the lion and made it into a cloak which he wore ever afterwards, sometimes with the lion's head covering his own head like a cap, sometimes with it slung backwards over his shoulders.

The next task given to Hercules by Eurystheus was to destroy a huge water snake, called the Hydra, which lived in the marshes of Argos, was filled with poison and had fifty venomous heads. Hercules, with his friend and companion, the young Iolaus, set out from Mycenae and came to the great cavern, sacred to Pan, which is a holy place in the hills near Argos. Below this cavern a river gushes out of the rock. Willows and plane-trees surround the source and the brilliant green of grass. It is the freshest and most delightful place. But, as the river flows downwards to the sea, it becomes wide and shallow, extending into pestilential marshes, the home of stinging flies and mosquitoes. In these marshes they found the Hydra, and Hercules, with his great club, began to crush the beast's heads, afterwards cutting them off with his sword. Yet the more he laboured, the more difficult his task became. From the stump of each head that he cut off two other heads, with forked and hissing tongues, immediately sprang. Faced with an endless and increasing effort, Hercules was at a loss what to do. It seemed to him that heat might prove more powerful than cold steel, and he commanded Iolaus to burn the root of each head with a red-hot iron immediately it was severed from the neck. This plan was successful. The heads no longer sprouted up again, and soon the dangerous and destructive animal lay dead, though still writhing in the black marsh water among the reeds. Hercules cut its body open and dipped his arrows in the blood. Henceforward these arrows would bring certain death, even if they only grazed the skin, so powerful was the Hydra's poison.

Eurystheus next ordered Hercules to capture and bring back alive a stag, sacred to Diana and famous for its great fleetness of foot, which lived in the waste mountains and forests, and never yet had been approached in the chase. For a whole year Hercules pursued this animal, resting for the hours of darkness and pressing on next day in its tracks. For many months he was wholly outdistanced; valleys and forests divided him from his prey. But at the end of the year the stag, weary of the long hunt, could run no longer. Hercules seized it in his strong hands, tied first its forelegs and then its hind legs together, put the body of the beast, with its drooping antlered head, over his neck, and proceeded to return to the palace of King Eurystheus. However, as he was on his way through the woods, he was suddenly aware of a bright light in front of him, and in the middle of the light he saw standing a tall woman or, as he immediately recognized, a goddess, grasping in her hands a bow and staring at him angrily with her shining eyes. He knew at once that this was the archer goddess Diana, she who had once turned Actaeon into a stag and who now was enraged at the loss of this other stag which was sacred to her. Hercules put his prey on the ground and knelt before the goddess. "It was through no desire of my own," he said, "that I have captured this noble animal. What I do is one at the command of my father Jupiter and of the oracle of your brother Apollo at Delphi." The goddess listened to his explanation, smiled kindly on him and allowed him to go on his way, when he had promised that, once the stag had been carried to Eurystheus, it would be set free again in the forests that it loved. So Hercules accomplished this third labour.

He was not, however, to be allowed to rest. Eurystheus now commanded him to go out to the mountains of Erymanthus and bring back the great wild boar that for long had terrorized all the neighbourhood. So Hercules set out once more and on his way he passed the country where the centaurs had settled after they had been driven down from the north in the battle that had taken place with the Lapiths at the wedding of Pirithous. In this battle they had already had experience of the hero's strength, but still their manners were rude and rough. When the centaur Pholus offered

Hercules some of the best wine to drink, the other centaurs became jealous. Angry words led to blows, and soon Hercules was forced to defend himself with his club and with his arrows, the poison of which not only caused death, but also the most extreme pain. Soon he scattered his enemies in all directions, driving them over the plains and rocks. Some he dashed to the ground with his club; others, wounded by the poisoned arrows, lay writhing in agony, or kicking their hooves in the air. Some took refuge in the house of the famous centaur Chiron, who had been schoolmaster to Hercules and who, alone among the centaurs, was immortal. As he pursued his enemies to this good centaur's house, shooting arrows at them as he went, Hercules, by an unhappy accident, wounded Chiron himself. Whether it was because of grief that his old pupil had so injured him, or whether it was because of the great pain of the wound, Chiron prayed to Jupiter that his immortality should be taken away from him. Jupiter granted his prayer. The good centaur died, but he was set in Heaven in a constellation of stars which is still called either Sagittarius or else The Centaur.

Hercules mourned the sad death of his old master. Then he went on to Erymanthus. It was winter and he chased the great boar up to the deep snow in the passes of the mountains. The animal's short legs soon grew weary of ploughing through the stiff snow and Hercules caught it up when it was exhausted and panting in a snowdrift. He bound it firmly and slung the great body over his back. They say that when he brought it to Mycenae, Eurystheus was so frightened at the sight of the huge tusks and flashing eyes that he hid for two days in the brass hiding place that he had had built for him.

The next task that Hercules was ordered to do would have seemed to anyone impossible. There was a king of Elis called Augeas, very rich in herds of goats and cattle. His stables, they say, held three thousand oxen and for ten years these stables had never been cleaned. The dung and muck stood higher than a house, hardened and caked together. The smell was such that even the herdsmen, who were used to it, could scarcely bear to go near. Hercules was now ordered to clean these stables, and, going to Elis, he first asked the king to promise him the tenth part of his herds if he was successful in his task. The king readily agreed, and Hercules made the great river Alpheus change his course and come foaming and roaring through the filthy stables. In less than a day all the dirt was cleared and rolled away to the sea. The river then went back to its former course and, for the first time in ten years, the stone floors and walls of the enormous stables shone white and clean.

Hercules then asked for his reward, but King Augeas, claiming that he had performed the task not with his own hands, but by a trick, refused to give it to him. He even banished his own son who took the side of

Hercules and reproached his father for not keeping his promise. Hercules then made war on the kingdom of Elis, drove King Augeas out and put his son on the throne. Then, with his rich reward, he returned to Mycenae, ready to undertake whatever new task was given him by Eurystheus.

Again he was ordered to destroy creatures that were harmful to men. This time they were great birds, like cranes or storks, but much more powerful, which devoured human flesh and lived around the black waters of the Stymphalian lake. In the reeds and rocky crags they lived in huge numbers and Hercules was at a loss how to draw them from their hiding places. It was the goddess Minerva who helped him by giving him a great rattle of brass. The noise of this rattle drove the great birds into the air in throngs. Hercules pursued them with his arrows, which rang upon their horny beaks and legs but stuck firm in the bodies that tumbled one after the other into the lake. The whole brood of these monsters was entirely destroyed and now only ducks and harmless water-fowl nest along the reedy shores.

Hercules had now accomplished six of his labours. Six more remained. After the killing of the Stymphalian birds he was commanded to go to Crete and bring back from there alive a huge bull which was laying the whole island waste. Bare-handed and alone he grappled with this bull, and, once again, when he brought the animal back into the streets of Mycenae, Eurystheus fled in terror at the sight both of the hero and of the great beast which he had captured.

From the southern sea Hercules was sent to the north to Thrace, over which ruled King Diomedes, a strong and warlike prince who savagely fed his famous mares on human flesh. Hercules conquered the king in battle and gave his body to the very mares which had so often fed upon the bodies of the king's enemies. He brought the mares back to King Eurystheus, who again was terrified at the sight of such fierce and spirited animals. He ordered them to be taken to the heights of Mount Olympus and there be consecrated to Jupiter. But Jupiter had no love for these unnatural creatures, and, on the rocky hillsides, they were devoured by lions, wolves, and bears.

Next Hercules was commanded to go to the country of the Amazons, the fierce warrior women, and bring back the girdle of their queen Hippolyte. Seas and mountains had to be crossed, battles to be fought; but Hercules in the end accomplished the long journey and the dangerous task. Later, as is well known, Hippolyte became the wife of Theseus of Athens and bore him an ill-fated son, Hippolytus.

Hercules had now travelled in the south, the north and the east. His tenth labour was to be in the far west, beyond the country of Spain, in an island called Erythia. Here lived the giant Geryon, a great monster with three bodies and three heads. With his herdsman, and his two-headed dog, called Orthrus, he looked after huge flocks of oxen, and, at the command of Eurystheus, Hercules came into his land to lift the cattle and to destroy the giant. On his way, at the very entrance to the Atlantic he set up two great marks, ever afterwards to be known by sailors and called the Pillars of Hercules. Later, as he wandered through rocks and over desert land, he turned his anger against the Sun itself, shooting his arrows at the great god Phoebus Apollo. But Phoebus pitied him in his thirst and weariness. He sent him a golden boat, and in this boat Hercules crossed over to the island of Erythia. Here he easily destroyed both watchdog and herdsman, but fought for long with the great three-bodied giant before he slew him, body after body. Then he began to drive the cattle over rivers and mountains and deserts from Spain to Greece. As he was passing through Italy he came near the cave where Cacus, a son of Vulcan, who breathed fire out of his mouth, lived solitary and cruel, since he killed all strangers and nailed their heads, dripping with blood, to the posts at the entrance of his rocky dwelling. While Hercules was resting, with the herds all round him, Cacus came out of his cave and stole eight of the best animals of the whole herd. He dragged them backwards by their tails, so that Hercules should not be able to track them down.

When Hercules awoke from his rest, he searched far and wide for the missing animals, but, since they had been driven into the deep recesses of Cacus's cave, he was unable to find them. In the end he began to go on his way with the rest of the herd, and, as the stolen animals heard the lowing of the other cattle, they too began to low and bellow in their rocky prison. Hercules stopped still, and soon out of the cave came the fire-breathing giant, prepared to defend the fruits of his robbery and anxious to hang the head of Hercules among his other disgusting trophies. This, however, was not to be. The huge limbs and terrible breath of Cacus were of no avail against the hero's strength and fortitude. Soon, with a tremendous blow of his club, he stretched out Cacus dead on the ground. Then he drove the great herd on over the mountains and plains, through forests and rivers to Mycenae.

Hercules' next labour again took him to the far west. He was commanded by Eurystheus to fetch him some of the golden apples of the Hesperides. These apples grew in a garden west even of the land of Atlas. Here the sun shines continually, but always cool well-watered trees of every kind give shade. All flowers and fruits that grow on earth grow here, and fruit and flowers are always on the boughs together. In the centre of the garden is the orchard where golden apples gleam among the shining green leaves and the flushed blossom. Three nymphs, the Hesperides, look after this orchard, which was given by Jupiter to Juno as a wedding present. It is guarded also by a great dragon that never sleeps, and coils its huge folds around the trees. No one except the gods knows exactly where this beautiful and remote garden is, and it was to this unknown place that Hercules was sent.

He was helped by Minerva and by the nymphs of the broad river Po in Italy. These nymphs told Hercules where to find Nereus, the ancient god of the sea, who knew the past, the present and the future. "Wait for him," they said, "until you find him asleep on the rocky shore, surrounded by his fifty daughters. Seize hold of him tightly and do not let go until he answers your question. He will, in trying to escape you, put on all kinds of shapes. He will turn to fire, to water, to a wild beast or to a serpent. You must not lose your courage, but hold him all the tighter, and, in the end, he will come back to his own shape and will tell you what you want to know."

Hercules followed their advice. As he watched along the sea god's shore he saw, lying on the sand, half in and half out of the sea, with seaweed trailing round his limbs, the old god himself. Around him were his daughters, the Nereids, some riding on the backs of dolphins, some dancing in the shore, some swimming and diving in the deeper water. As Hercules approached, they cried out shrilly at the sight of a man. Those on land leaped back into the sea; those in the sea swam further from the shore. But their cries did not awake their father till Hercules was close to him and able to grip him firmly in his strong hands. Immediately the old god felt the hands upon him, his body seemed to disappear into a running stream of water; but Hercules felt that body that he could not see, and did not relax his grasp. Next it seemed that his hands were buried in a great pillar of fire; but the fire did not scorch the skin and Hercules could still feel the aged limbs through the fire. Then it was a great lion with wide-open jaws that appeared to be lying and raging on the sands; then a bear, then a dragon. Still Hercules clung firmly to his prisoner, and in the end he saw again the bearded face and seaweed-dripping limbs of old Nereus. The god knew for what purpose Hercules had seized him, and he told him the way to the garden of the Hesperides.

It was a long and difficult journey, but at the end of it Hercules was rewarded. The guardian nymphs (since this was the will of Jupiter) allowed him to pick from the pliant boughs two or three of the golden fruit. The great dragon bowed its head to the ground at their command and left Hercules unmolested. He brought back the apples to Eurystheus, but soon they began to lose that beautiful sheen of gold that had been theirs in the western garden. So Minerva carried them back again to the place from which they came, and then once more they glowed with their own gold among the other golden apples that hung upon the trees.

. . . . . .

Now had come the time for the twelfth and last of the labours that Hercules did for his master Eurystheus. This labour would seem to anyone by far the hardest; for the hero was commanded to descend into the lower world, and bring back with him from the kingdom of Proserpine the terrible three-headed watch-dog Cerberus.

Hercules took the dark path which before him had been trodden only by Orpheus and Theseus and Pirithous. Orpheus had returned. Theseus and Pirithous, for their wicked attempt, were still imprisoned.

Hercules passed the Furies, undaunted by the frightful eyes beneath the writing serpents of their hair. He passed the great criminals, Sisyphus, Tantalus and the rest. He passed by his friend, the unhappy Theseus, who was sitting immovably fixed to a rock, and he came at last into the terrible presence of black Pluto himself, who sat on his dark throne with his young wife Proserpine beside him. To the King and Queen of the Dead Hercules explained the reason of his coming. "Go," said Pluto, "and, so long as you use no weapon, but only your bare hands, you may take my watch-dog Cerberus to the upper air."

Hercules thanked the dreadful king for giving him the permission which he had asked. Then he made one more request which was that Theseus, who had sinned only by keeping his promise to his friend, might be allowed to return again to life. This, too, was granted him. Theseus rose to his feet again and accompanied the hero to the entrance of hell, where the huge dog Cerberus, with his three heads and his three deep baying voices, glared savagely at the intruders. Even this tremendous animal proved no match for Hercules, who with his vice-like grip stifled the breath in two of the shaggy throats, then lifted the beast upon his shoulders and began to ascend again, Theseus following close behind, the path that leads to the world of men. They say that when he carried Cerberus to Mycenae, Eurystheus fled in terror to another city and was now actually glad that Hercules had completed what might seem to have been twelve impossible labours. Cerberus was restored to his place in Hell and never again visited the upper world. Nor did Hercules ever go down to the place of the dead, since, after further trials, he was destined to live among the gods above.

African: Wanjiru

The greatest of tests that faces the quest hero is death itself. Heroes who die and are later reborn resemble the dying god, and this aspect of their stories is closely related to that theme. The dying hero is the sacrificial victim whose death is part of a ritual act by which his or her society will be renewed or "saved." The story of the African maiden Wanjiru also contains the descent motif and the story of the rescue of the victim from the dark world that must remind us of the shamanistic rescues performed by Dionysos, Inanna, Jesus, Kutoyis, Herakles, and others.

•

The sun was very hot and there was no rain, so the crops died and hunger was great. This happened one year; and it happened again a second, and even a third year, that the rain failed. The people all gathered together on the great open space on the hilltop, where they were wont to dance, and they said to each other, "Why does the rain delay in coming?" And they went to the Medicine-Man and they said to him, "Tell us why there is no rain, for our crops have died, and we shall die of hunger."

And he took his gourd and poured out its contents. This he did many times; and at last he said, "There is a maiden here who must be bought if rain is to fall, and the maiden is named Wanjiru. The day after tomorrow let all of you return to this place, and every one of you from the eldest to the youngest bring with him a goat for the purchase of the maiden."

On the day after the morrow, old men and young men all gathered together, and each brought in his hand a goat. Now they all stood in a circle, and the relations of Wanjiru stood together, and she herself stood in the middle. As they stood there, the feet of Wanjiru began to sink into the ground, and she sank in to her knees and cried aloud, "I am lost!"

Her father and mother also cried and exclaimed, "We are lost!"

Those who looked on pressed close and placed goats in the keeping of Wanjiru's father and mother. Wanjiru sank lower to her waist, and again she cried aloud, "I am lost, but much rain will come!"

She sank to her breast; but the rain did not come. Then she said again, "Much rain will come."

Now she sank in to her neck, and then the rain came in great drops. Her people would have rushed forward to save her, but those who stood around pressed upon them more goats, and they desisted.

Then Wanjiru said, "My people have undone me," and she sank down to her eyes. As one after another of her family stepped forward to save her, someone in the crowd would give to him or her a goat, and he would fall back. And Wanjiru cried aloud for the last time, "I am undone, and my own people have done this thing." Then she vanished from sight; the earth closed over her, and the rain poured down, not in showers, as it sometimes does, but in a great deluge, and all the people hastened to their own homes.

Now there was a young warrior who loved Wanjiru and he lamented continually, saying, "Wanjiru is lost, and her own people have done this thing." And he said, "Where has Wanjiru gone? I will go to the same place." So he took his shield and spear. And he wandered over the country day and night until, at least, as the dusk fell, he came to the spot where Wanjiru had vanished. Then he stood where she had stood and, as he stood, his feet began to sink as hers had sunk; and he sank lower and lower until the ground closed over him, and he went by a long road under the earth as Wanjiru had gone and, at length, he saw the maiden. But, indeed, he pitied her sorely, for her state was miserable, and her raiment had per-

Paul Radin and James Sweeney, eds., *African Folktales and Sculpture* (New York, 1952), p. 272.

ished. He said to her, "You were sacrificed to bring the rain; now the rain has come, and I shall take you back." So he took Wanjiru on his back as if she had been a child and brought her to the road he had traversed, and they rose together to the open air, and their feet stood once more on the ground.

Then the warrior said, "You shall not return to the house of your people, for they have treated you shamefully." And he bade her wait until nightfall. When it was dark he took her to the house of his mother and he asked his mother to leave, saying that he had business, and he allowed no one to enter.

But his mother said, "Why do you hide this thing from me, seeing I am your mother who bore you?" So he suffered his mother to know, but he said, "Tell no one that Wanjiru has returned."

So she abode in the house of his mother. He and his mother slew goats, and Wanjiru ate the fat and grew strong. Then of the skins they made garments for her, so that she was attired most beautifully.

It came to pass that the next day there was a great dance, and her lover went with the throng. But his mother and the girl waited until everyone had assembled at the dance, and all the road was empty. Then they came out of the house and mingled with the crowd. When the relations saw Wanjiru, they said, "Surely that is Wanjiru whom we had lost."

And they pressed to greet her, but her lover beat them off, for he said, "You sold Wanjiru shamefully."

Then she returned to his mother's house. But on the fourth day her family again came and the warrior repented, for he said, "Surely they are her father and her mother and her brothers."

So he paid them the purchase price, and he wedded Wanjiru who had been lost.

Australian Aboriginal: The Pleiades

This Aboriginal version of the Pleiades story bears little surface resemblance to the Greek myth about the daughters of Atlas, priestesses of Artemis, being turned into stars. However, in nearly all parts of the ancient world the Pleiades constellation is associated with goddesses who were emanations of the moon goddess. The heroines of the Australian myth, like their sisters of other cultures, represent the light that can come from darkness, the renewal and salvation that can come from sacrifice, the life that can come from death. They are a representation of the aspect of the hero biography that entails a journey into the darkness.

•

In various parts of the world and among different races there are traditions that the lustre of the Pleiades is associated with acts in which women were concerned. There is an Australian legend on the subject. According to this story, it was the girls who had reached the age of adolescence who perceived the necessity for bringing the body under subjection to the mind in order to restrain physical appetite and control the effects of pain and fear. They saw that without such control there could be no real racial advancement. Accordingly, they presented themselves to the elders of the tribe in order to undergo the trial by ordeal. The elders explained to the girls that the test that they would have to submit to was a severe one. The girls, however, were firm in their resolve to undergo it. So every morning for three years, in a place apart from their brothers and sisters, the elders, to teach them moderation, gave them a small portion of the usual food, consisting perhaps of a piece of fish or flesh of the emu, kangaroo, or wombat. This they received twice a day, at the hour of sunrise and at the hour of sunset. At the end of the third year they were taken for a long journey through the dense bush, where the thorns scratched their flesh, and across the plains and rivers, travelling during the heat of the day, often almost fainting from fatigue, but ever pressing onward. After a week of such journeying had passed the elders called the girls before them and inquired whether they thought they were better able to control the appetite. To this the girls replied, "Our minds are made up. We will control the appetite." The elders then said, "You are asked to fast for three days, and during this fasting time we will all travel."

So the girls set out with the elders on the journey. The way was long and difficult, and they were weak from lack of food. The blazing sun seemed to them more ruthless and the way more rough and thorny than usual, but they were determined to conquer, and so they kept on their way undaunted. On the evening of the third day they arrived at the appointed camping-ground. The elders prepared the food for them for the following day. On the fourth morning they were given a flint knife, and were instructed to cut from the kangaroo or emu the amount of food they required. How tempting was the smell of the roasted flesh to the girls, who had travelled unceasingly for three days without breaking their fast! The temptation to cut a generous portion and satisfy the craving for food was very great. But each cut for herself only an ordinary portion. The elders praised the girls for their restraint. They said, "You have acquitted yourselves well so far; and now there are other appetites, and it is for you to control them as you have controlled your hunger." They replied, "We are ready to undergo any tests you please. Our minds are made up to subdue appetite and to conquer inclination." They then submitted themselves to various tests in order to learn to control other appetites, each test being more difficult than the former. In every case they were successful.

W. Ramsay Smith, *Myths and Legends of the Australian Aboriginals* (London, 1970), pp. 345–50.

When the elders told them that it was necessary to overcome pain they again submitted themselves to their guidance, and the elders decided the particular form of discipline that the girls should undergo. In the presence of the other girls and boys they took the girls away to a selected spot, where all sacred ceremonies were performed. They ordered them to lie upon the ground. Then they took a stone axe and a pointed stick about eight or nine inches long. They told the girls one by one to open their mouths. The elders placed the point of a stick against a front tooth of each, then raised an axe and brought it down upon the stick, breaking the tooth off, and leaving the nerves exposed and quivering. The girls then rose from the ground, and sat awaiting the further commands of the elders. They were asked whether they felt the pain, to which they replied, "Yes, we felt the pain." Then the elders said, "Are you willing to have another tooth knocked out?" And the girls replied, "Yes, our minds are made up. We are going to control pain." And again the elders asked at the conclusion of this test, "Are you willing to undergo more severe testing?" The girls replied as before, "Yes, our minds are made up. We will control pain." They were then led to another camping-ground and commanded to stand in a row. An elder of the tribe approached with a flint knife. He stood before each of the girls for a while, and then drew the knife silently across her breast, and the blood flowed. This he did to each girl in succession. Another elder took the ashes of a particular kind of wood, and rubbed them into the wound. The effect of this was twofold; it intensified the pain, and helped to heal the wound.

A day or two was given to allow the wounds to heal, and then the elders called the girls before them and inquired if they were still willing to submit themselves to further testing. They replied, "Yes, we are willing to go through any tests. Our minds are made up." The elders then went alone through the bush and selected another camping-ground for the girls. At bed-time they were led to the spot, and told, "It is time to retire to rest. This is your camping-ground." The girls, weary and eager for rest, threw their oppossum rugs on the ground. The night was dark and moonless and very warm. They lay there for a little while, and presently they felt things crawling over their bodies. They were afraid, but they refused to give way to fear. It may have been that each girl was afraid of what the others would think of her if she failed, and that thus each helped the others to be brave. By and by they discovered they were lying on a bed of ants. All through the night they lay there with the ants swarming over them. The time seemed very long. These girls had journeyed far, fasting, and their poor bodies were still tender with half-healed wounds. In the morning they presented themselves to the elders, smiling and showing no signs of the terrible night that they had passed.

Still their journey continued, and they underwent further tests, such

as the piercing of the nose and the wearing of a stick through it to keep
the wound open. Further, they were bidden to lie on a bed of hot cinders.
Before each fresh trial they were asked if they were willing to undergo the
tests. Their reply, which never varied, was, "Yes, we have made up our
minds to conquer pain."

Now the elders were very pleased with the girls, and very proud of
the powers of endurance that they showed, but they realized that it was
necessary for them to overcome fear as well as the appetites and pain, so
they called them together and said, "Girls! You have done very well, and
have proved that you possess wonderful courage and endurance. The next
stage is the control of fear. Do you wish to continue on the way?" The girls
stood there in all their youth, and with glowing eyes; and they repeated
the old phrase, "Yes, our minds are made up. We will conquer fear."

On a fresh camping-ground in the dark night, with the campfires
gleaming on the trees, and casting dark, gloomy shadows, the elders told
them tales about the *bunyip* and the *muldarpe*. This latter is a spirit which
assumes many shapes. It may come as a kangaroo, or a wombat, or a lizard.
The girls were told fearful stories of these dreadful beings, and of ghosts,
to which they listened tremblingly. The more highly strung among them
could scarcely refrain from crying out. They found themselves looking
over their shoulders, and imagining that the dark shadows were the *bunyip*
or the *muldarpe* or other spirits. For hours they listened, until it was time
to go to bed. After the elders had made the sign of good-night they told
them that the place where they were camping was the burial-place of their
great-grandfathers. They lay down to sleep, resolved not to be afraid of
any ghosts or spirits.

Then the elders crept round the camp, making weird noises, so that
the hair of the girls rose and their blood ran cold. Besides these sounds
there were the usual bush-noises, such as the howl of the dingo, the shriek
of the owl, and the falling of the decayed branches. But the girls were not
to be turned from their purpose, and they lay there until the break of day.
Then they rose and presented themselves to the elders, showing no signs
of their disturbed night, their faces placid and their eyes clear and shining.
The elders knew that the girls had conquered fear, and they rejoiced with
pride. They sent out invitations to the adjoining tribes, and they made
great rejoicing, and held many corrobberies in honour of the girls.

But the girls were not content with having conquered the appetites
and pain and fear. They desired that their sisters should do the same. So
the leader of the girls stepped out from the group, and said to the girls of
the assembled tribes, "We have passed through the testing that our elders
prescribed, and we have endured much pain. Now it is the desire of the
Great Spirit that you should go through the same course of testing. You
must know that the selfish person is not happy. This is because he thinks

only of himself. Happiness comes through thinking of others and forgetting self. Greed and pain and fear are caused by thinking too much of self, and so it is necessary to vanquish self. Will you not go and do as we have done?" The girls of the other tribes eagerly assented, so proud were they of the victory of their sisters.

Then the Great Spirit was so pleased with them that he sent a great star spirit to convey the girls to the heavens without death or further suffering, in order that they might shine there as a pattern and a symbol to their race. And on clear nights ever since that time the aboriginals look into the sky and revere this wonderful constellation, the Seven Sisters, and remember what the girls did, and always think of the story of how there came to be given to them a place in the heavens.

Hebrew: Abraham and Isaac

In this moving tale, which Christians see as a foreshadowing of the Crucifixion of Jesus, the boy hero Isaac is delivered at the last minute from death. For his father, Abraham, the hero-patriarch of Judaism, Christianity, and Islam, the event is a confrontation with death and a true test of his heroism.

•

And it came to pass after these things, that God did tempt Abraham, and said unto him, Abraham: and he said, Behold, here I am.

2 And he said, Take now thy son, thine only son Isaac, whom thou lovest, and get thee into the land of Mō-rī'-ăh; and offer him there for a burnt offering upon one of the mountains which I will tell thee of.

3 And Abraham rose up early in the morning, and saddled his ass, and took two of his young men with him, and Isaac his son, and clave the wood for the burnt offering, and rose up, and went unto the place of which God had told him.

4 Then on the third day Abraham lifted up his eyes, and saw the place afar off.

5 And Abraham said unto his young men, Abide ye here with the ass; and I and the lad will go yonder and worship, and come again to you.

6 And Abraham took the wood of the burnt offering, and laid it upon Isaac his son; and he took the fire in his hand, and a knife; and they went both of them together.

7 And Isaac spake unto Abraham his father, and said, My father: and he said, Here am I, my son. And he said, Behold the fire and the wood: but where is the lamb for a burnt offering?

Genesis 22:1–19

8 And Abraham said, My son, God will provide himself a lamb for a burnt offering: so they went both of them together.

9 And they came to the place which God had told him of; and Abraham built an altar there, and laid the wood in order, and bound Isaac his son, and laid him on the altar upon the wood.

10 And Abraham stretched forth his hand, and took the knife to slay his son.

11 And the angel of the Lord called unto him out of heaven, and said, Abraham, Abraham: and he said, Here am I.

12 And he said, Lay not thine hand upon the lad, neither do thou any thing unto him: for now I know that thou fearest God, seeing thou hast not withheld thy son, thine only son from me.

13 And Abraham lifted up his eyes, and looked, and beheld behind him a ram caught in a thicket by his horns: and Abraham went and took the ram, and offered him up for a burnt offering in the stead of his son.

14 And Abraham called the name of that place Jĕ-hō'-văh–jī'-rēh: as it is said to this day, In the mount of the Lord it shall be seen.

15 And the angel of the Lord called unto Abraham out of heaven the second time,

16 And said, By myself have I sworn, saith the Lord, for because thou hast done this thing, and hast not withheld thy son, thine only son:

17 That in blessing I will bless thee, and in multiplying I will multiply thy seed as the stars of the heaven, and as the sand which is upon the sea shore; and thy seed shall possess the gate of his enemies;

18 And in thy seed shall all the nations of the earth be blessed; because thou hast obeyed my voice.

19 So Abraham returned unto his young men, and they rose up and went together to Beer-sheba; and Abraham dwelt at Beer-sheba.

Mesopotamian: Gilgamesh

One of the earliest-known quest heroes is Gilgamesh. His quest includes a temptation by Ishtar (Inanna), an immortal femme fatale; fights with monsters; and a descent to the other world. It is a quest for immortality or eternal youth. Gilgamesh is guided by a goddess called Siduri, who reminds us of the later Kalypso in Homer's *Odyssey* and the Sybil in Vergil's *Aeneid*. Gilgamesh's story is found in the earliest of epic poems, a work in fragments that was composed perhaps as early as the second millennium B.C.E. This part of the myth is the story of Gilgamesh's descent into the dark world in search of his dead friend, Enkidu, and the Sumerian Noah, Utnapishtim.

•

Bitterly Gilgamesh wept for his friend Enkidu; he wandered over the wilderness as a hunter, he roamed over the plains; in his bitterness he cried,

"How can I rest, how can I be at peace? Despair is in my heart. What my brother is now, that shall I be when I am dead. Because I am afraid of death I will go as best I can to find Utnapishtim whom they call the Faraway, for he has entered the assembly of the gods." So Gilgamesh travelled over the wilderness, he wandered over the grasslands, a long journey, in search of Utnapishtim, whom the gods took after the deluge; and they set him to live in the land of Dilmun, in the garden of the sun; and to him alone of men they gave everlasting life.

At night when he came to the mountain passes Gilgamesh prayed: "In these mountain passes long ago I saw lions, I was afraid and I lifted my eyes to the moon; I prayed and my prayers went up to the gods, so now, O moon god Sin, protect me." When he had prayed he lay down to sleep, until he was woken from out of a dream. He saw the lions round him glorying in life; then he took his axe in his hand, he drew his sword from his belt, and he fell upon them like an arrow from the string, and struck and destroyed and scattered them.

So at length Gilgamesh came to Mashu, the great mountains about which he had heard many things, which guard the rising and the setting sun. Its twin peaks are as high as the wall of heaven and its paps reach down to the underworld. At its gate the Scorpions stand guard, half man and half dragon; their glory is terrifying, their stare strikes death into men, their shimmering halo sweeps the mountains that guard the rising sun. When Gilgamesh saw them he shielded his eyes for the length of a moment only; then he took courage and approached. When they saw him so undismayed the Man-Scorpion called to his mate, "This one who comes to us now is flesh of the gods." The mate of the Man-Scorpion answered, "Two thirds is god but one third is man."

Then he called to the man Gilgamesh, he called to the child of the gods: "Why have you come so great a journey; for what have you travelled so far, crossing the dangerous waters; tell me the reason for your coming?" Gilgamesh answered, "For Enkidu; I loved him dearly, together we endured all kinds of hardships; on his account I have come, for the common lot of man has taken him. I have wept for him day and night, I would not give up his body for burial, I thought my friend would come back because of my weeping. Since he went, my life is nothing; that is why I have travelled here in search of Utnapishtim my father; for men say he has entered the assembly of the gods, and has found everlasting life. I have a desire to question him concerning the living and the dead." The Man-Scorpion opened his mouth and said, speaking to Gilgamesh, "No man born of woman has done what you have asked, no mortal man has gone into the mountain; the length of it is twelve leagues of darkness; in it there is no light, but the heart is oppressed with darkness. From the rising of the sun

N. K. Sandars, trans., *The Epic of Gilgamesh*, rev. ed. (Harmondsworth, Eng., 1972), pp. 97–104.

to the setting of the sun there is no light." Gilgamesh said, "Although I should go in sorrow and in pain, with sighing and with weeping, still I must go. Open the gate of the mountain." And the Man-Scorpion said, "Go, Gilgamesh, I permit you to pass through the mountain of Mashu and through the high ranges; may your feet carry you safely home. The gate of the mountain is open."

When Gilgamesh heard this he did as the Man-Scorpion had said, he followed the sun's road to his rising, through the mountain. When he had gone one league the darkness became thick around him, for there was no light, he could see nothing ahead and nothing behind him. After two leagues the darkness was thick and there was no light, he could see nothing ahead and nothing behind him. After three leagues the darkness was thick, and there was no light, he could see nothing ahead and nothing behind him. After four leagues the darkness was thick and there was no light, he could see nothing ahead and nothing behind him. At the end of five leagues the darkness was thick and there was no light, he could see nothing ahead and nothing behind him. At the end of six leagues the darkness was thick and there was no light, he could see nothing ahead and nothing behind him. When he had gone seven leagues the darkness was thick and there was no light, he could see nothing ahead and nothing behind him. When he had gone eight leagues Gilgamesh gave a great cry, for the darkness was thick and he could see nothing ahead and nothing behind him. After nine leagues he felt the north wind on his face, but the darkness was thick and there was no light, he could see nothing ahead and nothing behind him. After ten leagues the end was near. After eleven leagues the dawn light appeared. At the end of twelve leagues the sun streamed out.

There was the garden of the gods; all round him stood bushes bearing gems. Seeing it he went down at once, for there was fruit of carnelian with the vine hanging from it, beautiful to look at; lapis lazuli leaves hung thick with fruit, sweet to see. For thorns and thistles there were haematite and rare stones, agate, and pearls from out of the sea. While Gilgamesh walked in the garden by the edge of the sea Shamash saw him, and he saw that he was dressed in the skins of animals and ate their flesh. He was distressed, and he spoke and said, "No mortal man has gone this way before, nor will, as long as the winds drive over the sea." And to Gilgamesh he said, "You will never find the life for which you are searching." Gilgamesh said to glorious Shamash, "Now that I have toiled and strayed so far over the wilderness, am I to sleep, and let the earth cover my head for ever? Let my eyes see the sun until they are dazzled with looking. Although I am no better than a dead man, still let me see the light of the sun."

Beside the sea she lives, the woman of the vine, the maker of wine; Siduri sits in the garden at the edge of the sea, with the golden bowl and the golden vats that the gods gave her. She is covered with a veil; and where she sits she sees Gilgamesh coming towards her, wearing skins, the flesh of the gods in his body, but despair in his heart, and his face like the face of one who has made a long journey. She looked, and as she scanned the distance she said in her own heart, "Surely this is some felon; where is he going now?" And she barred her gate against him with the cross-bar and shot home the bolt. But Gilgamesh, hearing the sound of the bolt, threw up his head and lodged his foot in the gate; he called to her, "Young woman, maker of wine, why do you bolt your door; what did you see that made you bar your gate? I will break in your door and burst in your gate, for I am Gilgamesh who seized and killed the Bull of Heaven, I killed the watchman of the cedar forest, I overthrew Humbaba who lived in the forest, and I killed the lions in the passes of the mountain."

Then Siduri said to him, "If you are that Gilgamesh who seized and killed the Bull of Heaven, who killed the watchman of the cedar forest, who overthrew Humbaba that lived in the forest, and killed the lions in the passes of the mountain, why are your cheeks so starved and why is your face so drawn? Why is despair in your heart and your face like the face of one who has made a long journey? Yes, why is your face burned from heat and cold, and why do you come here wandering over the pastures in search of the wind?"

Gilgamesh answered her, "And why should not my cheeks be starved and my face drawn? Despair is in my heart and my face is the face of one who has made a long journey, it was burned with heat and with cold. Why should I not wander over the pastures in search of the wind? My friend, my younger brother, he who hunted the wild ass of the wilderness and the panther of the plains, my friend, my younger brother who seized and killed the Bull of Heaven and overthrew Humbaba in the cedar forest, my friend who was very dear to me and who endured dangers beside me, Enkidu my brother, whom I loved, the end of mortality has overtaken him. I wept for him seven days and nights till the worm fastened on him. Because of my brother I am afraid of death, because of my brother I stray through the wilderness and cannot rest. But now, young woman, maker of wine, since I have seen your face do not let me see the face of death which I dread so much."

She answered, "Gilgamesh, where are you hurrying to? You will never find that life for which you are looking. When the gods created man they allotted to him death, but life they retained in their own keeping. As for you, Gilgamesh, fill your belly with good things; day and night, night and day, dance and be merry, feast and rejoice. Let your clothes be fresh, bathe yourself in water, cherish the little child that holds your hand, and make your wife happy in your embrace; for this too is the lot of man."

But Gilgamesh said to Siduri, the young woman, "How can I be silent, how can I rest, when Enkidu whom I love is dust, and I too shall die and be laid in the earth. You live by the sea-shore and look into the heart of it; young woman, tell me now, which is the way to Utnapishtim, the son of Ubara-Tutu? What directions are there for the passage; give me, oh, give me directions. I will cross the Ocean if it is possible; if it is not I will wander still farther in the wilderness." The wine-maker said to him, "Gilgamesh, there is no crossing the Ocean; whoever has come, since the days of old, has not been able to pass that sea. The Sun in his glory crosses the Ocean, but who beside Shamash has ever crossed it? The place and the passage are difficult, and the waters of death are deep which flow between. Gilgamesh, how will you cross the Ocean? When you come to the waters of death what will you do? But Gilgamesh, down in the woods you will find Urshanabi, the ferryman of Utnapishtim; with him are the holy things, the things of stone. He is fashioning the serpent prow of the boat. Look at him well, and if it is possible, perhaps you will cross the waters with him; but if it is not possible, then you must go back."

When Gilgamesh heard this he was seized with anger. He took his axe in his hand, and his dagger from his belt. He crept forward and he fell on them like a javelin. Then he went into the forest and sat down. Urshanabi saw the dagger flash and heard the axe, and he beat his head, for Gilgamesh had shattered the tackle of the boat in his rage. Urshanabi said to him, "Tell me, what is your name? I am Urshanabi, the ferryman of Utnapishtim the Faraway." He replied to him, "Gilgamesh is my name, I am from Uruk, from the house of Anu." Then Urshanabi said to him, "Why are your cheeks so starved and your face drawn? Why is despair in your heart and your face like the face of one who has made a long journey; yes, why is your face burned with heat and with cold, and why do you come here wandering over the pastures in search of the wind?

Gilgamesh said to him, 'Why should not my cheeks be starved and my face drawn? Despair is in my heart, and my face is the face of one who has made a long journey. I was burned with heat and with cold. Why should I not wander over the pastures? My friend, my younger brother who seized and killed the Bull of Heaven, and overthrew Humbaba in the cedar forest, my friend who was very dear to me, and who endured dangers beside me, Enkidu my brother whom I loved, the end of mortality has overtaken him. I wept for him seven days and nights till the worm fastened on him. Because of my brother I am afraid of death, because of my brother I stray through the wilderness. His fate lies heavy upon me. How can I be silent, how can I rest? He is dust and I too shall die and be laid in the earth for ever.

Greek: Orpheus and Eurydice

The most poignant of descent-rescue stories is that of Orpheus and Eurydice. Like the myth of Gilgamesh, it suggests human frustration over the inaccessibility of immortality.

From there Hymen, clad in his saffron robes, was summoned by Orpheus, and made his way across the vast reaches of the sky to the shores of the Cicones. But Orpheus' invitation to the god to attend his marriage was of no avail, for though he was certainly present, he did not bring good luck. His expression was gloomy, and he did not sing his accustomed refrain. Even the torch he carried sputtered and smoked, bringing tears to the eyes, and no amount of tossing could make it burn. The outcome was even worse than the omens foretold: for while the new bride was wandering in the meadows, with her band of naiads, a serpent bit her ankle, and she sank lifeless to the ground. The Thracian poet mourned her loss; when he had wept for her to the full in the upper world, he made so bold as to descend through the gate of Taenarus to the Styx, to try to rouse the sympathy of the shades as well. There he passed among the thin ghosts, the wraiths of the dead, till he reached Persephone and her lord, who holds sway over these dismal regions, the king of the shades. Then, accompanying his words with the music of his lyre, he said:

"Deities of this lower world, to which all we of mortal birth descend, if I have your permission to dispense with rambling insincerities and speak the simple truth, I did not come here to see the dim haunts of Tartarus, nor yet to chain Medusa's monstrous dog, with its three heads and snaky ruff. I came because of my wife, cut off before she reached her prime when she trod on a serpent and it poured its poison into her veins. I wished to be strong enough to endure my grief, and I will not deny that I tried to do so: but Love was too much for me. He is a god well-known in the world above; whether he may be so here too, I do not know, but I imagine that he is familiar to you also and, if there is any truth in the story of that rape of long ago, then you yourselves were brought together by Love. I beg you, by these awful regions, by this boundless chaos, and by the silence of your vast realms, weave again Eurydice's destiny, brought too swiftly to a close. We mortals and all that is ours are fated to fall to you, and after a little time, sooner or later, we hasten to this one abode. We are all on our way here, this is our final home, and yours the most lasting sway over the human race. My wife, like the rest, when she has completed her proper span of years will, in the fullness of time, come within your power. I ask as a gift from you only the enjoyment of her; but if the fates refuse her a reprieve, I have made up my mind that I do not wish to return either. You may exult in my death as well as hers!"

As he sang these words to the music of his lyre, the bloodless ghosts were in tears: Tantalus made no effort to reach the waters that ever shrank away, Ixion's wheel stood still in wonder, the vultures ceased to gnaw Tityus' liver, the daughters of Danaus rested from their pitchers, and Sisy-

Ovid, *The Metamorphoses*, trans. Mary M. Innes (London, 1955), pp. 225–27.

phus sat idle on his rock. Then for the first time, they say, the cheeks of
the Furies were wet with tears, for they were overcome by his singing. The
king and queen of the underworld could not bear to refuse his pleas. They
called Eurydice. She was among the ghosts who had but newly come, and
walked slowly because of her injury. Thracian Orpheus received her, but
on condition that he must not look back until he had emerged from the
valleys of Avernus or else the gift he had been given would be taken from
him.

Up the sloping path, through the mute silence they made their way,
up the steep dark track, wrapped in impenetrable gloom, till they had
almost reached the surface of the earth. Here, anxious in case his wife's
strength be failing and eager to see her, the lover looked behind him, and
straightway Eurydice slipped back into the depths. Orpheus stretched out
his arms, straining to clasp her and be clasped; but the hapless man
touched nothing but yielding air. Eurydice, dying now a second time, uttered no complaint against her husband. What was there to complain of,
but that she had been loved? With a last farewell which scarcely reached
his ears, she fell back again into the same place from which she had come.

At his wife's second death, Orpheus was completely stunned. He was
like that timid fellow who, when he saw three-headed Cerberus led along,
chained by the middle one of this three necks, was turned to stone in every
limb, and lost his fear only when he lost his original nature too: or like
Olenus and hapless Lethaea, once fond lovers, now stones set on well-
watered Ida, all because Lethaea was too confident in her beauty, while
Olenus sought to take her guilt upon his own shoulders, and wished to be
considered the culprit. In vain did the poet long to cross the Styx a second
time, and prayed that he might do so. The ferryman thrust him aside. For
seven days, unkempt and neglected, he sat on the river bank, without
tasting food: grief, anxiety and tears were his nourishment. Then he retired
to lofty Rhodope and windswept Haemus, complaining of the cruelty of
the gods of Erebus.

Three times the sun had reached the watery sign of Pisces, that brings
the year to a close. Throughout this time Orpheus had shrunk from loving
any woman, either because of his unhappy experience, or because he had
pledged himself not to do so. In spite of this there were many who were
fired with a desire to marry the poet, many were indignant to find themselves repulsed. However, Orpheus preferred to centre his affections on
boys of tender years, and to enjoy the brief spring and early flowering of
their youth: he was the first to introduce this custom among the people of
Thrace.

On the top of a certain hill was a level stretch of open ground, covered
with green turf. There was no shelter from the sun, but when the divinely-
born poet seated himself there and struck his melodious strings, shady
trees moved to the spot. The oak tree of Chaonia and poplars, Phaethon's

sisters, crowded round, along with Jupiter's great oak, with its lofty branches, and soft lime trees and beeches, and the virgin laurel, brittle hazels, and ash trees, that are used for spear shafts, smooth firs and the holm oak, bowed down with acorns, the genial sycamore, and the variegated maple, willows that grow by the rivers and the water-loving lotus, evergreen box, slender tamarisks, myrtles double-hued, and viburnum with its dark blue berries. There was ivy too, trailing its tendrils, and leafy vines, vine-clad elms and mountain ash, pitchpine and wild strawberry, laden with rosy fruit, waving palms, the victor's prize, and the pine, its leaves gathered up into a shaggy crest, the favourite tree of Cybele, the mother of the gods: for her priest Attis exchanged his human shape for this, and hardened into its trunk.

Greek: Odysseus

Before he can achieve his goal of returning home to Ithaca, Homer's Odysseus must meet with the dead. He learns of his destiny from Tiresias and of the nature of death. Having so "descended," he can begin to rise into his true self, in a motif that relates him and many other heroes to the ancient sun gods, who seem to die each night only to be reborn each day.

•

. . .

> We made the land, put ram and ewe ashore,
> and took our way along the Ocean stream
> to find the place foretold for us by Kirkê.
> There Perimêdês and Eurýlokhos
> pinioned the sacred beasts. With my drawn blade
> I spaded up the votive pit, and poured
> libations round it to the unnumbered dead:
> sweet milk and honey, then sweet wine, and last
> clear water; and I scattered barley down.
> Then I addressed the blurred and breathless dead,
> vowing to slaughter my best heifer for them
> before she calved, at home in Ithaka,
> and burn the choice bits on the altar fire;
> as for Teirêsias, I swore to sacrifice
> a black lamb, handsomest of all our flock.
> Thus to assuage the nations of the dead
> I pledged these rites, then slashed the lamb and ewe,
> letting their black blood stream into the wellpit.
> Now the souls gathered, stirring out of Erebos,
> brides and young men, and men grown old in pain,

Homer, *The Odyssey*, trans. Robert Fitzgerald (New York, 1961), pp. 198, 200–201.

and tender girls whose hearts were new to grief;
many were there, too, torn by brazen lanceheads,
battle-slain, bearing still their bloody gear.
From every side they came and sought the pit
with rustling cries; and I grew sick with fear.
But presently I gave command to my officers
to flay those sheep the bronze cut down, and make
burnt offerings of flesh to the gods below—
to sovereign Death, to pale Perséphonê.
Meanwhile I crouched with my drawn sword to keep
the surging phantoms from the bloody pit
till I should know the presence of Teirêsias.

                                                              . . .

Soon from the dark that prince of Thebes came forward
bearing a golden staff; and he addressed me:

"Son of Laërtês and the gods of old,
Odysseus, master of land ways and sea ways,
why leave the blazing sun, O man of woe,
to see the cold dead and the joyless region?
Stand clear, put up your sword;
let me but taste of blood, I shall speak true."

At this I stepped aside, and in the scabbard
let my long sword ring home to the pommel silver,
as he bent down to the sombre blood. Then spoke
the prince of those with gift of speech:

                                                              "Great captain,

a fair wind and the honey lights of home
are all you seek. But anguish lies ahead;
the god who thunders on the land prepares it,
not to be shaken from your track, implacable,
in rancor for the son whose eye you blinded.
One narrow strait may take you through his blows:
denial of yourself, restraint of shipmates.
When you made landfall on Thrinakia first
and quit the violet sea, dark on the land
you'll find the grazing herds of Hêlios
by whom all things are seen, all speech is known.
Avoid those kine, hold fast to your intent,
and hard seafaring brings you all to Ithaka.
But if you raid the beeves, I see destruction
for ship and crew. Though you survive alone,
bereft of all companions, lost for years,

under strange sail shall you come home, to find
your own house filled with trouble: insolent men
eating your livestock as they court your lady.
Aye, you shall make those men atone in blood!
But after you have dealt out death—in open
combat or by stealth—to all the suitors,
go overland on foot, and take an oar,
until one day you come where men have lived
with meat unsalted, never known the sea,
nor seen seagoing ships, with crimson bows
and oars that fledge light hulls for dipping flight.
The spot will soon be plain to you, and I
can tell you how: some passerby will say,
"What winnowing fan is that upon your shoulder?"
Halt, and implant your smooth oar in the turf
and make fair sacrifice to Lord Poseidon:
a ram, a bull, a great buck boar; turn back,
and carry out pure hekatombs at home
to all wide heaven's lords, the undying gods,
to each in order. Then a seaborne death
soft as this hand of mist will come upon you
when you are wearied out with rich old age,
your country folk in blessed peace around you.
And all this shall be just as I foretell."

When he had done, I said at once,

                                              "Teirêsias,

my life runs on then as the gods have spun it.
But come, now, tell me this; make this thing clear:
I see my mother's ghost among the dead
sitting in silence near the blood. Not once
has she glanced this way toward her son, nor spoken.
Tell me, my lord,
may she in some way come to know my presence?"

To this he answered:

                                              "I shall make it clear

in a few words and simply. Any dead man
whom you allow to enter where the blood is
will speak to you, and speak the truth; but those
deprived will grow remote again and fade."

When he had prophesied, Terêsias' shade
retired lordly to the halls of Death. . . .

The Rebirth, Return, and Apotheosis of the Hero

Blackfoot: Kutoyis

We have already encountered, literally or symbolically, the motif of the rebirth or resurrection of the dead hero or god in the myths of Jesus, Attis, Osiris, Odysseus, Jonah, Wanjiru, and others. The story of Kutoyis, a particularly comprehensive version of the world hero story, complete with miraculous birth and supernatural power, contains a dramatic death and rebirth that resembles the Orphic story of Dionysos' being chopped up and cooked. It has echoes in all those stories about children sacrificed and served up to evil fathers. The myth of Tereus and that of the House of Atreus contain this motif. The theme may have some connection with the ritual of the sacred meal, in which the dead god becomes the source of renewal for his society.

•

Long ago, down where Two Medicine and Badger Creeks come together, there lived an old man. He had but one wife and two daughters. One day there came to his camp a young man who was very brave and a great hunter. The old man said: "Ah! I will have this young man to help me. I will give him my daughters for wives." So he gave him his daughters. He also gave this son-in-law all his wealth, keeping for himself only a little lodge, in which he lived with his old wife. The son-in-law lived in a lodge that was big and fine.

At first the son-in-law was very good to the old people. Whenever he killed anything, he gave them part of the meat, and furnished plenty of robes and skins for their bedding and clothing. But after a while he began to be very mean to them.

Now the son-in-law kept the buffalo hidden under a big log jam in the river. Whenever he wanted to kill anything, he would have the old man go to help him; and the old man would stamp on the log jam and frighten the buffalo, and when they ran out, the young man would shoot one or two, never killing wastefully. But often he gave the old people nothing to eat, and they were hungry all the time, and began to grow thin and weak.

One morning, the young man called his father-in-law to go down to the log jam and hunt with him. They started, and the young man killed a fat buffalo cow. Then he said to the old man, "Hurry back now, and tell your children to get the dogs and carry this meat home, then you can have something to eat." And the old man did as he had been ordered, thinking to himself: "Now, at last, my son-in-law has taken pity on me. He will give

George Bird Grinnell, *Blackfoot Lodge Tales* (Lincoln, Neb., 1962), pp. 29–38.

me part of this meat." When he returned with the dogs, they skinned the cow, cut up the meat and packed it on the dog travois, and went home. Then the young man had his wives unload it, and told his father-in-law to go home. He did not give him even a piece of liver. Neither would the older daughter give her parents anything to eat, but the younger took pity on the old people and stole a piece of meat, and when she got a chance threw it into the lodge to the old people. The son-in-law told his wives not to give the old people anything to eat. The only way they got food was when the younger woman would throw them a piece of meat unseen by her husband and sister.

Another morning, the son-in-law got up early, and went and kicked on the old man's lodge to wake him, and called him to get up and help him, to go and pound on the log jam to drive out the buffalo, so that he could kill some. When the old man pounded on the jam, a buffalo ran out, and the son-in-law shot it, but only wounded it. It ran away, but at last fell down and died. The old man followed it, and came to where it had lost a big clot of blood from its wound. When he came to where this clot of blood was lying on the ground, he stumbled and fell, and spilled his arrows out of his quiver; and while he was picking them up, he picked up also the clot of blood, and hid it in his quiver. "What are you picking up?" called out the son-in-law. "Nothing," said the old man; "I just fell down and spilled my arrows, and am putting them back." "Curse you, old man," said the son-in-law, "you are lazy and useless. Go back and tell your children to come with the dogs and get this dead buffalo." He also took away his bow and arrows from the old man.

The old man went home and told his daughters, and then went over to his own lodge, and said to his wife: "Hurry now, and put the kettle on the fire. I have brought home something from the butchering." "Ah!" said the old woman, "has our son-in-law been generous, and given us something nice?" "No," answered the old man; "hurry up and put the kettle on." When the water began to boil, the old man tipped his quiver up over the kettle, and immediately there came from the pot a noise as of a child crying, as if it were being hurt, burnt or scalded. They looked in the kettle, and saw there a little boy, and they quickly took it out of the water. They were very much surprised. The old woman made a lashing to put the child in, and then they talked about it. They decided that if the son-in-law knew that it was a boy, he would kill it, so they resolved to tell their daughters that the baby was a girl. Then he would be glad, for he would think that after a while he would have it for a wife. They named the child Kŭt-o′-yis (Clot of Blood).

The son-in-law and his wives came home, and after a while he heard the child crying. He told his youngest wife to go and find out whether that baby was a boy or a girl; if it was a boy, to tell them to kill it. She came back and told them that it was a girl. He did not believe this, and sent his oldest wife to find out the truth of the matter. When she came back and told him the same thing, he believed that it was really a girl. Then he was glad, for he thought that when the child had grown up he would have another wife. He said to his youngest wife, 'Take some pemmican over to your mother; not much, just enough so that there will be plenty of milk for the child.''

Now on the fourth day the child spoke, and said, "Lash me in turn to each one of these lodge poles, and when I get to the last one, I will fall out of my lashing and be grown up." The old woman did so, and as she lashed him to each lodge pole he could be seen to grow, and finally when they lashed him to the last pole, he was a man. After Kŭt-o'-yis had looked about the inside of the lodge, he looked out through a hole in the lodge covering, and then, turning round, he said to the old people: "How is it there is nothing to eat in this lodge? I see plenty of food over by the other lodge." "Hush up," said the old woman, "you will be heard. That is our son-in-law. He does not give us anything at all to eat." "Well," said Kŭt-o'-yis, "where is your pis'kun?" The old woman said, "It is down by the river. We pound on it and the buffalo come out."

Then the old man told him how his son-in-law abused him. "He has taken my weapons from me, and even my dogs; and for many days we have had nothing to eat, except now and then a small piece of meat our daughter steals for us."

"Father," said Kŭt-o'-yis, "have you no arrows?" "No, my son," he replied; "but I have yet four stone points."

"Go out then and get some wood," said Kŭt-o'-yis. "We will make a bow and arrows. In the morning we will go down and kill something to eat."

Early in the morning Kŭt-o'-yis woke the old man, and said, "Come, we will go down now and kill when the buffalo come out." When they had reached the river, the old man said: "Here is the place to stand and shoot. I will go down and drive them out." As he pounded on the jam, a fat cow ran out, and Kŭt-o'-yis killed it.

Meantime the son-in-law had gone out, and as usual knocked on the old man's lodge, and called to him to get up and go down to help him kill. The old woman called to him that her husband had already gone down. This made the son-in-law very angry. He said: "I have a good mind to kill you right now, old woman. I guess I will by and by."

The son-in-law went on down to the jam, and as he drew near, he saw the old man bending over, skinning a buffalo. "Old man," said he, "stand up and look all around you. Look well, for it will be your last look." Now when he had seen the son-in-law coming, Kŭt-o'-yis had lain down and hidden himself behind the buffalo's carcass. He told the old man to say to his son-in-law, "You had better take your last look, for I am going to kill you, right now." The old man said this. "Ah!" said the son-in-law, "you make me angrier still, by talking back to me." He put an arrow to his bow and shot at the old man, but did not hit him. Kŭt-o'-yis told the old man to pick up the arrow and shoot it back at him, and he did so. Now they shot at each other four times, and then the old man said to Kŭt-o'-yis: "I am afraid now. Get up and help me." So Kŭt-o'-yis got up on his feet and said: "Here, what are you doing? I think you have been badly treating this old man for a long time."

Then the son-in-law smiled pleasantly, for he was afraid of Kŭt-o'-yis. "Oh, no," he said, "no one thinks more of this old man than I do. I have always taken great pity on him."

Then Kŭt-o'-yis said: "You lie. I am going to kill you now." He shot him four times, and the man died. Then Kŭt-o'-yis told the old man to go and bring down the daughter who had acted badly toward him. He did so, and Kŭt-o'-yis killed her. Then he went up to the lodges and said to the younger woman, "Perhaps you loved your husband." "Yes," she said, "I love him." So he killed her, too. Then he said to the old people: "Go over there now, and live in that lodge. There is plenty there to eat, and when it is gone I will kill more. As for myself, I will make a journey around about. Where are there any people? In what direction?" "Well," said the old man, "up above here on Badger Creek and Two Medicine, where the pis'kun is, there are some people."

Kŭt-o'-yis went up to where the pis'kun was, and saw there many lodges of people. In the centre of the camp was a large lodge, with a figure of a bear painted on it. He did not go into this lodge, but went into a very small one near by, where two old women lived; and when he went in, he asked them for something to eat. They set before him some lean dried meat and some belly fat. "How is this?" he asked. "Here is a pis'kun with plenty of fat meat and back fat. Why do you not give me some of that?" "Hush," said the old women. "In that big lodge near by, lives a big bear and his wives and children. He takes all those nice things and leaves us nothing. He is the chief of this place."

Early in the morning, Kŭt-o'-yis told the old women to get their dog travois, and harness it, and go over to the pis'kun, and that he was going to kill for them some fat meat. He reached there just about the time the buffalo were being driven in, and shot a cow, which looked very scabby, but was really very fat. Then he helped the old women to butcher, and when they had taken the meat to camp, he said to them, "Now take all the choice fat pieces, and hang them up so that those who live in the bear lodge will notice them."

They did this, and pretty soon the old chief bear said to his children: "Go out now, and look around. The people have finished killing by this

time. See where the nicest pieces are, and bring in some nice back fat." A
young bear went out of the lodge, stood up and looked around, and when
it saw this meat close by, at the old women's lodge, it went over and began
to pull it down. "Hold on there," said Kŭt-o'-yis. "What are you doing
here, taking the old women's meat?" and he hit him over the head with a
stick that he had. The young bear ran home crying, and said to his father,
"A young man has hit me on the head." Then all the bears, the father and
mother, and uncles and aunts, and all the relations, were very angry, and
all rushed out toward the old women's lodge.

Kŭt-o'-yis killed them all, except one little child bear, a female, which
escaped. "Well," said Kŭt-o'-yis, "you can go and breed bears, so there
will be more."

Then said Kŭt-o'-yis to the old women: "Now, grandmothers, where
are there any more people? I want to travel around and see them." The old
women said: "The nearest ones are at the point of rocks (on Sun River).
There is a pis'kun there." So Kŭt-o'-yis travelled off toward this place,
and when he reached the camp, he entered an old woman's lodge.

The old woman set before him a plate of bad food. "How is this?" he
asked. "Have you nothing better than this to set before a stranger? You
have a pis'kun down there, and must get plenty of fat meat. Give me some
pemmican." "We cannot do that," the old woman replied, "because there
is a big snake here, who is chief of the camp. He not only takes the best
pieces, but often he eats a handsome young woman, when he sees one."
When Kŭt-o'-yis heard this he was angry, and went over and entered the
snake's lodge. The women were cooking up some sarvis berries. He picked
up the dish, and ate the berries, and threw the dish out of the door. Then
he went over to where the snake was lying sleep, pricked him with his
knife, and said: "Here, get up. I have come to see you." This made the
snake angry. He partly raised himself up and began to rattle, when Kŭt-
o'-yis cut him into pieces with his knife. Then he turned around and killed
all his wives and children, except one little female snake, which escaped
by crawling into a crack in the rocks. "Oh, well," said Kŭt-o'-yis, "you
can go and breed young snakes, so there will be more. The people will not
be afraid of little snakes." Kŭt-o'-yis said to the old woman, "Now you go
into this snake's lodge and take it for yourself, and everything that is in
it."

Then he asked them where there were some more people. They told
him that there were some people down the river, and some up in the mountains. But they said: "Do not go there, for it is bad, because Ai-sin'-o-ko-
ki (Wind Sucker) lives there. He will kill you." It pleased Kŭt-o'-yis to
know that there was such a person, and he went to the mountains. When
he got to the place where Wind Sucker lived, he looked into his mouth,
and could see many dead people there,—some skeletons and some just
dead. He went in, and there he saw a fearful sight. The ground was white

as snow with the bones of those who had died. There were bodies with flesh on them; some were just dead, and some still living. He spoke to a living person, and asked, "What is that hanging down above us?" the person answered that it was Wind Sucker's heart. Then said Kŭt-o'-yis: "You who still draw a little breath, try to shake your heads (in time to the song), and those who are still able to move, get up and dance. Take courage now, we are going to have the ghost dance." So Kŭt-o'-yis bound his knife, point upward, to the top of his head and began to dance, singing the ghost song, and all the others danced with him; and as he danced up and down, the point of the knife cut Wind Sucker's heart and killed him. Kŭt-o'-yis took his knife and cut through Wind Sucker's ribs, and freed those who were able to crawl out, and said to those who could still travel to go and tell their people that they should come here for the ones who were still alive but unable to walk.

Then he asked some of these people: "Where are there any other people? I want to visit all the people." They said to him: "There is a camp to the westward up the river, but you must not take the left-hand trail going up, because on that trail lives a woman, a handsome woman, who invites men to wrestle with her and then kills them. You must avoid her." This was what Kŭt-o'-yis was looking for. This was his business in the world, to kill off all the bad things. So he asked the people just where this woman lived, and asked where it was best to go to avoid her. He did this, because he did not wish the people to know that he wanted to meet her.

He started on his way, and at length saw this woman standing by the trail. She called out to him, "Come here, young man, come here; I want to wrestle with you." "No," replied the young man, "I am in a hurry. I cannot stop." But the woman called again, "No, no, come now and wrestle once with me." When she had called him four times, Kŭt-o'-yis went up to her. Now on the ground, where this woman wrestled with people, she had placed many broken and sharp flints, partly hiding them by the grass. They seized each other, and began to wrestle over these broken flints, but Kŭt-o'-yis looked at the ground and did not step on them. He watched his chance, and suddenly gave the woman a wrench, and threw her down on a large sharp flint, which cut her in two; and the parts of her body fell asunder.

Then Kŭt-o'-yis went on, and after a while came to where a woman kept a sliding place; and at the far end of it there was a rope, which would trip people up, and when they were tripped, they would fall over a high cliff into deep water, where a great fish would eat them. When this woman saw him coming, she cried out," Come over here, young man, and slide with me." "No," he replied, "I am in a hurry." She kept calling him, and when she had called the fourth time, he went over to slide with her. "This sliding," said the woman, "is a very pleasant pastime." "Ah!" said Kŭt-o'-yis, "I will look at it." He looked at the place, and, looking carefully, he saw the hidden rope. So he started to slide, and took out his knife, and when he reached the rope, which the woman had raised, he cut it, and when it parted, the woman fell over backward into the water, and was eaten up by the big fish.

Again he went on, and after a while he came to a big camp. This was the place of a man-eater. Kŭt-o´-yis called a little girl he saw near by, and said to her: "Child, I am going into that lodge to let that man-eater kill and eat me. Watch close, therefore, and when you can get hold of one of my bones, take it out and call all the dogs, and when they have all come up to you, throw it down and cry out, 'Kŭt-o´-yis, the dogs are eating your bones!'"

Then Kŭt-o´-yis entered the lodge, and when the man-eater saw him, he cried out, "O'ki, O'ki," and seemed glad to see him, for he was a fat young man. The man-eater took a large knife, and went up to Kŭt-o´-yis, and cut his throat, and put him into a great stone kettle to cook. When the meat was cooked, he drew the kettle from the fire, and ate the body, limb by limb, until it was all eaten up.

Then the little girl, who was watching, came up to him, and said, "Pity me, man-eater, my mother is hungry and asks you for those bones." So the old man bunched them up together and handed them to her. She took them out, and called all the dogs to her, and threw the bones down to the dogs, crying out, "Look out, Kŭt-o´-yis; the dogs are eating you!" and when she said that, Kŭt-o´-yis arose from the pile of bones.

Again he went into the lodge, and when the man-eater saw him, he cried out, "How, how, how! the fat young man has survived," and seemed surprised. Again he took his knife and cut Kŭt-o´-yis' throat, and threw him into the kettle. Again, when the meat was cooked, he ate it up, and again the little girl asked for the bones, which he gave her; and, taking them out, she threw them to the dogs, crying, "Kŭt-o´-yis, the dogs are eating you!" and Kŭt-o´-yis again arose from the bones.

When the man-eater had cooked him four times, he again went into the lodge, and, seizing the man-eater, he threw him into the boiling kettle, and his wives and children too, and boiled them to death.

The man-eater was the seventh and last of the bad animals and people who were destroyed by Kŭt-o´-yis.

Christian: Jesus

After the rebirth, the hero returns to his society with a great boon. The Buddha returns from the Bodhi Tree with wisdom to share with his followers. Hiawatha returns with corn. Jesus returns with the gift of immortality. This is the story of Jesus' appearance before his disciples on the road to and in Emmaus after the Resurrection and of his eventual ascension into heaven. (See the story of the Passion of Jesus in the section on the Dying

God.) Such an end awaits many heroes and signifies the carrying of the hero idea, the continuing life of the eternal human, beyond the boundaries of death. The individual hero mask must die like all of us, but the hero behind the mask lives forever.

•

13 And, behold, two of them went that same day to a village called Em-mā'-ŭs, which was from Jerusalem about threescore furlongs.

14 And they talked together of all these things which had happened.

15 And it came to pass, that, while they communed together and reasoned, Jesus himself drew near, and went with them.

16 But their eyes were holden that they should not know him.

17 And he said unto them, What manner of communications are these that ye have one to another, as ye walk, and are sad?

18 And the one of them, whose name was Clē'-ŏ-păs, answering said unto him, Art thou only a stranger in Jerusalem, and hast not known the things which are come to pass there in these days?

19 And he said unto them, What things? And they said unto him, Concerning Jesus of Nazareth, which was a prophet mighty in deed and word before God and all the people:

20 And how the chief priests and our rulers delivered him to be condemned to death, and have crucified him.

21 But we trusted that it had been he which should have redeemed Israel: and beside all this, to-day is the third day since these things were done.

22 Yea, and certain women also of our company made us astonished, which were early at the sepulchre;

23 And when they found not his body, they came, saying, that they had also seen a vision of angels, which said that he was alive.

24 And certain of them which were with us went to the sepulchre, and found it even so as the women had said: but him they saw not.

25 Then he said unto them, O fools, and slow of heart to believe all that the prophets have spoken:

26 Ought not Christ to have suffered these things, and to enter into his glory?

27 And beginning at Moses and all the prophets, he expounded unto them in all the scriptures the things concerning himself.

28 And they drew nigh unto the village, whither they went: and he made as though he would have gone further.

29 But they constrained him, saying, Abide with us: for it is toward evening, and the day is far spent. And he went in to tarry with them.

Luke 24:13–53

30 And it came to pass, as he sat at meat with them, he took bread, and blessed it, and brake, and gave to them.

31 And their eyes were opened, and they knew him; and he vanished out of their sight.

32 And they said one to another, Did not our heart burn within us, while he talked with us by the way, and while he opened to us the scriptures?

33 And they rose up the same hour, and returned to Jerusalem, and found the eleven gathered together, and them that were with them.

34 Saying, The Lord is risen indeed, and hath appeared to Simon.

35 And they told what things were done in the way, and how he was known of them in breaking of bread.

36 And as they thus spake, Jesus himself stood in the midst of them, and saith unto them, Peace be unto you.

37 But they were terrified and affrighted, and supposed that they had seen a spirit.

38 And he said unto them, Why are ye troubled? and why do thoughts arise in your hearts?

39 Behold my hands and my feet, that it is I myself: handle me, and see; for a spirit hath not flesh and bones, as ye see me have.

40 And when he had thus spoken, he shewed them his hands and his feet.

41 And while they yet believed not for joy, and wondered, he said unto them, Have ye here any meat?

42 And they gave him a piece of a broiled fish, and of an honeycomb.

43 And he took it, and did eat before them.

44 And he said unto them, These are the words which I spake unto you, while I was yet with you, that all things must be fulfilled, which were written in the law of Moses, and in the prophets, and in the psalms, concerning me.

45 Then opened he their understanding, that they might understand the scriptures,

46 And said unto them, Thus it is written, and thus it behoved Christ to suffer, and to rise from the dead the third day:

47 And that repentance and remission of sins should be preached in his name among all nations, beginning at Jerusalem.

48 And ye are witnesses of these things.

49 And, behold, I send the promise of my Father upon you: but tarry ye in the city of Jerusalem, until ye be endued with power from on high.

50 And he led them out as far as to Bethany, and he lifted up his hands, and blessed them.

51 And it came to pass, while he blessed them, he was parted from them, and carried up into heaven.

52 And they worshipped him, and returned to Jerusalem with great joy:

53 And were continually in the temple, praising and blessing God. Amen.

Greek: Herakles

Herakles, the greatest of the Greek heroes, rises, phoenixlike, from flames and becomes an immortal.

·

And now Hercules himself cut down the trees on high Oeta, and with their trunks made a great funeral pyre. He was aided by his friend Philoctetes, who lit the pyre and to whom, as a reward, Hercules gave the famous bow which later was to to to Troy. Now, at the point of death, with burnt and withered flesh, Hercules grew calm again. On top of the pyre he spread the skin of the Nemean lion. He rested his head on his club as on a pillow, and lay down among the flames with peaceful face, as if, after cups of fine wine and crowned with garlands, he were lying on a couch at a banquet.

The gods from heaven looked down and saw that the defender of the earth was dying. Even Juno at last pitied him, and to all the gods and goddesses Jupiter spoke: "Fear not. Hercules has conquered everything, and he will conquer those flames. Part of him is immortal, and, as an immortal, he will live with the gods for ever."

So indeed it happened. As a snake changes its old skin, so Hercules, as the flames consumed his body, seemed to put on a new body, stronger, more heroic, more beautiful and more stately even than before. Thunder pealed, and through the hollow clouds Jupiter sent his four-horsed chariot which bore him to Heaven, where he was welcomed among the shining stars and in the assembly of the gods.

Aztec/Toltec: Quetzalcoatl

Quetzalcoatl was the feathered serpent god of the Aztec and Toltec cultures. His life, like that of the Buddha and of Herakles, ends in fire, and he, too, is taken off to the heavens, perhaps as a star. Like King Arthur and Jesus, he is a "once and future king" whose return to earth is expected.

> It ended on the beach
> It ended with a hulk of serpents formed into a boat

Rex Warner, *The Stories of the Greeks* (New York, 1967), pp. 106–07.

& when he'd made it, sat in it & sailed away
A boat that glided on those burning waters, no one knowing when he
    reached the country of Red Daylight
It ended on the rim of some great sea
It ended with his face reflected in the mirror of its waves
The beauty of his face returned to him
& he was dressed in garments like the sun
It ended with a bonfire on the beach where he would hurl himself
& burn, his ashes rising & the cries of birds
It ended with the linnet, with the birds of turquoise color, birds the color
    of wild sunflowers, red & blue birds
It ended with the birds of yellow feathers in a riot of bright gold
Circling till the fire had died out
Circling while his heart rose through the sky
It ended with his heart transformed into a star
It ended with the morning star with dawn & evening
It ended with his journey to Death's Kingdom with seven days of
    darkness
With his body changed to light
A star that burns forever in that sky

Christian: Mary

The early Christian people felt an instinctive desire to recognize the Great
Mother, even though that concept was thoroughly removed from the
young Church's official doctrine. They created an elaborate myth around
the figure of Mary, stressing the idea of the Immaculate Conception, in
which Mary is seen as having been conceived without original sin, and the
idea of her bodily assumption into heaven to reign there as queen. Both
ideas would eventually become doctrine.

•

Mary was also closely associated with the Great Goddess of Ephesus, whose
temples she took over. In the 5th century an Ephesian priest named Proclus delivered a sermon on the multiform nature of Mary, calling her "the
living bush, which was not burnt by the fire of the divine birth . . . virgin
and heaven, the only bridge between God and men, the awesome loom
. . . on which the garment of union was woven."
    Much was made of the reversal of Mary's Latin *Ave* and the name of
Eve (Eva). Mystics said Mary was Eve's purified reincarnation, as Jesus

From "The Flight of Quetzalcoatl," trans. Jerome Rothenberg, in *Shaking the Pumpkin: Traditional Poetry of the Indian North Americas*, ed. Jerome Rothenberg (New York, 1972), pp. 122–23.

Barbara G. Walker, *The Woman's Encyclopedia of Myths and Secrets* (San Francisco, 1983), pp. 605–06.

was the similar reincarnation of Adam. Somehow, theologians failed to recognize that the new incarnations apparently reversed the parent-child relationship. Then again, as Adam and Eve were spouses, so the relationship of Mary and Jesus sometimes verged on the sexual or conjugal. In a legend ascribed to St. John, Jesus welcomed Mary into heaven with the words, "Come, my chosen, and I shall set thee in my seat, for I have coveted the beauty of thee."

The Church's doctrine of the assumption of Mary was explained in a number of ways. Early churchmen declared that Jesus visited Mary's tomb—variously located in Ephesus, Bethlehem, Gethsemane, or Josaphat—and raised up her corpse, which he made to live again; then he personally escorted her into heaven as a live woman. She was not a soul or a spirit but an immortal person in her own original body. This became the official modern view when the doctrine of the assumption was declared an article of faith in 1950, when Pope Pius XII pronounced that "the immaculate mother of God, the ever Virgin Mary, when the course of her earthly life was run, was assumed in body and in soul to heavenly glory." But the point had already been argued for more than a thousand years.

The Church's problem was to take advantage of popular reverence for Mary but at the same time prevent her literal deification. Some theologians of the 13th century claimed Mary's mortality should bring more women to obey the Church, because the king of heaven "is no mere man but a mere woman is its queen. It is not a mere man who is set above the angels and all the rest of the heavenly court, but a mere woman is; nor is anyone who is merely man as powerful there as a mere woman."

Always the theologians feared to impute too much power and glory to Mary. Pope John XXIII, presuming to know Mary's inner thoughts, announced: "The Madonna is not pleased when she is put above her Son," though in fact it was the church who was not pleased. Catholic doctrines themselves attributed to her two of the three basic characteristics of divinity: she was immortal by reason of the assumption, and sinless by reason of the Immaculate Conception. The third requirement of divinity, omniscience, was conceded to her by popular belief.

Greek: Alcestis

Alcestis, the wife of the selfish Admetus, is the heroine of the myth told by Euripides in his *Alcestis* and by several other classical writers. She agrees to die for her husband, only to be brought back from the underworld by Herakles.

•

Alcestis, the most beautiful of Pelias's daughters, was asked in marriage by many kings and princes. Not wishing to endanger his political position by refusing any of them, and yet clearly unable to satisfy more than one, Pelias let it be known that he would marry Alcestis to the man who could yoke a wild boar and a lion to his chariot and drive them around the race-course. At this, Admetus King of Pherae summoned Apollo, whom Zeus had bound to him for one year as a herdsman, and asked: "Have I treated you with the respect due to your godhead?" "You have indeed," Apollo assented, "and I have shown my gratitude by making all your ewes drop twins." "As a final favour, then," pleaded Admetus, "pray help me to win Alcestis, by enabling me to fulfil Pelias's conditions." "I shall be pleased to do so," replied Apollo. Heracles lent him a hand with the taming of the wild beasts and presently Admetus was driving his chariot around the race-course at Iolcus, drawn by this savage team.

It is not known why Admetus omitted the customary sacrifice to Artemis before marrying Alcestis, but the goddess was quick enough to punish him. When, flushed with wine, anointed with essences and garlanded with flowers, he entered the bridal chamber that night, he recoiled in horror. No lovely naked bride awaited him on the marriage couch, but a tangled knot of hissing serpents. Admetus ran shouting for Apollo, who kindly intervened with Artemis on his behalf. The neglected sacrifice having been offered at once, all was well, Apollo even obtaining Artemis's promise that, when the day of Admetus's death came, he should be spared on condition that a member of his family died voluntarily for love of him.

This fatal day came sooner than Admetus expected. Hermes flew into the palace one morning and summoned him to Tartarus. General consternation prevailed; but Apollo gained a little time for Admetus by making the Three Fates drunk, and thus delayed the fatal scission of his life's thread. Admetus ran in haste to his old parents, clasped their knees, and begged each of them in turn to surrender him the butt-end of existence. Both roundly refused, saying that they still derived much enjoyment from life, and that he should be content with his appointed lot, like everyone else.

Then, for love of Admetus, Alcestis took poison and her ghost descended to Tartarus; but Persephone considered it an evil thing that a wife should die instead of a husband. "Back with you to the upper air!" she cried.

Some tell the tale differently. They say that Hades came in person to fetch Admetus and that, when he fled, Alcestis volunteered to take his place; but Herakles arrived unexpectedly with a new wild-olive club, and rescued her.

Robert Graves, *The Greek Myths*, vol. 1 (Baltimore, Md., 1955), pp. 223–24.

Bibliography

A classic work on the archetypal hero biography is Lord Raglan's *The Hero* (London, 1936). A more modern approach, one that owes much to Sigmund Freud and Carl Jung, is Joseph Campbell's *The Hero with a Thousand Faces* (New York, 1949). *Mythology: The Voyage of the Hero* (New York, 1981), by David Leeming, is a collection of hero myths arranged according to a reworking of Campbell and Raglan. *The Hero in Literature* (New York, 1969), edited by Victor Brombert, contains several essays on various kinds of literary heroes. Jung and Carl Kerenyi's *Essays on a Science of Mythology: The Myth of the Divine Child and the Mysteries of Eleusis* (New York, 1969) sheds much light on the *puer aeternus* motif. Otto Rank's *The Myth of the Birth of the Hero* (New York, 1959) is a Freudian interpretation of this motif. For a study of early cultic influences on the hero's life, see Mircea Eliade's *Rites and Symbols of Initiation* (New York, 1958). Other useful works on the hero are Lewis R. Farnell's *Greek Hero Cults and Ideas of Immortality* (Oxford, 1970) and Theodor Gaster's "Heroes" in *The Encyclopedia of Religion*, vol. 6, pp. 302–5. For an examination of the concept of a "new-age hero," see Carol Pearson's *The Hero Within: Six Archetypes We Live By* (San Francisco, 1986). George de Forest Lord's *Trials of the Self: Heroic Ordeals in the Epic Tradition* (Hamden, Conn., 1983) studies the hero concept in epic poetry.

PART IV

PLACE AND OBJECT MYTHS

In the world of myth, objects and places are endowed with properties of the sacred, the "other." This is logical, because myths are religious and assume the existence of a meaningful cosmos that is literally charged with the informing energy of the creator. In the modern literary or psychological sense, places and objects in myth are symbols, and like other mythological motifs—the descent into the underworld, the Supreme Being, the femme fatale, and so on—they have archetypal significance. The student of mythology understands quickly that a tree, a garden, a castle, or a city is a material reality that expresses a particular place or culture and at the same time a connotative one that transcends place and time. The cross is at once the one on which Jesus hangs at Golgatha and the sacred tree on which Attis and Odin hang as "victims" who bridge the world of death and the world of eternity. The rock out of which Arthur pulls his sword is also the maternal rock that is Jesus' tomb or Mithras' birth cave or the altar on which Isaac is nearly sacrificed.

It is this connotative or archetypally symbolic nature of certain places and objects that makes them, like other archetypes, so useful to the creative artist. When the child hero of the fairy tale enters the dark wood, we know in the depths of our collective being exactly where he or she is. And we recognize the tree that stands alone in the center of the grove or garden. Even in our nonmythological age, the poet can, by making use of such symbols, awaken understandings that still sleep in our collective unconscious. As Mircea Eliade writes, "It is through symbols that man finds his way out of his particular situation and 'opens himself' to the general and the universal" (*The Sacred and the Profane*, p. 211). This process of "opening" is a common concern of the religious person and the creative artist.

The sacred places and objects considered briefly here are only a very few of many. In order to make the archetypal character of these places and objects clear, they have been arranged according to type.

STORIES OF PLACES AND OBJECTS

The Mountain

The sacred mountain is the *mons veneris* of Mother Earth. It is the cosmic center on which the temple or the city is placed. It is the spot, nearest to the supreme sky god, where the word—the cosmic energy—can be received by Earth. It is Mount Parnassus, where the oracle of Delphi delivers dire predictions. It is the Golden Mountain, Meru—the *axis mundi* in India, where Shiva sits. It is the hill on which Athena builds her acropolis and temple in Athens. It is the mountain on which Moses receives the Ten Commandments, the mountain on which Jesus is "transfigured" (Mark 9).

Hebrew: Mount Sinai

Moses has led his people out of Egypt into Sinai when God calls him again.

•

Chapter 19

In the third month, when the children of Israel were gone forth out of the land of Egypt, the same day came they into the wilderness of Sinai.

2 For they were departed from Rĕph'-i-dim, and were come to the desert of Sinai, and had pitched in the wilderness; and there Israel camped before the mount.

3 And Moses went up unto God, and the Lord called unto him out of the mountain, saying, Thus shalt thou say to the house of Jacob, and tell the children of Israel;

4 Ye have seen what I did unto the Egyptians, and how I bare you on eagles' wings, and brought you unto myself.

5 Now therefore, if ye will obey my voice indeed, and keep my covenant, then ye shall be a peculiar treasure unto me above all people: for all the earth is mine:

6 And ye shall be unto me a kingdom of priests, and an holy nation. These are the words which thou shalt speak unto the children of Israel.

7 And Moses came and called for the elders of the people, and laid before their faces all these words which the Lord commanded him.

8 And all the people answered together, and said, All that the Lord hath spoken we will do. And Moses returned the words of the people unto the Lord.

9 And the Lord said unto Moses, Lo, I come unto thee in a thick

Exodus 19–20.

cloud, that the people may hear when I speak with thee, and believe thee for ever. And Moses told the words of the people unto the Lord.

10 And the Lord said unto Moses, Go unto the people, and sanctify them to-day and to-morrow, and let them wash their clothes,

11 And be ready against the third day: for the third day the Lord will come down in the sight of all the people upon mount Sinai.

12 And thou shalt set bounds unto the people round about, saying, Take heed to yourselves, that ye go not up into the mount, or touch the border of it: whosoever toucheth the mount shall be surely put to death:

13 There shall not an hand touch it, but he shall surely be stoned, or shot through; whether it be beast or man, it shall not live: when the trumpet soundeth long, they shall come up to the mount.

14 And Moses went down from the mount unto the people, and sanctified the people; and they washed their clothes.

15 And he said unto the people, Be ready against the third day: come not at your wives.

16 And it came to pass on the third day in the morning, that there were thunders and lightnings, and a thick cloud upon the mount, and the voice of the trumpet exceeding loud; so that all the people that was in the camp trembled.

17 And Moses brought forth the people out of the camp to meet with God; and they stood at the nether part of the mount.

18 And mount Sinai was altogether on a smoke, because the Lord descended upon it in fire: and the smoke thereof ascended as the smoke of a furnace, and the whole mount quaked greatly.

19 And when the voice of the trumpet sounded long, and waxed louder and louder, Moses spake, and God answered him by a voice.

20 And the Lord came down upon mount Sinai, on the top of the mount: and the Lord called Moses up to the top of the mount; and Moses went up.

21 And the Lord said unto Moses, Go down, charge the people, lest they break through unto the Lord to gaze, and many of them perish.

22 And let the priests also, which come near to the Lord, sanctify themselves, lest the Lord break forth upon them.

23 And Moses said unto the Lord, The people cannot come up to mount Sinai: for thou chargedst us, saying, Set bounds about the mount, and sanctify it.

24 And the Lord said unto him, Away, get thee down, and thou shalt come up, thou, and Aaron with thee: but let not the priests and the people break through to come up unto the Lord, lest he break forth upon them.

25 So Moses went down unto the people, and spake unto them.

Chapter 20

And God spake all these words, saying,

2 I am the Lord thy God, which have brought thee out of the land of Egypt, out of the house of bondage.

3 Thou shalt have no other gods before me.

4 Thou shalt not make unto thee any graven image, or any likeness of any thing that is in heaven above, or that is in the earth beneath, or that is in the water under the earth:

5 Thou shalt not bow down thyself to them, nor serve them: for I the Lord thy God am a jealous God, visiting the iniquity of the fathers upon the children unto the third and fourth generation of them that hate me;

6 And shewing mercy unto thousands of them that love me, and keep my commandments.

7 Thou shalt not take the name of the Lord thy God in vain; for the Lord will not hold him guiltless that taketh his name in vain.

8 Remember the sabbath day, to keep it holy.

9 Six days shalt thou labour, and do all thy work:

10 But the seventh day is the sabbath of the Lord thy God: in it thou shalt not do any work, thou, nor thy son, nor thy daughter, thy manservant, nor thy maidservant, nor thy cattle, nor thy stranger that is within thy gates:

11 For in six days the Lord made heaven and earth, the sea, and all that in them is, and rested the seventh day: wherefore the Lord blessed the sabbath day, and hallowed it.

12 Honour thy father and thy mother: that thy days may be long upon the land which the Lord thy God giveth thee.

13 Thou shalt not kill.

14 Thou shalt not commit adultery.

15 Thou shalt not steal.

16 Thou shalt not bear false witness against thy neighbour.

17 Thou shalt not covet thy neighbour's house, thou shalt not covet thy neighbour's wife, nor his manservant, nor his maidservant, nor his ox, nor his ass, nor any thing that is thy neighbour's.

18 And all the people saw the thunderings, and the lightnings, and the noise of the trumpet, and the mountain smoking: and when the people saw it, they removed, and stood afar off.

19 And they said unto Moses, Speak thou with us, and we will hear: but let not God speak with us, lest we die.

20 And Moses said unto the people, Fear not: for God is come to prove you, and that his fear may be before your faces, that ye sin not.

21 And the people stood afar off, and Moses drew near unto the thick darkness where God was.

22 And the Lord said unto Moses, Thus thou shalt say unto the children of Israel, Ye have seen that I have talked with you from heaven.

23 Ye shall not make with me gods of silver, neither shall ye make unto you gods of gold.

24 An altar of earth thou shalt make unto me, and shalt sacrifice thereon thy burnt offerings, and thy peace offerings, thy sheep, and thine oxen: in all places where I record my name I will come unto thee, and I will bless thee.

25 And if thou wilt make me an altar of stone, thou shalt not build it of hewn stone: for if thou lift up thy tool upon it, thou hast polluted it.

26 Neither shalt thou go up by steps unto mine altar, that thy nakedness be not discovered thereon.

The City

The city, whether Troy, Jerusalem, Thebes, or Uruk, is humanity's stand against chaos. Like so many other constructs in this world, it is feminine in nature—a representation of nourishment and protection, the gateways of which must be guarded against potential invaders. The city is our "mother," and her fall or corruption is among the most moving of tragedies.

Greek: Troy

Virgil describes the fall of Troy in the *Aeneid*. The Greek Sinon has convinced the Trojans that the giant wooden horse left outside their gates by the Greeks is a peace offering. In spite of the warnings of Laocoön, a priest of Apollo, who is killed by serpents sent from the sea by Poseidon, the Trojans receive the horse into their city. It is filled with Greek warriors. When they take the city, cosmos gives way to chaos.

•

> This fraud of Sinon, his accomplished lying,
> Won us over; a tall tale and fake tears
> Had captured us, whom neither Diomedes
> Nor Larisaean Achilles overpowered,
> Nor ten long years, nor all their thousand ships.
>
> And now another sign, more fearful still,
> Broke on our blind miserable people,
> Filling us all with dread. Laocoön,

Vergil, *Aeneid*, trans. Robert Fitzgerald (New York, 1983), pp. 40–52.

Acting as Neptune's priest that day by lot,
Was on the point of putting to the knife
A massive bull before the appointed altar,
When ah—look there!
From Tenedos, on the calm sea, twin snakes—
I shiver to recall it—endlessly
Coiling, uncoiling, swam abreast for shore,
Their underbellies showing as their crests
Reared red as blood above the swell; behind
They glided with great undulating backs.
Now came the sound of thrashed seawater foaming;
Now they were on dry land, and we could see
Their burning eyes, fiery and suffused with blood,
Their tongues a-flicker out of hissing maws.
We scattered, pale with fright. But straight ahead
They slid until they reached Laocoön.
Each snake enveloped one of his two boys,
Twining about and feeding on the body.
Next they ensnared the man as he ran up
With weapons: coils like cables looped and bound him
Twice round the middle; twice about his throat
They whipped their back-scales, and their heads towered,
While with both hands he fought to break the knots,
Drenched in slime, his head-bands black with venom,
Sending to heaven his appalling cries
Like a slashed bull escaping from an altar,
The fumbled axe shrugged off. The pair of snakes
Now flowed away and made for the highest shrines,
The citadel of pitiless Minerva,
Where coiling they took cover at her feet
Under the rondure of her shield. New terrors
Ran in the shaken crowd: the word went round
Laocoön had paid, and rightfully,
For profanation of the sacred hulk
With his offending spear hurled at its flank.

"The offering must be hauled to its true home,"
They clamored. "Votive prayers to the goddess
Must be said there!"
                        So we breached the walls
And laid the city open. Everyone
Pitched in to get the figure underpinned
With rollers, hempen lines around the neck.
Deadly, pregnant with enemies, the horse

Crawled upward to the breach. And boys and girls
Sang hymns around the towrope as for joy
They touched it. Rolling on, it cast a shadow
Over the city's heart. O Fatherland,
O Ilium, home of gods! Defensive wall
Renowned in war for Dardanus's people!
There on the very threshold of the breach
It jarred to a halt four times, four times the arms
In the belly thrown together made a sound—
Yet on we strove unmindful, deaf and blind,
To place the monster on our blessed height.
Then, even then, Cassandra's lips unsealed
The doom to come: lips by a god's command
Never believed or heeded by the Trojans.
So pitiably we, for whom that day
Would be the last, made all our temples green
With leafy festal boughs throughout the city.

As heaven turned, Night from the Ocean stream
Came on, profound in gloom on earth and sky
And Myrmidons in hiding. In their homes
The Teucrians lay silent, wearied out,
And sleep enfolded them. The Argive fleet,
Drawn up in line abreast, left Tenedos
Through the aloof moon's friendly stillnesses
And made for the familiar shore. Flame signals
Shone from the command ship. Sinon, favored
By what the gods unjustly had decreed,
Stole out to tap the pine walls and set free
The Danaans in the belly. Opened wide,
The horse emitted men; gladly they dropped
Out of the cavern, captains first, Thessandrus,
Sthenelus and the man of iron, Ulysses;
Hand over hand upon the rope, Acamas, Thoas,
Neoptolemus and Prince Machaon,
Menelaus and then the master builder,
Epeos, who designed the horse decoy.
Into the darkened city, buried deep
In sleep and wine, they made their way,
Cut the few sentries down,
Let in their fellow soldiers at the gate,
And joined their combat companies as planned.

That time of night it was when the first sleep,
Gift of the gods, begins for ill mankind,

Arriving gradually, delicious rest.
In sleep, in dream, Hector appeared to me,
Gaunt with sorrow, streaming tears, all torn—
As by the violent car on his death day—
And black with bloody dust,
His puffed-out feet cut by the rawhide thongs.
Ah god, the look of him! How changed
From that proud Hector who returned to Troy
Wearing Achilles' armor, or that one
Who pitched the torches on Danaan ships;
His beard all filth, his hair matted with blood,
Showing the wounds, the many wounds, received
Outside his father's city walls. I seemed
Myself to weep and call upon the man
In grieving speech, brought from the depth of me:

"Light of Dardania, best hope of Troy,
What kept you from us for so long, and where?
From what far place, O Hector, have you come,
Long, long awaited? After so many deaths
Of friends and brothers, after a world of pain
For all our folk and all our town, at last,
Boneweary, we behold you! What has happened
To ravage your serene face? Why these wounds?"

He wasted no reply on my poor questions
But heaved a great sigh from his chest and said:
"Ai! Give up and go, child of the goddess,
Save yourself, out of these flames. The enemy
Holds the city walls, and from her height
Troy falls in ruin. Fatherland and Priam
Have their due; if by one hand our towers
Could be defended, by this hand, my own,
They would have been. Her holy things, her gods
Of hearth and household Troy commends to you.
Accept them as companions of your days;
Go find for them the great walls that one day
You'll dedicate, when you have roamed the sea."

As he said this, he brought out from the sanctuary
Chaplets and Vesta, Lady of the Hearth,
With her eternal fire.
                              While I dreamed,
The turmoil rose, with anguish, in the city.
More and more, although Anchises' house

Lay in seclusion, muffled among trees,
The din at the grim onset grew; and now
I shook off sleep, I climbed to the roof top
To cup my ears and listen. And the sound
Was like the sound a grassfire makes in grain,
Whipped by a Southwind, or a torrent foaming
Out of a mountainside to strew in ruin
Fields, happy crops, the yield of plowing teams,
Or woodlands borne off in the flood; in wonder
The shepherd listens on a rocky peak.
I knew then what our trust had won for us,
Knew the Danaan fraud: Deïphobus'
Great house in flames, already caving in
Under the overpowering god of fire;
Ucalegon's already caught nearby;
The glare lighting the straits beyond Sigeum;
The cries of men, the wild calls of the trumpets.

To arm was my first maddened impulse—not
That anyone had a fighting chance in arms;
Only I burned to gather up some force
For combat, and to man some high redoubt.
So fury drove me, and it came to me
That meeting death was beautiful in arms.
Then here, eluding the Achaean spears,
Came Panthus, Othrys' son, priest of Apollo,
Carrying holy things, our conquered gods,
And pulling a small grandchild along: he ran
Despairing to my doorway.
                  "Where's the crux,
Panthus," I said. "What strongpoint shall we hold?"

Before I could say more, he groaned and answered:
"The last day for Dardania has come,
The hour not to be fought off any longer.
Trojans we have been; Ilium has been;
The glory of the Teucrians is no more;
Black Jupiter has passed it on to Argos.
Greeks are the masters in our burning city.
Tall as a cliff, set in the heart of town,
Their horse pours out armed men. The conqueror,
Gloating Sinon, brews new conflagrations.
Troops hold the gates—as many thousand men
As ever came from great Mycenae; others
Block the lanes with crossed spears; glittering

In a combat line, swordblades are drawn for slaughter.
Even the first guards at the gates can barely
Offer battle, or blindly make a stand."

Impelled by these words, by the powers of heaven,
Into the flames I go, into the fight,
Where the harsh Fury, and the din and shouting,
Skyward rising, calls. Crossing my path
In moonlight, five fell in with me, companions:
Ripheus, and Epytus, a great soldier,
Hypanis, Dymas, cleaving to my side
With young Coroebus, Mygdon's son. It happened
That in those very days this man had come
To Troy, aflame with passion for Cassandra,
Bringing to Priam and the Phrygians
A son-in-law's right hand. Unlucky one,
To have been deaf to what his bride foretold!
Now when I saw them grouped, on edge for battle,
I took it all in and said briefly,
                              "Soldiers,
Brave as you are to no end, if you crave
To face the last fight with me, and no doubt of it,
How matters stand for us each one can see.
The gods by whom this kingdom stood are gone,
Gone from the shrines and altars. You defend
A city lost in flames. Come, let us die,
We'll make a rush into the thick of it.
The conquered have one safety: hope for none."

The desperate odds doubled their fighting spirit:
From that time on, like predatory wolves
In fog and darkness, when a savage hunger
Drives them blindly on, and cubs in lairs
Lie waiting with dry famished jaws—just so
Through arrow flights and enemies we ran
Toward our sure death, straight for the city's heart,
Cavernous black night over and around us.
Who can describe the havoc of that night
Or tell the deaths, or tally wounds with tears?
The ancient city falls, after dominion
Many long years. In windrows on the streets,
In homes, on solemn porches of the gods,
Dead bodies lie. And not alone the Trojans
Pay the price with their heart's blood; at times
Manhood returns to fire even the conquered

And Danaan conquerors fall. Grief everywhere,
Everywhere terror, and all shapes of death.

Androgeos was the first to cross our path
Leading a crowd of Greeks; he took for granted
That we were friends, and hailed us cheerfully:

"Men, get a move on! Are you made of lead
To be so late and slow? The rest are busy
Carrying plunder from the fires and towers.
Are you just landed from the ships?"
                           His words
Were barely out, and no reply forthcoming
Credible to him, when he knew himself
Fallen among enemies. Thunderstruck,
He halted, foot and voice, and then recoiled
Like one who steps down on a lurking snake
In a briar patch and jerks back, terrified,
As the angry thing rears up, all puffed and blue.
So backward went Androgeos in panic.
We were all over them in a moment, cut
And thrust, and as they fought on unknown ground,
Startled, unnerved, we killed them everywhere.
So Fortune filled our sails at first. Coroebus,
Elated at our feat and his own courage,
Said:
      "Friends, come follow Fortune. She has shown
The way to safety, shown she's on our side.
We'll take their shields and put on their insignia!
Trickery, bravery: who asks, in war?
The enemy will arm us."
                 He put on
The plumed helm of Androgeos, took the shield
With blazon and the Greek sword to his side.
Ripheus, Dymas—all were pleased to do it,
Making the still fresh trophies our equipment.
Then we went on, passing among the Greeks,
Protected by our own gods now no longer;
Many a combat, hand to hand, we fought
In the black night, and many a Greek we sent
To Orcus. There were some who turned and ran
Back to the ships and shore; some shamefully
Clambered again into the horse, to hide
In the familiar paunch.

                                        When gods are contrary
They stand by no one. Here before us came
Cassandra, Priam's virgin daughter, dragged
By her long hair out of Minerva's shrine,
Lifting her brilliant eyes in vain to heaven—
Her eyes alone, as her white hands were bound.
Coroebus, infuriated, could not bear it,
But plunged into the midst to find his death.
We all went after him, our swords at play,
But here, here first, from the temple gable's height,
We met a hail of missiles from our friends,
Pitiful execution, by their error,
Who thought us Greek from our Greek plumes and shields.
Then with a groan of anger, seeing the virgin
Wrested from them, Danaans from all sides
Rallied and attacked us: fiery Ajax,
Atreus' sons, Dolopians in a mass—
As, when a cyclone breaks, conflicting winds
Will come together, Westwind, Southwind, Eastwind
Riding high out of the Dawnland; forests
Bend and roar, and raging all in spume
Nereus with his trident churns the deep.
Then some whom we had taken by surprise
Under cover of night throughout the city
And driven off, came back again: they knew
Our shields and arms for liars now, our speech
Alien to their own. They overwhelmed us.
Coroebus fell at the warrior goddess' altar,
Killed by Peneleus; and Ripheus fell,
A man uniquely just among the Trojans,
The soul of equity; but the gods would have it
Differently. Hypanis, Dymas died,
Shot down by friends; nor did your piety,
Panthus, nor Apollo's fillets shield you
As you went down.
                                        Ashes of Ilium!
Flames that consumed my people! Here I swear
That in your downfall I did not avoid
One weapon, one exchange with the Danaans,
And if it had been fated, my own hand
Had earned my death. But we were torn away
From that place—Iphitus and Pelias too,
One slow with age, one wounded by Ulysses,

Called by a clamor at the hall of Priam.
Truly we found here a prodigious fight,
As though there were none elsewhere, not a death
In the whole city: Mars gone berserk, Danaans
In a rush to scale the roof; the gate besieged
By a tortoise shell of overlapping shields.
Ladders clung to the wall, and men strove upward
Before the very doorposts, on the rungs,
Left hand putting the shield up, and the right
Reaching for the cornice. The defenders
Wrenched out upperworks and rooftiles: these
For missiles, as they saw the end, preparing
To fight back even on the edge of death.
And gilded beams, ancestral ornaments,
They rolled down on the heads below. In hall
Others with swords drawn held the entrance way,
Packed there, waiting. Now we plucked up heart
To help the royal house, to give our men
A respite, and to add our strength to theirs,
Though all were beaten. And we had for entrance
A rear door, secret, giving on a passage
Between the palace halls; in other days
Andromachë, poor lady, often used it,
Going alone to see her husband's parents
Or taking Astyanax to his grandfather.
I climbed high on the roof, where hopeless men
Were picking up and throwing futile missiles.
Here was a tower like a promontory
Rising toward the stars above the roof:
All Troy, the Danaan ships, the Achaean camp,
Were visible from this. Now close beside it
With crowbars, where the flooring made loose joints,
We pried it from its bed and pushed it over.
Down with a rending crash in sudden ruin
Wide over the Danaan lines it fell;
But fresh troops moved up, and the rain of stones
With every kind of missile never ceased.
Just at the outer doors of the vestibule
Sprang Pyrrhus, all in bronze and glittering,
As a serpent, hidden swollen underground
By a cold winter, writhes into the light,
On vile grass fed, his old skin cast away,
Renewed and glossy, rolling slippery coils,

With lifted underbelly rearing sunward
And triple tongue a-flicker. Close beside him
Giant Periphas and Automedon,
His armor-bearer, once Achilles' driver,
Besieged the place with all the young of Scyros,
Hurling their torches at the palace roof.
Pyrrhus shouldering forward with an axe
Broke down the stony threshold, forced apart
Hinges and brazen door-jambs, and chopped through
One panel of the door, splitting the oak,
To make a window, a great breach. And there
Before their eyes the inner halls lay open,
The courts of Priam and the ancient kings,
With men-at-arms ranked in the vestibule.
From the interior came sounds of weeping,
Pitiful commotion, wails of women
High-pitched, rising in the formal chambers
To ring against the silent golden stars;
And, through the palace, mothers wild with fright
Ran to and fro or clung to doors and kissed them.
Pyrrhus with his father's brawn stormed on,
No bolts or bars or men availed to stop him:
Under his battering the double doors
Were torn out of their sockets and fell inward.
Sheer force cleared the way: the Greeks broke through
Into the vestibule, cut down the guards,
And made the wide hall seethe with men-at-arms—
A tumult greater then when dykes are burst
And a foaming river, swirling out in flood,
Whelms every parapet and races on
Through fields and over all the lowland plains,
Bearing off pens and cattle. I myself
Saw Neoptolemus furious with blood
In the entrance way, and saw the two Atridae;
Hecuba I saw, and her hundred daughters,
Priam before the altars, with his blood
Drenching the fires that he himself had blessed.
Those fifty bridal chambers, hope of a line
So flourishing; those doorways high and proud,
Adorned with takings of barbaric gold,
Were all brought low: fire had them, or the Greeks.

What was the fate of Priam, you may ask.
Seeing his city captive, seeing his own

Royal portals rent apart, his enemies
In the inner rooms, the old man uselessly
Put on his shoulders, shaking with old age,
Armor unused for years, belted a sword on,
And made for the massed enemy to die.
Under the open sky in a central court
Stood a big altar; near it, a laurel tree
Of great age, leaning over, in deep shade
Embowered the Penatës. At this altar
Hecuba and her daughters, like white doves
Blown down in a black storm, clung together,
Enfolding holy images in their arms.
Now, seeing Priam in a young man's gear,
She called out:
                "My poor husband, what mad thought
Drove you to buckle on these weapons?
Where are you trying to go? The time is past
For help like this, for this kind of defending,
Even if my own Hector could be here.
Come to me now: the altar will protect us,
Or else you'll die with us."
                            She drew him close,
Heavy with years, and made a place for him
To rest on the consecrated stone.
                        Now see
Politës, one of Priam's sons, escaped
From Pyrrhus' butchery and on the run
Through enemies and spears, down colonnades,
Through empty courtyards, wounded. Close behind
Comes Pyrrhus burning for the death-stroke: has him,
Catches him now, and lunges with the spear.
The boy has reached his parents, and before them
Goes down, pouring out his life with blood.
Now Priam, in the very midst of death,
Would neither hold his peace nor spare his anger.

"For what you've done, for what you've dared," he said,
"If there is care in heaven for atrocity,
May the gods render fitting thanks, reward you
As you deserve. You forced me to look on
At the destruction of my son: defiled
A father's eyes with death. That great Achilles
You claim to be the son of—and you lie—

Was not like you to Priam, his enemy;
To me who threw myself upon his mercy
He showed compunction, gave me back for burial
The bloodless corpse of Hector, and returned me
To my own realm."
                              The old man threw his spear
With feeble impact; blocked by the ringing bronze,
It hung there harmless from the jutting boss.
Then Pyrrhus answered:
                              "You'll report the news
To Pelidës, my father; don't forget
My sad behavior, the degeneracy
Of Neoptolemus. Now die."
                              With this,
To the altar step itself he dragged him trembling,
Slipping in the pooled blood of his son,
And took him by the hair with his left hand.
The sword flashed in his right; up to the hilt
He thrust it in his body.
                              That was the end
Of Priam's age, the doom that took him off,
With Troy in flames before his eyes, his towers
Headlong fallen—he that in other days
Had ruled in pride so many lands and peoples,
The power of Asia.
                              On the distant shore
The vast trunk headless lies without a name.

Hebrew: Jerusalem

Jerusalem has traditionally been the "beloved of God," sacred to Christians
and Muslims as well as to Jews. For some, the holy city takes on a purely
metaphorical rather than physical form—the "heavenly Jerusalem" or the
"new Jerusalem," which might be anywhere or might simply be a phrase
to describe the newly discovered Kingdom of God. The feminine nature
of Jerusalem is clear in the Old Testament's Lamentations of Jeremiah,
written perhaps during the exile of the Jews in Babylon.

●

How doth the city sit solitary, that was full of people! how is she become
as a widow! she that was great among the nations, and princess among the
provinces, how is she become tributary!

2 She weepeth sore in the night, and her tears are on her cheeks: among all her lovers she hath none to comfort her: all her friends have dealt treacherously with her, they are become her enemies.

3 Judah is gone into captivity because of affliction, and because of great servitude: she dwelleth among the heathen, she findeth no rest: all her persecutors overtook her between the straits.

4 The ways of Zion do mourn, because none come to the solemn feasts: all her gates are desolate: her priests sigh, her virgins are afflicted, and she is in bitterness.

5 Her adversaries are the chief, her enemies prosper; for the Lord hath afflicted her for the multitude of her transgressions: her children are gone into captivity before the enemy.

6 And from the daughter of Zion all her beauty is departed: her princes are become like harts that find no pasture, and they are gone without strength before the pursuer.

7 Jerusalem remembered in the days of her affliction and of her miseries all her pleasant things that she had in the days of old, when her people fell into the hand of the enemy, and none did help her: the adversaries saw her, and did mock at her sabbaths.

8 Jerusalem hath grievously sinned; therefore she is removed: all that honoured her despise her, because they have seen her nakedness: yea, she sigheth, and turneth backward.

9 Her filthiness is in her skirts; she remembereth not her last end; therefore she came down wonderfully: she had no comforter. O Lord, behold my affliction: for the enemy hath magnified himself.

10 The adversary hath spread out his hand upon all her pleasant things: for she hath seen that the heathen entered into her sanctuary, whom thou didst command that they should not enter into thy congregation.

11 All her people sigh, they seek bread; they have given their pleasant things for meat to relieve the soul: see, O Lord, and consider; for I am become vile.

12 Is it nothing to you, all ye that pass by? behold, and see if there by any sorrow like unto my sorrow, which is done unto me, wherewith the Lord hath afflicted me in the day of his fierce anger.

13 From above hath he sent fire into my bones, and it prevaileth against them: he hath spread a net for my feet, he hath turned me back: he hath made me desolate and faint all the day.

14 The yoke of my transgressions is bound by his hand: they are wreathed, and come up upon my neck: he hath made my strength to fall,

Lamentations of Jeremiah 1.

the Lord hath delivered me into their hands, from whom I am not able to
rise up.

15 The Lord hath trodden under foot all my mighty men in the midst
of me: he hath called an assembly against me to crush my young men: the
Lord hath trodden the virgin, the daughter of Judah, as in a wine-press.

16 For these things I weep; mine eye, mine eye runneth down with
water, because the comforter that should relieve my soul is far from me:
my children are desolate, because the enemy prevailed.

17 Zion spreadeth forth her hands, and there is none to comfort her;
the Lord hath commanded concerning Jacob, that his adversaries should
be round about him: Jerusalem is as a menstruous woman among them.

18 The Lord is righteous; for I have rebelled against his command-
ment: hear, I pray you, all people, and behold my sorrow: my virgins and
my young men are gone into captivity.

19 I called for my lovers, but they deceived me: my priests and mine
elders gave up the ghost in the city, while they sought their meat to relieve
their souls.

20 Behold, O Lord; for I am in distress: my bowels are troubled;
mine heart is turned within me; for I have grievously rebelled: abroad the
sword bereaveth, at home there is as death.

21 They have heard that I sigh; there is none to comfort me: all mine
enemies have heard of my trouble; they are glad that thou hast done it:
thou wilt bring the day that thou hast called, and they shall be like unto
me.

22 Let all their wickedness come before thee; and do unto them, as
thou hast done unto me for all my transgressions: for my sighs are many,
and my heart is faint.

Greek: Delphi

Although a sacred precinct rather than a city, Delphi, like the great cities
and temples of the ancient world, is the navel or omphalos—the very center—of the world. The conical stone in Apollo's temple at Delphi is the
navel that gives significance to Earth herself. The chasm in the earth at the
sacred precinct gave access to the very womb of Mother Earth.

•

But the most celebrated of the Grecian oracles was that of Apollo at Delphi,
a city built on the slopes of Parnassus in Phocis.

It had been observed at a very early period that the goats feeding on
Parnassus were thrown into convulsions when they approached a certain
long deep cleft in the side of the mountain. This was owing to a peculiar

Thomas Bulfinch, *Bulfinch's Mythology: The Age of Fable* (New York, 1962). p. 337.

vapor arising out of the cavern, and one of the goatherds was induced to try its effects upon himself. Inhaling the intoxicating air, he was affected in the same manner as the cattle had been, and the inhabitants of the surrounding country, unable to explain the circumstance, imputed the convulsive ravings to which he gave utterance while under the power of the exhalations to a divine inspiration. The fact was speedily circulated widely, and a temple was erected on the spot. The prophetic influence was at first variously attributed to the goddess Earth, to Neptune, Themis, and others, but it was at length assigned to Apollo, and to him alone. A priestess was appointed whose office it was to inhale the hallowed air, and who was named the Pythia. She was prepared for this duty by previous ablution at the fountain of Castalia, and being crowned with laurel, was seated upon a tripod similarly adorned, which was placed over the chasm whence the divine afflatus proceeded. Her inspired words while thus situated were interpreted by the priests.

The Temple

The temple is a microcosmic version of the city. It, too, is feminine, representative also of the Mother Mountain, the maternal womb into which the hero enters and plants his seed. The great cathedrals of Europe are the body of Christ on the horizontal plane and a representation of the cavernous and monumental Mother Mountain on the vertical. Often named after Mary, the Christian version of the Great Mother, they are architectural depictions of the union of the hero and the mother-wife—Mother Church, the church as the bride of the Lamb. The symbols within the church building reinforce this theme: the feminine font into which the pascal candle is plunged on Holy Saturday, the feminine altar-tomb-throne that is the place of the lover-god's sacrifice. The pyramids of Egypt, the Ziggurat of Babylon at the top of which the king marries the Goddess, the towering *gopuram* of the Tamilnad temples to Shiva and Vishnu and the Goddess, the Chapel Perilous where Galahad rediscovers the blood vessel, the Holy Grail—all are symbols of the feminine cosmic mound, the primeval mound of Earth from which life itself is born.

Judeo-Christian: The Temple at Jerusalem

The temple being always the sacred center for Jews, Jesus cleanses it and makes it a metaphor for himself and for his "kingship," much as in ancient India the invader king's taking of the women of his victims was a symbolic plowing and occupation of the land newly acquired in battle. Here Jesus enters the city as a king and immediately claims his rights to the temple.

Chapter 19

. . . 28 And when he had thus spoken, he went before, ascending up to Jerusalem.

29 And it came to pass, when he was come nigh to Bĕth'-phă-ġē and Bethany, at the mount called the mount of Olives, he sent two of his disciples,

30 Saying, Go ye into the village over against you; in the which at your entering ye shall find a colt tied, whereon yet never man sat: loose him, and bring him hither.

31 And if any man ask you, Why do ye loose him? thus shall ye say unto him, Because the Lord hath need of him.

32 And they that were sent went their way, and found even as he had said unto them.

33 And as they were loosing the colt, the owners thereof said unto them, Why loose ye the colt?

34 And they said, The Lord hath need of him.

35 And they brought him to Jesus: and they cast their garments upon the colt, and they set Jesus thereon.

36 And as he went, they spread their clothes in the way.

37 And when he was come nigh, even now at the descent of the mount of Olives, the whole multitude of the disciples began to rejoice and praise God with a loud voice for all the mighty works that they had seen;

38 Saying, Blessed be the King that cometh in the name of the Lord: peace in heaven, and glory in the highest.

39 And some of the Pharisees from among the multitude said unto him, Master, rebuke thy disciples.

40 And he answered and said unto them, I tell you that, if these should hold their peace, the stones would immediately cry out.

41 And when he was come near, he beheld the city, and wept over it,

42 Saying, If thou hadst known, even thou, at least in this thy day, the things which belong unto thy peace! but now they are hid from thine eyes.

43 For the days shall come upon thee, that thine enemies shall cast a trench about thee, and compass thee round, and keep thee in on every side,

44 And shall lay thee even with the ground, and thy children within thee; and they shall not leave in thee one stone upon another; because thou knewest not the time of thy visitation.

Luke 19:28–20:8.

45 And he went into the temple, and began to cast out them that sold therein, and them that bought;

46 Saying unto them, It is written, My house is the house of prayer: but ye have made it a den of thieves.

47 And he taught daily in the temple. But the chief priests and the scribes and the chief of the people sought to destroy him,

48 And could not find what they might do: for all the people were very attentive to hear him.

Chapter 20

And it came to pass, that on one of those days, as he taught the people in the temple, and preached the gospel, the chief priests and the scribes came upon him with the elders,

2 And spake unto him, saying, Tell us, by what authority doest thou these things? or who is he that gave thee this authority?

3 And he answered and said unto them, I will also ask you one thing; and answer me:

4 The baptism of John, was it from heaven, or of men?

5 And they reasoned with themselves, saying, If we shall say, From heaven; he will say, Why then believed ye him not?

6 But and if we say, Of men; all the people will stone us: for they be persuaded that John was a prophet.

7 And they answered, that they could not tell whence it was.

8 And Jesus said unto them, Neither tell I you by what authority I do these things.

European: The Chapel Perilous

The Chapel Perilous is perhaps related to the Seat (or Siege) Perilous. It is one form of the "Mount of Joy," the maternal place where the womb symbol and later Christian symbol called the Holy Grail was kept. The virginal *puer aeternus* Galahad may sit in the chapel in his quest for the Holy Grail, just as over the main doors of so many cathedrals the Christ Child as king is depicted seated on the lap of Mary, who thus, like the altar and the church itself, becomes the feminine throne for the seed-bearing hero. The Chapel Perilous appears in several versions of the Grail myth, not always in connection with Galahad.

•

Students of the Grail romances will remember that in many of the versions the hero—sometimes it is a heroine—meets with a strange and terrifying adventure in a mysterious Chapel, an adventure which, we are given to

understand, is fraught with extreme peril to life. The details vary: sometimes there is a Dead Body laid on the altar; sometimes a Black Hand
extinguishes the tapers; there are strange and threatening voices, and the
general impression is that this is an adventure in which supernatural, and
evil, forces are engaged.

Such an adventure befalls Gawain on his way to the Grail castle. He
is overtaken by a terrible storm, and coming to a Chapel, standing at a
crossways in the middle of a forest, enters for shelter. The altar is bare,
with no cloth, or covering, nothing is thereon but a great golden candle-
stick with a tall taper burning within it. Behind the altar is a window, and
as Gawain looks a Hand, black and hideous, comes through the window,
and extinguishes the taper, while a voice makes lamentation loud and dire,
beneath which the very building rocks. Gawain's horse shies for terror,
and the knight, making the sign of the Cross, rides out of the Chapel, to
find the storm abated, and the great wind fallen. Thereafter the night was
calm and clear.

The Genitals

As we have seen in the myth of the dying god, the loss of genitals is directly
associated with the god's role as seed planted in the earth-womb of the
Great Goddess. The conjunction of genitals in this case, as in the case of
the many Indian depictions of sex acts between Shiva and Parvati—his
feminine soul, or *Shakti* (*anima*)—and between Vishnu and his spouse, is
a symbol of union or wholeness. The Shiva phallus, or *lingam* (often
painted blood red), standing within the temple inner sanctum, the *yoni* or
Great Goddess vulva, is the iconographic correlative of the essence of the
Shivite cult. It is related to the ritual of the flower-bedecked maypole or
such mythological images as the Christian *Pietà*, in which the mythic son-
lover is joined with the mother-wife after the Crucifixion. The archetypal
image of Arthur's sword in the rock takes another form in the little stone
lingam-yoni combinations that are to be found in and around Shiva temples.

Greek: Tiresias

The rather bizarre story of Tiresias must have its roots in the archetype of
the androgyne, the person of both sexes who becomes another version of
the yin-yang/lingam-yoni unity, which carries with it the powers of proph-

Jessie L. Weston, *From Ritual to Romance: An Account of the Holy Grail from Ancient Ritual to Christian Symbol* (1920; New York, 1957), p. 175.

ecy. (See Ovid's version of the story in the collection of miscellaneous stories of the gods and lesser spirits in Part II of this book.)

Apache: The Vagina Girls

This Apache tale is almost certainly a patriarchal myth of the taming of the female powers associated in other traditions—India's, for example— with the destructive nature of the Great Goddess of death and rebirth.

•

According to [a myth]—told in New Mexico by the Jicarilla Apache Indians—there once was a murderous monster called Kicking Monster, whose four daughters at that time were the only women in the world possessing vaginas. They were "vagina girls." And they lived in a house that was full of vaginas. "They had the form of women," we are told, "but they were in reality vaginas. Other vaginas were hanging around on the walls, but these four were in the form of girls with legs and all body parts and were walking around." As may be imagined, the rumor of these girls brought many men along the road; but they would be met by Kicking Monster, kicked into the house, and never returned. And so Killer-of-Enemies, a marvelous boy hero, took it upon himself to correct the situation.

Outwitting Kicking Monster, Killer-of-Enemies entered the house, and the four girls approached him, craving intercourse. But he asked, "Where have all the men gone who were kicked into this place?" "We ate them up," they said, "because we like to do that"; and they attempted to embrace him. But he held them off, shouting, "Keep away! That is no way to use the vagina." And then he told them, "First I must give you some medicine, which you have never tasted before, medicine made of sour berries; and then I'll do what you ask." Whereupon he gave them sour berries of four kinds to eat. "The vagina," he said, "is always sweet when you do like this." The berries puckered their mouths, so that finally they could not chew at all, but only swallowed. "They liked it very much, though," declared the teller of the story. "It felt just as if Killer-of-Enemies was having intercourse with them. They were almost unconscious with ecstasy, though really Killer-of-Enemies was doing nothing at all to them. It was the medicine that made them feel that way.

"When Killer-of-Enemies had come to them," the story-teller then concluded, "they had had strong teeth with which they had eaten their victims. But this medicine destroyed their teeth entirely." And so we see how the great boy hero, once upon a time, domesticated the toothed vagina to its proper use.

Joseph Campbell, *The Masks of God: Primitive Mythology* (New York, 1969), pp. 74–75.

Greek: The Fig Phallus of Dionysos

This myth is perhaps a narrative for the ritual in which the phallus of
Dionysos was carried in procession by an impersonator of the Great Goddess during fertility festivals.

●

When Dionysus had firmly established his worship throughout the lands
of the eastern Mediterranean and as far east as India, he withdrew from
earth and took his place with the other gods on Mount Olympus. First,
however, he descended into Hades to bring up his mother. Several Greek
cities later claimed that this memorable event had occurred in their terri-
tory. Instead of going by a land route, Dionysus apparently dived into the
water, either the bottomless Alcyonian Lake, at Lerna, or the bay of Troezen. He was shown this route by a native guide named Prosymnus, Polymnus, or Hypolipnus. On meeting the handsome young god, the guide demanded that he lie with him. Dionysus, unwilling to delay his rescue of
his mother,* vowed to pay Prosymnus on his return. When the time came,
Prosymnus was dead. The god discharged his debt by whittling out of fig-
wood an image of the organ that the guide had admired, and leaving it at
the tomb.

The Stone

In myth, the stone is often a place of sacrifice. Again, the symbolism seems
to be maternal, or at least feminine. Arthur proves his powers by pulling
the phallic sword from the maternal rock. Theseus does the same by re-
moving the sword and sandals from under the rock.

Phrygian: The Agdos Rock

The Phrygian earth religion, in which Cybele, the Great Goddess, is central, contains this tale in which the mother is identified with the rock. This
myth also makes use of the genital archetype and is a virgin birth story.

●

The Agdos rock—so the story runs—had assumed the shape of the Great
Mother. [The Phrygian sky-god, Papas] . . . fell asleep upon it. As he
slept, or as he strove with the goddess, his semen fell upon the rock. In

Edward Tripp, ed., *Crowell's Handbook of Classical Mythology* (New York, 1970), p. 209.
    *Semele in this version.

C. Kerenyi, *The Gods of the Greeks* (London, 1951), pp. 89–90.

the tenth month the Agdos rock bellowed and brought forth an untamable, savage being, of twofold sex and twofold lust, named Agdistis. With cruel joy Agdistis plundered, murdered and destroyed whatever it chose, cared for neither gods nor men, and held nothing mightier on earth or in heaven than itself. The gods often consulted together as to how this insolence could be tamed. When they all hesitated, Dionysos took over the task. There was a certain spring to which Agdistis came to assuage its thirst when it was overheated with sport and hunting. Dionysos turned the springwater into wine. Agdistis came running up, impelled by thirst, greedily drank the strange liquor and fell perforce into deepest sleep. Dionysos was on the watch. He adroitly made a cord of hair, and with it bound Agdistis's male member to a tree. Awakened from its drunkenness, the monster sprang up and castrated itself by its own strength. The earth drank the flowing blood, and with it the torn-off parts. From these at once arose a fruit-bearing tree: an almond-tree or—according to another tale— a pomegranate-tree. Nana, the daughter of the king or river-god Sangarios (Nana is another name for the great goddess of Asia Minor), saw the beauty of the fruit, plucked it and hid it in her lap. The fruit vanished, and Nana conceived a child of it. Her father imprisoned her, as a woman deflowered, and condemned her to death by starvation. The Great Mother fed her on fruits and on the foods of the gods. She gave birth to a little boy. Sangarios had the child left out in the open to perish. A he-goat tended the suckling, who, when he was found, was fed upon a liquor called "he-goat's milk." He was named Attis, either because *attis* is Lydian for a handsome boy or because *attagus* was Phrygian for a he-goat.

Australian Aboriginal: Erathipa

This fertility stone has a feminine opening on one side.

•

The tribes of central Australia have . . . a hugh rock known as Erathipa which has an opening in one side from which the souls of the children imprisoned in it watch for a woman to pass by so that they may be reborn in her. When women who do not want children go near the rock, they pretend to be old, and walk as if leaning on a stick, crying: "Don't come to me, I am an old woman!"*

The idea implicit in all these rites is that certain stones have the power to make sterile women fruitful, either because of the spirits of the ancestors

*The Native Tribes of Central Australia, London, 1899, p. 337.

Mircea Eliade, Patterns in Comparative Religion (New York, 1958), p.220–221.

that dwell in them, or because of their shape (the pregnant woman, "woman stone"), or because of their origin (*svayambhū*, "autogenesis").

Hebrew: The Bethel

The bethel stone, like the Ka'ba at Mecca or the omphalos stone at Delphi, is in Genesis "the house of God" and "the gate of heaven," another version of the world navel.

Chapter 28

. . .10 And Jacob went out from Beer-sheba, and went toward Haran.

11 And he lighted upon a certain place, and tarried there all night, because the sun was set; and he took of the stones of that place, and put them for his pillows, and lay down in that place to sleep.

12 And he dreamed, and behold a ladder set up on the earth, and the top of it reached to heaven: and behold the angels of God ascending and descending on it.

13 And, behold, the Lord stood above it, and said, I am the Lord God of Abraham thy father, and the God of Isaac: the land whereon thou liest, to thee will I give it, and to thy seed;

14 And thy seed shall be as the dust of the earth, and thou shalt spread abroad to the west, and to the east, and to the north, and to the south: and in thee and in thy seed shall all the families of the earth be blessed.

15 And, behold, I am with thee, and will keep thee in all places whither thou goest, and will bring thee again into this land; for I will not leave thee, until I have done that which I have spoken to thee of.

16 And Jacob awaked out of his sleep, and he said, Surely the Lord is in this place; and I knew it not.

17 And he was afraid, and said, How dreadful is this place! this is none other but the house of God, and this is the gate of heaven.

18 And Jacob rose up early in the morning, and took the stone that he had put for his pillows, and set it up for a pillar, and poured oil upon the top of it.

19 And he called the name of that place Beth-el: but the name of that city was called Luz at the first.

20 And Jacob vowed a vow, saying, If God will be with me, and will keep me in this way that I go, and will give me bread to eat, and raiment to put on,

Genesis 28:10–29:11

21 So that I come again to my father's house in peace; then shall the Lord be my God:

22 And this stone, which I have set for a pillar, shall be God's house: and of all that thou shalt give me I will surely give the tenth unto thee.

Chapter 29

Then Jacob went on his journey, and came into the land of the people of the east.

2 And he looked, and behold a well in the field, and, lo, there were three flocks of sheep lying by it; for out of that well they watered the flocks: and a great stone was upon the well's mouth.

3 And thither were all the flocks gathered: and they rolled the stone from the well's mouth, and watered the sheep, and put the stone again upon the well's mouth in his place.

4 And Jacob said unto them, My brethren, whence be ye? And they said, Of Haran are we.

5 And he said unto them, Know ye Laban the son of Nā'-hôr? And they said, We know him.

6 And he said unto them, Is he well? And they said, He is well: and, behold, Rachel his daughter cometh with the sheep.

7 And he said, Lo, it is yet high day, neither is it time that the cattle should be gathered together: water ye the sheep, and go and feed them.

8 And they said, We cannot, until all the flocks be gathered together, and till they roll the stone from the well's mouth; then we water the sheep.

9 And while he yet spake with them, Rachel came with her father's sheep: for she kept them.

10 And it came to pass, when Jacob saw Rachel the daughter of Laban his mother's brother, and the sheep of Laban his mother's brother, that Jacob went near, and rolled the stone from the well's mouth, and watered the flock of Laban his mother's brother.

11 And Jacob kissed Rachel, and lifted up his voice and wept.

The Tree

The roots of the sacred tree extend to the depths of the earth and its branches reach to the heavens. It brings together the temporal and the eternal. Furthermore, it is a symbol of life and of wholeness. The cross of the Crucifixion is a tree, the Buddha found enlightenment under the Bodhi Tree, Osiris was found in a tree, Adonis was born of a tree. Many cultures possess world trees or axle trees, which, like temples and primeval mounds, are the center of the world.

India: The Cosmic Tree

In the ancient Upanishads the cosmic tree, Asvattha, represents Brahman itself, the cosmos in full bloom. In the *Bhagavad-Gita* it incorporates the world of humanity.

•

Indian tradition, according to its earliest writings, represents the cosmos in the form of a giant tree. This idea is defined fairly formally in the Upanisads: the Universe is an inverted tree, burying its roots in the sky and spreading its branches over the whole earth. (It is not impossible that this image was suggested by the downpouring of the sun's rays. Cf. *Rg Veda:* "The branches grow towards what is low, the roots are on high, that its rays may descend upon us!") The *Katha-Upanisad* describes it like this: "This eternal Aśvattha, whose roots rise on high, and whose branches grow low, is the pure [*śukram*], is the Brahman, is what we call the Non-Death. All the worlds rest in it!" The *aśvattha* tree here represents the clearest possible manifestation of Brahman in the Cosmos, represents, in other words, creation as a descending movement. Other texts from the Upanisads restate still more clearly this notion of the cosmos as a tree. "Its branches are the ether, the air, fire, water, earth," etc. The natural elements are the expression of this "Brahman whose name is Aśvattha."

In the *Bhagavad-Gitā*, the cosmic tree comes to express not only the universe, but also man's condition in the world: "It is said that there is an indestructible tree, its roots above, its branches below, its leaves the hymns of the Veda; whoever knows it knows the Veda also. Its branches increase in height and depth, growing on the *gunas;* its buds are the objects of sense; its roots spread out from below, bound to actions in the world of men. In this world one cannot perceive the shape, nor the end, nor the beginning, nor the expanse of it. With the strong weapon of renunciation, one must first cut down this *aśvattha* with its powerful roots, and then seek the place from which one never returns . . ."; The whole universe, as well as the experience of man who lives in it and is not detached from it, are here symbolized by the cosmic tree. By everything in himself which corresponds with the cosmos or shares in its life, man merges into the same single and immense manifestation of Brahman. "To cut the tree at its roots" means to withdraw man from the cosmos, to cut him off from the things of sense and the fruits of his actions. We find the same motif of detachment from the life of the cosmos, of withdrawal into oneself and

Mircea Eliade, *Patterns in Comparative Religion* (New York, 1958), pp. 273–274.

recollection as man's only way of transcending himself and becoming free, in a text from the *Mahābhārata*. "Sprung from the Unmanifested, arising from it as only support, its trunk is *bodhi*, its inward cavities the channels of the sense, the great elements its branches, the objects of the senses its leaves, its fair flowers good and evil [*dharmādharmav*], pleasure and pain the consequent fruits. This eternal Brahma-tree [*brahma-vrksa*] is the source of life [*abjīva*] for all beings . . . Having cut asunder and broken the tree with the weapon of *gnosis* [*jananeña*], and thenceforth taking pleasure in the Spirit, none returneth thither again.

Norse: Yggdrasil

The most famous cosmic tree is the Norse Yggdrasil, which is not only the Tree of Wisdom or Knowledge but also the Tree of Life.

•

Then Gangleri asked: "Where is the chief place or sanctuary of the gods?"

High One replied: "It is by the ash Yggdrasil.. There every day the gods have to hold a court."

Then Gangleri asked: "In what way is that place famous?"

Then Just-as-high said: "The ash is the best and greatest of all trees; its branches spread out over the whole world and reach up over heaven. The tree is held in position by three roots that spread far out; one is among the Æsir, the second among the frost ogres where once was Ginnungagap, and the third extends over Niflheim, and under that root is the well Hvergelmir; but Nídhögg[1] gnaws at the root from below. Under the root that turns in the direction of the frost ogres lies the spring of Mímir, in which is hidden wisdom and understanding; Mímir is the name of the owner of the spring. He is full of wisdom because he drinks [water] from the spring out of the horn Gjöll. All-father came there and asked for a single drink from the spring, but he did not get it until he had given one of his eyes as a pledge. As it says in the *Sibyl's Vision:*

> I know for certain Ódin
> where you concealed your eye,
> in the famous
> spring of Mímir;
> mead he drinks
> every morning
> from the pledge of the Father-of-the-slain.
> Do you know any more or not?

Snorri Sturluson, *The Prose Edda* (Berkeley, Calif., 1954), pp. 42–44.
[1]Striker-that-destroys.

The third root of the ash tree is in the sky, and under that root is the very sacred spring called the Spring of Urd.[2] There the gods hold their court of justice. The Æsir ride up to that place every day over the bridge Bifröst, which is also known as the Bridge of the Æsir. The names of the horses of the gods are as follows: Sleipnir is the best, Ódin owns him, he has eight legs; the second is Glad;[3] the third, Gyllir; the fourth, Glen; the fifth, Skeidbrimir;[4] the sixth, Silfr[in]topp;[5] the seventh, Sinir;[6] the eighth, Gils, the ninth, Falhófnir;[7] the tenth, Gulltopp;[8] the eleventh, Léttfet[i].[9] Baldr's horse was burned with him, and Thór walks to the court wading through the rivers that have these names:

> Körmt and Örmt
> and both the Kerlaugar
> these must Thór wade through
> every day,
> when he goes to give judgment
> at Yggdrasil's ash,
> since the Bridge of the Æsir
> is flaming with fire
> the sacred waters glow."

Hebrew: The Tree of Knowledge

The Tree of Knowledge in Genesis is central to the mythic tradition of our culture. It is the source of knowledge as well as of death. It is, for Christians, the precursor to the Tree of Life—the Cross—on which Christ is crucified in order to reverse the events in Eden and therefore, as the New Adam, to overcome death. (For the Tree of Life myth, see Genesis 3 in the Creation section of this book.)

The Garden, the Grove, and the Cave

The garden, the grove, and the cave are sacred spaces in myth. Their connotative energy derives from the fact that they are originally associated with the Mother Goddess. They are places of birth (Jesus, the Buddha,

---

[2]Destiny.
[3]Shining One.
[4]Fast-galloper.
[5]Silver Forelock.
[6]Strong-of-sinew.
[7]Shaggy Fetlock.
[8]Golden Forelock.
[9]Lightfoot.

Dionysos in some stories). They are places of withdrawal for meditation, which can lead to a second birth (Muhammad, Endymion, Jesus in Gethsemane). They are enclosed, protective places that, like temples and walled cities, are metaphors for cosmos in the face of chaos. The Tree of Life and other forms of the Cosmic Tree are often found in gardens (the Bodhi Tree, the Tree of Knowledge), forming still another version of union in the tradition of the lingam-yoni conjunction, the tree being the standing phallus in the womb-garden.

Muslim: Muhammad's Cave

The prophet retires to the cave to receive the word of Allah.

•

Mohammad was now approaching his fortieth year. Always pensive, he had of late become even more thoughtful and retiring. Contemplation and reflection engaged his mind. The debasement of his people pressed heavily on him; the dim and imperfect shadows of Judaism and Christianity excited doubts without satisfying them; and his soul was perplexed with uncertainty as to what was the true religion. Thus burdened, he frequently retired to seek relief in meditation amongst the solitary valleys and rocks near Mecca. His favourite spot was a cave in the declivities at the foot of mount Hira, a lofty conical hill two or three miles north of Mecca. Thither he would retire for days at a time; and his faithful wife sometimes accompanied him. The continued solitude, instead of stilling his anxiety, magnified into sterner and more impressive shapes the solemn realities which agitated his soul. Close by was the grave of the aged Zeid, who, after spending a lifetime in the same inquiries, had now passed into the state of certainty;—might he himself not reach the same assurance without crossing the gate of death?

All around was bleak and rugged. To the east and south, the vision from the cave of Hira is bounded by lofty mountain ranges, but to the north and west the weary prospect is thus described by Burckhardt:— "The country before us had a dreary aspect, not a single green spot being visible; barren, black, and grey hills, and white sandy valleys, were the only objects in sight." There was harmony here between external nature, and the troubled world within. By degrees the impulsive and susceptible mind of Mohammad was wrought up to the highest pitch of excitement; and he would give vent to his agitation in wild rhapsodical language, enforced often with incoherent oaths, the counterpart of inward struggling after truth. The following fragments [from the Koran] belong probably to this period:

Sir William Muir, *The Life of Mohammad* (1923; New York, 1975), pp. 37–38, 138–139.

By the declining day I swear!
Verily, man is in the way of ruin;
Excepting such as possess faith,
And do the things which are right,
And stir up one another unto truth and steadfastness.

And again—

By the rushing panting steeds!
Striking fire with flashing hoof,
That scour the land at early morn!
And, darkening it with dust,
Cleave thereby the Enemy!
Verily Man is to his Lord ungrateful,
And he himself is witness of it.
Verily he is keen after this world's good.
Ah! witteth he not that when what is in the graves shall be brought forth,
And that which is in men's breasts laid bare;—
Verily in that day shall the Lord be will informed of them.

Nor was he wanting in prayer for guidance to the great Being who, he felt, alone could give it. The following petitions (though probably adapted subsequently to public worship) contain perhaps the germ of frequent prayer at this early period.

Praise be to God, the Lord of creation,
The most merciful, the most compassionate!
Ruler of the day of Reckoning!
Thee we worship, and invoke for help.
Lead us in the straight path;—
The path of those towards whom Thou hast been gracious;
Not of those against whom Thy wrath is kindled, or that walk in error.

. . .

Several years after, Mohammad thus alludes in the Koran to the position of himself and his friend [Abu Bekr] in the cave of mount Thaur:

If ye will not assist the Prophet, verily God assisted him aforetime when the Unbelievers cast him forth, in the company of a Second only; when they two were in the cave alone, when the Prophet said unto his companion, *Be not cast down, for verily God is with us.* And God caused to descend tranquillity upon him, and strengthened him with hosts which ye saw not, and made the word of the Unbelievers to be abased; and the word of the Lord, that is exalted, for God is mighty and wise.

The "sole companion," or in Arabic phraseology *The Second of the Two*, became one of Abu Bekr's most honoured titles. Hassan, the contemporary poet of Medina, thus sings of him:—

> And the Second of the two in the glorious Cave, while the foes were
>   searching around, and they two had ascended the mountain;
> And the Prophet of the Lord, they well knew, loved him,—more than all
>   the world; he held no one equal unto him.

Legends cluster around the cave. A spider wove its web across the entrance. Branches sprouted, covering it in on every side. Wild pigeons settled on the trees to divert attention, and so forth. Whatever may have been the real peril, Mohammad and his companion felt it, no doubt, to be a time of jeopardy. Glancing upwards at a crevice through which the morning light began to break, Abu Bekr whispered: "What if one were to look through the chink, and see us underneath his very feet." *"Think not thus, Abu Bekr!"* said the Prophet; "WE ARE TWO, BUT GOD IS IN THE MIDST A THIRD."

The Labyrinth

The labyrinth appears in the myths of many cultures, but most prominently in the story of Theseus. The word derives from the Greek *labrys*, ax. Presumably, in Crete, where the labyrinth was built in the form of a double ax by Daedalus to house the half-bull Minotaur, it referred to the sacred double ax used there for sacrifices. The labyrinth has always connoted the idea of a difficult journey into the unknown. To escape from it and from the monster within is to have faced death and been reborn (see the Theseus story in the Hero Myths section of this book).

An interesting outgrowth of the labyrinth myth is the tragic story of Daedalus and Icarus, who longed to escape Crete and the Labyrinth, which Daedalus himself had designed and built.

Greek: Daedalus and Icarus

It was not easy, however, to escape from Crete, since Minos kept all his ships under military guard, and now offered a large reward for his apprehension. But Daedalus made a pair of wings for himself, and another for Icarus, the quill feathers of which were threaded together, but the smaller ones held in place by wax. Having tied on Icarus's pair for him, he said

Robert Graves, *The Greek Myths*, vol. 1 (Baltimore, Md., 1955), pp. 312–313.

with tears in his eyes: "My son, be warned! Neither soar too high, lest the sun melt the wax; nor swoop too low, lest the feathers be wetted by the sea." Then he slipped his arms into his own pair of wings and they flew off. "Follow me closely," he cried, "do not set your own course!"

As they sped away from the island in a north-easterly direction, flapping their wings, the fishermen, shepherds, and ploughmen who gazed upward mistook them for gods.

They had left Naxos, Delos, and Paros behind them on the left hand, and were leaving Lebynthos and Calymne behind on the right, when Icarus disobeyed his father's instructions and began soaring towards the sun, rejoiced by the lift of his great sweeping wings. Presently, when Daedalus looked over his shoulder, he could no longer see Icarus; but scattered feathers floated on the waves below. The heat of the sun had melted the wax, and Icarus had fallen into the sea and drowned. Daedalus circled around, until the corpse rose to the surface, and then carried it to the nearby island now called Icaria, where he buried it. . . .

Bibliography

The most stimulating discussions of sacred places and objects are those of Mircea Eliade, particularly in his *Patterns in Comparative Religion* (New York, 1958) and *The Sacred and the Profane* (New York, 1959). For useful discussions of biblical places and objects, see Walter Beltz, *God and the Gods: Myths of the Bible* (Baltimore, Md., 1983). For a strong and convincing analysis of sacred places and objects and much of mythology in general, see Barbara Walker, *The Woman's Encyclopedia of Myths and Secrets* (New York, 1983). Jessie Weston's *From Ritual to Romance* (New York, 1957) is still the most exciting analysis of the Holy Grail myth. For the poetic and philosophical implications of sacred space, places, and objects, see Gaston Bachelard, *The Poetics of Space* (Boston, 1969).

INDEX

Aaron, 317
Abhidhamma Pitaka, 266
Abraham, 134, 287–88
Acamas, 321
Acheron. *See* River of Woe
Achilles, 8, 67, 322, 328–29
Acropolis, 245, 248
Adad, 45
Adam, 27–29, 157, 309
Admetus, 309–10
Adonis, 96, 105, 112, 147, 153, 162, 183, 218, 341
Aegeus, 245–46
Aeneas, 68, 219, 244, 257–58
Aeneid (Virgil), 67, 258, 288, 319
Aeschylus, 192, 258
Æsir, 87, 118, 343–44
Aesop, 163
Africa, 85
African myths, 6, 39, 281–83
  Bantu, 229, 234–35
  Wanjiru, 281–83, 298
Afterlife, 14, 64–75, 96
  Buddhist, 69–72
  Egyptian, 65–67
  Greco-Roman, 67–68
  Hopi, 72–75
  Judeo-Christian, 68
  Muslim, 68–69
Agamemnon, 192, 258
Agdistis, 339
Agdos rock, 338–39
Agenor, 196

Agni, 31
Ahura Mazda, 124
Aisinokoki (Wind Sucker), 302
Ajax, 326
Akhenaton, 95
Alcestis, 309–10
Alcestis (Euripides), 309
Alcmene, 100, 228–29
Alcyonian Lake. *See* Lerna
Allah, 93, 124, 345
Alpheus, 277
Amaterasu, 199–202
Amazons, 278
Amen-Ra. *See* Amun
American Dream, myth of, 4
American Indian myths, 6
  Apache, 337
  Aztec, 175, 221, 307–8
  Aztec-Toltec, 157
  Blackfoot Indian, 221, 298–304
  Hopi. *See* Hopi myth
  Navaho, 16, 134
American South, 220
Amida, 69–72. *See also* Buddha
Amphitryon, 228–29
Amun (Amen-Ra), 95. *See also* Atum
Anatolia, 109
Anchises, 322
Ancient Greek view of history, 89
Ancient Hebrews, 85
Ancient mythmaker, 8
Ancient myths, 3
Androgeos, 325

Androgyne, archetype of, 336
Andromache, 327
Anima, 220. See also *Shakti*
Anshar, 19
Antichrist, 79
Antigone (Sophocles), 239–43
Anu, 18, 22, 44, 46, 291
Anunnaki, 23, 45
Apache, 337
Aphrodite, 33, 104, 118, 153, 185, 247
Apocalypse, 8, 14, 76–89
    Armageddon, 76, 85
    Ragnarok (Norse), 18
Apocalyptic stories, 77–89
    Christian, 79–81
    Hebrew, 77–79
    Hopi, 84–85
    Indian, 81–84
    Modern, 88–89
    Norse, 85–88
Apollo, 108–9, 112, 118, 178, 183, 185–88,
    192, 245–46, 275–76, 310, 319, 326,
    332–33
Apollodorus, 185
Apollonius of Rhodes, 258
Apotheosis of hero, 298–310
Appollodorus, 104
Apsu, 19–22
Apuleius, 185
Ararat, 50
Archetype(s), 5, 6, 43, 315
    of androgyne, 336
    of dying god, 183
    of femme fatale, 5
    of God, 123–74
    journey quest, 5
    of productive sacrifice, 43
    of trickster, 5
    of wise old guide, 5
Architecture, 4, 333
Ares, 104, 118
Argive fleet, 321
Argonauts, 258
Argos, 275, 323
Ariadne, 247–48
Aristophanes, 67
Arjuna, 125–29
Armageddon, 76, 85
Artemis, 108–9, 118, 134, 185, 283, 310
Arthur (King). *See* King Arthur
Artist, modern, 8, 315
Asiatic god, 108

Assumption of Mary, 309
Astyanax, 327
Asvattha, 342
Athena, 100, 103–4, 108–9, 118, 192, 316
Athens, 101, 192
Atlantic, 279
Atlantis, 81
Atlas, 111, 175, 185, 279, 283
Atman (Soul), 29, 31
Atreus, 326
Atridae, 328
Attagus, 339
Attis, 96, 112, 118, 146–47, 155, 162, 183,
    221, 295, 298, 315, 339
Atum (Re), 17–18, 95–96
    cult of, 17
Augeas, 277–78
Australian Aboriginal myth, 283–87, 339–
    40
Autogenesis, 339
Automedon, 328
Avernus, 294
Axis mundi, 316
Aztec myth, 175, 221, 307–8
Aztec-Toltec, 157

Babylon, 330, 333
Babylonia, 97
Babylonian captivity, 24
Babylonian-Greco-Roman myth, 153–55
Babylonian/Mesopotamian myth, 44–47
Babylonian New Year Festival, 16
Bacchae (Euripides), 112, 239
Bacchus, 118
Baldr, 118, 162, 344
Bantu myth, 39–44, 229, 234–35
Baruch, 79
Bastian, Adolf, 5
Bateson, Gregory, 133
Bear, The (Faulkner), 220
Beatrice, 68, 220
Beersheba, 340
Bekr, Abu, 347
"Belle dame sans merci, La" (Keats), 220
Bellerophon, 274
Berry, Thomas, 41
Bethany, 306
Bethel, 340–41
Bethel stone, 340
Bethlehem, 309
Bhagavad-Gita, 125, 342
Bhagavata Purana, 165, 225

Bhuvarloka, 83
Bifrost, 344
Big bang theory, 89
Blackfoot Indian myth, 221, 298–304
Black Jupiter, 323
Boas, Franz, 5
Bodde, Derk, 53
Bodhisatta, 262–65
Bodhi Tree, 257, 262, 304, 341, 343, 345
Boeotia, 57
Book of Going Forth by Day, 17
Book of the Dead, 17, 35, 65
Book of the Two Ways, 66
Boshongo (Bantu) myth, 39–40
Bo Tree, 223. *See also* Bodhi Tree
Brahma, 29, 31, 84
Brahmaloka, 84
Brahman, 93, 124–25, 342
Brahma-tree, 343
Brahmavaivarta Purana, 207
Breaking of bread, 306
Brer Rabbit, 163
Brhadaranyaka Upanishad, 29–30
Briareus, 32
Bridge of the Æsir, 344
Brown, Norman O., 32
Buddha, 71, 218–19, 221, 229–33, 257,
    262–67, 274, 304, 307, 341, 344
Buddhahood, 70–71
Buddhism, 69–72, 262
Buffalo, 6, 298–301
Bull of Heaven, 291–92
Bumba, 39–40
Bunyip, 286
Burckhardt, Titus, 345

Cacus, 279
Calymne, 348
Campbell, Joseph, 5, 6, 8, 217
Cǎ′-nǎ-ǎn, 53
Cappadocia, 109
Carthage, 258
Cassandra, 320, 324–25
Cassirer, Ernst, 5
Castalia, 333
Castle, 315
Castor, 100
Cathedrals of Europe, 333
Cave, 315, 344, 345–47
Cawka Paho, 39
Celtic myth, 243–44, 252–55
Centaur, 277

Cephisus, 59
Cerberus, 67, 102, 281, 294
Ceres, 117
Chaonia, 294
Chapel Perilous, 333, 335–36
Chedi Bumba, 40
Chimaera, 274
Chimalman, 221
China, 85
Chinese myth, 7, 53–55
Chiron, 275, 277
Chonganda, 40
Chou Dynasty, 53
Christ, 33, 118, 135, 344. *See also* Jesus
Christ figure, 156
Christian church, 218. *See also* Church
Christianity, 197, 278, 344–45, 262
Christian myths, 3, 35–36, 79–81, 134–35,
    157–61, 304–9
  assumption of Mary, 309
Christians, 330
Church, 16, 308–9
Circe, 219
City, 315, 316, 319–33
Clark, R. T. Rundle, 65
Cleopas, 305
Clot of Blood, 299. *See also* Kutoyis
Clytemnestra, 100, 103, 192, 258
Cobra, 6
Coelus, 117
Coeus, 32
Coffin Texts, 17, 65–66
Collective "folk" mind, 7
Collective unconscious, 123, 315. *See also*
    Jung, Carl Gustav
Colum, Padraic, 199
Consciousness, 64–65, 217
Corn, 304
  discovery of, 267–74
Coroebus, 324–26
Corycian nymphs, 58
Cosmic energy, 316
Cosmic myths, 8, 13
Cosmic tree, 341–45
Cosmogony, 15
Cosmological theory, 89
Cosmology, 14
Cosmos, 16, 315
  nature of, 95
Cottus, 32
Country of Two Hearts, 71
Covenant, 49, 52–53, 316

Coyote, 163
Creation, 4, 8, 14, 15–42
    Bantu, 39–40
    Christian, 35–36
    Egyptian, 17–18
    Greek, 32–35
    Hebrew, 24–29
    Hopi, 41–42
    Indian, 29–30
    Mesopotamian, 18–23
    Modern, 41–42
Creon, 239, 274
Crete, 278, 347
    ancient, 100
Crime and Punishment (Dostoevsky), 221
Crius, 32
Cronus, 32–34
Cross, 344
Crucifixion, the, 217, 233, 262, 278, 341,
    336
Cults, 3
    of Atum (Re), 17
    of Demeter, 101
    of Dionysos, 101
    fertility, 101, 163
Cupid, 118. See also Eros
Cybele, 109, 134, 155, 295, 338
Cyclopes, 32, 56
Cyprus, 33
Cythera, 33

Daedalus, 347
Dahomey. See Fon tribe of West Africa
Damkina, 21
Danaan(s), 321–27
Danaus, 293
Daniel, book of, 77
Daniélou, Jean, 43
Dante, 68, 124, 220
Daphne, 185–88
Dardanelles, 4
Dardania, 322–23
Dardanus, 320
Dat, 65–66
Davy Crockett, 163
Day of Yahweh, 77
Dead King, 66
Death God, the, 37
Deiphobus, 323
Delilah, 219, 260
Delos, 108, 348

Delphi, 108, 245–46, 275–76, 316, 332–33,
    340
Deluge, 43
Demeter, 34, 43, 97–103, 109, 117, 134–
    36, 148
Demodocus, 8
Demons. See Herods
Descent of hero, 281
    into darkness, 290
    into death, 147, 220, 308
    descent-rescue, 292
    Herakles, 280
    to underworld, 119, 217, 219, 221, 244,
        274, 293–95, 315, 338
Deucalion, 56–58
Devadaha, 232–33
Devaki, 225
Devi, 134–35
Dhoulkefl, 69
Diana, 109–11, 118, 276
Dido, 258
Dilmun, 289
Diomedes, 319, 278
Dionysos, 67, 97–98, 100, 108, 112–13,
    118, 135, 147, 156–57, 162, 188, 217,
    239, 255, 281, 298, 338–39, 345
Dionysus. See Dionysos
Dios, 124
Div, 124
Divine child. See Puer aeternus
Divine Comedy (Dante), 68
Dolopians, 326
Dostoevsky, Fyodor, 221
Dreams, 5–6
Dumuzi-Tammuz, 136, 147
Durga, 135
Dying god, 123, 136, 146–62, 220–21, 281,
    298, 336
    archetype of, 183
    Aztec-Toltec, 157
    Babylonian-Greco-Roman, 153–55
    Christian, 157–61
    Egyptian, 147–53
    Greek, 156–57
    Norse, 162–63
    Phyrgian, 155
Dymas, 324–26

Ea, 20–23, 44–45, 47
Earth. See Gaia; Geb

Earth Goddess, 36, 148, 178. *See also* Great Mother
Earth Mother, 227. *See also* Great Mother
Earth Woman, 134
East Indian myths, 6
Echo, 178–83
Eden, 27–29, 69, 344
Egypt, 85, 134
Egyptian gods, 8
Egyptian myth, 65–67, 95–98, 134
Eightfold Path, 266
Elder Edda, 118, 162
Elektra, 258
Elektra complex, 5
Elephants, 6
Eleusinian Mysteries, 101, 103
Eleusinian myth, 135
Eleusis, 101, 103
Eliade, Mircea, 6, 15, 43, 93, 315
Eliot, T. S., 147
Elis, 277–78
Elisha, 69
Elysian Field, 67
Emmaus, 304–5
Enchantresses, 220. *See also* Femme fatale
Endymion, 345
Energy of creator, 315
Enki, 44
Enkidu, 288–89, 291–92
Enlightenment, 263, 265
Enlil, 22, 44–47, 124
Ennead, 96
Ennugi, 44
Entropic equilibrium, 16, 77
Entropy, 6, 88–89
Entropy Law, 89
Enuma elish, 18, 24
Epeos, 321
Ephesus, 35, 79, 109, 134, 308, 309
Epic tradition, 7
Epytus, 324
Erathipa, 339–40
Erebos, 295
Erebus, 294
Erinnyes, 33. *See also* Eumenides
Eros, 32, 33, 104, 118, 183. *See also* Cupid
Erythia, 278–79
Esdras, 79
Esharra, 22
Etruscans, 117
Eucharist, 16

Eumenides, 192
Euphrates, 44
Euripides, 112, 239, 258, 309
Europa, 67, 196–97
European myth, 335–36
Eurydice, 292
Eurylokhos, 295
Eurystheus, 275–81
Eve, 29, 157, 177, 308–9
Ezekiel, book of, 77

Fairy tale, 7
Fall, the, 14, 15, 157
Fates, Three, 310
Father, 218
Father Creator, 123
Father-god, 224
Faulkner, William, 123, 136, 220
Feather Gulf, 54
Feather Mountain, 54
Feathered Serpent, 60, 157
Female creative principle, 36
Feminine, 319
  cosmic, 333
  nature of city, 330
Femme fatale, 5, 105, 177, 219, 220, 243, 258, 260, 288, 315
Fenrir, 86–88, 118
Fertility, 118, 147
  cults, 101, 163
  rites, 183
  stone, 339
Fertility Daimon, 66
Fielding, Henry, 220
Fifth World, 84–85
Flood, 8, 14, 43–62
  Babylonian/Mesopotamian, 44–47
  Chinese, 53–55
  Greco-Roman, 56–60
  Hebrew, 47–53
  Indian, 55
  Mayan, 60–62
Folk world, 7
Fon tribe of West Africa, 171–72
Fortune, 325
Frazer, Sir James, 5, 147, 155, 156, 158
French myth, 235–36
Freud, Sigmund, 5, 100, 133, 155
Freudian psychology, 5
Freyja, 118
Freyr, 118

Frigg, 118
Frogs, The, 67
Frye, Northrop, 4
Furies, 281, 294. *See also* Eumenides
Fury, 324

Gaia (Earth), 32, 99–100, 117, 124, 134,
    145–46. *See also* Geb
Galahad, 333, 335
Gangleri, 85–86, 343
Ganymede, 183
Garden, 235, 315, 344
    of Gethsemane, 248, 309, 345
    of the gods, 290
Gawain, 336
Geb (Earth), 17, 96–97, 99, 134. *See also*
    Gaia
Genesis, 16, 24–29, 340, 344
Genitals, 336
    archetype of, 338
German, 227
Germanic myths, 5
Germany, 5
Geryon, 278
Gethsemane. *See* Garden, of Gethsemane
Gilgamesh, 44–47, 288–92
Gils, 344
Ginnungagap, 343
Gjoll, 343
Glen, 344
Gnosis, 343
Gnostic, 35
God, 5, 16, 35, 68, 77, 93, 124, 134, 155,
    219, 248
Goddess Earth, 333. *See also* Great Mother
Gods and heroes, 3
Gods, nature of, 4
Golden Ass, The, 185
Golden Bough, The (Frazer), 147
Golden Fleece, 3, 6, 8, 258
Golden Mountain, 316
Golgatha, 315
Gopuram, 333
Gorgon, 274
Gospel of John, 16, 35
Gostrey, Maria, 220
Graves, Robert, 175, 163
Great Goddess, 146–47, 218, 220, 336–38.
    See also Great Mother
Great Mother, 43, 93, 96, 101, 109, 123–
    24, 134–46, 308, 333, 338–39
Great pyramids, 17

Great Spirit, 274, 286–87
Greco-Roman myth, 3, 56–60, 67–68
Greece, 97, 98, 101, 134, 163, 279
Greek myth, 32–35, 163–65, 227–29, 237–
    43, 244–48, 257–58, 274–81, 292–97,
    307, 309–10, 319–30, 332–38, 336–38
Greek Titans, 118
Grove, 344
Guernica (Picasso), 8
Gunas, 342
Gyes, 32
Gyllir, 344

Hades, 34, 67, 101–3, 117, 294, 310, 338
Ham, 48–49, 53
Hamlet, 123, 147, 221
Hanish, 45
Haran, 340–41
Hari, 84
Harrison, Jane, 177
Hassan, 347
Havomal, 162
Hawthorne, Nathaniel, 220
    Chillingworth, 220
Heaven, 64–65, 68
Hebrew myth, 79, 248, 255, 260, 287–88,
    316–19, 330–32, 340–41, 344
Hector, 322, 329–30
Hecuba, 328–29
Hedda Gabler, 147
Hel, 119, 162
Helen of Troy, 67, 100, 224, 258
Heliopolis, 17–18, 95–96
Helios, 109, 296
Hell, 64–65, 68, 221, 281
Helmholtz, 89
Helper god, 123
Hephaistos, 104–5, 118
Hera, 3, 34, 93, 99, 192, 228–29
Herakles, 67, 100, 217, 224, 228–29, 233,
    245, 274–81, 307, 309–10
Hercules. *See* Herakles
Herm, 163, 171
Hermes, 111–12, 118, 163–65, 228, 310
Herod, 219
Hero myths, 8, 219
    apotheosis, 298–310
    birth, 16
    descent, 44. *See also* Descent of hero
    search for father, 218
Hesiod, 7, 32–34, 98, 100, 104, 175, 177,
    192

Hesperides, 279
Hestia, 34, 101, 117
Hiawatha, 267–74, 304
Hicanavaiya, 37
High God, 17, 35, 39
Hiiaka, 202–7
Hinduism, 69
Hindu myths, 3, 77, 88
Hippolyte, 278
Hippolytus, 278
Hira, 345
Hitler, 5
Hittite, 175
Hoder, 118
Holocaust, 77
Holy Grail, 219, 243, 252, 333, 335–36
Homer, 7, 8, 32, 64, 66–67, 98, 108–9,
    175, 192, 288, 295
Homeric Hymns (Boer), 98, 102, 113, 163,
    188
Honen, 71
Hopi myth, 36–40, 72–75, 84–85, 134, 136
    creation myth, 36–39
    rituals, 85
Horus, 96–97
House of Atreus, 298
Hsia Dynasty, 54
Human ritual sacrifice, 4
Humbaba, 291–92
Huwinyamu, 38
Huzuiwuhti, 37–38
Hvergelmir, 343
Hyacinth, 4
Hyacinthus, 183–85
Hydra, 275–76
Hymen, 293
Hypanis, 324, 326
Hyperion, 32
Hypolipnus, 338

Iago, 220
Iapetus, 32
Icaria, 348
Icarus, 347
Icelandic myth, 118
Ida, 294
Igigi, 23
Iliad (Homer), 258
Ilium, 320, 323, 326
Immaculate Conception, 308–9
Inanna, 134, 136–45, 281, 288. *See also*
    Ishtar

India, 85, 134–35, 316, 333, 337
Indian epic, 258
Indian myth, 207–12, 225–27, 229, 262–67,
    336, 342–43
Individuality, 15
Individuation, 44, 217, 218, 220, 221
Indra, 124, 207–12
Inundation Spirit, 66
Io, 99, 192–96
Iolaus, 275, 310
Iphitus, 326
Ireland, 220
Iris, 56
Irish myth, 233–34
Irw, 66
Isaac, 134, 221, 287–88, 315
Isaiah, book of, 77
Ishmael, 69
Ishtar, 46. *See also* Inanna
Isis, 3, 16, 97, 101, 118, 134–36, 147–53,
    217
Islam, 278
Isolde, 258
Israel, 305
Itaka. *See* Ithaca
Italy, 279, 280
Ithaca, 295–96
Ixion, 293
Izanagi, 134, 199
Izanami, 199

Jā'-phĕth, 48–50, 53
Jacob, 332, 340–41
James, Henry, 220
Janaloka, 83–84
Janardana, 83
Japan, 69–72
Japanese myth, 134, 199–202
Jason, 257–58, 275
Jerome, 153
Jerusalem, 305–6, 319, 330–32, 333–35
Jesus, 8, 35, 135, 146, 147, 153, 155, 217–
    21, 224, 228, 244, 248, 262, 274, 278,
    281, 298, 304–9, 315–16, 333–35, 344
    Jesus/Christ, 157–58
    resurrection, 68
Jewish myths, 3
Joan of Arc, 235–36
Job, 8, 134
    book of, 130
Jocasta, 155, 237

Joel, book of, 77
John, 16, 35, 79
    Gospel of, 16, 35
John the Baptist, 335, 221
Jonah, 219, 255, 298
Josaphat, 309
Journey quest, 5
Jove, 56, 117
Joyce, James, 136, 217, 220
Judah, 331–32
Judaism, 68, 278, 345
Judeo-Christian myth, 4, 68, 333–34
Jung, Carl Gustav, 123, 163, 220
Juno, 56, 274, 279, 307
Jupiter, 56–58, 117, 276–80, 295, 307

Ka, 96
Kachinas, 72–74, 85
Kahgahgee. *See* Raven
Kali, 43, 135
Kali Age, 81–82
Kalypso, 288
Kammapa, 235
Karma, 69
Karna, 226
Katha-Upanisad, 342
Keats, John, 220
Kerlaugar, 344
Khepri. *See* Atum
Khoper (Khepri), 17, 18
Kicking Monster, 337
Killer-of-Enemies, 337
King Arthur, 219, 243–44, 252, 307, 315
    sword of, 8, 336, 338
Kingdom of God, 6, 64, 77, 79, 330
Kingu, 23
Kirke, 295
Kishar, 19
Kiva, 136
Kohoninos, 38
Kokyanwuhti, 37–38
Koran, 68, 345–46
Kore. *See* Persephone
Kormt, 344
Kosmos, 14, 15
Koyona, 38
Krishna, 125–29, 163, 165–69, 225, 233
Kronos, 99–101, 117
Kun, 54
Kutoyis, 218, 221, 229, 281, 298–304

Laban, 341
Labyrinth, 8, 247, 347–48
Labyrs, 347
Lada, 108
Lady of the Lake, 243
Lady of the Hearth, 322
La Fontaine, 163
Lahamu, 19
Lahmu, 19
Lakshmi, 135
Lamb, 333
Lamentations, 330
Land of the Dead, 64, 67, 219
Land of the good spirits, 85
Laocoön, 319–20
Larisaean Achilles, 319
Last Judgment, 76
Lear, King, 147, 221
Lebynthos, 348
Leda, 100
Legba, 171–72
Lemaitre, Canon Georges, 89
Lerna, 338
Lethaea, 294
Lethe. *See* River of Forgetfulness
Leto, 108
Lévi-Strauss, Claude, 6
Lingam, 336
Lingam-yoni union, 345
Literary mythmakers, 7
Literary world, 7
Literature, 4
Lituolone, 229, 234–35
Logos, 35, 36
Loki, 118, 163
Loko Yima, 40
Longfellow, Henry Wadsworth, 267
Lovelock, James, 145
Lugaldimmerankia, 23
Luz, 340
Lycidas (Milton), 147
Lyctus, 34

Ma, 109
Madame Merle, 220
Madhu, 84
Madonna, 134–35, 309. *See also* Mary
Magic Twins, 37
Magna Mater, 134
Mahabharata, 7, 8, 125, 226, 343
Maharloka, 83

Maia, 111
Malinowski, Bronislaw, 5
Manas (Mind), 29
Mandala, 16
Man-eater, 304
Man-Scorpion, 289–90
Manu, 43, 55
Maori, 134
Marduk, 18, 21–23, 24
Mars, 118, 327
Marxist traditions, 4
Mary, 16, 308–9, 333, 335
Mary Magdalene, 135
Masauwuh, 37
Mashu, 289–90
Matriarch, 4, 36, 258
Matthew, 158
Maui, 227
Maya, 16, 229
Mayas, 60–62
Mecca, 340, 345
Medea, 258
Medicine-Man, 282
Medieval Christian view of history, 89
Medina, 347
Medusa, 101, 293. *See also* Gorgon
Memea, 275
Memory. *See* Mnemosyne
Menelaos, 67
Menelaus, 321
Mercury, 118
Meru, 316
Mesopotamia, 134
Mesopotamian myth, 18–23, 136, 288–92
Metamorphoses, The (Ovid), 153
Metaphor, 3, 4, 8, 15–16, 95, 123, 200
Middle East, 146
  culture, 18
  fertility cults, 68
Middle Kingdom, 17, 66
Midgard Serpent, 86–88
Milton, John, 147
Mimir, 343
Minerva, 118, 278, 280, 320, 326
Minos, 347
Minotaur, 244, 245–47, 347
Mithras, 197–99, 218, 315
Mnemosyne, 32, 192
Mondamin, 269–74
Monomyth, 217

Mons veneris, 316
Morgan le Fay, 243
Moses, 8, 219, 227, 248, 305–6, 316–19
Mother, 319–20
Mother Church, 333
Mother Earth, 33–34, 185, 316, 332. *See also* Great Goddess; Great Mother
Mother Goddess, 344. *See also* Great Goddess; Great Mother
Mother Mountain, 333
Mount Aegeum, 34
Mount Ararat, 55
Mount of Joy, 335
Mount of Olives, 334
Mount Olympus, 95, 98, 101, 108, 112, 278, 332, 338
Mount Parnassus, 56, 57, 316
Mount Sinai, 316–19
Mountain, sacred, 316–19
Muhammad, 68, 345–47
Muiyinwuh, 37, 39
Muldarpe, 286
Mummu, 19–21
Muses, 192
Muslim myth, 68–69, 345–47
Muslims, 332
Mycenae, 275, 277–81, 323
Mygdon, 324
Myrmidons, 321
Mystery (fertility) cults, 135
Myth, definition of, 3
Mythic cosmology, 14
Mythologists, modern, 6
Mythology(ies), definition of, 3
Mythos, 6
Myths
  of afterlife, 64–75
  cosmic, 8, 13
  and culture, 5, 6
  etiological aspect, 4
  of origin, 15
  origin of, 7
  as sacred, 315
  theistic, 8
  universal, 6, 93

Nana, 155, 221, 339
Narcissus, 4, 178–83
Native American Indian myths. *See* American Indian myths
Native Americans, 163

Navaho, 134
  sand-painting ceremonies, 16
Naxos, 348
Nebuchadrezzar, 18
Nembutsu, 70
Nemea, 275
Nemean lion, 307
Nemesis, 100
Neoptolemus, 321, 328, 330
Nephthys, 97
Neptune, 57, 58, 117, 320, 333
Nereids, 57, 280
Nereus, 280, 326
Nergal, 45
Netherworld, 83
New Adam, 344
New Jerusalem, 330
New Kingdom, 17, 66
New Mexico, 337
New physics, 4
New Testament, 35, 77
Newtonian mythic structure, 4
Nibbana, 266
Niflheim, 343
Nigrodha tree, 266
Nile, 60, 95, 96
Ninurta, 44, 45, 47
Nirvana, 6, 64
Nisir, 46
Njord, 118
Noah, 43, 44, 47–53, 55, 288
Nokomis, 272–74
Norse myth, 85–88, 118–21, 162–63, 343–
  44
Nothingness, 77, 93
Nudimmud, 19, 22
Nut (Sky), 17, 65, 96–97, 99, 134
Nymphs, 279–80
Nyonye Ngana, 40

Odin, 87, 118, 146, 162, 315, 343
Odysseus, 3, 8, 64, 67, 101, 257, 295–97,
  298, 326
Odyssey (Homer), 7, 8, 64, 67, 101, 103,
  258, 288
Oedipus, 100, 108, 147, 155, 220, 227,
  237–39, 274
Oedipus at Colonus, 220
Oedipus Rex (Sophocles), 100
Oedipus the King, 237
Oeta, 57, 307
Old Kingdom, 17

Old Testament, 18, 44, 77, 79, 330
Old Man Coyote, 169–71
Olenus, 294
Olympians, 98–99
Omphalos, 332
  stone, 340
Ops, 117
Oracle, 58, 59, 237, 275, 316
Oraibi, 85
Oral epic tradition, 7
Orcus, 325
Oresteia (Aeschylus), 258
Orestes, 103, 108, 192, 258
Origen, 153
Origin stories, 15
Orion, 185
Ormt, 344
Orpheus, 183, 217, 281, 292–95
Orthrus, 279
Osiris, 3, 18, 65–67, 96–97, 112, 118, 136,
  147–53, 157, 298, 341
Othrys, 323
Ovid, 7, 56, 102, 109, 153, 178, 183

Paho, 38–39
Pah-Utes, 38
Palestine, 85
Palunhoya, 37
Pan, 188–92, 275
Pandora, 175, 177–78
Pannikar, Raimundo, 93
Pantheon, 95–121
  Egyptian, 95–98
  Greek, 95, 98–117
  Hebrew, 95
  Norse, 118–21
  Roman, 117–18
Panthus, 323, 326
Papa, 134
Papas, 338
Parade of Ants, 207–12
Paradiso, 124
Parcival, 252–55
Parnassus, 34, 332
Paros, 348
Parvati, 135, 336
Pascal candle, 333
Passion, Christ's, 33, 157
Path of Sages, 71
Patriarchy, 93, 100, 109, 124, 178, 218,
  239
  cultures, 219, 220

myth of, 337
  tradition, 258
Patrilineal culture, 39
Pegasus, 101, 274
Pele, 202–7
Pelias, 310, 326
Pelias's daughters, 309
Pelides, 330
Penates, 329
Peneleus, 326
Pentheus, 239, 255
Percival. See Parcival
Perimedes, 295
Periphas, 328
Persephone, 4, 109, 101–3, 117, 136, 293,
  296, 310
Perseus, 3, 274
Persian myth, 197, 228
Personal mythology, 6
Phaethon's sisters, 294
Phaiakians, 7
Phallus, 345, 338–39
Pherae, 310
Philoctetes, 307
Phocis, 57, 332
Phoebe, 32
Phoebus Apollo, 279
Phoenix, 18
Pholus, 276
Phrygia, 96, 109, 134
Phrygian Cybele, 117
Phrygian myth, 135, 155, 221, 338–39
Phrygians, 324
Pieta, 336
Pillars of Hercules, 279
Pindar, 104, 258
Pine tree, 295
Pink Panther, The, 163
Pirithous, 281
Pisces, 294
Pisisbaiya, 38
Place, 8
Pleiades, 185, 283–87
Plutarch, 147
Pluto, 117, 281
Po, 280
Poet, 7, 315, 347
Poetic Edda, 118, 162
Poetry, 16
Polites, 329
Pollux, 100
Polymnus, 338

Polynesian myth, 202–7, 227
Polyphemus, 101
Pope Pius XII, 309
Popol-Vuh, 60–62
Portrait of the Artist as a Young Man, A
  (Joyce), 220
Posedion, 34, 101–3, 117, 245, 247, 297, 319
Prajapati. See Brahma
Prem Sagara, 225
Priam, 322, 324–25, 327–30
Prima materia, 15, 135
Primal Vow, 70–72
Prince Machaon, 321
Proclus, 308
Prometheus, 59, 175–77, 192
Prometheus Bound, 192
Promised Land, 248
Prose Edda, 85
Proserpina, 117
Proserpine, 281
Prosymnus, 338
Psalms, 24, 89
Psyche, 135, 183
Psyche, 185
Psychological aspect of myth, 76, 315
  descent, 147
  process, 221
  reality, 218–19
Psychology, modern, 5
Puer aeternus, 97, 227, 229, 335
Puranas, 81
Purgatory, 68
Purusa, 31
Puukonhoya, 37
Puzur-Amurri, 45
Pyramid Texts, 17, 65–66, 96, 97, 148
Pyramids of Egypt, 333
Pyrrha, 56–59
Pyrrhus, 327–28, 330
Pythian Ode, 258
Pythis, 333
Pytho, 34

Queen Guinevere, 243
Quest, 5, 6, 202, 217, 219
  descent. See Descent of hero
  for father, 237
  of hero, 235–97
  for identity, 8
  loss, death, rebirth, 8
  for New Troy, 258
  refusal of call, 252, 255

Quetzalcoatl, 157, 175, 218, 221, 229, 307–8

Rachel, 341
Ragnarök, 85–88, 162
Rahab, 24
Rajayatana tree, 266
Rama, 258
Ramayana, 258
Rangi, 134
Raskolnikov, 221
Raven, 6, 163, 271
Rebirth, of hero, 147, 298–310
Red Daylight, 308
Resurrection, 262, 298, 302, 304
Resurrection god, 65
Return, of hero, 298–310
Revelation, book of, 76, 78–81
Rhadamanthos, 67
Rhea, 32, 34, 99–101, 117
Rhodope, 294
Rig Veda, 29–30
Ripheus, 324–26
Rites of passage, 17, 218, 220
Ritual, 4, 5, 17, 36, 43
  of sacred meal, 298
Ritual cleansing, 76
River of Forgetfulness, 67
River of Woe, 67
Rock, 315
  Agdos rock, 338–39
Roman gods, 117
Roman myth, 117–18, 258–59
Romans, 7
Rome, 257
Rose, H. J., 102
Rudra, 82–83

Sacramental, 15
Sacred and the Profane, The, 315
Sacred, places and objects, 315
Sacrifice, 14, 338. *See also* Scapegoat
Sacrificial rites, 147
Sagittarius. *See* Centaur
Saint George, 274
Saint John, 79, 309
Sakyamuni, 71
Samson, 219, 260
Sanaka, 84
Sangarios, 339
Sangreal. *See* Holy Grail
Satanic characters of myth, 220

Saw, 21
Scapegoat, 147, 158, 221
Science, modern, 88
Scorpions, 289
Scyros, 328
Search for the father, 221, 244
Second Coming of Christ, 79
Selene, 109
Self, 6
  identity, 69
  knowledge, 108
  realization, 5
Semele, 99, 100, 113, 124
Set. *See* Seth
Seth, 97
Seven Sisters, 287
Shakespeare, William, 220, 221
  Hamlet, 123, 147, 221
  Iago, 220
  King Lear, 147, 221
Shakespearean sonnet, 108
Shakti (anima), 135, 336
Shaman, 16, 217, 281
  modern-day, 5
  rituals, 217, 218
Shamash, 45, 290, 292
Shang Ti, 54
Shan-tao, 71
Shatapatha-Brahman, 55
Shem, 48–49, 53
Sheol, 68
Shino cult, 199
Shinran, 70
Shiva, 124, 135, 316, 333, 336
Shivite cult, 336
Shoshoni Indian tale, 169–71
Shu, 17, 18, 96
Shu ching, 53–54
Shullat, 45
Shun, 54
Shurrupak, 44
Sibyl, 219
Sibyl's Vision, 86, 343
Siddhartha Gautama, 229. *See also* Buddha
Siduri, 288, 290–91
Siegfried, 227–29
Sigeum, 323
Simon, 305
Sinon, 319, 321, 323
Sir Lancelot, 243
Sirens, 219
Sisyphus, 281, 293–94

Sita, 258
Sky god, 316
Sky Man, 134
Sleipnir, 344
Sophia, 135
Sophocles, 100, 237
Sotuknang, 85
Spain, 278–79
Sphinx, 274
Spider Woman, 36–39, 134–35
Spretnak, Charlene, 178
Sthenelus, 321
Stone, 338–39
    Bethel, 340
    fertility, 339
    Omhalos, 340
Strether, Lambert, 220
Sturluson, Snorri, 84, 118, 162
Stymphalian lake, 278
Styx, 67, 293–94
Subconscious, 5
Sumerian myth, 4, 44
Sumero-Babylonian creation myth, 16
Sun God, 134
Sun River, 302
Supreme Being, 124, 133, 175, 218, 220–
    21, 315
    archetype, 124
Susanowo, 199–202
Svarloka, 83
Svayambhu, 339
Swimme, Brian, 41
Sybil, 288
Symbols, 315

Taiowa, 85
Tamilnad temples, 333
Tammuz, 112, 153
Tannisho, 70
Tantalus, 281, 293
Tartarus, 293, 310
Tawa, 36–39
Tefnut, 18, 96
Teilhard de Chardin, Pierre, 217
Teiresias, 229
Telipinu, 157
Temple, 316, 332–36, 342, 345
Temptress. See Femme fatale
Ten Commandments, 316–19
Tenedos, 320–21
Tereus, 298

Terra, 117
Tethys, 32
Teucrians, 321, 323
Teutonic myths, 118
Tewa, 221
Thea, 32
Thebes, 95, 237, 274, 296, 319
Theistic myths, 8
Themis, 32, 58, 59, 333
Theogony, 7, 32–34, 98, 100
Theseus, 3, 8, 101, 224, 233, 244–48, 278,
    281, 338, 347
Thessandrus, 321
Third Reich, 5
Thoas, 321
Thompson, Benjamin, 88
Thor, 87, 118, 124, 344
Thrace, 278, 294
Thracian Orpheus, 294
Three Fates, 310
Thrinakia, 296
Ti, 54
Tiamat, 19–23, 24
Tiresias, 178–83, 295–97, 336–37
Titans, 34, 99–101
Tityus, 293
Tiyo, 135
Toltec, 307–8
Tom Jones, 220
Tree, 315, 339, 341–44
    of Knowledge, 27, 343–44
    of Life, 343–45
    of Wisdom, 263, 265–66, 343
Tribal myths, 5
Trickster, 123, 163–69, 219
    Greek, 163–65
    Indian, 165–69
    Shoshoni Indian, 169–71
    West African Fon Tribe, 171–72
Tristan, 258
Triton, 57
Troezen, 101, 338
Trojan Horse, 319–30
Trojan War, 105, 258
Trojans, 319–30
Troy, 307, 319–30
Tsetse, 40
Tso chuan history, 55
Twelfth Dynasty, 66
Twelve Olympians, 8
Tylor, E. B., 5
Tyr, 87

Ubara-Tut, 44, 291
Ucalegon, 323
Ulysses. *See* Odysseus
Ulysses (Joyce), 321
Unconscious, 147, 219
Underworld, 36, 38, 43, 65, 102, 119, 309
Undying gods, 297
United States, 85
Universal mythology, 6, 93
Universal Mind, 133
Universal dream, 93, 175
Universal search for self-knowledge, 217
Upanishads, 342
Uranos, 99–100, 117, 124, 134
Urshanabi, 292
Uruk, 291, 319
Utnapishtim, 43, 44, 47, 55, 288–89,
    291–92

Vagina Girls (Apache tale), 337
Vanir, 118
Vasudeva, 83–84
Veda, 342
Venus, 118
Victim, 315. *See also* Scapegoat
Virgil, 7, 105, 66–68, 258, 288, 319
Virgin goddess, 109
Virgin Mary, 135, 155, 221, 309
Virgin Mother, 16
Virgin Sybil, 68
Vishnu, 81–84, 124, 125–29, 135, 165, 225,
    333, 336
Vishnu Purana, 225
Vishvakarman, 207–8, 212
Viviane, 243
Voluspa, 85
Volva, 85
Vulcan, 118, 279
Vulva, 336
Vyasa, 7

Wagner, 5
Walker, Barbara, 197
Wanjiru, 281–83, 298
War and Peace, 8

Waste Land, The (Eliot), 147
Water Jar Boy, 221–24, 229
Western culture, 79, 221
Wide old guide figure, 5
Wind Sucker. *See* Aisinokoki
Woman of the Hard Substances, 39
Womb-garden, 345
Woolf, Virginia, 136
Word, the, 16, 17, 35
World mythology, 6, 65, 93, 123, 175
World Serpent, 118
World War I, 85
World War II, 85
World hero, 298
Wunzh. *See* Hiawatha
Wupo Paho, 38
Wuwuchim ceremony, 85

Yahweh, 124, 130, 134, 248
Yajnavalkya, 31
Yang, 135
Yao, 54
Yeats, William Butler, 4, 100
Yggdrasil, 87, 343–44
Yin, 135
Yin-yang, 336
Yoni, 336
Young, Carl, 5, 43
Younger or Prose Edda, 118
Yu, 54

Zarathustra. *See* Zoroaster
Zechariah, book of, 77
Zeid, 345
Zeus, 3, 32, 34–35, 67, 93, 98–104, 108,
    111–13, 117, 124, 177, 183, 192–97,
    228–29, 245–48, 310
Zevi, Bruno, 4
Ziggurat, 333
Zimmer, Heinrich, 207
Zion, 331–32
Ziusudra, 44
Zoroaster, 228
Zoroastrian Day of Judgment, 77
Zunis, 38